Pro HTML5 with
Visual Studio 2015

Mark J. Collins

Apress®

Pro HTML5 with Visual Studio 2015

ISBN-13 (pbk): 978-1-4842-1148-9

ISBN-13 (electronic): 978-1-4842-1147-2

Managing Director: Welmoed Spahr
Lead Editor: James DeWolf
Development Editor: Douglas Pundick
Technical Reviewer: Damien Foggon
Editorial Board: Steve Anglin, Mark Beckner, Gary Cornell, Louise Corrigan, Jim DeWolf,
    Jonathan Gennick, Robert Hutchinson, Michelle Lowman, James Markham, Susan McDermott,
    Matthew Moodie, Jeffrey Pepper, Douglas Pundick, Ben Renow-Clarke, Gwenan Spearing,
    Matt Wade, Steve Weiss
Coordinating Editor: Melissa Maldonado
Copy Editor: Kim Wimpsett
Compositor: SPi Global
Indexer: SPi Global
Artist: SPi Global

Distributed to the book trade worldwide by Springer Science+Business Media New York, 233 Spring Street, 6th Floor, New York, NY 10013. Phone 1-800-SPRINGER, fax (201) 348-4505, e-mail orders-ny@springer-sbm.com, or visit www.springeronline.com. Apress Media, LLC is a California LLC and the sole member (owner) is Springer Science + Business Media Finance Inc (SSBM Finance Inc). SSBM Finance Inc is a Delaware corporation.

For information on translations, please e-mail rights@apress.com, or visit www.apress.com.

Apress and friends of ED books may be purchased in bulk for academic, corporate, or promotional use. eBook versions and licenses are also available for most titles. For more information, reference our Special Bulk Sales–eBook Licensing web page at www.apress.com/bulk-sales.

Any source code or other supplementary material referenced by the author in this text is available to readers at www.apress.com. For detailed information about how to locate your book's source code, go to www.apress.com/source-code/.

To my beautiful and precious wife, Donna.
Thank you for sharing your life with me.

Contents at a Glance

Contents

About the Author

Mark J. Collins has been developing software solutions for more than 30 years. Some of the key technology areas of his career include COM, .NET, SQL Server, and SharePoint. He has built numerous enterprise-class applications in a variety of industries. He currently serves as an application and data architect for multiple organizations. You can see more info on his web site, www.TheCreativePeople.com. For questions and comments, contact Mark at markc@thecreativepeople.com.

About the Technical Reviewer

Damien Foggon is a developer, writer, and technical reviewer in cutting-edge technologies and has contributed to more than 50 books on .NET, C#, Visual Basic, and ASP.NET. He is the cofounder of the Newcastle-based user group NEBytes (www.nebytes.net), is a multiple MCPD in .NET 2.0 onward, and can be found online at http://blog.fasm.co.uk.

Acknowledgments

First and foremost, I acknowledge my Lord and Savior, Jesus Christ. The divine and eternal perspective on life, which can be found only in You, is an anchor, steadfast and sure. I humbly conclude that Your hand has guided me, often carrying me, through every endeavor, great and small. I submit that nothing of any value or significance is possible without You.

I want to say a very big thank-you to my beautiful wife, Donna. I can honestly say that I would not be who I am if it were not for what you have sown in my life. I am truly blessed to be able to share my life with you. Thank you for your loving support and for making life fun!

Also, I want to thank Kevin Belknap for your help on this project. You have a keen eye and a seemingly innate ability to design great user experiences. I appreciate your friendship and willingness to jump in and help.

Next, I'd like to thank all the people at Apress who made this book possible and for all their hard work that turned it into the finished product you see now; this is truly a team effort. Jim, thank you for another opportunity to work with Apress; Melissa, thanks for keeping everything rolling smoothly and for being patient with all the last-minute changes; Damien, thank you for your input and critique, helping to improve the quality and accuracy of this book; Douglas, Kim, and all the other contributors at Apress, thanks for overseeing the details. Everyone at Apress has made writing this book a pleasure.

Introduction

HTML5 is such an exciting opportunity for software developers. For a long time, the Web has been the favorite platform for providing software applications to both external and internal users because of its reach and ease of deployment and maintenance. The primary limitation has been the client-side support, which can severely limit the user experience. With the lack of cross-browser standardization, using any of the advanced features often meant broken pages on older browsers or difficult polyfills.

HTML5 is a game-changer. Not only does it bring browser vendors together with a common set of specifications, the features included in HTML5 enable web applications to provide a user experience that rivals even client applications. With mobile devices rapidly jumping on the HTML5 bandwagon, the number of HTML5 devices is expected to exceed 2 billion in the next year. I have seen the rise of many technologies and standards that promised to change the future of software development, but the momentum and support for HTML5 seem unprecedented.

Having said that, we are not quite there yet. Many of the specifications are still in draft form, and browsers, even current releases of them, do not support all the features that have been agreed upon. However, there are already enough features that are generally supported by browser vendors to make the switch to HTML5 attractive. And the future is even more promising.

Who This Book Is For

HTML5 consists of changes in the markup, CSS improvements, and JavaScript enhancements and can be used with any implementation platform. However, this book presents these new features with the professional Visual Studio developer in mind. My goal is to answer the question "What would most ASP.NET developers need to know to incorporate the benefits of HTML5?" The sample applications are written using Visual Studio 2015, and some of the examples are specific to the ASP.NET platform, including web forms and MVC 6.

Each chapter covers a different topic, providing both an explanation of how the feature is used and hand-on exercises that will reinforce the important concepts.

How This Book Is Structured

I've split the book into four parts, each going a bit deeper into the more advanced features.

Part 1 provides a quick introduction to web application technologies. This part explains the operating environment that web developers find themselves in and where the HTML5 umbrella fits in.

Part 2 covers the basics of HTML5, including form development with both traditional web forms and the MVC model. Chapter 4 provides a really good overview of CSS with a focus on the new features available in CSS3. This part also demonstrates some of the scripting enhancements in Visual Studio 2015 and includes discussions on how to use web workers and how to support mobile devices with HTML5.

Part 3 takes this further and demonstrates some of the really cool features including the new audio and video elements. I then demonstrate the graphics support available using both SVG and canvas. This part also discusses how to use polyfills to deal with older browsers.

Part 4 explains some of the more advanced features such as Indexed DB, which provides a persistent, client-side data store. This part also demonstrates geolocation and mapping using Bing Maps. Finally, it explains how web sockets and drag-and-drop can be used for advanced applications.

Downloading the Code

The code for the examples shown in this book is available on the Apress web site, `www.apress.com`. You can find a link on the book's information page on the Source Code/Downloads tab, which is located in the Related Titles section of the page. The download file also contains resources that you'll need when working through the exercises in this book.

Contacting the Author

Should you have any questions or comments—or even spot a mistake you think I should know about—you can contact me at `markc@thecreativepeople.com`.

PART I

What is HTML5?

■ ■ ■

CHAPTER 1

Before You Begin

Throughout this book I will be demonstrating how you can take advantage of the really cool new features included in Hypertext Markup Language (HTML5). It will be very hands-on with lots of code samples and working web pages. Before we get started, however, I will set the stage and provide some context for where we will be going. What is generally referred to as HTML5 includes many technologies, and HTML is just the tip of the iceberg.

In this chapter, I will briefly review the operating environments that host web sites, currently and historically. I will also describe the development tools that are available. While this book is specifically focused on Visual Studio 2015, there are some free alternatives that will enable you to work through most of these exercises. Finally, I'll take a quick inventory of the HTML5 support in current and future browsers.

Reviewing the Web Environment

So you can better understand where HTML5 sits from the web developer's view, I will first review the web environment that we find ourselves in. This will be a basic overview and quite familiar to most readers. However, I often find it useful to step back, once in a while, and get a better perspective.

The Basic HTTP Page

In the early days of the Web, the model was quite simple. It included a web server that was responsible for serving up web pages and a browser that would render them on the client. In the Microsoft stack, Internet Information Services (IIS) provided the server component, and Internet Explorer was the de facto browser. There were other browsers, of course, such as Netscape. The browser would request a page from the web server by passing the address (URL) in a Hypertext Transfer Protocol (HTTP) GET request. The server would respond by providing an HTML document, which was then rendered by the browser, as illustrated in Figure 1-1.

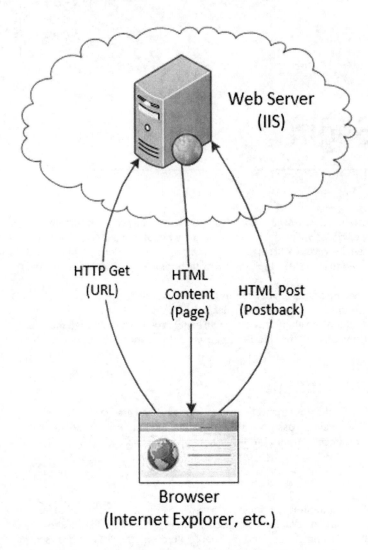

Figure 1-1. *A simple page-centric web model*

If the web page included a form with input fields, the browser would provide for this data to be entered. When the page was submitted, this data was sent to the web server through an HTTP POST request. The web application would do something with this data and then return an updated web page. The browser would then render the entire page on the client.

There are two key aspects that I want to focus on here that still have a significant influence even with today's web environment:

- The model is very page-centric.

- There are both server and client aspects to web development.

Page-Centric Web

As I mentioned, web sites are predominantly focused on web pages. A page is requested, returned, and rendered. Data on a page is posted to the server and processed, and an updated page is returned and rendered. Because the web server is stateless, it has no knowledge of previous pages that were returned. This is why the entire page must be submitted and returned. Current and future technology is helping to move away from this paradigm, and I'll demonstrate many of these techniques throughout this book. However, page-centric designs are still prevalent and will likely to continue to be for some time.

Client-Server Model

There are both server and client components to consider when building a web application. On the server, IIS responds to the HTTP requests as I mentioned. For static content, the HTML files can be simply stored in a virtual folder within IIS, and no programming is required. For dynamic content, a web application is needed to generate HTML. Enter ASP.NET.

ASP.NET allows you to write code to dynamically create HTML. For example, the page can query a database and populate a grid using the data returned from the database. Likewise, the data presented in an HTTP POST request can be written to a database. Also, while a web application is generally considered stateless, ASP.NET provides several techniques for saving information between requests.

On the client side, the browser is responsible for rendering the content. This content is provided as HTML, which is essentially text with embedded formatting tags. In addition, Cascading Style Sheets (CSS) can be used to instruct the browser how to format the content. The support for these HTML tags and CSS constructs will vary, however, between the available browsers and herein lies some of the biggest challenges of web development.

Improving the Web Experience

The page-centric approach is a major obstacle in raising the bar of the overall user experience. Refreshing an entire page is not very efficient. To address this issue, two key improvements were introduced:

- Client-side scripting
- Asynchronous JavaScript and XML (AJAX)

Using Client-Side Scripting

All browsers now provide the ability to run client-side scripts, which are predominantly written in JavaScript, although others such as VBScript are also possible in some browsers. The ability to run scripts in the browser is a huge improvement. For example, a script can hide or show a section or modify the format of the content based on the user input. Since this happens on the client, no round-trip to the server is necessary. This makes the web site seem much more responsive.

▓ **Caution**   JavaScript can be disabled on the client, and you should consider, and test, how your page will function with scripting disabled.

Using AJAX

AJAX is an acronym for Asynchronous JavaScript and XML. While a bit of a misnomer since it doesn't have to be asynchronous, use JavaScript, or use XML, the term refers to a collection of technologies that enable client-side scripting to communicate with the web server outside of the typical page refresh scenario. In a nutshell, AJAX uses JavaScript to request data from the web server. It then updates the page content using the Document Object Model (DOM). This allows portions of the web page to be updated as needed without a complete refresh.

AJAX can also be used to call web services independently from the web server that is hosting the web page. You can use AJAX to access data provided by a third party such as stock quotes or currency conversion. You can also call your own web services to perform real-time updates or load data based on user input. For example, you can provide a product search feature and use AJAX to call a web service that returns the matching products. Again, this is all independent of the standard page-refresh paradigm.

Figure 1-2 illustrates the more robust model that most web sites use today.

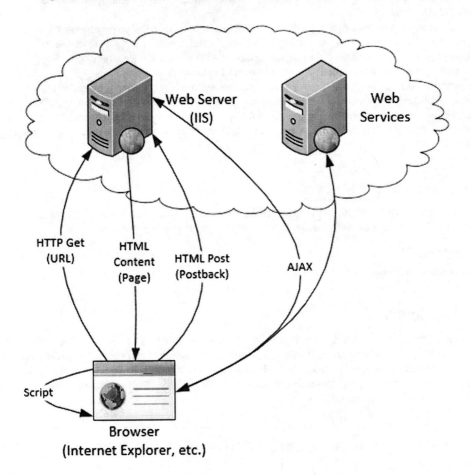

Figure 1-2. *A more robust web environment*

With the inclusion of client-side scripting and AJAX requests, you can now create much more interactive and responsive web-based solutions. Of course, this requires more complex web applications and a broad set of technologies to work with on both the server and the client.

Reviewing Web Technologies

Let's quickly review the various technologies that you will likely need to use when building great-looking interactive web applications.

- *HTML*: Hypertext Markup Language is the primary means for delivering content to the browser. In addition to the actual text that is displayed, HTML contains embedded tags that control how the content is formatted. Tags are used to align the content in sections and tables, modify text attributes, and include nontextual content including links and graphics.

- *CSS*: Cascading Style Sheets are used as a central place for controlling visual aspects of the web pages such as fonts, colors, background images, and margins. They are called *cascading* because the style options are defined at various levels in the DOM. You can define site-level styles in one style sheet and then provide additional style sheets as necessary to either further define or override these for specific pages, sections, or classes.

- *DOM*: The HTML that is rendered by the browser is similar to an XML document, and the Document Object Model defines the structure of this document. This is used for programmatically accessing and modifying the document's content.

- *ECMAScript*: Client-side scripts are interpreted and executed by the browser. To improve cross-browser compatibility, the ECMAScript standard defines the syntax and features of the scripting language. JavaScript is a dialect of the ECMAScript standard.

■ **Note** Historically, JavaScript and JScript were two implementations of the same scripting language. Microsoft named its implementation JScript to avoid trademark issues with Sun, but they are essentially the same and follow the evolving ECMAScript standards. With Internet Explorer 10, Microsoft is moving away from this distinction and referring to its scripting language as JavaScript. And just to keep things interesting, Microsoft still provides a JScript language, which provides access to .NET and is very different from JavaScript. I will refer to JavaScript throughout this book as the standard ECMAScript-compliant scripting language.

Exploring HTML5

So, where does HTML5 fit in to this equation? Just about everywhere! What is generally classified as HTML5 is actually a broad set of specifications related to web browser standardization, many of which having nothing to do with HTML. I will briefly summarize these here and then demonstrate these features in detail throughout the rest of this book. The following are a few things that you should keep in mind:

- Many of the specifications have not been finalized yet. Much of the core specifications are completed, but some of the advanced features are still subject to change.

- Browser-support for these features will vary. Browser vendors are aggressively incorporating new features in each subsequent release.

- The specifications leave room for each browser vendor to decide how each feature is implemented. For example, all compliant browsers will provide a date picker control for entering dates, but each browser may implement this in a different way.

The general trend with HTML5 is to provide more native support in the browser. As you will see throughout this book, browsers are providing an increasingly impressive set of features. This will enable you to build better web applications with less work.

Reviewing Markup Changes

As you would expect, HTML5 includes some important improvements in the markup elements. There is a sizeable list of new markup elements, and I will demonstrate many of these in Chapters 2, 3, and 4.

The generic `<div>` element is still supported, but new, more context-specific elements are also provided. I will explain and demonstrate this in Chapter 4. The new content tags are as follows:

- `<article>`
- `<aside>`
- `<footer>`
- `<header>`
- `<hgroup>`
- `<nav>`
- `<section>`

Several new input type elements are provided that allow native formatting and validation capabilities. These will be described in Chapters 2 and 3. The new types are as follows:

- `color`
- `datetime` (as well as `datetime-local`, `date`, `time`, `month`, and `week`)
- `email`
- `number`
- `range`
- `search`
- `tel`
- `url`

There are also some new elements that enable you to use browser-implemented controls such as the following:

- `<audio>`
- `<figcaption>`
- `<figure>`
- `<meter>`
- `<output>`
- `<progress>`
- `<video>`

There are a few other elements introduced with HTML5 that I will describe in more detail later. I will demonstrate the `<audio>` and `<video>` tags in Chapter 8. The new `<canvas>` element provides some significant graphics capabilities, and I will demonstrate this in Chapter 10.

Understanding Cascading Style Sheets

Like HTML, CSS capabilities are defined by an evolving set of specifications. The current published *recommendation* is CSS 2.1, and the next version being drafted is referred to as CSS3. However, it has been broken down into more than 50 "modules" with a separate specification for each. As of this writing, only a few of these modules have become official W3C Recommendations (REC) and several more are at W3C Candidate Recommendation (CR) status.

■ **Tip** Since the status of each CSS module is ever changing, for complete information about the current status of each, see the article at www.w3.org/Style/CSS/current-work.

So, the actual CSS3 "specification" is very much a moving target at the moment, and browser support for these specifications will also vary. However, there are already a number of cool features that are generally available, and I will demonstrate some of these in Chapter 4.

Reviewing Other HTML Functionality

The actual scripting syntax is defined by the ECMAScript specification I mentioned earlier. The current version, 5.1, was published in June 2011. While it's not actually part of the HTML5 specifications, HTML5-compliant browsers are expected to support the ECMAScript 5.1 standard. As I said, however, this specification describes the language syntax and some built-in functions such as element selectors.

In addition to the language specification, there are quite a few other specifications that are loosely included under the HTML5 umbrella that define specific client-side functionality. I will demonstrate many of these in Chapter 5, and the rest will be covered in later chapters. The new functionality includes the following:

- *Drag and Drop*: This provides the ability to select an item and drop it on another item on the web page. I will demonstrate this in Chapter 14.

- *Web workers*: This allows you to execute a script on a separate thread. This includes mechanisms to communicate with workers and the ability to share workers between multiple web pages. I will explain this in Chapter 5.

- *Web storage*: This includes `sessionStorage` for isolating session data between multiple tabs connected to the same site as well as `localStorage` for storing data on the client that persists after the session is closed. IndexedDB is another technique for client-side data storage, which I will demonstrate in Chapter 11.

- *Geolocation*: This is not part of the official specifications but has been generally included when discussing HTML5 features. Geolocation defines an API that can be called from JavaScript to determine the current geographic location. How the browser implements this is determined by the available hardware. On a GPS-enabled device, it will use a GPS satellite. If GPS support is not available, it will use Wi-Fi, if possible, to determine the location. Mobile devices can use cell tower triangulation. If all else fails, the IP address can at least provide some estimate of location. Obviously, the accuracy will vary greatly, and the API handles this. I will demonstrate geolocation in Chapter 12.

- *Web sockets*: This provides asynchronous communication between the web page (browser) and the server. Once the connection is established, the server can send real-time updates to the client. This will be demonstrated in Chapter 13.

Choosing a Development Tool

There are several development environments that you can use to create ASP.NET applications that take advantage of the HTML5 features. I will present them here briefly and cover them in a little more detail in subsequent chapters. The key thing to know is that there are some free alternatives to Visual Studio.

Using Visual Studio 2015

Visual Studio 2015 is the premier development environment for building ASP.NET applications. I won't say much about it here because I will be using it predominantly throughout this book to demonstrate HTML5 implementations. However, if acquiring Visual Studio is cost prohibitive, there are some free alternatives that will still allow you to work most of the exercises in this book.

■ **Tip** You can use earlier versions of Visual Studio for most of the exercises. Some of the details for configuring projects will vary with older versions, especially in Chapters 2 and 3. However, most of the HTML, CSS, and JavaScript examples in this book are also relevant to any version of Visual Studio.

Using Microsoft's WebMatrix

Microsoft's WebMatrix is a lightweight integrated development environment (IDE) that is specifically targeted for building web sites. While not limited to just ASP.NET pages, you can build full-fledged ASP.NET applications. It includes SQL Server Compact, which is a file-based version of SQL Server. It also uses IIS Express to host a local web site for debugging. This is the same hosting environment provided in Visual Studio 2012, which replaces the ASP.NET Development Server used in previous versions of Visual Studio.

The ASP pages are based on ASP.NET MVC and use the Razor view engine. Consequently, the file extensions are .cshtml (or .vbhtml if you're using Visual Basic). The classic ASP model with an .aspx markup file and separate .cs code-behind file is not supported, however. You can create .aspx files, but adding a code-behind file is not a practical option.

You can download and install WebMatrix version 3 from this site: www.microsoft.com/web/webmatrix. When creating a new site, if you use the Starter Site template, it will create a familiar default ASP web application, as shown in Figure 1-3.

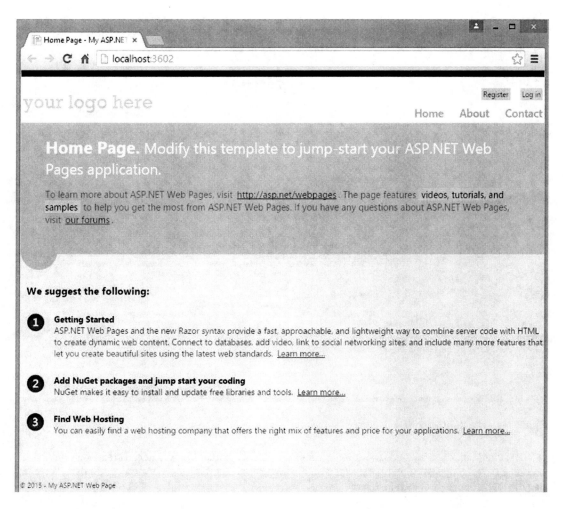

Figure 1-3. *The default ASP application*

■ **Note** When selecting the Starter Site template, I got a 404 error trying to download the template. I found that others experienced this error as well. However, it seems to be intermittent because it worked fine when I tried it again sometime later.

Figure 1-4 shows the IDE. Notice the .cshtml extensions and the Razor syntax for the page implementation.

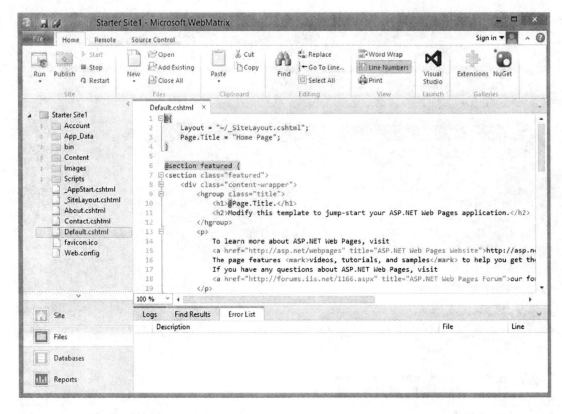

Figure 1-4. *The WebMatrix IDE*

The WebMatrix IDE includes the ability to manage SQL Server databases. You can create new databases or connect to existing SQL Server databases. You can create and alter tables and view and edit data. You can also run SQL queries, as shown in Figure 1-5.

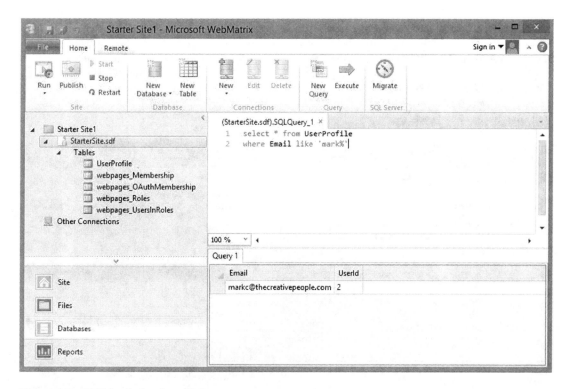

Figure 1-5. *WebMatrix database IDE*

For more information on using WebMatrix, I suggest starting with the tutorial at www.microsoft.com/web/post/how-to-use-the-starter-site-template-for-aspnet-web-pages.

Using Visual Studio Community Edition

Microsoft announced a free version of Visual Studio in November 2014, called Community Edition. There have been other free editions, such as Visual Studio Express for Web; however, the Community Edition is significant in that it looks and functions just like the full retail version of Visual Studio Professional. Visual Studio Express editions were targeted to specific technologies (for example, for Web or for Desktop). Also, the Express editions were not integrated with Team Foundation Server, and they did not support Visual Studio extensions.

The Community Edition is functionally equivalent to the Professional Edition. Its restrictions are primarily based on who is allowed to use it. Generally, any academic or nonprofit use is allowed. Enterprise organizations can also use it with some limitations. For more details, see the article at www.visualstudio.com/en-us/products/visual-studio-community-vs. If these restrictions are a problem, you should consider one of the Express versions of Visual Studio, which are also free but with some limited capability.

You can download Visual Studio Community Edition at https://www.visualstudio.com/en-us/downloads/visual-studio-2015-downloads-vs.

ASP.NET 5

The latest version of ASP.NET 5 is a pretty significant departure from previous versions. This article, http://docs.asp.net/en/latest/conceptual-overview/aspnet.html, provides good overview of the changes introduces with ASP.NET 5. When creating a new project, Visual Studio 2015 provides separate templates for version 5 as well as 4.6 since the structures are very different. Figure 1-6 shows the available templates.

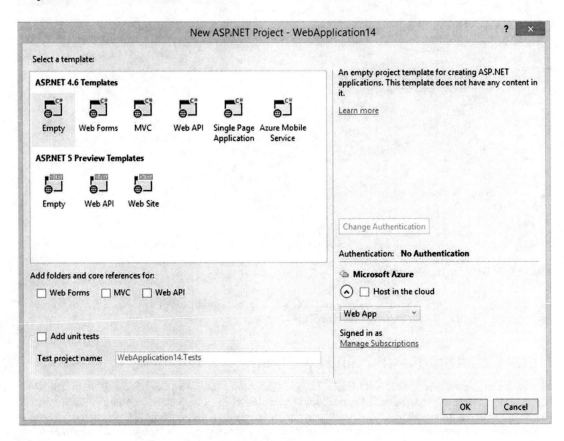

Figure 1-6. *The ASP.NET project templates*

Most of the topics in this book will work equally well in both versions. For the sample projects that you will build, the differences lie only in how the projects are created and which files you'll need to add and edit.

Chapter Exercises

The exercises in this book will use both 4.6 and 5 as well as the WebMatrix application. Chapters 2 and 3 will use ASP.NET 4.6 and you'll be modifying standard Web Forms and MVC applications. Chapter 4 will use WebMatrix as will Chapter 6, since it uses the completed Chapter 4 project as its starting point. The remaining chapter exercises use the new ASP.NET 5 structure. Chapter 9 uses SQL Server and Entity Framework, but most of the chapters are just basic HTML, CSS, and JavaScript. If you prefer to use a single project type, you can adjust the initial steps to suit your needs.

Project Structure

When you create an ASP.NET 5 project for the first time, you'll find the folder structure has changed sigficantly. A typical structure is shown in Figure 1-7.

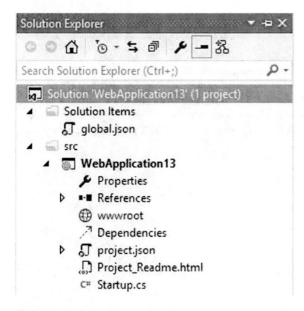

Figure 1-7. *A sample project structure*

The wwwroot folder is were you'll put your static web files such as HTML, CSS, JavaScript files as well as other content including images and audio and video files. The compiled files such as controllers, views, and web forms are placed in other folders. You will be working mostly with files in the wwwroot folder.

Notice that there is no web.config file. With ASP.NET 5, configuration information can be placed in multiple files and in various formats including JSON, .ini files, and environment variables. The project template generates JSON files such as global.json and project.json files shown in Figure 1-7. I will explain this further in Chapter 5.

Deciphering Browser Support for HTML5

All of the work to move applications to HTML5 is based on the assumption that the majority of browsers will be HTML5 compatible. This requires that the browser vendors step up to the plate and provide HTML5-compatible browsers and that the public at large will adopt them. This also includes mobile devices, which are a key part of the push for HTML5 compliance. The general consensus is that everyone is moving in that direction at a pretty good clip.

As I mentioned earlier, the actual HTML5 specifications are still being defined. Initial estimates were as late as 2022 before the final recommendation was complete, according to HTML5 editor Ian Hickson. However, as large parts of the specification are being finalized, vendors are implementing them, so much is already available in browsers that are currently in use. As web developers, we should focus on the features that are generally available now or expect to be soon, and these are the features that I will cover in this book.

There is a really good web site at `http://html5test.com` that provides a summary of the browsers that are currently available and those that are still in development. Each browser is awarded points based on the HTML5 features it supports. In addition to an overall score that allows you to compare browsers, the scores are also broken down by functional area so you can see which areas have good support from most browsers.

Summary

HTML5 covers a broad set of technologies that include improvements to the HTML markup, Cascading Style Sheets, and client-side scripting. In addition, there are some significant enhancements to browsers that make it easier to provide some great web applications. While the official specifications are still a work-in-progress and the browser vendors are playing catch-up, there is quite a bit of functionality already available. Also, as you'll see in the next few chapters, Visual Studio and the ASP.NET platform have been expanded to leverage the HTML feature set.

PART II

Using the New HTML5 Features

■ ■ ■

CHAPTER 2

ASP.NET Web Forms

In this chapter, I will demonstrate some of the new input types defined by HTML5 and show you how to use these in an ASP.NET web form. Typically, the TextBox control is used when data needs to be entered on a form. Users can enter all kinds of data in a TextBox including strings, numbers, dates, and so on. To ensure valid data, the form needs to supply either server-side or client-side validation logic. The HTML5 specification provides several new input types that can do much of this for you and implement a better customer experience.

The following input types are defined (however, not all browsers support all of them yet):

- select

- color

- datetime (including datetime-local, date, time, month, and week)

- email

- number

- range

- tel

- url

When you build a web form using ASP.NET, the actual HTML that is sent to the browser is generated by .NET. I'll show you the ASP.NET way of inserting the new input types. Also, using some of the new HTML elements requires a little extra manipulation, so I'll demonstrate how to handle that as well.

Introducing the New Input Types

I'll start with a fairly simple example to demonstrate how to use the new e-mail control combined with the placeholder attribute to quickly provide client-side instructions and validation. You'll start by creating a standard ASP project using the Visual Studio template and then modify the registration page. Then you'll inspect the HTML that is being rendered.

Creating an ASP.NET Project

In this chapter, you'll create an ASP.NET project using the standard Web Forms template in Visual Studio 2015. Start Visual Studio 2015. From the Start Page, click the New Project link. In the New Project dialog box, select the Web category and select the ASP.NET Web Application template, enter **Chapter 2** for the project name and select an appropriate location, as shown in Figure 2-1. Turn off Application Insights if it's selected.

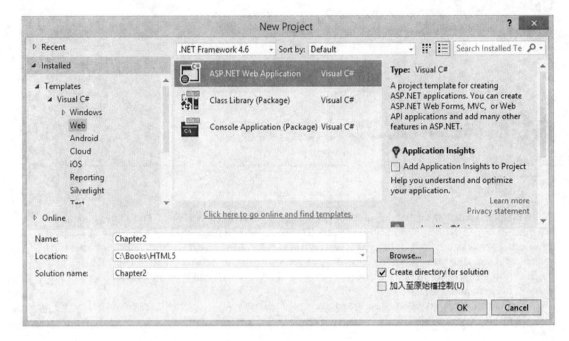

Figure 2-1. *Creating an ASP.NET Web Application project*

Prior versions of Visual Studio provided three different ways of creating web applications.

- Web Forms are best suited for fairly lightweight web pages.

- MVC provides a framework for building more complex web applications.

- Web API is primarily used for creating web services.

While some of the concepts were similar across all three technologies, they were implemented on completely different stacks. From a developer's perspective, once you chose one approach, it was not easy to transition to another one. Also, skill sets were not readily transferrable to other technologies. With MVC 6, Microsoft merged all three onto a single implementation.

If you have used previous versions of Visual Studio, you'll notice one of the subtle differences resulting from this. When selecting the project type, you simply choose ASP.NET Web Application. The choice of which style of application to use is deferred to the next step, where you select the template. A template defines the files that are created for you when you build a new project. An MVC app will need different files and folders than a Web Forms application.

In the next dialog box, shown in Figure 2-2, select the Web Forms template. Notice one of the available styles (Web Forms, MVC, or Web API) is automatically checked based on the selected template.

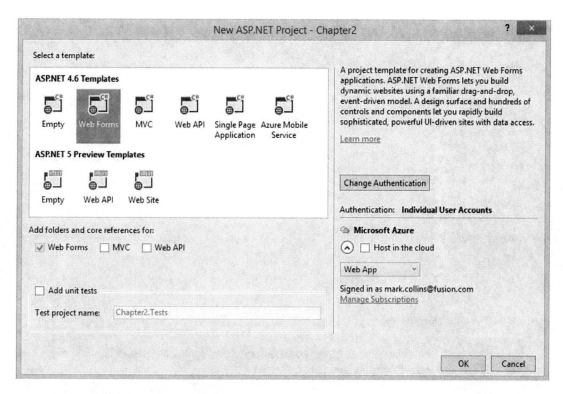

Figure 2-2. *Choosing the Web Forms template*

Using the Email Control

For the first exercise, you'll use the placeholder attribute to let the users know that an e-mail address is needed in the field.

EXERCISE 2-1. MODIFYING THE REGISTRATION PAGE

1. In the Chapter2 project, open the Register.aspx page, which you'll find in the Account folder.

2. There are several div elements in the fieldset node that include the input fields. The first one is for the Email field. Change this as follows by entering the attributes shown in bold:

   ```
   <asp:TextBox runat="server" ID="Email" CssClass="form-control"
   TextMode="Email"
       placeholder="use your email address" Width="200" />
   <asp:RequiredFieldValidator runat="server" ControlToValidate="Email"
       CssClass="text-danger" ErrorMessage="The email field is required." />
   ```

3. Start the application by pressing F5. Using the Chrome browser, the Register page will look like Figure 2-3. Notice the text in the Email field.

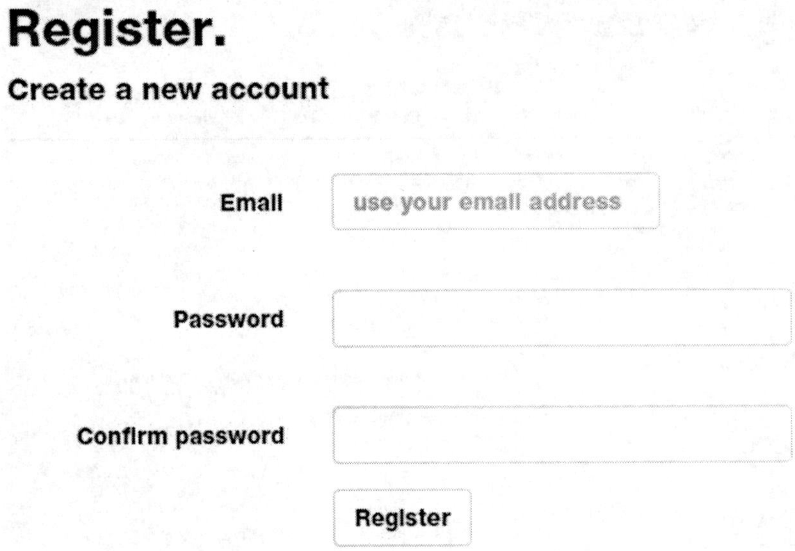

Register.

Create a new account

Email	use your email address
Password	
Confirm password	
	Register

Figure 2-3. The initial Register page

4. If you enter an invalid email address, you should see the error message shown in Figure 2-4 when you attempt to submit the page.

Email   Invalid email address|

> ⚠ Please include an '@' in the email address. 'invalid email address' is missing an '@'.

sword

The passwo...

Figure 2-4. The invalid email error message

5. Close the browser and stop debugging.

6. For this example, we used Google Chrome as the browser. If you want to use a different browser, you can select it from the drop-down list in the menu, as shown in Figure 2-5.

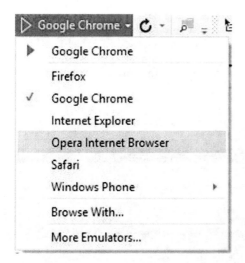

Figure 2-5. Selecting the browser to use for debugging

7. Try viewing this page with several different browsers. Notice that the email validation message looks different in each. In Firefox this will look like Figure 2-6, and in Opera it looks like Figure 2-7.

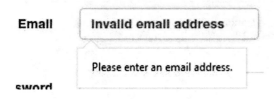

Figure 2-6. The invalid e-mail message in Firefox

Figure 2-7. The invalid e-mail message in Opera

■ **Tip** This drop-down list automatically includes all of the browsers that are currently installed. You don't have to do anything to add them. If you install a new browser, you will need to restart Visual Studio before it will be included in the list. If you use Internet Explorer, the browser will be more integrated with the debugger. For example, when you close the browser, Visual Studio will automatically stop debugging. However, when testing HTML5 support, you'll need to use other browsers in addition to Internet Explorer.

Using the Page Inspector

Display the Register page using Internet Explorer. Select the Tools drop-down menu and click the F12 Developer Tools link. This will allow you to look at the actual HTML that was generated. Press Ctrl+B to enable element selection and then click the Email field. This will show the relevant markup highlighted, as shown in Figure 2-8.

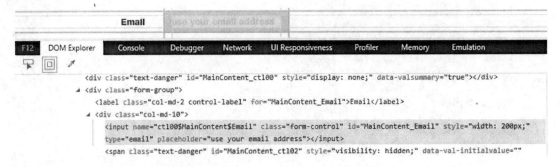

Figure 2-8. *The HTML generated for the email control*

■ Tip   Most of the other browsers have a similar feature that lets you inspect the form content, which is usually accessed through their Tools menu.

Except for the rather cryptic control name and id, this is standard HTML5 syntax. In particular, notice the following attributes; the email type value and the placeholder attribute are new in HTML5:

```
type="email"
placeholder="use your email address"
```

The placeholder attribute that you entered in the Register.aspx page is not an ASP.NET attribute. It was not processed by .NET but passed directly to the generated HTML.

Notice also the pane to the right that provides several tabs for viewing the CSS styles. We've selected the Attributes tab, which shows the values for all of the element's attributes. The other tabs show you the styles that are applied. Stop the debugger to close the page inspector.

Exploring the Other Input Types

HTML5 introduces several other input types. To see them in action, you'll add a feedback form with some rather contrived questions. These will implement the other types that are available to you.

■ Tip   To get a detailed explanation of each of the input elements, check out the actual HTML5 specification. This address will take you to the section on input elements: www.whatwg.org/specs/web-apps/current-work/multipage/the-input-element.html#the-input-element.

Implementing a Feedback Form

In the next exercise, you'll create a new form and add several input controls, one of each type. After you have created the form, I'll discuss each of the controls.

EXERCISE 2-2. ADDING A FEEDBACK FORM

1. Open the Chapter2 project in Visual Studio if not already open.

2. In the Solution Explorer, right-click the Chapter2 project and click the Add and Webform links. Enter **Feedback** when prompted for the form name.

3. This will create a new form with a single div, as shown in Listing 2-1.

Listing 2-1. The Blank Form Implementation

```
<%@ Page Language="C#" AutoEventWireup="true" CodeBehind="Feedback.aspx.cs"
    Inherits="Chapter2.Feedback" %>

<!DOCTYPE html>

<html xmlns="http://www.w3.org/1999/xhtml">
<head runat="server">
    <title></title>
</head>
<body>
    <form id="form1" runat="server">
    <div>

    </div>
    </form>
</body>
</html>
```

4. Within the empty div, enter the code shown in Listing 2-2. This will add several fields that each demonstrate one of the new input types.

Listing 2-2. Adding Feedback Fields

```
<fieldset>
    <legend>Feedback Form</legend>
    <ol>
        <li>
            <asp:Label ID="lblURL" runat="server"
                AssociatedControlID="URL">Default home page</asp:Label>
            <asp:textbox runat="server" ID="URL" TextMode="Url"></asp:textbox>
        </li>
        <li>
            <asp:Label ID="lblOptions" runat="server"
                AssociatedControlID="Options">Default browser</asp:Label>
            <asp:DropDownList ID="Options" runat="server">
```

```
                    <asp:ListItem Text="Internet Explorer" Value="1">
                    </asp:ListItem>
                    <asp:ListItem Text="Google Chrome" Value="2" Selected>
                    </asp:ListItem>
                    <asp:ListItem Text="Firefox" Value="3"></asp:ListItem>
                    <asp:ListItem Text="Opera" Value="4"></asp:ListItem>
                </asp:DropDownList>
        </li>
        <li>
            <asp:Label ID="lblBirthday" runat="server"
                AssociatedControlID="Birthday">Birthday</asp:Label>
            <asp:TextBox runat="server" ID="Birthday" TextMode="Date">
            </asp:TextBox>
        </li>
        <li>
            <asp:Label ID="lblMonth" runat="server"
                AssociatedControlID="Month">Favorite Month</asp:Label>
            <asp:TextBox runat="server" ID="Month" TextMode="Month">
            </asp:TextBox>
        </li>
        <li>
            <asp:Label ID="lblWeek" runat="server"
                AssociatedControlID="Week">Busiest Week</asp:Label>
            <asp:TextBox runat="server" ID="Week" TextMode="Week">
            </asp:TextBox>
        </li>
        <li>
            <asp:Label ID="lblStart" runat="server"
                AssociatedControlID="DateTime">Start Date/Time</asp:Label>
            <asp:TextBox runat="server" ID="DateTime"
                TextMode="DateTimeLocal"></asp:TextBox>
        </li>
        <li>
            <asp:Label ID="lblTime" runat="server"
                AssociatedControlID="Time">Current Time</asp:Label>
            <asp:TextBox runat="server" ID="Time" TextMode="Time" >
            </asp:TextBox>
        </li>
        <li>
            <asp:Label ID="lblPhone" runat="server"
                AssociatedControlID="Phone">Phone</asp:Label>
            <asp:TextBox runat="server" ID="Phone" TextMode="Phone">
            </asp:TextBox>
        </li>
        <li>
            <asp:Label ID="lblRange" runat="server"
                AssociatedControlID="Range">Overall satisfaction</asp:Label>
            <asp:TextBox runat="server" ID="Range" TextMode="Range"
                Width="200" Height="30"></asp:TextBox>
        </li>
```

```
        <li>
            <asp:Label ID="lblColor" runat="server"
                AssociatedControlID="Color">Preferred color</asp:Label>
            <asp:TextBox runat="server" ID="Color" TextMode="Color">
            </asp:TextBox>
        </li>
        <li>
            <asp:Label ID="lblScore" runat="server"
                AssociatedControlID="Score">Overall Rating</asp:Label>
            <asp:TextBox ID="Score" runat="server" TextMode="Number"
                MaxLength="1"></asp:TextBox>
        </li>
        <li>
            <asp:Label ID="lblComments" runat="server"
                AssociatedControlID="Multi">Comments</asp:Label>
            <asp:TextBox runat="server" ID="Multi" TextMode="Multiline"
                Rows="5" Columns="30"></asp:TextBox>
        </li>
    </ol>
    <asp:Button ID="Submit" runat="server" CommandName="Submit" Text="Submit" />
</fieldset>
```

5. Save the changes and press F5 to display the new page in the browser. Figure 2-9 shows the feedback form as rendered by the Opera browser.

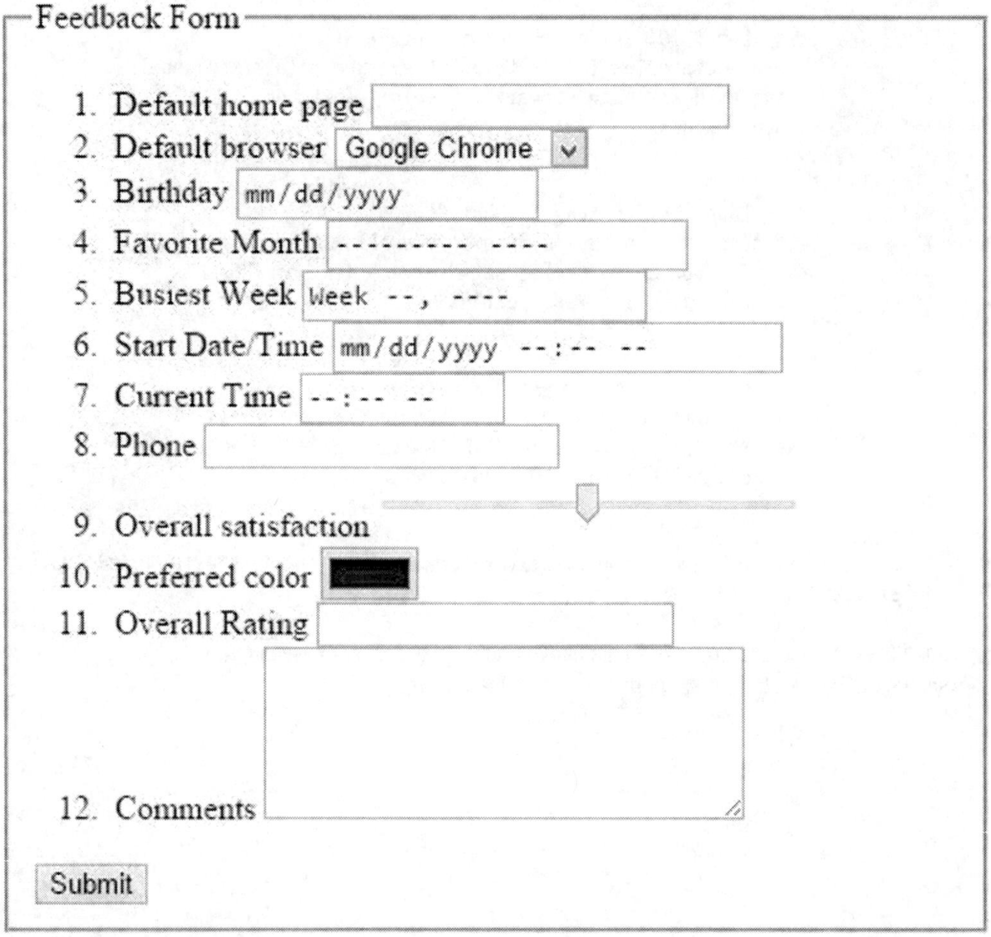

Feedback Form

1. Default home page [   ]
2. Default browser [Google Chrome ▾]
3. Birthday [mm/dd/yyyy   ]
4. Favorite Month [--------- ----]
5. Busiest Week [Week --, ----]
6. Start Date/Time [mm/dd/yyyy --:-- --]
7. Current Time [--:-- --]
8. Phone [   ]

9. Overall satisfaction
10. Preferred color [▆]
11. Overall Rating [   ]

12. Comments [   ]

[Submit]

Figure 2-9. *The initial feedback form*

___

■ **Note**   I'm using the Opera browser to render the feedback form because it has the best support for the new input types, as of this writing. I'll explain that more later in this chapter. You can download Opera from www.opera.com. Chrome also has excellent support for these features.

___

Reviewing the New Input Types

Now let's look at each of the new input types and see how they have been implemented in Opera. Keep in mind that different browsers may present the control differently.

URL

The first field uses the url input type, which expects a valid web address. If you enter an invalid address, when the page is submitted, you'll see the validation error shown in Figure 2-10

1. Default home page bad address

2. Default browse
   Please enter a valid web address

3. Birthday

Figure 2-10. *The URL field*

■ **Note** The protocol, such as http://, is required in the URL. For example, if you enter www.apress.com and try to submit the form, the address is considered invalid. Enter http://www.apress.com instead.

Selection List

The next field provides a drop-down list of available browsers. In ASP.NET this is coded as a DropDownList that contains a number of ListItem elements. The generated HTML uses a select element that contains option elements like this:

```
<select name="Options" id="Options">
  <option value="1">Internet Explorer</option>
  <option selected="selected" value="2">Google Chrome</option>
  <option value="3">Firefox</option>
  <option value="4">Opera</option>
</select>
```

Notice that the selected item is indicated with the selected attribute. This is a boolean and doesn't need a value. Visual Studio will show a warning, and the generated markup has the value set to selected. The browser will ignore the value and simply look for the existence of the selected attribute.

Date/Time Fields

The feedback form contains the following date/time fields that demonstrate the browser support for various date-type fields:

- *Birthday:* (Date) a single date (no time portion)

- *Favorite Month:* (Month) an entire month, including the year

- *Busiest Week:* (Week) an entire week, including the year

- *Start Date/Time:* (DateTime) a single date including the time portion

- *Current Time:* (Time) the time without any date

The date fields are text boxes where you can key the desired value but with intelligence built in. For example, go to the Birthday field and type **7**, and the cursor will automatically go to the day portion of the date. If you type a **1** instead, you'll need to either enter a **0**, **1**, or **2** to complete the month entry or just hit Tab to move to the day.

There is also an icon that displays a date picker control. The different formats of this control (date, month, and week) are shown in Figures 2-11, 2-12, and 2-13, respectively. These controls are essentially the same except that the month and week versions will only allow you to select the entire month or week. Notice that the week format also displays the week number (from 1 to 52).

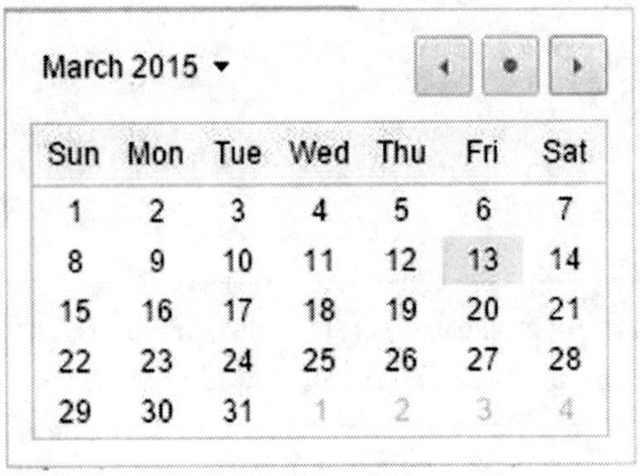

Figure 2-11. *The date picker control*

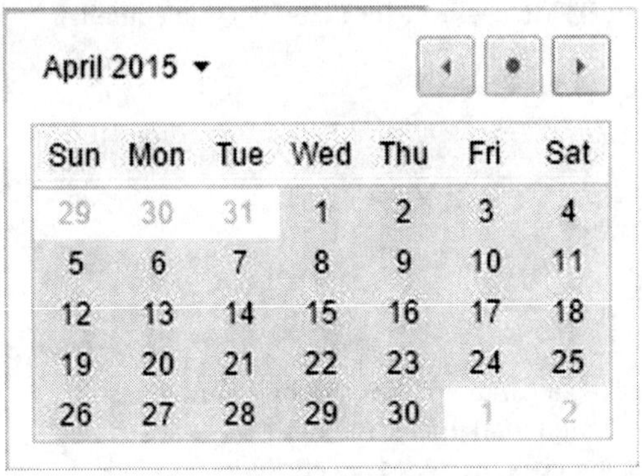

Figure 2-12. *The date picker selecting an entire month*

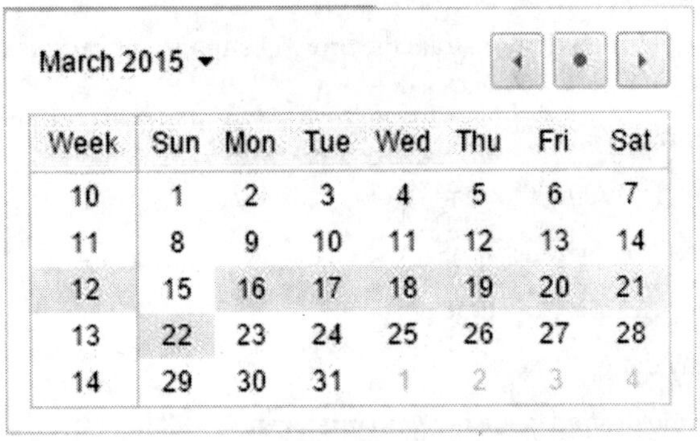

Figure 2-13. *The date picker selecting an entire week*

Both the Start Date/Time and Current Time fields include a time control that allows the hour and minute to be entered separately, shown in Figure 2-14. You can also use the up/down arrows to increment the hour or minute portion depending on which is currently in focus. But there is no drop-down where you can select the hour or minute.

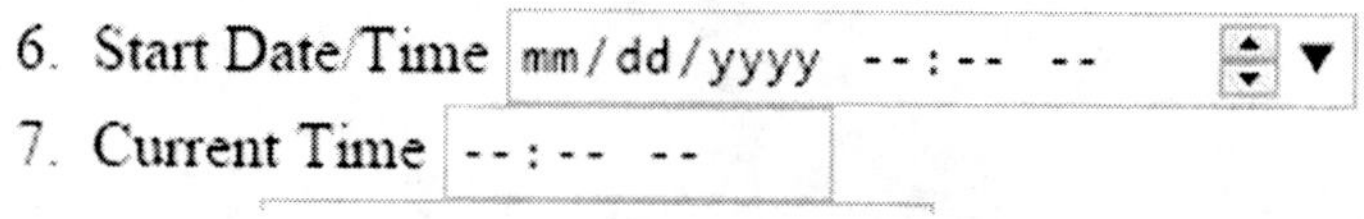

6. Start Date/Time `mm/dd/yyyy --:-- --` ▲▼ ▼

7. Current Time `--:-- --`

Figure 2-14. *The time control*

■ **Caution**   As of this writing, ASP.NET supports both `DateTime` and `DateTimeLocal` text modes. These are translated to the HTML types `datetime` and `datetime-local`. However, `datetime` has been deprecated in favor of `datetime-local`. So, be sure to use the `DateTimeLocal` text mode in your forms.

Phone

The feedback form includes a Phone field that uses the new `tel` input type. At the time of this writing, none of the desktop browsers supports this type. I included it in the exercise with the hope that by the time you read this you'll have a browser that will support it. As with all nonsupported types, the browser treats this as a standard TextBox control.

Range

The next control uses the is similar to a fuel gauge in a car where the specific value is not as important as the relative value such as new range input type. This allows you to slide the indicator across the extent of the control, providing a relative value such as three-quarters full. I defined this with a width of 300 and a height of 30.

There are some other attributes of the range control that you can manipulate in HTML that are not supported in ASP.NET. You could still specify these in the `.aspx` page, and they would be passed to the generated HTML just like the `placeholder` attribute. However, I will show you another way to configure the range control later in this chapter.

Color

The color control includes a small rectangle that displays the selected color. If you click this, you can select a color from the color picker, as shown in Figure 2-15.

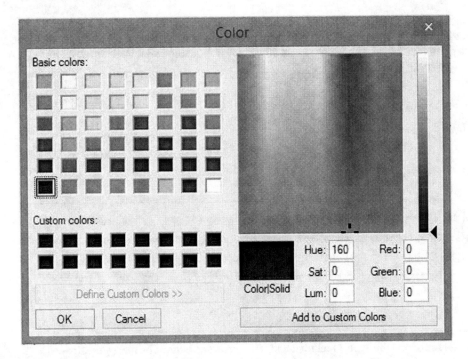

Figure 2-15. *The color-picker control*

Number

The Overall Rating field uses the number input type. Several browser now include up and down arrows that allow you to increment and decrement the current value. When the form is submitted, if a non-numeric value was entered, an error will be displayed, as shown in Figure 2-16.

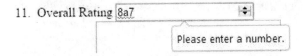

Figure 2-16. *A non-numeric value error*

Text Area

The last field uses the text area input type. I specified this to use 5 rows and 30 columns. This affects only how the field is displayed on the page. The text is stored as a single string. The text will be wrapped to fit into the allotted size on the page, but it can contain any number of rows.

Reviewing the Form

Figure 2-17 shows a completed form.

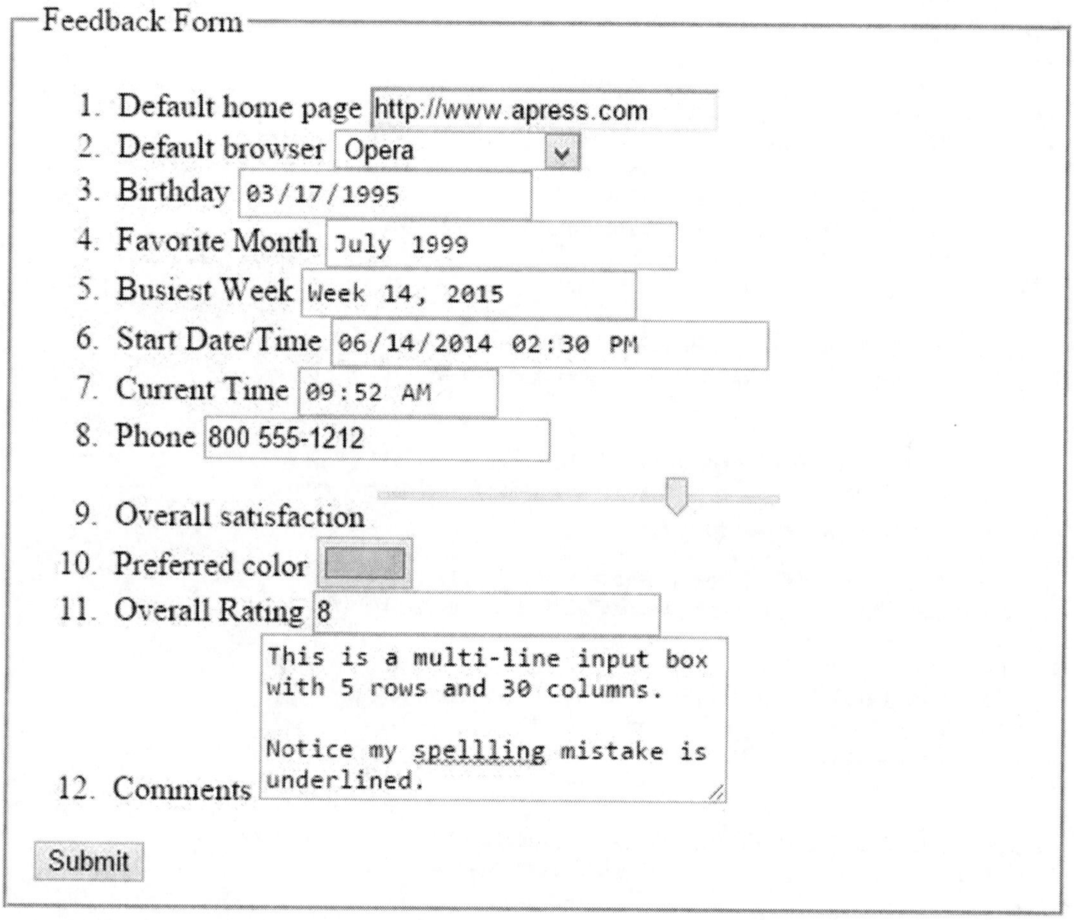

Figure 2-17. *The completed feedback form*

Browsers try to be smart about performing spell-check on the contents of appropriate fields. Notice in the Comments field, misspelled words are underlined. You can explicitly turn this on or off using the spellcheck attribute. To disable spell-checking, add the code shown in bold here:

```
<asp:TextBox runat="server" ID="Multi" TextMode="Multiline"
    Rows="5" Columns="30" spellcheck="false"></asp:TextBox>
```

After entering values for each of the fields, click the Submit button and then view the page's source. Each of the fields will now have a value attribute that contains the value that was included when the page was submitted. This is what the server-side code would use to store and/or process the submitted data. I extracted a portion of this, which is shown in Listing 2-3. Look at how the various date/time field values are formatted. These are shown in bold. Also, notice that the color is stored as a hexadecimal representation of the selected RGB values.

Listing 2-3. The Source with Submitted Values

```
<li>
    <label for="URL" id="lblURL">Default home page</label>
    <input name="URL" type="url" value="http://www.apress.com" id="URL" />
</li>
<li>
    <label for="Options" id="lblOptions">Default browser</label>
    <select name="Options" id="Options">
        <option value="1">Internet Explorer</option>
        <option value="2">Google Chrome</option>
        <option value="3">Firefox</option>
        <option selected="selected" value="4">Opera</option>
    </select>
</li>
<li>
    <label for="Birthday" id="lblBirthday">Birthday</label>
    <input name="Birthday" type="date" value="1995-03-17" id="Birthday" />
</li>
<li>
    <label for="Month" id="lblMonth">Favorite Month</label>
    <input name="Month" type="month" value="1999-07" id="Month" />
</li>
<li>
    <label for="Week" id="lblWeek">Busiest Week</label>
    <input name="Week" type="week" value="2015-W14" id="Week" />
</li>
<li>
    <label for="DateTime" id="lblStart">Start Date/Time</label>
    <input name="DateTime" type="datetime-local"
        value="2014-06-14T14:30" id="DateTime" />
</li>
<li>
    <label for="Time" id="lblTime">Current Time</label>
    <input name="Time" type="time" value="09:52" id="Time" />
</li>
<li>
    <label for="Phone" id="lblPhone">Phone</label>
    <input name="Phone" type="tel" value="800 555-1212" id="Phone" />
</li>
<li>
    <label for="Range" id="lblRange">Overall satisfaction</label>
    <input name="Range" type="range" value="76" id="Range"
        style="height:30px;width:200px;" />
</li>
```

```
<li>
    <label for="Color" id="lblColor">Preferred color</label>
    <input name="Color" type="color" value="#ffbe7d" id="Color" />
</li>
<li>
    <label for="Score" id="lblScore">Overall Rating</label>
    <input name="Score" type="number" value="8" maxlength="1" id="Score" />
</li>
<li>
    <label for="Multi" id="lblComments">Comments</label>
    <textarea name="Multi" rows="5" cols="30" id="Multi">
This is a multi-line input box with 5 rows and 30 columns.
Notice my spellling mistake is underlined.
    </textarea>
</li>.
```

Using the HTML5Test Web Site

I mentioned that we're using Opera for this exercise. Each browser may implement a different subset of HTML5 features. The HTML5Test.com web site mentioned in the previous chapter is a really useful tool for figuring out which browser works best for a specific set of features.

If you go to the Compare tab, you can select up to five different browsers to see a side-by-side comparison for each feature. For example, I selected Opera, Google Chrome, Firefox, IE, and Safari to see how they stack up for the form features. The results are displayed in Figure 2-18. Opera and Chrome are significantly more advanced when it comes to supporting forms.

forms	73	73	49	34	47
Field types					
▶ input type=text	Yes ✓	Yes ✓	Yes ✓	Partial ○	Yes ✓
▶ input type=search	Yes ✓	Yes ✓	Yes ✓	Yes ✓	Yes ✓
▶ input type=tel	Yes ✓	Yes ✓	Yes ✓	Yes ✓	Yes ✓
▶ input type=url	Yes ✓	Yes ✓	Yes ✓	Yes ✓	Yes ✓
▶ input type=email	Yes ✓	Yes ✓	Yes ✓	Yes ✓	Yes ✓
▶ input type=date	Yes ✓	Yes ✓	No ✕	No ✕	No ✕
▶ input type=month	Yes ✓	Yes ✓	No ✕	No ✕	No ✕
▶ input type=week	Yes ✓	Yes ✓	No ✕	No ✕	No ✕
▶ input type=time	Yes ✓	Yes ✓	No ✕	No ✕	No ✕
▶ input type=datetime	No ✕	No ✕	No ✕	No ✕	No ✕
▶ input type=datetime-local	Yes ✓	Yes ✓	No ✕	No ✕	No ✕
▶ input type=number	Yes ✓	Yes ✓	Yes ✓	Yes ✓	Yes ✓
▶ input type=range	Yes ✓	Yes ✓	Yes ✓	Yes ✓	Yes ✓
▶ input type=color	Yes ✓	Yes ✓	Yes ✓	No ✕	No ✕
▶ input type=checkbox	Yes ✓	Yes ✓	Yes ✓	Yes ✓	Yes ✓
▶ input type=image	Yes ✓	Yes ✓	Yes ✓	Yes ✓	Yes ✓
▶ input type=file	Yes ✓	Yes ✓	Yes ✓	Yes ✓	Yes ✓
▶ textarea	Yes ✓	Yes ✓	Yes ✓	Yes ✓	Yes ✓
▶ select	Yes ✓	Yes ✓	Yes ✓	Yes ✓	Yes ✓
▶ fieldset	Yes ✓	Yes ✓	Yes ✓	Partial ○	Yes ✓
▶ datalist	Yes ✓	Yes ✓	Yes ✓	Yes ✓	No ✕
▶ keygen	Yes ✓	Yes ✓	No ✕	No ✕	Yes ✓
▶ output	Yes ✓	Yes ✓	Yes ✓	No ✕	Yes ✓
▶ progress	Yes ✓	Yes ✓	Yes ✓	Yes ✓	Yes ✓
▶ meter	Yes ✓	Yes ✓	Yes ✓	No ✕	Yes ✓

Figure 2-18. A side-by-side comparison of Opera, Chrome, Firefox, IE, and Safari

Another way to use this site is to see how all browsers support a specific feature. From the Features subtab (in the Compare tab), you can select up to three specific features to see which browsers support it. We selected three features related to the range input type, as shown in Figure 2-19. Currently, Chrome and Opera are the only desktop browsers that fully support these features.

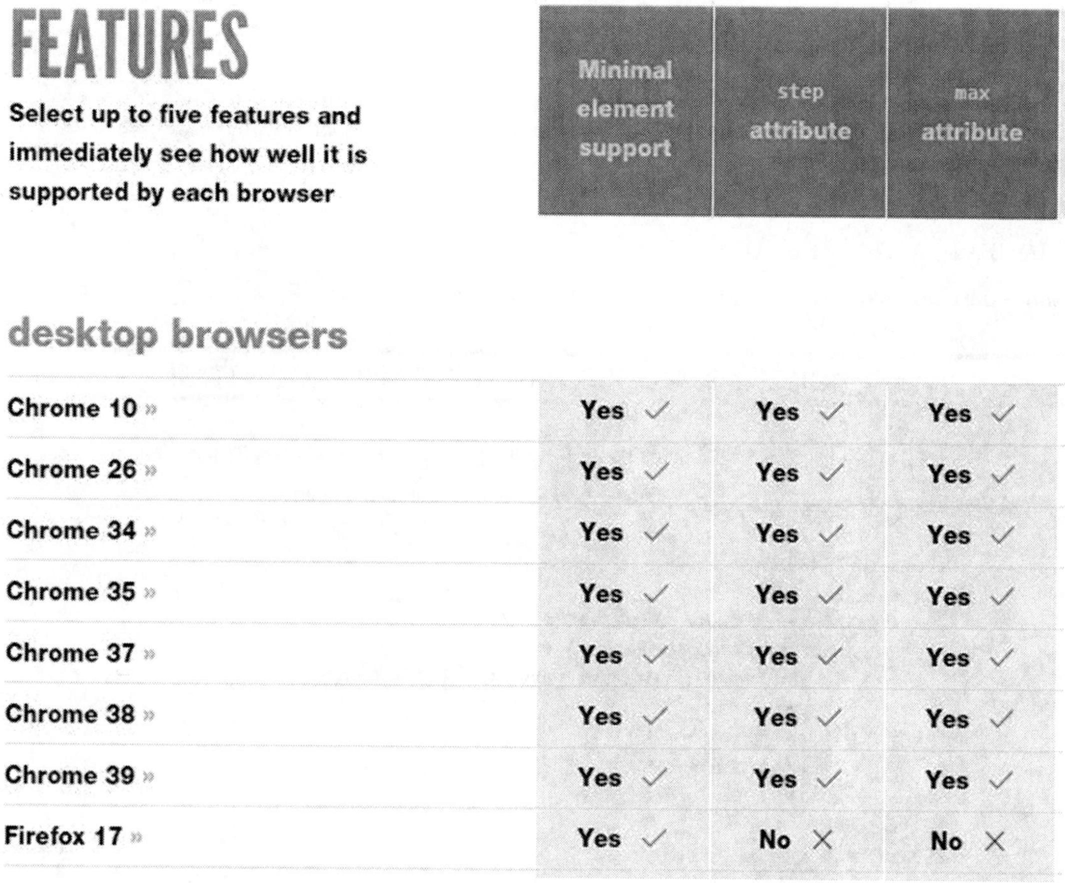

FEATURES

Select up to five features and immediately see how well it is supported by each browser

	Minimal element support	step attribute	max attribute

desktop browsers

	Minimal element support	step attribute	max attribute
Chrome 10 »	Yes ✓	Yes ✓	Yes ✓
Chrome 26 »	Yes ✓	Yes ✓	Yes ✓
Chrome 34 »	Yes ✓	Yes ✓	Yes ✓
Chrome 35 »	Yes ✓	Yes ✓	Yes ✓
Chrome 37 »	Yes ✓	Yes ✓	Yes ✓
Chrome 38 »	Yes ✓	Yes ✓	Yes ✓
Chrome 39 »	Yes ✓	Yes ✓	Yes ✓
Firefox 17 »	Yes ✓	No ✗	No ✗

Figure 2-19. Viewing each browser's support of the range control

■ **Caution** These comparisons and analysis are provided only for demonstration purposes. Browser support is changing at a pretty rapid pace, and by the time you're reading this, you may have different results. The method for comparing browser support will still be valid, however.

Using the Range Control

The range control supports attributes that allow you to configure its behavior. For example, you can specify the min and max attributes that define the value of the field when the slider is at each end of the control. You can also indicate the step attribute that controls stops along the scale where the slider can stop at. For example, if the min is 0, the max is 100, and the step is 20, the control will allow you to stop only at increments of 20 (for example, 0, 20, 40, 60, 80, and 100).

You would code this in HTML like this:

```
<!DOCTYPE html>

<input name="Range" type="range" id="Range"
    min="0" max="200" step="20"
    style="height:30px;width:200px;" />
```

Even though IntelliSense does not support these attributes, you could specify them in your .aspx page, and they would be included in the final HTML. Another way to do this is to modify the control when the page is loaded using JavaScript.

Modifying the Step Attribute

Now you'll write a simple script to configure the range attributes.

EXERCISE 2-3. MODIFYING THE RANGE CONTROL

1. Load the Chapter 2 project in Visual Studio and open the Feedback.aspx page.

2. Inside the head tag, add the following script element shown in bold:

```
<head runat="server">
    <title></title>
    <script type="text/javascript">
        function configureRange() {
            var range = document.getElementById("Range");
            range.min = 0;
            range.max = 200;
            range.step = 20;
        }
    </script>
</head>
```

3. This simple JavaScript function modifies the attributes of the range control. The document property represents the HTML document of the current page. The getElementById() function is a selector that returns the specified element, the range control in this case. (I will cover selectors in JavaScript in more detail in Chapter 5.)

4. Now that the function has been implemented, you need to tell the page to execute it. To do that, add the following code in bold to the <body> tag:

```
<body onload="configureRange()">
    <form id="form1" runat="server">
```

5. This instructs the page to call the configureRange() function when the OnLoad event occurs.

6. Save your changes and press F5 to load the page.

7. The range control will look just like it did before, but when you move the slider, it will stop only at the preset values.

Adding Custom Tick Marks

Previous versions of Opera would display tick marks to help graduate the scale of the range control, but the current version does not, and neither does Chrome. However, you can add these yourself using a datalist tag. As of this writing, Firefox doesn't support this feature.

EXERCISE 2-4. ADDING CUSTOM TICK MARKS

1. Add the following anywhere inside the fieldset tag. This defines the list of values where the tick marks should be placed.

```
<datalist id="ticks">
    <option>0</option>
    <option>20</option>
    <option>40</option>
    <option>60</option>
    <option>80</option>
    <option>100</option>
    <option>120</option>
    <option>140</option>
    <option>160</option>
    <option>180</option>
    <option>200</option>
</datalist>
```

2. In the Range control, add the list attribute shown in bold. This specifies the datalist tag that defines where the tick marks should be.

```
<asp:Label ID="lblRange" runat="server"
    AssociatedControlID="Range">Overall satisfaction</asp:Label>
<asp:TextBox runat="server" ID="Range" TextMode="Range"
    Width="200" Height="30" list="ticks"> </asp:TextBox>
```

3. Save your changes and press F5 to display the modified form.

4. You should see tick marks at each step, as shown in Figure 2-20.

9. Overall satisfaction

Figure 2-20. The Range control with tick marks

Displaying the Range Value

While you're working on the Range control I will show you a simple trick to display its value. You'll add a TextBox control next to the range control and then use JavaScript to update its value when the range control is modified.

▉ **Note** Internet Explorer 11 automatically displays the current value of the range control while the user is moving it. This is an example of how each browser can implement features in different ways.

EXERCISE 2-5. DISPLAYING THE RANGE VALUE

1. In the `Feedback.aspx` page, add the following code in bold to the range item:

```
<li>
    <asp:Label ID="lblRange" runat="server"
        AssociatedControlID="Range">Overall satisfaction</asp:Label>
    <asp:TextBox runat="server" ID="Range" TextMode="Range"
        Width="200" Height="30" list="ticks"></asp:TextBox>
    <asp:TextBox runat="server" ID="RangeValue" Width="50"></asp:TextBox>
</li>
```

2. Next, add the code in bold to the script section:

```
<script type="text/javascript">
    function configureRange() {
        var range = document.getElementById("Range");
        range.min = 0;
        range.max = 200;
        range.step = 20;
        updateRangeValue();
    }
    function updateRangeValue() {
        document.getElementById("RangeValue").value
            = document.getElementById("Range").value;
    }
</script>
```

3. The `updateRangeValue()` function takes the current value of the `Range` control and stores it in the text box. Also, the `configureRange()` function that is called when the page is loaded calls `updateRangeValue()` to set its initial value.

4. Now you'll need to call the `updateRangeValue()` function whenever the range control is updated. To do that, add the code in bold to the `Page_Load()` event handler in the `Feedback.aspx.cs` code-behind file.

```
public partial class Feedback : System.Web.UI.Page
{
    protected void Page_Load(object sender, EventArgs e)
    {
        Range.Attributes.Add("onChange", "updateRangeValue()");
    }
}
```

5. Save your changes and execute the page. As you move the slider, the selected value is displayed. Notice that it is updated in increments of 20 (if the step attribute is still set at 20).

Summary

In this chapter, you created a basic ASP.NET web form application using the template provided by Visual Studio. After briefly trying the email control, you then created a feedback page that demonstrated many of the other input types. Using some simple JavaScript, you configured the range control and provided a real-time display of its value.

Along the way, I also provided some useful information regarding the development environment including the following:

- Configuring browsers to test with

- Inspecting the page elements in Internet Explorer

- Using the HTML5Test.com web site to research browser support

▩ ▩ ▩

CHAPTER 3

MVC Web Applications

In this chapter, you will use ASP.NET MVC to create a feedback form that will demonstrate several of the new input types. I will first provide a brief introduction of the Model-View-Controller (MVC) framework included with the .NET platform and then show you how to build an HTML5-based web page using MVC. The end result will be something similar to what you did in Chapter 2, but the implementation will be quite different. As you will see, the solution will rely heavily on the ability to extend the MVC framework to incorporate the new HTML5 features.

Model-View-Controller is an architectural pattern that has been around since as early as the late 1970s. The primary benefit of this pattern is the separation of concerns, allowing independent development, testing, and maintenance of each. The model provides the data and business logic. If the application is presenting a product catalog, for example, the model will provide the product details. If changes are made, the model is responsible for persisting the data, when invoked by the controller. The view provides the user experience, both formatting the presentation of data as well as enabling user interaction with input controls, buttons, and links. The controller handles the user requests, passing this to the model and invoking the appropriate view. Figure 3-1 illustrates this process.

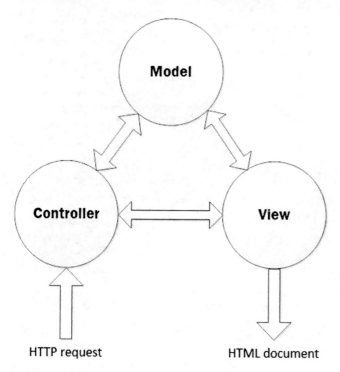

Figure 3-1. *The MVC architectural pattern*

Introducing ASP.NET MVC6

ASP.NET MVC is a framework based on .NET that was first released in 2009 and implements the MVC pattern. The initial release used the same .aspx Web Forms syntax that was used in the traditional ASP.NET framework. In 2010, a new view engine called Razor was released, which generates web pages in a more natural, HTML-like syntax. Also, instead of a code-behind file, the Razor engine allows the code to be included in the markup file. MVC version 6, included with the Visual Studio 2015 release, has merged much of the implementation stack with Web Forms and Web API.

Like the traditional ASP.NET Web Forms I discussed in the previous chapter, MVC6 does not support many of the new HTML5 tags out of the box. However, the MVC framework is much more extensible, making it relatively easy to add HTML5 support. In this chapter, I will explain different techniques for extending the MVC framework to incorporate the new HTML5 features. There are also several open source extensions that you can install, and I will briefly demonstrate one of these as well.

Creating an ASP.NET MVC Project

In this chapter, you'll create an ASP.NET MVC project using the standard template in Visual Studio 2015. Start Visual Studio 2015. From the Web category, select the ASP.NET Web Application template, enter **Chapter3** for the project name, and select an appropriate location, as shown in Figure 3-2. Click the OK button to continue.

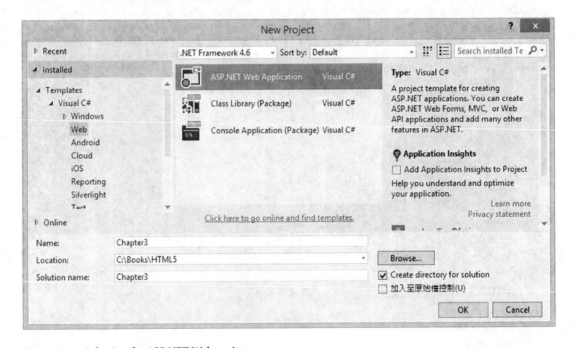

Figure 3-2. *Selecting the ASP.NET Web project*

This is the same way you created the project in the previous chapter. However, in the next dialog box, select the MVC template, as shown in Figure 3-3. This will create a web application that looks just like the project in Chapter 2, but it is implemented using the MVC style.

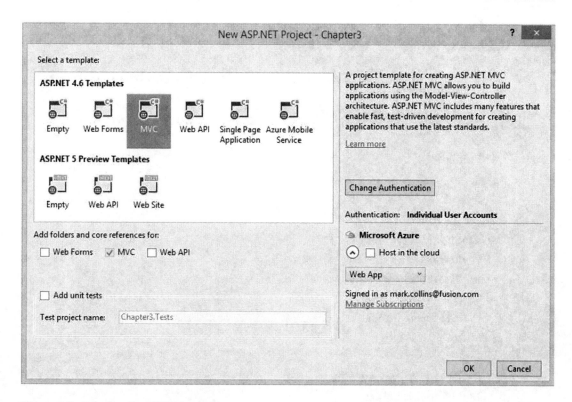

Figure 3-3. *Selecting the MVC template*

After the project has been created, you'll see a number of folders in the Solution Explorer. Notice there are separate folders for controllers, models, and views, as shown in Figure 3-4. The sample project includes several examples of each of these items.

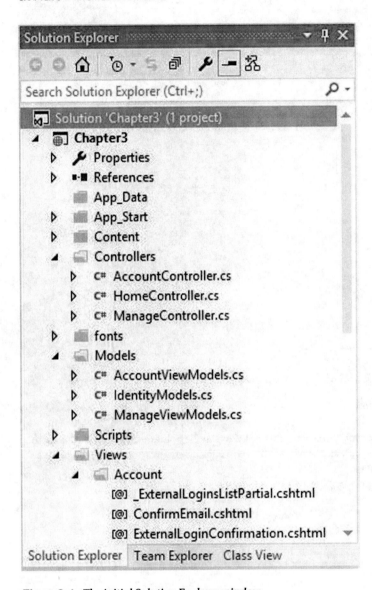

Figure 3-4. The initial Solution Explorer window

Exploring a Razor View

For a quick demonstration of the Razor view syntax you can look at the existing views provided by the project template. Open the Register.cshtml file, which you'll find in the Views\Account folder. This implements the view for the registration page. Listing 3-1 shows the main portion of the page.

Listing 3-1. The Initial Register.cshtml Implementation

```
<h4>Create a new account.</h4>
<hr />
@Html.ValidationSummary("", new { @class = "text-danger" })
<div class="form-group">
    @Html.LabelFor(m => m.Email, new { @class = "col-md-2 control-label" })
    <div class="col-md-10">
        @Html.TextBoxFor(m => m.Email, new { @class = "form-control" })
    </div>
</div>
<div class="form-group">
    @Html.LabelFor(m => m.Password, new { @class = "col-md-2 control-label" })
    <div class="col-md-10">
        @Html.PasswordFor(m => m.Password, new { @class = "form-control" })
    </div>
</div>
<div class="form-group">
    @Html.LabelFor(m => m.ConfirmPassword, new { @class = "col-md-2 control-label" })
    <div class="col-md-10">
        @Html.PasswordFor(m => m.ConfirmPassword, new { @class = "form-control" })
    </div>
</div>
<div class="form-group">
    <div class="col-md-offset-2 col-md-10">
        <input type="submit" class="btn btn-default" value="Register" />
    </div>
</div>
```

In the Razor syntax, an @ indicates the text that follows is code instead of literal markup. The code will generate HTML content at runtime. You'll notice that much of the code uses the Html class. This is a helper class with methods that generate HTML markup. The LabelFor() method, for example, generates markup to insert a Label control.

For each of the fields in the form, the code uses the LabelFor() and TextBoxFor() methods of the Html helper class. (The password fields use the PasswordFor() method.) Each of these methods takes a lambda expression (for example, m => m.Email) that specifies a data element from the associated model. The model that is used for the view is defined by the following instruction at the top of the file:

```
@model Chapter3.Models.RegisterViewModel
```

If you look at the AccountViewModels.cs file, you'll find the definition of the RegisterViewModel class. This class has three public properties.

- Email
- Password
- ConfirmPassword

Each of these properties has some metadata attributes such as Required and DataType that are used to generate the correct HTML. I will explain this further later in the chapter.

47

Using Editor Templates

The TextBoxFor() method will output a standard TextBox control. To use the new HTML5 input types, you'll need to modify this implementation. The MVC framework allows you to use the EditorFor() method instead of TextBoxFor(). By itself that doesn't change the markup that is generated since the default implementation of EditorFor() will still use the type="text" attribute. I'll show you how to create an editor template to override this default behavior.

EXERCISE 3-1. ADDING AN EDITOR TEMPLATE

1. Open the Register.cshtml file, which you'll find in the Views\Account folder.

2. For the Email field, replace TextBoxFor with **EditorFor**. The code will look like this:

```
<div class="form-group">
  @Html.LabelFor(m => m.Email, new { @class =
"col-md-2 control-label" })
    <div class="col-md-10">
      @Html.EditorFor(m => m.Email, new { @class = "form-control" })
    </div>
</div>
```

3. In the Solution Explorer, right-click the Views\Shared folder and choose Add and New Folder. Enter **EditorTemplates** for the folder name.

■ **Caution**   Later in the chapter I will explain how the appropriate editor template is selected for each property. Editor templates must be in the EditorTemplates folder for the MVC framework to be able to use them. Because this folder was added to the Views\Shared folder, the templates are available to all views in your projects. You could create the EditorTemplates folder in the Views\Account folder. This would make them available to all views in the Account folder but not in other folders such as the Home folder. This would also allow you to create a separate set of editor templates for each folder if you wanted the Home templates to be different from the Account templates. If you have the same name in both folders, the one in the Home or Account folder will override the Shared version.

---

4. Right-click the Views\Shared\EditorTemplates folder and choose Add and View links.

5. In the Add View dialog box, enter **EmailAddress** as the view name and make sure all the check boxes are unselected, as shown in Figure 3-5. Click the Add button to create the template.

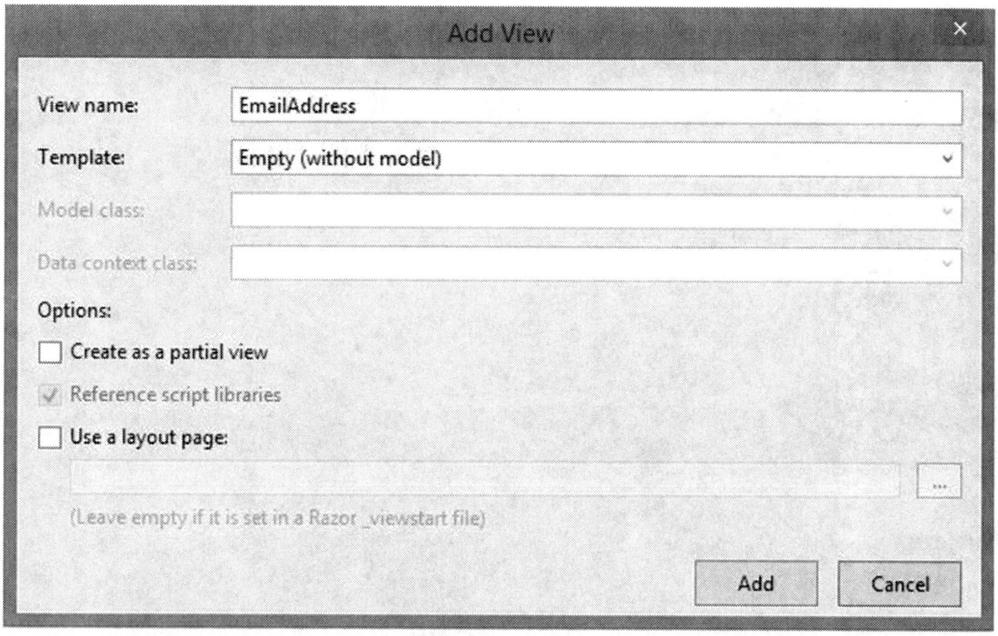

Figure 3-5. *Adding the EmailAddress template*

6. This will generate a view page named EmailAddress.cshtml. Delete the entire content and replace it with the following code. This uses the TextBox() method but specifies some additional attributes including type and placeholder.

```
@Html.TextBox("", null, new
{
  @class = "text-box single-line",
  type = "email",
  placeholder = "Enter an e-mail address"
})
```

7. Save your changes and debug the application. By default, the debugger will try to display the page you have open. Open the Register.cshtml file before pressing F5, and that page will be opened in the browser. Go to the Registration page, and you should see the placeholder text displayed in the empty Email field, as shown in Figure 3-6.

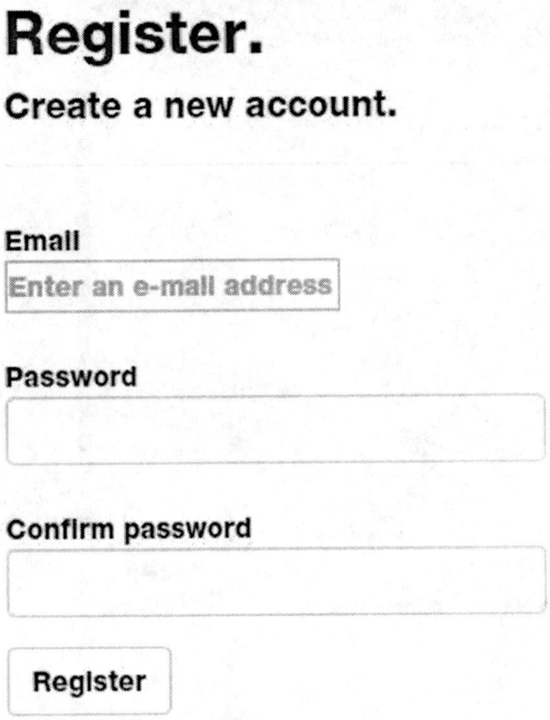

Register.

Create a new account.

Email

Enter an e-mail address

Password

Confirm password

Register

Figure 3-6. *The blank register form*

8. If you look at the page's source or the Page Inspector, the actual HTML will look similar to this:

```
<input name="Email"
    class="text-box single-line"
    id="Email"
    type="email"
    placeholder="Enter an e-mail address"
    value=""
    data-val-required="The Email field is required."
    data-val-email="The Email field is not a valid e-mail address."
    data-val="true" >
```

9. Close the browser and stop the debugger.

■ **Tip**   As with the previous chapter, I will be using the Opera browser for most of the exercises since it has the best support for the new input types.

Notice the data-val tags in the generated markup. They are used to control the client-side validation logic.

ATTRIBUTE DRIVEN VALIDATION

Data validation in ASP.NET MVC starts with the model. If you look at the AccountViewModel.cs file, you'll see metadata attributes such as Required attached to each property. For example, the Email property looks like this:

```
[Required]
[EmailAddress]
[Display(Name = "Email")]
public string Email { get; set; }
```

The TextBoxFor() helper function uses the metadata attributes to generate HTML like you saw with the Email field. Specifically, the data-val and data-val-required HTML attributes are generated. The view also includes these jQuery libraries:

```
<script src="~/Scripts/jquery.validate.js"></script>
<script src="~/Scripts/jquery.validate.unobtrusive.js"></script>
```

These JavaScript libraries use the HTML attributes such as data-val to perform client-side validation. For more information, see the article at www.datahaunting.com/mvc/client-and-server-side-validation-using-dataannotation-in-mvc.

Adding a Feedback Page

You will now create a feedback form and use this to demonstrate how to implement the new HTML5 capabilities. You'll start by creating a model and then implement a strongly typed view based on this model. You'll then add a controller action as well as a link to the new page.

■ **Tip**   Adding a page to the web application usually involves adding a model, adding a view, and creating or modifying a controller. The MVC pattern allows these to be developed separately, and in a large project, you will often have different people responsible for the views and models. You may be able to use an existing model. However, in a small project like this, where you are the sole developer, you will generally need to touch all three areas to add a page.

Creating the Feedback Model

A model defines the data elements that can be included on your page. By designing the model first, you can simplify the view implementation.

In the Solution Explorer, right-click the Models folder, choose Add and Class, and enter **FeedbackModel.cs** for the class name. Click the OK button to create the class. For the class implementation, enter the code shown in Listing 3-2.

Listing 3-2. The FeedbackModel Class

```
using System;
using System.Collections.Generic;
using System.Linq;
using System.Web;
using System.ComponentModel.DataAnnotations;

namespace Chapter3.Models
{
    public class FeedbackModel
    {
        [Display(Name = "Name", Prompt = "Enter your full name"),
         Required]
        public string Name { get; set; }

        [Display(Name = "Average Score", Prompt = "Your average score"),
         Range(1.0, 100.0),
         Required]
        public decimal Score { get; set; }

        [Display(Name = "Birthday"),
         DataType(DataType.Date)]
        public DateTime? Birthday { get; set; }

        [Display(Name = "Home page", Prompt = "Personal home page"),
         DataType(DataType.Url),
         Required]
        public string Homepage { get; set; }

        [Display(Name = "Email", Prompt = "Preferred e-mail address"),
         DataType(DataType.EmailAddress),
         Required]
        public string Email { get; set; }

        [Display(Name = "Phone number", Prompt = "Contact phone number"),
         DataType(DataType.PhoneNumber),
         Required]
        public string Phone { get; set; }

        [Display(Name = "Overall Satisfaction")]
        public string Satisfaction { get; set; }
    }
}
```

■ **Note** The view files use the Razor syntax and have the `.cshtml` (or `.vbhtml`) extension. However, the model and controller files are standard C# (or VB) classes.

Rebuild the application. This will make the model available when defining the view.

Defining the Feedback View

Now you'll define a new view based on this model. Initially, this will be a simple form with a single field. Then you will add a link on the home page and a controller action to handle this. Later in the chapter you'll add more fields to the form.

EXERCISE 3-2. DESIGNING THE INITIAL FEEDBACK FORM

1. In the Solution Explorer, expand the Views folder. Right-click the Home folder and choose Add and View. Enter the name **Feedback**, select the Empty template, and select the FeedbackModel, as shown in Figure 3-7. Click the Add button to create the view.

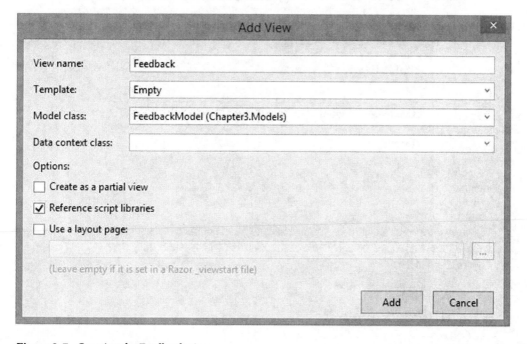

Figure 3-7. *Creating the Feedback view*

2. The new view is generated with a single empty div inside the body tag. Enter the code shown in bold in Listing 3-3. This code includes an input control for the Email property using the EditorFor() method.

Listing 3-3. Defining the Initial Form

```
@model Chapter3.Models.FeedbackModel

@{
    Layout = null;
}

<!DOCTYPE html>

<html>
<head>
    <meta name="viewport" content="width=device-width" />
    <title>Feedback</title>
</head>
<body>
    <div>
        @using (Html.BeginForm((string)ViewBag.FormAction, "Home"))
        {
            <fieldset>
            <legend>Feedback Form</legend>
            <div>
                @Html.EditorFor(m => m.Email)
            </div>
            <p>
                <input type="submit" value="Submit" />
            </p>
            </fieldset>
        }
    </div>
</body>
</html>
```

3. Views are invoked by a controller, so you'll need to add a controller action that will load this page. Open the HomeController.cs class, which you'll find in the Controllers folder.

4. Add the following method:

```
public ActionResult Feedback()
{
    return View();
}
```

5. Finally, you'll need a link that triggers this controller action. Open `_Layout.cshtml` in the `View\Shared` folder.

6. Add the line shown in bold:

```
<ul id="menu">
  <li>@Html.ActionLink("Home", "Index", "Home")</li>
  <li>@Html.ActionLink("About", "About", "Home")</li>
  <li>@Html.ActionLink("Contact", "Contact", "Home")</li>
  <li>@Html.ActionLink("Feedback", "Feedback", "Home")</li>
</ul>
```

7. Save your changes and press F5 to debug. You should now have a Feedback link on the home page, as shown in Figure 3-8.

Figure 3-8. *The Feedback link on the home page*

8. Click this link to display the feedback form, which is shown in Figure 3-9.

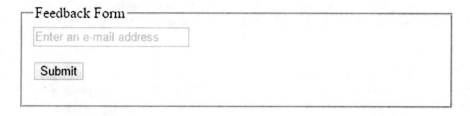

Figure 3-9. *The initial feedback form*

9. Enter an invalid email address and click the Submit button. You should see the standard HTML5 validation error, as shown in Figure 3-10.

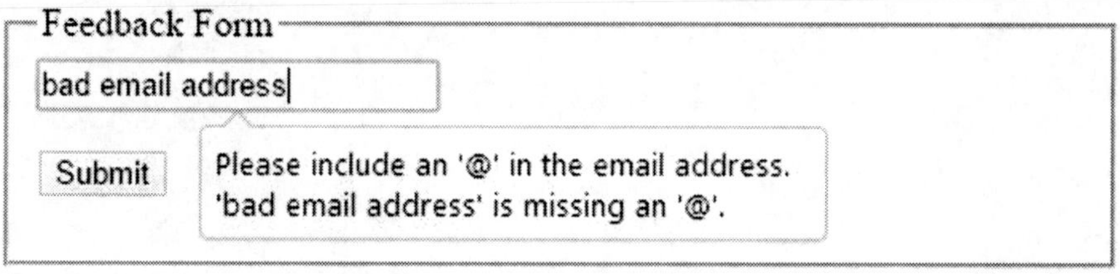

Figure 3-10. *The standard HTML5 validation error*

10. View the source of the feedback form, which should be similar to this:

```
<form action="/Home/Feedback" method="post">
  <fieldset>
    <legend>Feedback Form</legend>
    <div>
      <input class="text-box single-line" data-val="true"
          data-val-required="The Email field is required."
          id="Email"
          name="Email" placeholder="Enter an e-mail address"
          type="email" value="" />
    </div>
    <p>
      <input type="submit" value="Submit" />
    </p>
  </fieldset>
</form>
```

Completing the Feedback Form

Now you'll add the remaining fields to the feedback form. You'll also need to provide editor templates for the additional data types. I will show you how the framework determines which template to use.

Adding the Other Fields

You'll start by adding the other fields that are defined in the FeedbackModel.cs class. For each one you'll include a label and use the EditorFor() method to generate the input field.

EXERCISE 3-3. COMPLETING THE FEEDBACK FORM

1. Open the `Feedback.cshtml` file and add the code shown in bold in Listing 3-4.

Listing 3-4. The Feedback View Implementation

```
<div>
    @Html.EditorFor(m => m.Email)
</div>
<div class="editor-label">
    @Html.LabelFor(m => m.Name)
</div>
<div class="editor-field">
    @Html.EditorFor(m => m.Name)
</div>
<div class="editor-label">
    @Html.LabelFor(m => m.Birthday)
</div>
<div class="editor-field">
    @Html.EditorFor(m => m.Birthday)
</div>
<div class="editor-label">
    @Html.LabelFor(m => m.Homepage)
</div>
<div class="editor-field">
    @Html.EditorFor(m => m.Homepage)
</div>
<div class="editor-label">
    @Html.LabelFor(m => m.Phone)
</div>
<div class="editor-field">
    @Html.EditorFor(m => m.Phone)
</div>
<div class="editor-label">
    @Html.LabelFor(m => m.Score)
</div>
<div class="editor-field">
    @Html.EditorFor(m => m.Score)
</div>
<div class="editor-label">
    @Html.LabelFor(m => m.Satisfaction)
</div>
<div class="editor-field">
    @Html.EditorFor(m => m.Satisfaction)
</div>
<p>
    <input type="submit" value="Submit" />
</p>
```

2. Save your changes and press F5 to view the modified form. Click the Feedback link to display the page, which will look similar to Figure 3-11.

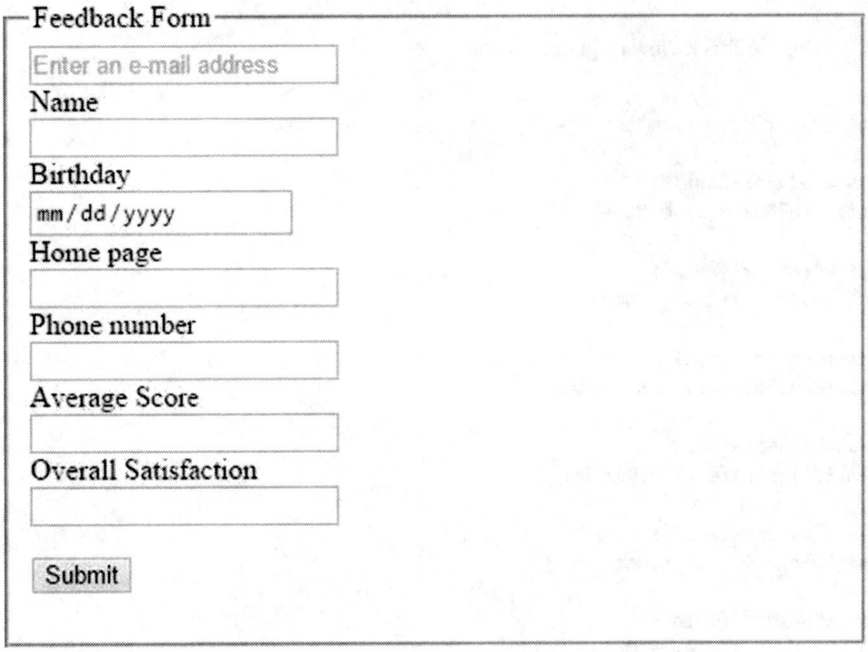

Figure 3-11. *The feedback form*

3. Notice that all the new fields, except `Birthday`, use the standard `TextBox` control and do not include a `placeholder` text. This is because there is no editor template defined for these data types. The `Birthday` property was defined in the model as a `DateTime` value, and the implementation of the `Textbox` control uses this placeholder for dates.

Adding Editor Templates

You may have been asking yourself, how does the framework know which editor template to use? The framework tries to use the correct template based on the data type of the property. This is not very reliable because e-mail, URLs, and phone numbers are all stored in a `string` variable. The preferred method is to define this using metadata.

If you include the `System.ComponentModel.DataAnnotations` namespace in your model class, you can include metadata in your model. There are two metadata attributes that are used to determine the appropriate template.

- `DataType`
- `UIHint`

The DataType attribute is specified using the DataType enum. This includes a fairly large but fixed set of values, such as the contextual types EmailAddress, CreditCard, Currency, PostalCode, and Url. If you add a DataType attribute, the editor template with the matching name is used. You included the DataType attributes when you implemented the FeedbackModel.

The UIHint attribute is specified with a string, and you can therefore use any value to want. If you want a property displayed in green font, you can specify the UIHint("GreenFont") attribute in the model and then provide a GreenFont.cshtml template. The UIHint takes precedence over the DataType attribute when determining the appropriate template to use.

■ **Tip** My GreenFont example was used to illustrate how the UIHint attribute works. You should not use it for setting style properties because this is the role of the style sheets. A more appropriate application of the UIHint attribute will be demonstrated later in this chapter when you implement a range control.

---

4. Right-click the Views\Shared\EditorTemplates folder and choose Add and View. In the Add View dialog box, enter the name **Date** and unselect all of the check boxes. Replace the view implementation with the following code:

```
@Html.TextBox("", null, new
{
    @class = "text-box single-line",
    type = "date"
})
```

5. In the same way, add another editor template named **Url** and use the following implementation:

```
@Html.TextBox("", null, new
{
    @class = "text-box single-line",
    type = "url",
    placeholder = "Enter a web address"
})
```

6. Create a **PhoneNumber** template using the following code:

```
@Html.TextBox("", null, new
{
    @class = "text-box single-line",
    type = "tel",
    placeholder = "Enter a phone number"
})
```

7. Create a **Number** template using the following code (you will be using this in a later exercise):

```
@Html.TextBox("", null, new
{
    @class = "text-box single-line",
    type = "number",
    placeholder = "Enter a number"
})
```

8. Save your changes and press F5 to debug your application. The feedback form should now use the HTML5 controls, as shown in Figure 3-12.

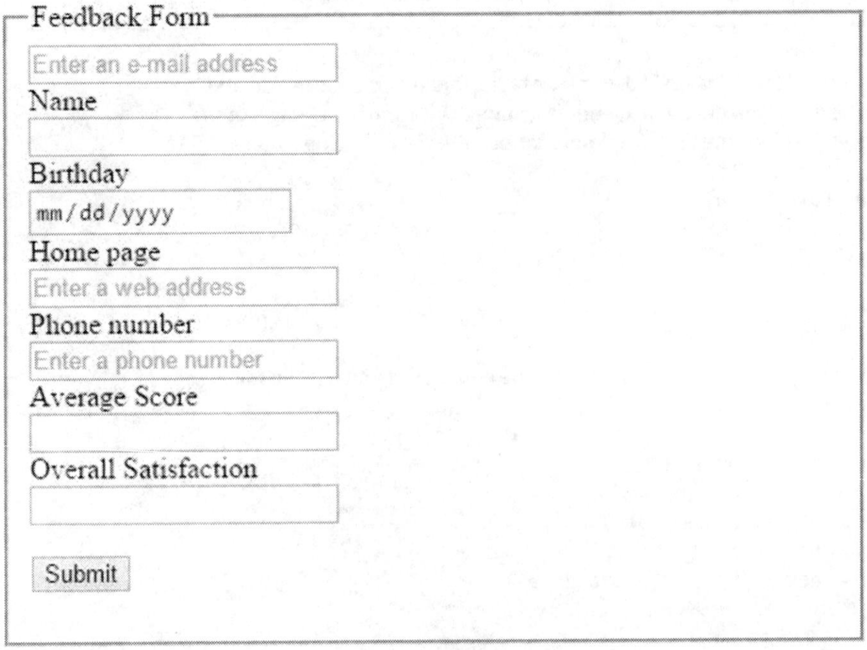

Figure 3-12. *The form using HTML5 controls*

Generating Custom HTML

The editor templates that you have implemented are all based on the TextBox() method of the Html helper class. The templates simply add some additional attributes such as type and placeholder. However, you can implement templates that will output any HTML content you want. To demonstrate that, I'll show you how to build your own helper extension that generates the markup from scratch. You will use this to replace the EmailAddress template.

Adding a Custom Helper Class

You can create your own helper class and add it as a property of the existing Html helper class. You can then access your custom method as follows:

```
@Html.<CustomClass>.<CustomMethod>()
```

EXERCISE 3-4. CREATING A HELPER EXTENSION

1. In the Solution Explorer, right-click the Chapter3 project and choose Add and Class links. Enter the name **Html5.cs** when prompted for the class name.

2. Enter the source shown in Listing 3-5.

   Listing 3-5. The Initial HTML5 Helper Class

   ```
   using System;
   using System.Collections.Generic;
   using System.Linq;
   using System.Web;
   using System.Globalization;

   namespace System.Web.Mvc
   {
       public class Html5Helper
       {
           private readonly HtmlHelper htmlHelper;

           public Html5Helper(HtmlHelper htmlHelper)
           {
               this.htmlHelper = htmlHelper;
           }
           private static CultureInfo Culture
           {
               get
               {
                   return CultureInfo.CurrentCulture;
               }
           }

           // Add custom methods here...

       }

       public static class HtmlHelperExtension
       {
           public static Html5Helper Html5(this HtmlHelper instance)
           {
               return new Html5Helper(instance);
           }
       }
   }
   ```

There are a couple of things to point out here. First, note that the namespace is set as System.Web.Mvc and not your application's namespace, Chapter3. Your custom helper class is named Html5Helper, and its constructor takes an HtmlHelper parameter. This is a reference to the standard helper class, which is stored as a private class member. Your custom methods will need this to access data from the framework such a view and model information. Finally, this code also declares a static HtmlHelperExtension class, which provides a static method that returns your custom class. Notice that the method name is Html5, so you will access your custom class from the view as follows:

```
@Html.Html5().<CustomMethod>()
```

The purpose of having your own custom helper class is to be able to implement custom helper methods. So, let's add one now. The first method will generate an e-mail input control. You will then use this in your EmailAddress.cshtml template.

3. Add the code shown in Listing 3-6 to your custom class where the // Add custom methods here placeholder is.

Listing 3-6. The EmailControl Implementation

```
public IHtmlString EmailControl()
{
    string id;
    string name;
    string placeHolder;
    string value;
    string valueAttribute;

    ViewDataDictionary viewData = htmlHelper.ViewData;
    ModelMetadata metaData = viewData.ModelMetadata;

    // Build the HTML attributes
    id = viewData.TemplateInfo.GetFullHtmlFieldId(string.Empty);
    name = viewData.TemplateInfo.GetFullHtmlFieldName(string.Empty);

    if (string.IsNullOrWhiteSpace(metaData.Watermark))
        placeHolder = string.Empty;
    else
        placeHolder = "placeholder=\"" + metaData.Watermark + "\"";

    value = viewData.TemplateInfo.FormattedModelValue.ToString();
    if (string.IsNullOrWhiteSpace(value))
        valueAttribute = string.Empty;
    else
        valueAttribute = "value=\"" + value + "\"";

    // Determine the css class
    string css = "text-box single-line";
```

```
            ModelState state;
            if (viewData.ModelState.TryGetValue(name, out state)
                && (state.Errors.Count > 0))
                css += " " + HtmlHelper.ValidationInputCssClassName;

            // Format the final HTML
            string markup = string.Format(Culture,
                "<input type=\"email\" id=\"{0}\" name=\"{1}\" {2} {3} " +
                "class=\"{4}\"/>", id, name, placeHolder, valueAttribute, css);

            return MvcHtmlString.Create(markup);
        }
```

This method gathers the various HTML attributes such as id, name, class, and placeholder. This information is extracted from the model or the model metadata. At the end of this method, the markup string is built using the standard string.Format() method, which assembles the various attributes. This is then passed to the static MvcHtmlString.Create() method to provide this as the IHtmlString interface that the MVC framework requires.

The primary difference in this implementation of the EmailAddress template is that the placeholder attribute is set using the model metadata. The previous implementation used a hard-coded placeholder, "Enter an e-mail address." Unfortunately, the property names are completely inconsistent. In the model, this is specified using the Prompt attribute (Prompt = "Preferred e-mail address"). In the ModelMetadata class, this value is provided as the Watermark property. And, of course, this is included in the HTML document as a placeholder attribute.

Re-implementing the Custom E-mail Template

Now you'll replace the EmailAddress template with a much simpler one that uses the new helper extension that you've just implemented.

EXERCISE 3-5. RE-IMPLEMENTING THE E-MAIL TEMPLATE

1. Save the changes and open the EmailAddress.cshtml template.

2. Replace the entire implementation with the following:

   ```
   @Html.Html5().EmailControl()
   ```

3. Save the changes and press F5 to debug. The placeholder text should now reflect the prompt specified in the model metadata, as demonstrated in Figure 3-13.

Figure 3-13. *The modified Email field*

4.   View the source of this page, and the HTML markup for the Email field should look
     like this:

```
<input type="email"
    id="Email"
    name="Email"
    placeholder="Preferred e-mail address"
    class="text-box single-line">
```

Implementing a Range Control

As you saw in the previous chapter, the range control supports some additional attributes that are not
available in the standard TextBoxFor (or even EditorFor) implementations. To implement this using the
MVC framework, you'll implement a custom helper method. You'll then provide an editor template that calls
this custom method. Finally, you'll add a UIHint attribute in the model metadata that will tell the framework
to use the new template.

Implementing a Custom Helper Method

The first step is to create a custom helper method that will generate the appropriate markup for a range
control. This will be similar to the EmailControl() method that you just implemented except that is doesn't
include the placeholder attribute. Also, the min, max, and step attributes are passed in to the method.

   Add the code in Listing 3-7 to the Html5.cs file (inside the Html5Helper class).

Listing 3-7.   The RangeControl Implementation

```
public IHtmlString RangeControl(int min, int max, int step)
{
    string id;
    string name;
    string value;
    string valueAttribute;

    ViewDataDictionary viewData = htmlHelper.ViewData;

    // Build the HTML attributes
    id = viewData.TemplateInfo.GetFullHtmlFieldId(string.Empty);
    name = viewData.TemplateInfo.GetFullHtmlFieldName(string.Empty);

    value = viewData.TemplateInfo.FormattedModelValue.ToString();
    if (string.IsNullOrWhiteSpace(value))
        valueAttribute = string.Empty;
    else
        valueAttribute = "value=\"" + value + "\"";

    // Determine the css class
    string css = "range";
```

```
ModelState state;
if (viewData.ModelState.TryGetValue(name, out state)
    && (state.Errors.Count > 0))
    css += " " + HtmlHelper.ValidationInputCssClassName;

// Format the final HTML
string markup = string.Format(Culture,
    "<input type=\"range\" id=\"{0}\" name=\"{1}\" " +
    "min=\"{2}\" max=\"{3}\" step=\"{4}\" {5} class=\"{6}\"/>",
    id, name, min.ToString(), max.ToString(), step.ToString(),
    valueAttribute, css);

return MvcHtmlString.Create(markup);
}
```

Adding the Range Template

Now you'll need to create an editor template for the range control that will use this new custom method.

EXERCISE 3-6. ADDING A RANGE TEMPLATE

1. Right-click the Views\Shared\EditorTemplates folder and choose Add and View.

2. In the Add View dialog box, enter the name **Range** and unselect all of the text boxes.

3. Replace the default implementation with the following:

    ```
    @Html.Html5().RangeControl(0, 200, 20)
    ```

4. Open the FeedbackModel.cs file and add the UIHint attribute to the Satisfaction property like this:

    ```
    [Display(Name = "Overall Satisfaction"), UIHint("Range")]
    public string Satisfaction { get; set; }
    ```

5. While you have the FeedbackModel.cs file open, add a UIHint attribute for the Score property as follows:

    ```
    [Display(Name = "Average Score", Prompt = "Your average score"),
    Range(1.0, 100.0), UIHint("Number"),
    Required]
    public decimal Score { get; set; }
    ```

6.   Save your changes and press F5 to debug. Go to the Feedback page; the page should look like Figure 3-14.

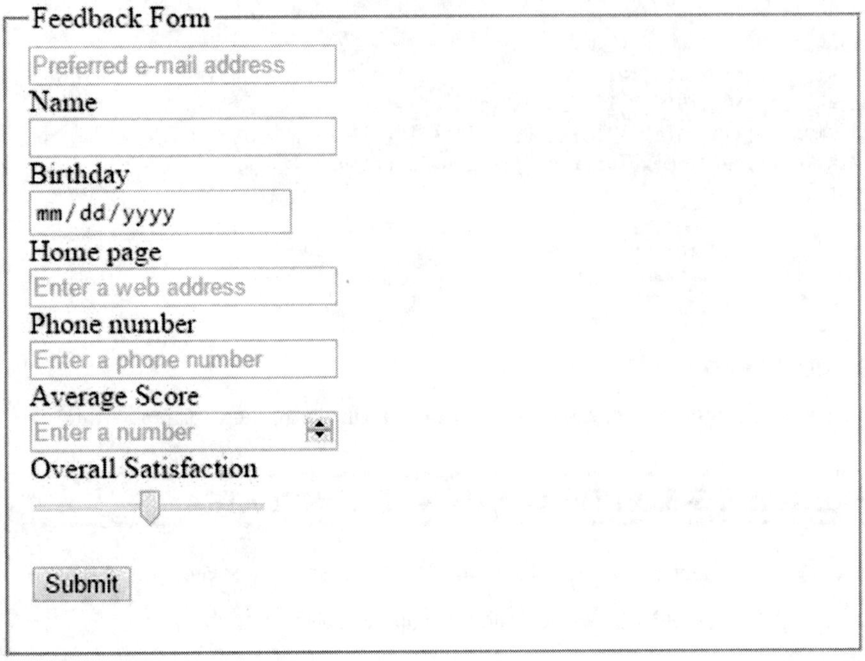

Figure 3-14. *The updated score and range control*

Using Open Source Extensions

So far you have created two editor templates that are based on custom helper methods and four simple templates based on the TextBox() method. However, you will likely need quite a few other templates beside these. Before you spend all that time implementing them, you might be wondering if someone else has already done this for you. Well, the answer is yes.

There are a lot of third-party libraries and tools that are available to you. Visual Studio provides a package manager called NuGet that makes it easy to find, download, install, and manage these third-party packages. I'll show you how to use NuGet to install a package of editor templates so you don't have to write them yourself. Of course, now that you know how to write your own, feel free to do so if any of these don't work quite like you want them to.

EXERCISE 3-7. INSTALLING EDITOR TEMPLATES

1. When the third-party package is installed, it will prompt you before overwriting any existing templates. So before you begin, you should delete the existing editor templates. Delete all of the files in the EditorTemplates folder except for Range.cshtml (the third-party package does not include this template).

2. In Visual Studio, with the Chapter3 project still open, choose Tools and NuGet Package Manager and Manage NuGet Packages for Solution.

3. This will display the Manage NuGet Packages dialog box. If you select Installed in the Filter drop-down, it will list the packages currently installed. You might be surprised to find that quite a few have already been installed by the project template. The blue icon to the right of each package indicates whether there is an update available for it, as demonstrated in Figure 3-15.

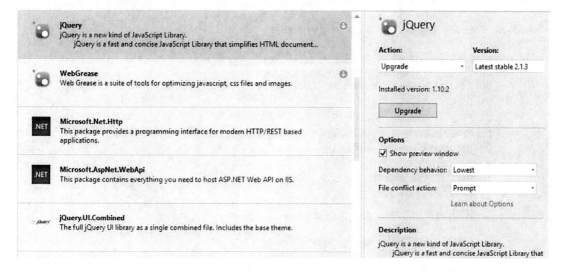

Figure 3-15. *Listing the installed packages*

4. Change the Filter drop-down to All, and enter **html5 editor templates** in the search field.

5. Select the package named Html5EditorTemplates, as shown in Figure 3-16. The pane on the right displays details of this package including author, description, and links for more information.

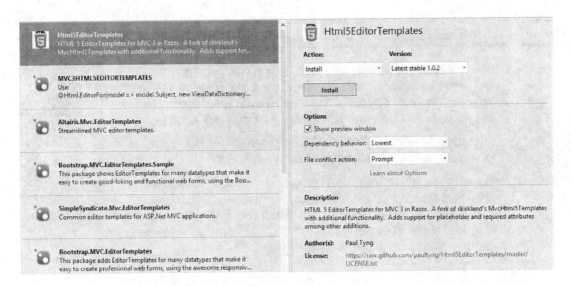

Figure 3-16. *Selecting the Html5EditorTemplates package*

6. Click the Install button.

7. Once the install has completed, you should now see quite a few templates in the `EditorTemplates` folder. Open the `EmailAddress.cshtml` file. Listing 3-8 shows the third-party implementation for this template. While this is implemented differently from yours, it accomplishes basically the same thing, including getting the placeholder from the metadata.

Listing 3-8. The Open Source Email Template

```
@{
    var attributes = new Dictionary<string, object>();

    attributes.Add("type", "email");

    attributes.Add("class", "text-box single-line");
    attributes.Add("placeholder", ViewData.ModelMetadata.Watermark);

    //since this is a constraint, IsRequired and other constraints
    //won't necessarily apply in the browser, but in case script
    //turns off readonly we want the constraints passed
    if (ViewData.ModelMetadata.IsReadOnly)
    {
        attributes.Add("readonly", "readonly");
    }

    if (ViewData.ModelMetadata.IsRequired)
    {
        attributes.Add("required", "required");
    }
}
@Html.TextBox("", ViewData.TemplateInfo.FormattedModelValue, attributes)
```

8.   Press F5 to debug the Feedback page, which should look like Figure 3-17.

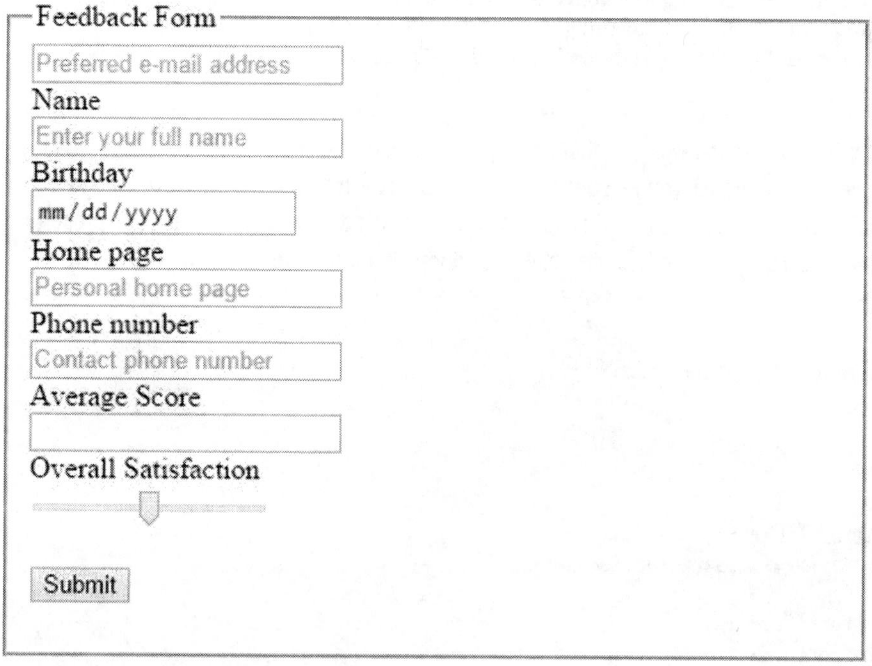

Figure 3-17. The feedback page using third-party templates

Adding Literal HTML

Using the Html helper class, including the EditorFor() method, is the recommended way to implement forms with ASP.NET MVC. This provides tight integration with the model including the model metadata and the separation of concerns (business rules and user experience). However, you can always embed the actual HTML markup in your view. An appropriate use of this would be to include static content or a control that is not connected to a model, such as a progress bar.

I'll now demonstrate three examples, each inserting one of the new HTML5 controls into the feedback form using direct HTML markup.

- Range

- Progress

- Meter

Adding a Range Control

You already included a range control using a custom editor template. Now you'll insert another one by simply adding the appropriate HTML markup. And just for fun, you'll make this a vertical slider by setting the transform to rotate 90 degrees. To do this, add the code in bold in Listing 3-9 to the Feedback.cshtml view.

■ **Caution** Previous versions of Opera would render a range control vertically if the height was larger than the width. The current version (as of this writing) does not do that. There seems to be little agreement between browser implementations on how this should be implemented. I have found that using the transform property is the most consistent way to accomplish this. I will explain transforms in more detail in Chapter 4.

Listing 3-9. Adding a range Control in HTML

```
<fieldset>

    . . .

    <div class="editor-label">
        @Html.LabelFor(m => m.Satisfaction)
    </div>
    <div class="editor-field">
        @Html.EditorFor(m => m.Satisfaction)
    </div>
    <div>
        Custom range
        <input type="range" id="CustomRange" name="CustomRange"
               class="range"
               style="width: 100px; height: 30px; transform: rotate(90deg)"
               min="0" max="200" step="20" />
    </div>
    <p>
        <input type="submit" value="Submit" />
    </p>
</fieldset>
```

Save your changes and press F5 to debug. The form should look like Figure 3-18.

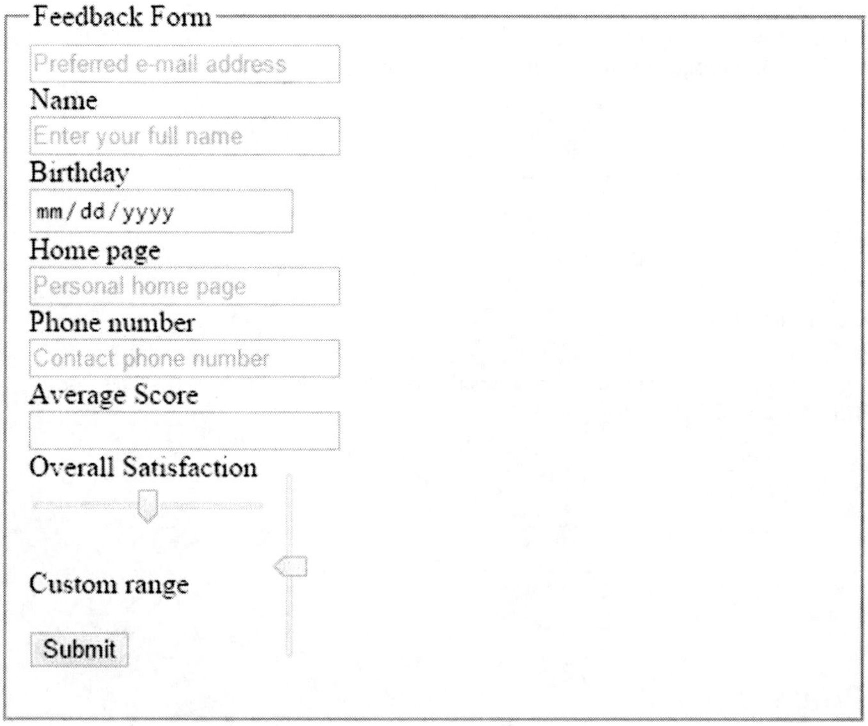

Figure 3-18. *Adding a vertical range control*

■ **Note** The value of this control is not part of the model and will not be saved with the form. This is appropriate if the control is used solely to aid the user experience and does not need to be persisted. For example, it could control the volume of a video or audio clip.

Adding a Progress Bar

Next, you'll add a progress bar by inserting a progress tag in the form. Add the following code in bold after the Submit button:

```
<p>
    <input type="submit" value="Submit" />
</p>
<div>
    <progress id="FormProgress" value="60" max="100">
        <strong>Progress: 60%</strong>
    </progress>
</div>:
</fieldset>
```

The progress tag does not support a min attribute but only a max attribute. The minimum value is assumed to be zero. The value attribute specifies the current progress. Press F5 to debug the application and navigate to the feedback form. The progress should appear as shown in Figure 3-19.

Figure 3-19. *The progress control in Opera*

The content within the progress tag is used for browsers that do not support the progress tag. For example, in IE9, the form would look like Figure 3-20.

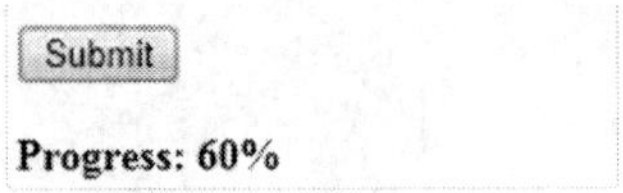

Submit

Progress: 60%

Figure 3-20. *The progress control in IE9*

Updating the Progress Bar

However, a static progress bar is not very interesting; one might even find a progress bar that never changes to be frustrating. Now you'll add some JavaScript code to update the progress bar as fields on the form have been entered.

First, you'll create a function called calculateProgress() that iterates through all the input fields to see which ones have a value. There are six fields, so you'll give each one a value of 17 (6 × 17 = 102). Setting the value to anything over 100 will just show as 100 percent complete. This code uses the document. getElementsByClassName() selector that returns all elements with the specified class attribute. In this case, you want elements with the text=box single-line class. The function then updates the value of the progress bar using the computed value.

Then, you'll need to call this function whenever an input field is changed. To do that, you'll create a function named bindEvents() and use the same getElementsByClassName() selector. This time, you'll use the addEventListener() function to bind the calculateProgress() function to the onChange event. Finally, you'll call bindEvents() function in the onLoad event handler.

Enter the code in bold in Listing 3-10 to your feedback form.

Listing 3-10. Adding JavaScript to Update the Progress Bar

```
<head>
    <meta name="viewport" content="width=device-width" />
    <title>Feedback</title>
    <script type="text/javascript">
        function calculateProgress() {
            var value = 0;
            var fieldList = document.getElementsByClassName("text-box single-line");
            for (var i = 0; i < fieldList.length; i++) {
                if (fieldList[i].value > "")
                    value += 17;
            }
            if (value > 100)
                value = 100;
            var progress = document.getElementById("FormProgress");
            progress.value = value;
        };
        function bindEvents() {
            var fieldList = document.getElementsByClassName("text-box single-line");
            for (var i = 0; i < fieldList.length; i++) {
                fieldList[i].addEventListener("change", calculateProgress, false);
            }
        }
    </script>
</head>
<body onload="bindEvents();">
```

___

■ **Note** In calculating the progress, this code ignores the range control used for the Satisfaction field as well as the overall score. This was done because these controls always have a value and so you can't tell when a value was "entered."

___

Also, change the initial value property of the progress tag from 60 to 0 like this:

```
<progress id="FormProgress" value="0" max="100">
```

Press F5 to debug the application. As you enter values in the input fields, notice that the progress bar is automatically updated, as shown in Figure 3-21.

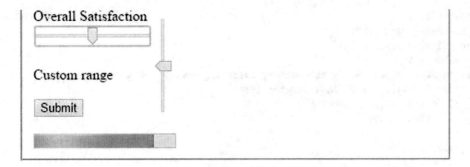

Figure 3-21. *The progress and range controls in Chrome*

■ **Tip** As I mentioned, the text inside the progress tag is displayed when the browser does not support the progress control. You could update this dynamically with JavaScript; however, you could also just leave it blank and not show the progress when this is not supported.

Using the Meter Control

For the last example, you'll add a meter control, which is similar to the progress bar. A meter allows you to define intervals within the range that will enable the color-coding of the status indicator. For example, consider an oil-pressure gauge on a car. A "normal" range is indicated on the gauge, and low or high values are highlighted. I don't need to know what the oil pressure is or even what it should be; I just want to know whether it's in the normal range.

Like the range control, the meter control supports the min and max attributes as well as the current value. It also provides low, high, and optimum attributes that define the normal range. Enter the following code in bold:

```
<div>
    <progress id="FormProgress" value="0" max="100">
        <strong>Progress: 60%</strong>
    </progress>
</div>
<div>
    <meter id="Meter" value="50" min="20" max="120"
        low="50" high="100" optimum="75">
        <strong>Meter:</strong>
    </meter>
</div>
</fieldset>
```

To demonstrate how different values are displayed, you'll add some JavaScript code to update the control with a random value every second. To do that, add the following code in bold to the `bindEvents()` function:

```
function bindEvents() {
    var fieldList = document.getElementsByClassName("text-box single-line");
    for (var i = 0; i < fieldList.length; i++) {
        fieldList[i].addEventListener("change", calculateProgress, false);
    }
    setInterval(function () {
            var meter = document.getElementById("Meter");
            meter.value = meter.min + Math.random() * (meter.max - meter.min);
    }, 1000);
}
```

This code uses the `setInterval()` function, so the anonymous function is called every 1,000 milliseconds. Press F5 to start the application. Depending on the value, the color will change from green to yellow, as shown in Figure 3-22.

Figure 3-22. *The meter control*

Summary

In case you've gotten lost in all the various updates, Listing 3-11 shows the complete implementation of the `Feedback.cshtml` view.

Listing 3-11. The Final Feedback.cshtml Implementation

```
@model Chapter3.Models.FeedbackModel

@{
    Layout = null;
}

<!DOCTYPE html>

<html>
<head>
    <meta name="viewport" content="width=device-width" />
    <title>Feedback</title>
    <script type="text/JavaScript">
```

```
        function calculateProgress() {
            var value = 0;
            var fieldList = document.getElementsByClassName("text-box single-line");
            for (var i = 0; i < fieldList.length; i++) {
                if (fieldList[i].value > "")
                    value += 17;
            }
            if (value > 100)
                value = 100;
            var progress = document.getElementById("FormProgress");
            progress.value = value;
        };
        function bindEvents() {
            var fieldList = document.getElementsByClassName("text-box single-line");
            for (var i = 0; i < fieldList.length; i++) {
                fieldList[i].addEventListener("change", calculateProgress, false);
            }
            setInterval(function () {
                var meter = document.getElementById("Meter");
                meter.value = meter.min + Math.random() * (meter.max - meter.min);
            }, 1000);

        }
    </script>
</head>
<body onload="bindEvents();">
    <div>
        @using (Html.BeginForm((string)ViewBag.FormAction, "Home"))
        {
            <fieldset>
                <legend>Feedback Form</legend>
                <div>
                    @Html.EditorFor(m => m.Email)
                </div>
                <div class="editor-label">
                    @Html.LabelFor(m => m.Name)
                </div>
                <div class="editor-field">
                    @Html.EditorFor(m => m.Name)
                </div>
                <div class="editor-label">
                    @Html.LabelFor(m => m.Birthday)
                </div>
                <div class="editor-field">
                    @Html.EditorFor(m => m.Birthday)
                </div>
                <div class="editor-label">
                    @Html.LabelFor(m => m.Homepage)
                </div>
                <div class="editor-field">
                    @Html.EditorFor(m => m.Homepage)
                </div>
```

```
                    <div class="editor-label">
                        @Html.LabelFor(m => m.Phone)
                    </div>
                    <div class="editor-field">
                        @Html.EditorFor(m => m.Phone)
                    </div>
                    <div class="editor-label">
                        @Html.LabelFor(m => m.Score)
                    </div>
                    <div class="editor-field">
                        @Html.EditorFor(m => m.Score)
                    </div>
                    <div class="editor-label">
                        @Html.LabelFor(m => m.Satisfaction)
                    </div>
                    <div class="editor-field">
                        @Html.EditorFor(m => m.Satisfaction)
                    </div>
                    <div>
                        Custom range
                        <input type="range" id="CustomRange" name="CustomRange"
                            class="range vertical"
                            style="width: 100px; height: 30px; transform: rotate(90deg)"
                            min="0" max="200" step="20" />
                    </div>
                    <p>
                        <input type="submit" value="Submit" />
                    </p>
                    <div>
                        <progress id="FormProgress" value="0" max="100">
                            <strong>Progress: 0%</strong>
                        </progress>
                    </div>
                    <div>
                        <meter id="Meter" value="50" min="20" max="120"
                            low="50" high="100" optimum="75">
                            <strong>Meter:</strong>
                        </meter>
                    </div>
                </fieldset>
            }
        </div>
    </body>
</html>
```

In this chapter, you used some of the new HTML5 input types in an ASP.NET MVC project. As with the traditional Web Forms project, you have to do a little extra work to use them, but it's fairly easy to incorporate the new HTML5 features. In particular, the MVC framework is designed to be extensible, which provides a clean platform for building HTML5 applications.

The MVC pattern provides models that define the data elements used on the forms. By including some metadata attributes in the model and then providing custom templates, you can take advantage of the HTML5 semantic-specific controls. There are open source extensions that you can download and install, making it easy to build HTML5-compliant applications. However, in this chapter I showed you how to build your own custom helper extension and build your own editor templates. If you find yourself in a unique situation where you need a specific implementation, you can always build your own.

With the MVC Razor view engine, you can also include literal HTML markup so you have ultimate control of the user experience. I also introduced two new HTML controls, `progress` and `meter`, and demonstrated how these work with some simple JavaScript to manipulate them.

CHAPTER 4

■ ■ ■

Cascading Style Sheets

In Chapters 2 and 3, I showed you the some of the new HTML elements and how to use them in ASP.NET applications. The second major area in the overall HTML5 umbrella includes the improvements in the style sheets. As I explained in Chapter 1, the CSS3 recommendations are broken down into more than 50 modules, most of which are still in draft (as of this writing). However, there is quite a bit of new functionality that is already available in most browsers.

In this chapter, I will demonstrate many of the more useful features. I will start by explaining the basics of creating style sheets. If you have some experience with CSS, this may seem like review, but some of this is new with CSS3, especially the selectors, which have been significantly improved with CSS3. You'll then create a single web page using some of the new structural elements such as nav, aside, and footer. With the page content complete, I'll then explain some of the fun things you can do with CSS.

Reviewing Style Syntax

A style sheet is comprised of a set of rules. Each rule consists of a selector that indicates what elements the rule applies to and one or more declarations. Each declaration contains a property-value pair. A rule is specified with the following syntax:

```
<selector> {<property:value>; <property:value>; ... }
```

For example, if you wanted all the paragraph tags to use a green 12px font, the rule would look like this:

```
p {color:green; font-size:12px;}
```

As with HTML, white space is ignored in a style sheet, so this rule could also be written as follows:

```
p
{
    color:green;
    font-size:12px;
}
```

I will use this format throughout the rest of this chapter because I think it's a little easier to read.

Using Selectors

There were a lot of different ways to select elements from the document, and the CSS3 specifications nearly double this list. I'll provide an overview of the selectors that are available. Many of these will be demonstrated later in the chapter.

Element Selectors

The first one that I just showed you is an *element* selector. To use this, simply specify the element type such as p, h1, input, ol, div, and so on. HTML5 introduces a large number of new tags that you can take advantage of when applying styles. These context-specific elements, such as article, footer, and nav, communicate their purpose more clearly and therefore make it more likely that consistent formatting will be applied to all pages. These new element types are as follows:

- article: A stand-alone portion of content such as a blog entry
- aside: Content usually put to one side of the page; typically used for related information
- details: Used for expandable content that can be hidden or displayed based on user input
- figcaption: Used with figure to associate a caption with an image
- figure: Used to wrap embedded content such as an image or graphic
- footer: The page or section footer
- header: The page or section header
- hgroup: Used to group header elements such as h1, h2, and so on
- nav: Used to contain navigation links
- output: Contains output such as the result of a user action
- section: Used to organize content into logical sections
- summary: Usually used in conjunction with one or more details elements

Using Combinators

If you want to apply the same declarations to more than one element type, you can group them like this:

```
p, h1, h2
{
    color:green;
    font-size:12px;
}
```

The comma (,) character serves as a logical OR operation, for example, "all elements of type p OR h1 OR h2". This is just a special case of a selector combinator. You can also combine selectors to specify certain element hierarchies. By combining elements with one of the following operators, you can create a more complex selector:

- **, (for example, p, h1)**: Selects all p elements as well as all h1 elements.

- **space (for example, header p)**: Selects the second element when it is inside the first element. For example, if you want all p elements that are inside a header element, use header p. The header element does not have to be the immediate parent, just somewhere in the node's parentage.

- *** (for example, header*p)**: Selects the second element when it is a grandchild or later descendant of the first element.

- **> (for example, header>p)**: Selects the second element when the first element is the immediate parent. The header>p selector returns all p elements whose parent (immediate) is a header element.

- **+ (for example, header+p)**: Selects the second element when the first element is the preceding sibling.

- **~ (for example, p~header)**: Selects the second element when it follows the first element (not necessarily immediately).

To illustrate the last two, if your document looks like the following, the h1+p selector will not return any element, but both h2+p and h1~p will both return the p element:

```
<h1>Some header</h1>
<h2>Some sub-header</h2>
<p>Some text</p>
```

Class and ID Selectors

The class selector allows you to select elements with a specific class attribute. For this reason, the class attribute is often referred to as the CSS class. A class selector is created by prefixing the class name with a dot (.) like this:

```
.featured
{
    background-color:yellow;
}
```

This will apply the background color for all elements that have the class="featured" attribute. The class selector looks for whole words that match the selector value. An element can have multiple words in the class attribute like class="the featured article", and the .featured selector will return it.

> ■ **Caution** In the HTML document, the `class` attribute is a string that can have any value you want to give it. However, to be able to use it in a class selector, it must not have any white space or other characters that are not compatible with the CSS syntax. For example, you cannot select the whole `class="featured content"` in a class selector. If you really want a class for featured content, use `featured_content` or `featuredContent`. However, you will not be able to select just `featured` with a class selector. Instead, you'll need to use an attribute selector, which I will demonstrate later.

An ID selector works just like a class selector except that it uses the `id` attribute instead of `class` and you prefix it with a hash symbol (#) like this:

```
#Submit
{
    color:blue;
}
```

An ID selector specifies a single element based on its unique ID, so, by definition, the style will not be reused. It is better to define styles based on elements or classes so similar elements can be styled the same way. ID selectors should be used sparingly and only for unique situations where the style does not need to be reused.

Using Attribute Selectors

Attribute selectors give you a great deal of flexibility, allowing you to select elements based on any of the element's attributes. These are specified as `[attribute=value]` like this:

```
[class="book"]
{
    background-color:yellow;
}
```

This is functionally equivalent to using the `.book` class selector; however, the attribute selector allows you to select using only portions of the attribute's value. To do that, prefix the equal sign (=) with one of the following:

- ~ (for example, `[class~="book"]`): The attribute value must include the word indicated by the selector value (for example, `class="some book titles"`). This is exactly how the class selector works.

- | (for example, `[class|="book"]`): The attribute value must begin with a word that matches the selector value (for example, `class="book titles"`)

- ^= (for example, `[class^="book"]`): The attribute value must begin with the selector value (for example, `class="books"`)

- $ (for example, `[class$="book"]`): The attribute value must end with the selector value (for example, `class="checkbook"`)

- * (for example, `[class*="book"]`): The attribute value must contain the selector value (for example, `class="overbooked"`)

You can specify the attribute without a value, which will return all elements that have the attribute. A good example of this is the [href] selector, which will select all elements that have the href attribute, regardless of its value. You can also include an element selector before an attribute selector to further restrict the selected elements. For example, img[src^="https"] will return all img elements whose src attribute begins with https.

Pseudo-class Selectors

Quite a few selectors are based on the dynamic properties of an element. Consider a hyperlink, for example. If the page referenced by the link has been displayed, the link is usually displayed with a different color. This is achieved using a CSS rule that uses the visited property like this:

```
a:visited
{
    color: purple;
}
```

This will change the color of all a elements that have the visited flag set. Several of these selectors have been available for some time, but CSS3 defines a fairly large set of new ones. Here is the complete list:

- :active: Selects the active link

- :checked: Selects elements that are checked (applies to check boxes)

- :disabled: Selects elements that are currently disabled (typically used for input elements)

- :empty: Selects elements that have no children (elements that include text are not selected)

- :enabled: Selects elements that are enabled (typically used for input elements)

- :first-child: Selects the elements that are the first child of its immediate parent

- <tag>:first-of-type: Selects the elements that is the first of the specified type within its parent

- :focus: Selects the element that currently has the focus

- :hover: Selects the element that the mouse is currently hovering over

- :in-range: Selects input elements that have values within the specified range

- :invalid: Selects input elements that do not have a valid value

- :lang(value): Selects the elements that have a lang attribute that start with the specified value

- :last-child: Selects the elements that are the last child within its parent

- :link: Selects all unvisited links

- <tag>:last-of-type: Selects the elements that are the last of the specified type within its parent

- :nth-child(n): Selects the elements that are the nth child within its parent

- :nth-last-child(n): Selects the elements that are the nth child within its parent, counting in reverse

- <tag>:nth-last-of-type(n): Selects the nth child of the specified type within its parent, counting in reverse

- `<tag>:nth-of-type(n)`: Selects the nth child of the specified type within its parent

- `:only-child`: Selects the elements that are the only child element of its parent

- `<tag>:only-of-type`: Selects the elements that are the only sibling of the specified type within its parent

- `:optional`: Selects input elements that are not required (that is, do not have the `required` attribute)

- `:read-only`: Selects input elements that have the `readonly` attribute

- `:read-write`: Selects input elements that do not have the `readonly` attribute

- `:required`: Selects input elements that have the `required` attribute

- `:root`: Selects the root element of the document

- `:target`: Selects the elements with a target attribute where the target is the active element

- `:valid`: Selects input elements that have a valid value

- `:visited`: Selects all visited links

The `nth-child(n)` selector counts all child elements of the parent, while the `nth-of-type(n)` counts only child elements of the specified type. The distinction here is subtle but important. The same is true with the `only-child` and `only-of-type` selectors.

■ **Caution**   There are four pseudo-classes that can be used with an anchor (a) element (`:link`, `:visited`, `:hover`, and `:active`). If you use more than one, they should appear in this order in the style rules. For example, `:hover` must come after `:link` and `:visited` if they are used. Likewise, `:active` must come after `:hover`.

These pseudo-elements can be used to return a portion of the selected elements:

- `:first-letter`: Selects the first character of every selected element

- `:first-line`: Selects the first line of every selected element

- `:selection`: Returns the portion of an element that is selected by the user

You can add the `:before` or `:after` qualifiers to a selector to insert content in the document before or after the selected elements. Use the `content:` keyword to specify the content and include any desired style commands (the style applies only to the inserted content). For example, to add "Important!" before each p tag that immediately follows a header tag, use the following rule:

```
header+p:before
{
    content:"Important! ";
    font-weight:bold;
    color:red;
}
```

You can also prefix a selector with `:not` to return all the elements not selected. For example, `:not(header+p)` selects all elements except p tags that immediately follow a header tag.

Understanding Unions

You can also combine complex selectors in a logical OR relationship by separating them with commas. For example, the p, h1, h2 selector I showed earlier in this chapter is an example of a union. It will return all elements that satisfy any of the included selectors. Each selector can be any of the more complex types. This is also a valid selector:

```
header+p, .book, a:visited
```

It will return all elements that are either a p element that immediately follows a header element, an element with the book class, or a visited a element.

■ **Tip** For a definitive list of available selectors, see the article at www.w3schools.com/cssref/css_selectors.asp.

Using CSS Properties

All of these selectors are provided so you can specify the appropriate elements that you want to apply the desired style properties to. This is the real meat of CSS. There are hundreds of CSS properties available, and I can't describe them all here. I will demonstrate many of the newer, more useful features in the rest of this chapter. You will find a really good reference of all CSS properties at www.w3schools.com/cssref/default.asp.

Using Vendor Prefixes

Oh, the joys of living on the edge! As with other areas of HTML5, browser vendors will have varying support for the CSS specifications. In many cases, however, these vendors implement new properties before they become part of the official recommendation. In fact, much of what is being included in the CSS3 specification has already been available from one or more browsers.

When a browser vendor adds a new feature that is not part of the CSS3 recommendation, the property is given a vendor-specific prefix to indicate this is a nonstandard feature. If this becomes part of the recommendation, the prefix is eventually dropped. To take advantage of some of the newer properties, you may need to use the vendor-specific properties, and since you want your page to work on all vendors, you'll need to add all of them. For example, to specify the border radius, in addition to the standard border-radius property, you may need to set all of the vendor-specific properties as well like this:

```
header
{
    -moz-border-radius: 25px;
    -webkit-border-radius: 25px;
    -ms-border-radius: 25px;
    border-radius: 25px;
}
```

Table 4-1 lists the most common prefixes. There are others, but this table covers the vast majority of browsers.

Table 4-1. *Vendor Prefixes*

Prefix	Browser Vendor
-moz-	Firefox
-webkit-	Chrome, Safari, Opera
-ms-	Internet Explorer

You can't blindly assume that all vendor-prefixed properties have the same name as the standard property, with the prefix added, although that is true most of the time. Here is a good article that lists many of the vendor-specific properties: http://peter.sh/experiments/vendor-prefixed-css-property-overview. Unfortunately, this page has not been updated for a while and may be out of date. If you find that a standard property doesn't work in a particular browser, you may need to do some research to see whether there is a prefixed property available from their developer's site. For example, use this link for Webkit extensions: https://developer.mozilla.org/en-US/docs/Web/CSS/Reference/Webkit_Extensions.

■ **Caution**   You should always list the standard property last so it will override the vendor-specific version. Some browsers will support both, and while most of the time the implementation is identical, sometimes the vendor-specific version behaves differently.

Understanding the Box Model

Each element in the document takes up a certain amount of space, which depends on the content of that element. In addition, factors such as padding and margin affect this. *Padding* is the space between the content and the element's border. The *margin* is the space between the border and adjacent elements. This is illustrated in Figure 4-1.

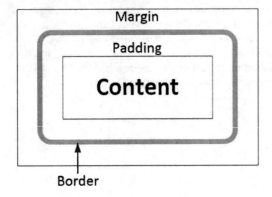

Figure 4-1. *The box model*

You can specify the margin with the `margin` declaration and specify the values either in pixels or as a percentage of the page size. You can specify the top, right, bottom, and left margins individually using the `margin-top`, `margin-right`, `margin-bottom`, and `margin-left` declarations or with the `margin` declaration specifying all four values (in that order—top, right, bottom, and left). You can also use the `margin` declaration with a single value, which will set all four margins to this value. If you pass two values, the first will set the top and bottom margins, and the second will specify the left and right margins. You set the padding the same way using the `padding` declaration.

When determining the space used, remember to include the border width. For example, if the padding is set to 10px, the margin set to 5px, and the border-width set to 3px, the space used (in addition to the actual element content) will be (2 * 10) + (2 * 5) + (2 * 3) = 36px.

Applying Style Rules

Styles are specified from various sources and in several different ways, and as the name suggests, they are cascaded, or inherited. It's important to understand how this works, especially when there are conflicting declarations.

Including Style Specifications

There are three sources of style sheets:

- *Author*: These are the style sheets created by the web developer and what you normally think of when referring to a style sheet.

- *User*: A user can also create a style to control how web pages are displayed for them specifically.

- *User Agent*: A user agent (web browser) will have a default style sheet. For example, if you create a document with no style rules, the browser will display the content using a default font family and size. These are actually defined in a style sheet that is specific to the browser.

For author styles, which are the only source you can control, there are three ways to include style rules in an HTML document.

- *Inline*: The style is set directly in the element using the `style` attribute like this: `<p style="color:red">This is red text</p>`. Of course, with this method, you don't use a selector since the style applies only to the current element (as well as all child elements).

- *Internal*: Style rules can be included in the actual HTML document using the `style` element. This is normally placed in the head tag and applies to the entire document. Styles defined this way will require a selector to indicate on which elements the style should be used. This approach is sometimes referred to as *embedded* styles.

- *External*: The most common way to apply styles is to place all of the style rules in a separate file with a `.css` extension. The style rules are formatted just like the internal styles. The obvious benefit of using an external style sheet is that the same set of rules can be applied to multiple pages. Each page references this style sheet with a `link` element like this:

```
<link rel="stylesheet" type="text/css" href="MyStyleSheet.css"
```

Cascading Rules

When rendering a page, the browser has to process styles from all of these sources to determine the appropriate style for each element. When there are conflicting rules, the author style sheet takes precedence over the user style sheet, which takes precedence over the user agent styles (browser defaults). The author styles can be specified using the three methods I explained earlier (inline, internal, and external). Within the author styles, inline declarations take precedence over internal declarations and external style sheets. If a page uses an internal style element and also uses the link element to include an external style sheet, the internal declarations will override conflicting rules in the external style sheet as long as it comes after the link element.

■ **Caution**   If an external style sheet is referenced after the style tag, it will take precedence over the internal styles. If you have both external style sheets and an internal style element, you should reference the external sheet first so the precedence rules work as expected.

In addition, consider that even within a single style sheet there may be conflicting declaration. For example, a style sheet may include the following:

```
p
{
    color: black;
}

header p
{
    color: red;
}
```

A p element within a header element is selected by both rules, so which one is used? In this case, the specificity rule applies, which states that the more specific selector is used, which is the header p selector. With all the selectors that are available, determining which one is more *specific* is not as straightforward as you might think. ID selectors are considered more specific than class or attribute selectors, which are more specific than element selectors. If there are only element selectors, the rule with the most elements takes precedence, so header p, which contains two elements, is more specific than just p.

Finally, what if the same selector is used twice in the same style sheet with different declarations? Say p { color:black; } appears in the style sheet and later p { color:green } appears. In this case, the rule that appears last takes precedence, so you'll have green text.

Using the Important Keyword

The one sort of "ace-in-the-hole" is the important keyword. If this is used in a style rule, this trumps all other rules. You can add the important keyword like this:

```
p
{
    color: red;
    !important;
}
```

If two conflicting rules both have the important keyword, then the precedence is determined based on the rules I already mentioned. There is one significant difference, however. Normally rules in the author style sheet override rules in the user style sheet. If they have the important keyword, this is reversed; the user style sheet will override the author rules. That may seem odd at first, but this has an important application. This allows the user to override the author styles for certain properties. For example, someone who is visually impaired may need to increase the font size. The important tag will ensure that this style does not get overridden.

■ **Caution**   You might be tempted to use the important keyword to make a quick fix and override a cascaded style rule. With all the precedence rules that I just described, you shouldn't need to do this. I recommend using this as a last resort. Overuse of the important keyword can make your style sheets difficult to maintain.

Creating a Web Page

For the rest of this chapter I will show you how to build a single web page that will demonstrate many of the new CSS features. For variety, I will be using the WebMatrix application instead of Visual Studio to create a single web page. The style rules will use the internal style element so everything can be placed in a single file. The small amount of JavaScript will also be included in the single file.

I will be using the Chrome browser for this project because it supports most of the CSS features that I will be demonstrating. At the time of this writing, the other browsers do not support one or more of these features. By the time you read this, other browsers may support these also.

■ **Note**   I explained how to install the WebMatrix application in Chapter 1. This is a free download provided by Microsoft. If you prefer, you can also implement the web site using Visual Studio with the MVC project template. Follow the instructions in the rest of this chapter using the Index.cshtml file, which you'll find in the Views\Home folder, instead of Default.cshtml. You can also download the completed Visual Studio project that is included in the source code from www.apress.com.

Planning the Page Layout

Before creating a new web page, it's a good idea to sketch out the basic page structure. This will help you visualize the overall layout and see how the elements are nested together.

The page that you will develop in this chapter will use header and nav elements at the top and a footer element at the bottom. The main area in the middle will use a div element and have two side-by-side areas, each with a series of article tags. The larger area will be enclosed with another div element and provide the primary content, which is organized into articles. The smaller area, on the right, will use an aside element and will contain a section element. This will contain a series of article elements that will present related information. Figure 4-2 illustrates the page layout.

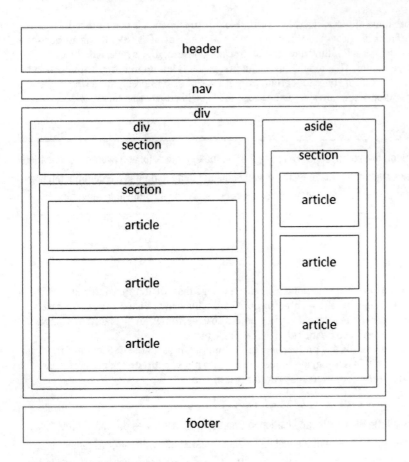

Figure 4-2. *Planning the page layout*

■ **Note**   This diagram shows spaces between each of the elements to make it easier to understand. In the actual web page, in most cases this space is removed by setting the padding attribute to 0.

Creating the Web Project

With the content planned out, you're ready to begin building the web page. You'll start by creating a project using WebMatrix. Then you'll enter the basic page structure and add content to each element. Later, I'll show how to implement the style rules.

Start the WebMatrix application, click the New icon, and then click the Template Gallery button, as shown in Figure 4-3.

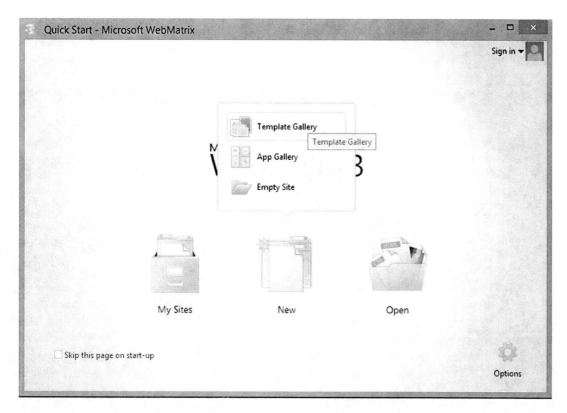

Figure 4-3. *Launching the WebMatrix application*

■ **Tip** For future reference, the App Gallery button will display a fairly large list of prebuilt web applications that you can download and use to build your web project. This includes packages such as WordPress, Joomla, and Drupal.

There are several templates to choose from. The Starter Site template, for example, will create an ASP.NET MVC project. For this chapter, you'll use the Empty Site template. Select this and enter **Chapter4** for the site name, as shown in Figure 4-4. Click the OK button to create the project.

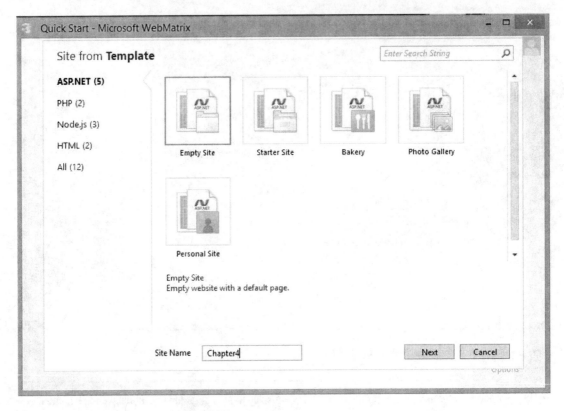

Figure 4-4. *Selecting the Empty Project template*

When the project has been created, click the Files button in the navigation pane. The files and folders that were created for you should look like Figure 4-5

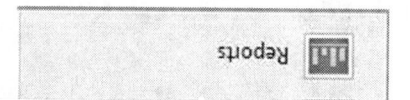

Figure 4-5. The initial files and folders

There should be a single web page named Default.cshtml. Double-click the file name in the navigation pane to open it. The initial contents will look like this:

```
@{
}
<!DOCTYPE html>
<html lang="en">
<head>
<meta charset="utf-8" />
<title>My Site's Title</title>
<link href="~/favicon.ico" rel="shortcut icon" type="image/x-icon" />
</head>
<body>
</body>
</html>
```

Defining the Page Structure

I find it helpful to start by entering the structural elements first before adding the contents. This will give you an opportunity to see the structure clearly, uncluttered by the actual content. Open the Default.cshtml file and enter the elements shown in Listing 4-1.

Listing 4-1. Entering the Page Structure

```
<!DOCTYPE html>

<html lang="en">
    <head>
        <meta charset="utf-8" />
        <title>Chapter 4 - CSS Demo</title>
    </head>
    <body>
        <header class="intro">
        </header>

        <nav>
        </nav>

        <div id="contentArea">

            <div id="mainContent">
                <section class="rounded">
                    <header>
                    </header>
                </section>

                <section>
                    <article class="featuredContent">
                        <a id="feature"></a>
                        <header>
                        </header>

                        <div>
                        </div>
                    </article>

                    <article class="otherContent">
                        <a id="other"></a>
                        <header>
                        </header>

                        <div>
                        </div>
                    </article>
```

```
            <article class="otherContent">
                <a id="another"></a>
                <header>
                </header>

                <div>
                </div>
            </article>
        </section>
    </div>

    <aside id="sidebar">
        <section id="titles">
            <article class="book">
                <header>
                </header>
            </article>

            <article class="book">
                <header>
                </header>
            </article>

            <article class="book">
                <header>
                </header>
            </article>

            <article class="book">
                <header>
                </header>
            </article>

            <article class="book">
                <header>
                </header>
            </article>
        </section>
    </aside>
</div>

<footer>
</footer>

    </body>
</html>
```

This is just a basic HTML structure that you could have inferred from the diagram shown in Figure 4-2. The article elements have the class attribute assigned because you will use this for styling purposes. I assigned the id attribute to a few of the top-level elements. I also added an anchor element (`<a id="feature"></a>`) to each of the main content articles. You will set up navigation links to these in the nav element.

Adding the Content

There's nothing particularly special about the content. It's a lot of text (mostly *Lorem ipsum*), a few images, and some links.

In the Navigation pane, right-click the Chapter4 project and click the New Folder link. Enter **Images** for the folder name. An Images.zip file is included with the downloadable source code. Copy the images from this file to the new Images folder in your project.

I recommend downloading the content rather than entering it manually. There is a Default_content.cshtml file available in the source code. Replace your current implementation of this with the code in this file. It contains only the content of this page without any styles defined. If you want to enter the content manually, you can find it in Appendix A.

■ **Note** I wanted to point out one minor detail in the content. The footer element uses the new time element that was added with HTML5. The text between the begin and end tags (March 7th 2015) is displayed, but the datetime attribute contains a machine-readable format that can be used by the browser, search engines, or JavaScript. Check out this article for more details: www.sitepoint.com/html5-time-element-guide.

After the content has been added, click the Run button in the ribbon to see what the page looks like so far. It should be similar to Figure 4-6.

CSS Demo

Introducing the new HTML5 features

Use the new CSS3 features to build some of the most visually appealing web sites.

- Feature
- Article
- Archives
- Apress

Main content area

Lorem ipsum dolor sit amet, consectetur adipisicing elit, sed do eiusmod tempor incididunt ut labore et dolore magna aliqua. Ut enim ad minim veniam, quis nostrud exercitation ullamco laboris nisi ut.

Featured Article

This is really cool...

Figure 4-6. The initial page with only default styles

Implementing the Style Rules

Now you are at the fun part, adding style. There is a huge number of style attributes that are available to you, and I will demonstrate some of the more useful techniques that are new to CSS3. Many of these styles have been used for a while, but prior to CSS3, their implementation was more complicated, often requiring JavaScript. After assigning some basic style rules, I'll show you how to use more advance features including the following:

- Rounded corners

- Gradient backgrounds

- Tables

- Multiple columns

- Box shadows

- Zebra striping Text decorations

- 3D transforms

- CSS animation

Adding Basic Styles

Before you start adding the new styling features, you'll need to define the basic style formats. Add a `style` element inside the head element at the top of the `Default.cshtml` file. Then add the rules shown in Listing 4-2. Again, if you prefer, you can download the `Default_styled.cshtml` file and copy the code from there.

Listing 4-2. Adding the Basic Styles

```
<style>
    /* Basic tag settings */
    body
    {
        margin: 0 auto;
        width: 940px;
        font: 13px/22px Helvetica, Arial, sans-serif;
        background: #f0f0f0;
    }

    h2
    {
        font-size: 18px;
        line-height: 5px;
        padding: 2px 0;
    }

    h3
    {
        font-size: 12px;
        line-height: 5px;
        padding: 2px 0;
    }
```

```css
h1, h2, h3
{
    text-align: left;
}


p
{
    padding-bottom: 2px;
}

.book
{
    padding: 5px;
}

/* Content sections */
.featuredContent
{
    background-color: #ffffff;
    border: 2px solid #6699cc;
    padding: 15px 15px 15px 15px;
}


.otherContent
{
    background-color: #c0c0c0;
    border: 1px solid #999999;
    padding: 15px 15px 15px 15px;
}

aside
{
    background-color: #6699cc;
    padding: 5px 5px 5px 5px;
}

footer
{
    margin-top: 12px;
    text-align:center;
    background-color: #ddd;
}

footer p
{
    padding-top: 10px;
}
```

```
    /* Navigation Section */
    nav
    {
        left: 0;
        background-color: #003366;
    }

    nav ul
    {
        margin: 0;
        list-style: none;
    }

    nav ul li
    {
        float: left;
    }

    nav ul li a
    {
        display: block;
        margin-right: 20px;
        width: 140px;
        font-size: 14px;
        line-height: 28px;
        text-align: center;
        padding-bottom: 2px;
        text-decoration: none;
        color: #cccccc;
    }

    nav ul li a:hover
    {
        color: #fff;
    }
</style>
```

I won't say much about this because it's all pretty standard CSS stuff. It uses mostly element selectors with an occasional class selector. If you preview your web page now, it should look like Figure 4-7.

CSS Demo

Introducing the new HTML5 features

Use the new CSS3 features to build some of the most visually appealing web sites.

Feature   Article   Archives   Apress   **Main content area**

Lorem ipsum dolor sit amet, consectetur adipisicing elit, sed do eiusmod tempor incididunt ut labore et dolore magna aliqua. Ut enim ad minim veniam, quis nostrud exercitation ullamco laboris nisi ut.

Featured Article

This is really cool...

Lorem ipsum dolor sit amet, consectetur adipisicing elit, sed do eiusmod tempor incididunt ut labore et dolore magna aliqua. Ut enim ad minim veniam, quis nostrud exercitation ullamco laboris nisi ut.

Lorem ipsum dolor sit amet, consectetur adipisicing elit, sed do eiusmod tempor incididunt ut labore et dolore magna aliqua. Ut enim ad minim veniam, quis nostrud exercitation ullamco laboris nisi ut.

Lorem ipsum dolor sit amet, consectetur adipisicing elit, sed do eiusmod tempor incididunt ut labore et dolore magna aliqua. Ut enim ad minim veniam, quis nostrud exercitation ullamco laboris nisi ut.

Rounded Borders

Details about rounded corners

Figure 4-7. *The web page with only basic styling*

■ **Note**   To simplify the sample code, I will use only the Chrome vendor prefix, -webkit-, and only when the current version (43) doesn't support the standard attribute. I can get away with this because I am expecting the page to work only in the Chrome browser. Normally, you cannot make this assumption and will need to include all of the vendor prefixes.

Using Rounded Corners

Adding rounded corners is easy to do with CSS3; just define the border-radius attribute. Your web page will use rounded corners for the aside, nav, and footer elements as well as elements with the rounded class.

■ **Note** In Chapter 7, I will show you how to implement rounded corners in older browsers that do not support this feature. After reading that chapter, you'll likely have a better appreciation for having features like this supported natively in the browser.

Add the rules shown in Listing 4-3 to the end of the style element.

Listing 4-3. Using Rounded Borders

```
/* Rounded borders */
.rounded
{
    border: 1px solid;
    border-color:#999999;
    border-radius:25px;
    padding: 24px;
}

aside
{
    border: 1px solid #999999;
    border-radius:12px;
}

/* Make the radius half of the height */
nav
{
    height: 30px;
    border-radius:15px;
}

footer
{
    height: 50px;
    border-radius:25px;
}
```

For the nav and footer elements, since they are fairly short sections, you'll set the radius to be half of the height. This will form a semicircle on both ends. The top navigation section should look like Figure 4-8.

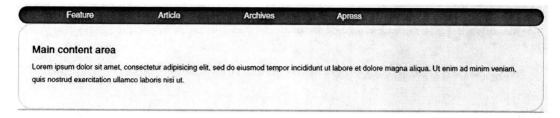

Figure 4-8. Using rounded borders

Working with Gradients

With CSS3 you can easily create a gradient by setting the background-image attribute using the linear-gradient function. With this function you can specify the beginning and ending colors as well as the angle at which the gradient should be applied. You'll use a gradient in the main heading, which has the intro class.

Add the following rule at the end of the style element:

```
/* Gradients */
.intro
{
    border: 1px solid #999999;
    text-align: left;
    padding-left: 15px;
    margin-top: 6px;
    border-radius: 25px;
    background-image: linear-gradient(45deg, #ffffff, #6699cc);
}
```

This will apply the gradient as a 45° angle. This also creates a rounded border. The top of the page should now look like Figure 4-9.

Figure 4-9. Using a gradient background

Creating Tables

It is generally considered bad practice to use tables in your markup for formatting purposes. This type of formatting is better done in the style sheet. You can then update the style if a different format is needed. You might have noticed that the current web page has the aside element following the main content instead of the two aligned side-by-side. You'll set up a table now using CSS to correct that.

Add the rules shown in Listing 4-4 at the end of the style element.

Listing 4-4. Creating a Table

```
/* Setup a table for the content and sidebar */
#contentArea
{
    display: table;
}

#mainContent
{
    display: table-cell;
    padding-right: 2px;
}

aside
{
    display: table-cell;
    width: 280px;
}
```

These rules set the display attribute on the top-level elements. The contentArea element is set to table, and the mainContent and aside elements are set to table-cell. These elements are then rendered as cells within the overall content element. To complete the alignment, the padding on the mainContent is set to 2px, and the width of the aside element is set to 280px. The width of the mainContent is calculated automatically using the remaining space.

The page layout should now look like Figure 4-10.

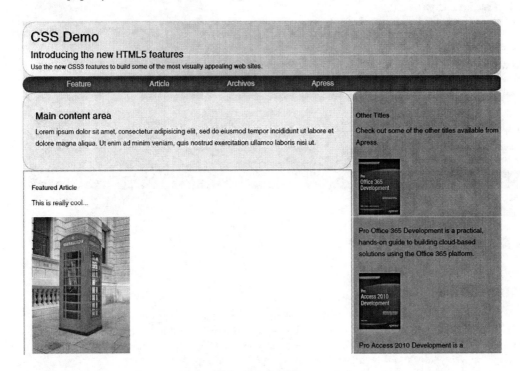

Figure 4-10. *The page layout with the sidebar on the right*

Adding Column Layout

Another neat feature that is new with CSS3 is the ability to format the content into columns like you would see in a newspaper or magazine. This is done using the `column-count` attribute. You should also specify the `column-gap` attribute that defines the vertical space between the columns.

Add the following rules at the end of the `style` element:

```
/* Setup multiple columns for the articles */
.otherContent
{
    text-align:justify;
    padding:6px;

    -webkit-column-count: 2;
    column-count: 2;

    -webkit-column-gap: 20px;
    column-gap: 20px;
}
```

The articles should now be formatted with two columns, as demonstrated in Figure 4-11.

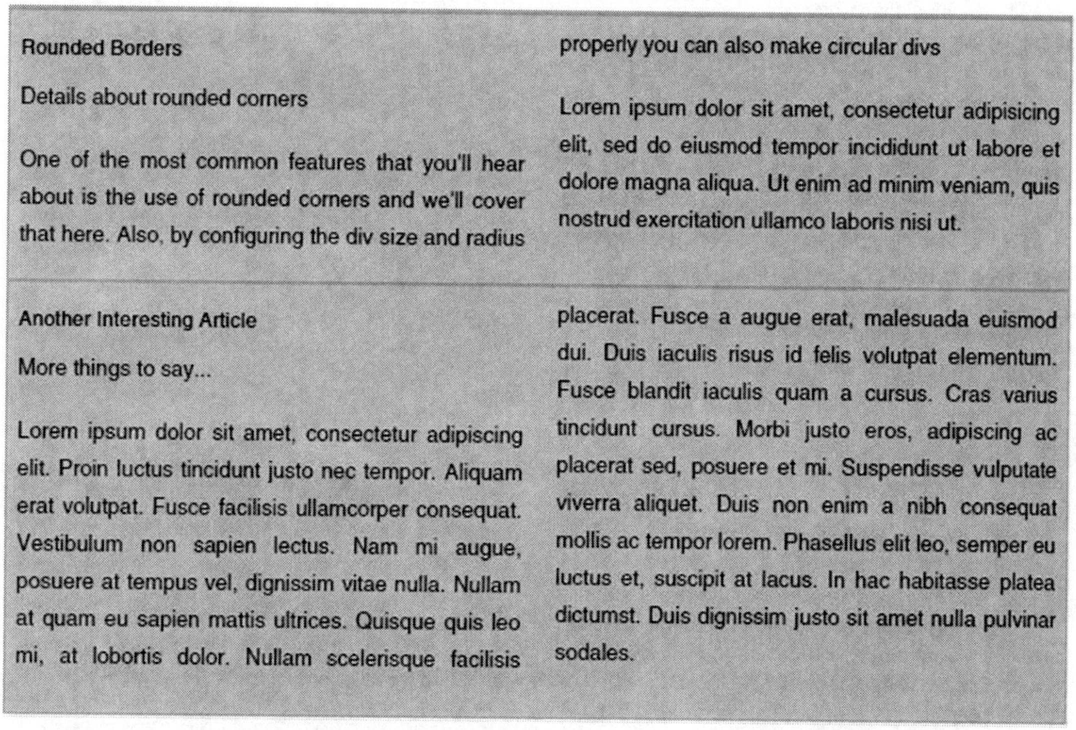

Rounded Borders

Details about rounded corners

One of the most common features that you'll hear about is the use of rounded corners and we'll cover that here. Also, by configuring the div size and radius

properly you can also make circular divs

Lorem ipsum dolor sit amet, consectetur adipisicing elit, sed do eiusmod tempor incididunt ut labore et dolore magna aliqua. Ut enim ad minim veniam, quis nostrud exercitation ullamco laboris nisi ut.

Another Interesting Article

More things to say...

Lorem ipsum dolor sit amet, consectetur adipiscing elit. Proin luctus tincidunt justo nec tempor. Aliquam erat volutpat. Fusce facilisis ullamcorper consequat. Vestibulum non sapien lectus. Nam mi augue, posuere at tempus vel, dignissim vitae nulla. Nullam at quam eu sapien mattis ultrices. Quisque quis leo mi, at lobortis dolor. Nullam scelerisque facilisis

placerat. Fusce a augue erat, malesuada euismod dui. Duis iaculis risus id felis volutpat elementum. Fusce blandit iaculis quam a cursus. Cras varius tincidunt cursus. Morbi justo eros, adipiscing ac placerat sed, posuere et mi. Suspendisse vulputate viverra aliquet. Duis non enim a nibh consequat mollis ac tempor lorem. Phasellus elit leo, semper eu luctus et, suscipit at lacus. In hac habitasse platea dictumst. Duis dignissim justo sit amet nulla pulvinar sodales.

Figure 4-11. *Using two columns*

Adding Box Shadows

Images can look a bit harsh, and adding a shadow can soften the look and make the page more visually appealing. A shadow is easily added using the box-shadow attribute, which takes the following values:

- *Horizontal position*: The position of the horizontal shadow. If negative, the shadow is on the left side.

- *Vertical position*: The position of the vertical shadow. If negative, the shadow is at the top.

- *Blur*: The size of the blurred area just after the shadow.

- *Spread*: The width of the shadow.

- *Color*: The color of the shadow.

- *Inset*: Makes the image appear lower than the surrounding area, causing the shadow be on the image rather that outside the image.

The values are specified in a comma-separated list. It expects from two to four position/size values, an optional color property, and the optional inset keyword. Only the first two are required, which are the horizontal and vertical positions. The blur and spread values will default to zero if not specified. Add the following rules to the end of the style element:

```
/* Add the box shadow */
article img
{
    margin: 10px 0;
    box-shadow: 3px 3px 12px #222;
}

.book img
{
    margin: 10px 0;
    display: block;
    box-shadow: 2px 2px 5px #444;
    margin-left: auto;
    margin-right: auto;
}

aside
{
    box-shadow: 3px 3px 3px #aaaaaa;
}
```

The .book img rule also includes both the margin-left and margin-right attributes, which are both set to auto. This causes the images to be centered horizontally. Figures 4-12 and 4-13 show a close-up of the images in the featured content and the sidebar items. Notice the first image has a larger blur area than the sidebar images.

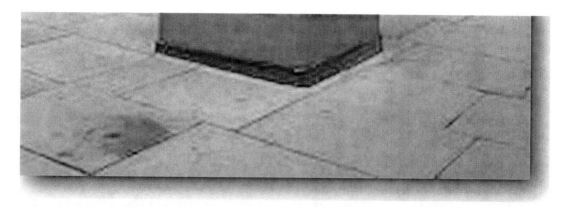

Figure 4-12. *The shadow of the phone in booth image the featured content section*

Figure 4-13. *The shadow on the sidebar images*

Using Zebra Striping

One styling approach that has been used for a long time is to alternate the background when there is a list of items, which is sometimes referred to as *zebra-striping*. This goes back to the old blue-bar paper used to enter accounting journals. The alternating backgrounds make it easier to distinguish between each item. Prior to CSS3 this was accomplished with JavaScript that would programmatically change the background on every other element.

CSS3 introduces the `nth-child` selector, which is perfect for this application because it returns every nth element. Using this with n set to 2 will return every other element. Add the following code to the end of the style element:

```
/* Stripe the title list */
#titles article:nth-child(2n+1)
{
    background: #c0c0c0;
    border: 1px solid #6699cc;
    border-radius: 10px;
}

#titles article:nth-child(2n+0)
{
    background: #6699cc;
    border: 1px solid #c0c0c0;
    border-radius: 10px;
}
```

This rule uses a complex selector #titles `article:nth-child(2n+1)`, which first selects the #titles element. This is a section element that contains the book titles. Each book title is in a separate article element. The article:nth-child selector then returns every nth article element inside the #titles element. The 2n+1 parameter may seem a bit odd, however. To get every other element, you specify 2n as the parameter, which would return the odd items (first, third, fifth, and so on). By using 2n+1, the list is offset by 1, so you will get the even items (second, fourth, sixth and so on). So, the first rule formats the even items, and the second rule, which uses 2n+0, will format the odd items. You could simply use 2n instead of 2n+0 because these are equivalent, but I like using 2n+0 for consistency. The only difference between these two style rules is the background and border colors. Figure 4-14 shows the effect.

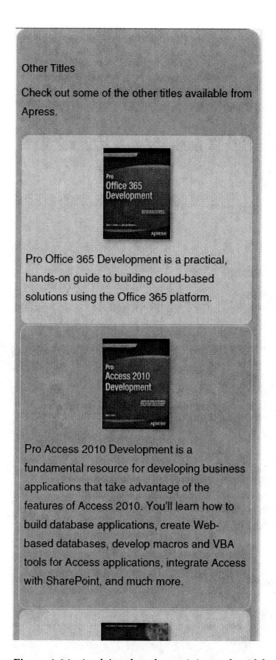

Figure 4-14. Applying the zebra striping to the sidebar

Adding Text Decorations

Text decorations allow you to embellish text with various effects. There are three types of decorations that have been defined: lines (such as underline and strikethrough), emphasis marks, and shadows. The official recommendation defines this capability although browser implementation is a bit sketchy and inconsistent. I'll first explain how the standard has been defined and then show you the workarounds that you may need to do to make it work.

■ **Note**   The text decoration details are explained well in the WC3 recommendation, which you can access at www.w3.org/TR/css-text-decor-3.

Line Decorations

Line decorations are defined by a combination of three attributes:

- text-decoration-line: Specifies whether the line should be above the text (overline), below the text (underline), or through the middle of the text (line-through)

- text-decoration-style: Defines the style of the line such as solid, dashed, dotted, double, or wavy

- text-decoration-color: Indicates the color of the line

The recommendation also allows for the text-decoration shortcut where you can specify all three properties in one attribute. For example, you could use this to define a red, wavy underline:

```
text-decoration: underline wavy red;
```

If the style and color are omitted from the shortcut, this is backward compatible with CSS levels 1 and 2. And, as of this writing, this is all most browsers support. So, you can add an underline, an overline, or a strikethrough, but you cannot adjust its style or color. To try it, add the following at the end of the style element:

```
h2
{
    text-decoration: underline overline line-through;
}
```

This will display all three lines in your text. Save these changes and refresh the browser window, and the header text should look like Figure 4-15.

CSS Demo

Introducing the new HTML5 features

Use the new CSS3 features to build some of the most visu

Figure 4-15. *Adding line decorations*

Firefox supports some of the line decoration styles, but you'll need to use their vendor prefix. To demonstrate how to do that, replace the h2 selector that you just added with the following:

```
h2
{
    text-decoration: underline;
    -moz-text-decoration-line: underline;
    -moz-text-decoration-style: wavy;
    -moz-text-decoration-color: red;
    text-decoration-line: underline;
    text-decoration-style: wavy;
    text-decoration-color: red;
}
```

The first line uses the backward-compatible attribute that most browsers will support. This will define a solid underline using the same color as the text. The next three lines define the same wavy red line using the Firefox vendor prefix, which will be ignored by all other browsers. The last three lines define a wavy red line using the CSS3 standards. If you display this page using most browsers, you'll have a solid black line like you saw previously. If you use Firefox, the page will look like Figure 4-16.

CSS Demo

Introducing the new HTML5 features

Use the new CSS3 features to build some of the most visua

Figure 4-16. *Displaying line decorations in Firefox*

Over time, however, as browsers adopt the CSS3 standards, the wavy underline will replace the solid line. This is a good example of how you can design your page to use the features that are currently available and position it to take advantage of emerging capabilities.

111

Emphasis Marks

The use of emphasis marks is similar to adding lines; they add a symbol or mark to emphasize the specified text. As of this writing, none of the desktop browsers supports this feature. Emphasis marks are defined using a combination of three attributes.

- `text-emphasis-style`: Specifies the type of symbol to use such as `dot`, `triangle`, `double-circle`, or `sesame`.

- `text-emphasis-color`: Indicates color to use for the emphasis mark.

- `text-emphasis-position`: Defines the position of the mark relative to the text; possible values are `over`, `under`, `left`, and `right`. You can include combinations such as `over right`.

A shortcut definition is also allowed so you can specify this with a single attribute like this:

```
text-emphasis: dot red;
```

Text Shadows

Text shadows are defined like box shadows, which I explained earlier. Unlike some of the other text decoration features, text shadows are supported by all major browsers.

A text shadow is defined with a single attribute that contains the following parameters:

- Horizontal offset

- Vertical offset

- Blur radius

- Color

The offset values can be negative. A negative vertical offset will place the shadow above the text, and a negative horizontal shadow will put the shadow to the left. If the color parameter is omitted, the shadow will be the same color as the text.

■ **Caution** The blur radius for text shadows should be small. Unless you have a really large font, using values more than 1px or 2px will make the text unreadable. You can specify 0px, which will cause the shadow to not be blurred at all.

To demonstrate text shadows, add the following to the end of your `style` element:

```
h3:first-letter
{
    text-shadow: 2px -5px 1px blue;
}
```

Save your changes and refresh the browser. The header text should look like Figure 4-17.

Featured Article

Figure 4-17. Adding a text shadow

■ **Tip** This example also demonstrates the `first-letter` pseudo-class. This selects the first letter from each h3 element.

Using 3D Transforms

Adding a 3D transform can add some pizzazz to your web page. I'll demonstrate a fairly simple application where you can flip the phone booth image in 3D. You'll also add some JavaScript to animate the rotation.

To format the 3D transformation, you'll specify a couple of attributes. First, you'll set the `perspective` property on the `div` that contains the image. This establishes the vanishing point that is used to determine how the 3D effect is rendered. Then, you'll set the `preserve-3d` attribute on the image itself, which tells the browser to maintain the 3D perspective when rotating the image. To do this, add the following to the end of the `style` section:

```
/* Transforms */
.rotateContainer
{
    -webkit-perspective: 360;
    perspective: 360px;
}

.rotate
{
    -webkit-transform-style: preserve-3d;
    transform-style: preserve-3d;
}
```

■ **Note** The standard `perspective` attribute expects the units (for example, `360px`), but the IntelliSense in WebMatrix doesn't recognize this and will show this as a CSS validation error. You can ignore this. Also note that the vendor-prefixed attribute, `-webkit-perspective`, does not require the units.

Now you'll add a JavaScript function that will animate the image rotation. Enter the code in bold in the head element:

```
<head>
    <meta charset="utf-8" />
    <title>Chapter 4 - CSS Demo</title>

    <script type="text/javascript">
        var angle = 0;
        var t;
        function rotateImage(value) {
            document.getElementById("phone").style.transform
                = "rotateY(" + value + "deg)";
        }
        function toggleAnimation() {
            if (angle == 0) {
                t = setInterval(function () {
                    rotateImage(angle);
                    angle += 1;
                    if (angle >= 360)
                        angle = 0;
                }, 100);
            }
            else {
                clearInterval(t);
                angle = 0;
                rotateImage(angle);
            }
        }
    </script>

    <style>
```

The angle variable stores the current rotation angle of the image, and the t variable is a reference to the interval timer. The rotateImage() function simply sets the rotateY style for the image element. This is equivalent to adding this to the CSS:

```
transform: rotate(20deg);
```

This is done in JavaScript because it will specify a different angle every time this is called. The toggleAnimation() function will either start or stop the animation. To start the animation, this calls the setInterval() function, supplying an anonymous function that will be called every 100 milliseconds. The anonymous function calls rotateImage() at the current angle and then increments the angle. To cancel the animation, the clearInterval() method is called, and then the image is set back to the initial rotation.

Lastly, add the code shown in bold, which calls the toggleAnimation() function when the image is clicked:

```
<div id="rotateContainer">
    <p>This is really cool...</p>
    <img class="rotate" id="phone"
        src="images/phonebooth.jpg"
```

```
          alt="phonebooth"
          onclick="toggleAnimation()"/>
<br />
```

Save these changes and refresh your browser window. To start the animation, click the image. You should see the image rotate slowly, as demonstrated in Figure 4-18.

Figure 4-18. *The rotated phonebooth—in 3D!*

■ **Tip**   As of this writing, Chrome, Opera, and Safari have an interesting bug. The transformation is a simple 2D transform until you inspect the element. Right-click the `image` element and choose Inspect Element. Once the transform has changed to 3D, you can close the inspection window.

Adding Animation

For the last effect, I'll show you how to create an animation effect without using any JavaScript. You can't modify the image with CSS because that is considered content, not format. However, you can change the background image, and you'll take advantage of that to achieve the animation effect.

The `aside` element has a `div` defined as follows:

```
<div id="moon"></div>
```

Because there is no content or size defined, this has no effect on the page layout currently. Now you'll use the animation feature in CSS3 to iterate through various images that illustrate the phases of the moon.

In CSS, animation is achieved by defining a set of keyframes. Each frame defines one or more CSS attributes. In this application you'll specify the appropriate background image, but you could just as easily change the color or size or any other CSS attribute. For each frame you also specify the percentage of the animation duration when this frame should appear. You should always have a 0% and 100% frame, which specify the beginning and ending properties. You can include any number of steps in between. In this example, there are eight images, so, to keep the frames spaced evenly, the frames will transition at 0%, 12%, 25%, 37%, 50%, 62%, 75%, 87%, and 100%.

Once you have defined the `keyframes`, you then then set the animation attributes on the element that you want to animate. You'll specify the name of the `keyframes` by setting the `animation-name` attribute. You can also set the duration (in seconds) that the animation will take using the `animation-duration` attribute. Add the code shown in Listing 4-5 to the end of the style section.

Listing 4-5. Defining the Animation Effect

```
/* Animate the moon phases */
@@-webkit-keyframes moonPhases
{
0%    {background-image:url("images/moon1.png");}
12%   {background-image:url("images/moon2.png");}
25%   {background-image:url("images/moon3.png");}
37%   {background-image:url("images/moon4.png");}
50%   {background-image:url("images/moon5.png");}
62%   {background-image:url("images/moon6.png");}
75%   {background-image:url("images/moon7.png");}
87%   {background-image:url("images/moon8.png");}
100%   {background-image:url("images/moon1.png");}
}

@@keyframes moonPhases
{
0%    {background-image:url("images/moon1.png");}
12%   {background-image:url("images/moon2.png");}
25%   {background-image:url("images/moon3.png");}
37%   {background-image:url("images/moon4.png");}
```

```
50%     {background-image:url("images/moon5.png");}
62%     {background-image:url("images/moon6.png");}
75%     {background-image:url("images/moon7.png");}
87%     {background-image:url("images/moon8.png");}
100%    {background-image:url("images/moon1.png");}
}

#moon
{
    width:115px;
    height:115px;
    background-image: url("images/moon1.png");
    background-repeat: no-repeat;
    -webkit-animation-name:moonPhases;
    -webkit-animation-duration:4s;
    -webkit-animation-delay:3s;
    -webkit-animation-iteration-count:10;

    animation-name:moonPhases;
    animation-duration:4s;
    animation-delay:3s;
    animation-iteration-count:10;
}
```

This code sets the total duration at four seconds, so the image should transition every half second. It also specifies to wait three seconds before starting and to repeat the animation ten times. When you refresh the web page, after about three seconds it should cycle through the phases of the moon, as shown in Figure 4-19.

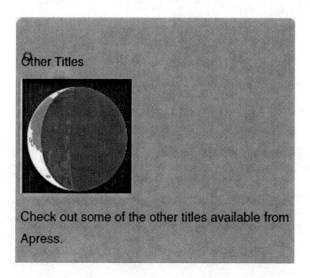

Figure 4-19. *Animating the moon's phases*

■ **Tip** If you want the animation to continue indefinitely, set the `animation-iteration-count` attribute to `infinite`.

There are two other animation properties that were not applicable here, `timing-function` and `direction`. If you're using a simple animation and define only the begin and end values, the `timing-function` defines the speed of the transition. For example, if you're moving an element to a different position, setting this to `linear` will move the object at a constant rate. However, using the default value, `ease`, the transition will start out slow and then speed up and then slow down near the end. There are other options, like `ease-in`, which will start out slow and then speed up for the remainder of the transition. The `direction` property, if set to `alternate`, will reverse the transition on alternating iterations. The default value, `normal`, will replay the same transition each time.

Summary

In this chapter, I covered a lot of information about CSS, especially the new features in CSS3. The selectors are quite powerful and offer a great deal of flexibility when applying styles. Prior to CSS3, much of this had to be done with a lot of JavaScript functions. I also showed you how to plan and structure a sample web page using a lot of the new structural HTML5 elements. Appendix B shows the complete `style` element.

Using the WebMatrix application, you created a simple web page, defined the basic structure, and then populated the content. Using some of the new CSS3 features, you then added some significant style features including the following:

- Rounded borders
- Gradients
- Tables
- Multiple columns
- Shadows
- Zebra striping
- Text decorations
- 3D transforms
- Animation

In the next chapter, I'll introduce some of the new features of HTML5 related to scripting.

CHAPTER 5

■ ■ ■

Scripting Enhancements

In this chapter, I will demonstrate a few miscellaneous improvements that affect the scripting aspect of web development. So far, I have introduced the markup changes and the CSS enhancements. Scripting is the third leg of the overall HTML5 umbrella, and a significant amount of attention was given to this area. This chapter will explain some improvements that have broad application.

- Query selectors
- Web workers
- Managing packages and builds

Package management is not actually part of HTML5 but is accomplished through open source tools such as Bower and Gulp, which have been integrated into Visual Studio.

Using Query Selectors

In Chapter 4, I explained the CSS selectors that you can use to create powerful style rules. CSS3 introduced a significant improvement in this area. With the robust attribute selectors and quite a few new pseudo-classess such as nth-child that you used in Chapter 4, there is considerable functionality for selecting DOM elements. But it gets even better: all of this ability is available from JavaScript as well.

The HTML5 specification includes two new functions, querySelector() and querySelectorAll(). The querySelector() function returns a single element, the first one that matches the specified selector. The querySelectorAll() function returns an array of matching elements. For both functions, you pass in the CSS selector, formatted just like you would in a style sheet. So, once you've learned how to use CSS selectors, you can apply that same experience to JavaScript.

To try these functions, you will use the same web page you created in Chapter 4. The final version of the Chapter 4 project is available in the source code download if you want to use that.

Using querySelector

The querySelector() function can be used to replace the getElementById() function. Of course, it is much more useful than that because you can pass in any type of CSS selector.

Open the Default.cshtml file and modify the rotateImage() function, replacing the getElementById() function like this:

```
function rotateImage(value){
    document.querySelector("#phone").style.transform
        ="rotateY(" + value + "deg)";
}
```

■ **Caution**   Don't forget to prefix the ID with #. Because the querySelector() function can be used with any type of selector, you'll need the hash symbol to indicate this is an ID selector.

Run the web page using Firefox and verify the 3D rotation still works.

Using querySelectorAll

That was a fairly trivial example, so now I'll demonstrate a more complex selector. You'll add a JavaScript function that will change the color on all of the internal links in the nav element. Arguably you could just do this in the style sheet, but sometimes you need to do it in code as well. For example, you might need to change the style programmatically based on user input.

Add the following function to the script element in the Default.cshtml page:

```
function adjustInternalLinks(){
    var links = document.querySelectorAll("nav ul li a[href ^='#']");
    for (var i=0; i < links.length; i++){
        links[i].style.color = "green";
    }
}
```

The CSS selector is nav ul li a[href ^='#'], which returns all a elements with an href attribute that begins with the # character. This is further filtered to only elements that have the nav, ul, and li parentage. This will exclude links that may appear in other sections.

The querySelectorAll() function returns an array, so this code iterates through the array making each element green. Now you'll need to call this function. Add the following code shown in bold to the body element:

```
<body onload="adjustInternalLinks()">
```

This will call the function when the page is loaded, but you could just as easily call this based on some appropriate user input to make the style dynamic. Save the changes and reload the page. You should now have green links. Note that the link to www.apress.com is not green because it is an external link and doesn't start with #.

Creating the Visual Studio Project

For the rest of the exercises in this chapter you'll use a Visual Studio project. Start Visual Studio 2015 and click New Project. Select the ASP.NET Web Application project template and enter **Chapter5** for the name, as shown in Figure 5-1.

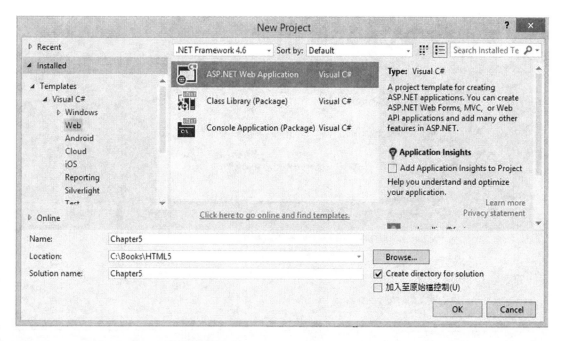

Figure 5-1. *Creating the Chapter5 project*

In the second dialog, select the ASP.NET 5 Web Site template.

Employing Web Workers

With more and more work being done on the client, making the client application multithreaded becomes more important. Fortunately, the use of web workers is a convenient way to accomplish that. Functions that are CPU intensive or may take some time to complete can be executed on a background thread leaving the main UI thread available to respond to user actions.

Web workers use a fairly simple concept. You create a worker and pass it a JavaScript file that defines its execution. The web page can then communicate with the worker through messages. The worker implements the onmessage event handler to respond to an incoming message from the page and uses the postMessage() function to send data back to the caller. The caller must also handle the onmessage event to receive the messages from the worker. This is illustrated in Figure 5-2.

121

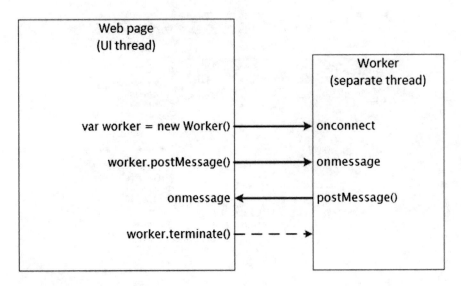

Figure 5-2. *Communicating with a dedicated web worker*

■ **Tip**   For the demo application that you'll create in this chapter, the messages between the caller and the worker will be simple text messages. However, they can be any format you want, including JSON-encoded data.

One of the most significant limitations of web workers is that they cannot access the DOM, so you can't use them to update the page content or style. Also, they cannot access the window object, which means, among other things, that you can't use timers. With these limitations in mind, you might be wondering when you would use a web worker.

Web workers are great for performing tasks such as retrieving data. For example, if you need to look up information from an external source (such as a database, local file system, or web), you can pass the lookup parameters to the worker, and when the lookup finishes, the data can be passed back as a JSON message. This allows the web page to respond to user actions while the data is being retrieved.

Web workers come in two varieties: dedicated and shared. A dedicated worker can be used by only a single page, whereas a shared worker can be used by multiple web pages. Both dedicated and shared workers function the same basic way, but the communication is a little different. You'll start by implementing a dedicated web worker.

Using a Dedicated Worker

A dedicated web worker, as its name implies, is dedicated to the web page that created it. The web page creates it, uses it as needed, and closes it when it no longer needs it. A web page can create as many workers as it needs.

To demonstrate a dedicated web worker, you'll build a simple web page that will allow you to create a worker and send messages to it. It will also display the response so you can see the two-way communication. The worker implementation is trivial, simply echoing back the message that was sent to it.

EXERCISE 5-1. USING A DEDICATED WEB WORKER

1. In the Chapter5 project you created earlier, open the Index.cshtml file, which you'll find in the Views\Home folder. Replace the default implementation of this view using the code shown in Listing 5-1. This will create a simple form with a text area for displaying messages and three buttons for communicating with the worker.

   Listing 5-1. The Index View Implementation

   ```
   <!DOCTYPE html>

   <html lang="en">
       <head>
           <meta charset="utf-8" />
           <title>Chapter 5 - Web Workers</title>
           <link rel="stylesheet" type="text/css" href="~/css/Sample.css" />
           <script type="text/javascript" src="~/controlWorker.js"></script>
       </head>
       <body>
           <header>
               <h1>Web Workers Demo</h1>
           </header>

           <div>
               <textarea id="output"></textarea>
           </div>

           <form id="control" method="post" action="">
               <input id="create" type="button" class="button" value="Create Worker"
                   onclick="createWorker()"> <br>
               <input id="send" type="button" class="button" value="Send Message"
                   onclick="sendWorkerMessage()">
               <input id="message" type="text" class="text" value="Hello,
               World!"><br>
               <input id="kill" type="button" class="button" value="Close Worker"
                   onclick="closeWorker()">
           </form>

       </body>
   </html>
   ```

2. From the Solution Explorer, right-click the wwwroot\css folder and choose Add and New Item. Select the Style Sheet item and enter **Sample.css** for the file name, as shown in Figure 5-3. Click the Add button to create the file.

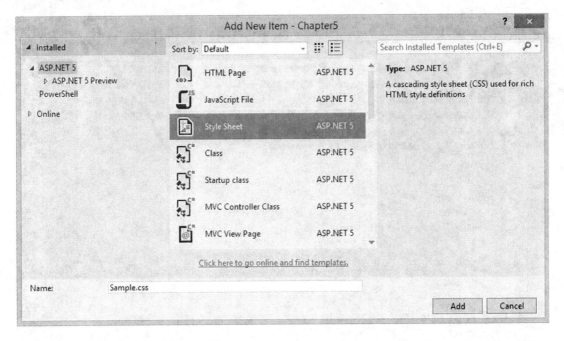

Figure 5-3. Adding the Sample.css style sheet

3.   Replace the default implementation with the code shown in Listing 5-2.

Listing 5-2. The Sample.css style Sheet

```
h1
{
    font-size:22px;
    color:purple;
}

#output
{
    width: 500px;
    height: 250px;
    background-color:#dfcaca;
}

.button
{
    width:125px;
    height:25px;
    color:green;
}
.text
{
    width:260px;
}
```

4. Press F5 to debug the application; the form should look similar to Figure 5-4.

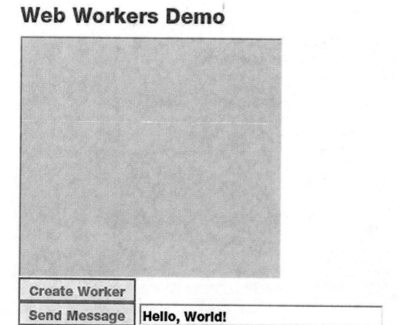

Figure 5-4. The initial form design

5. Close the browser and stop the debugger.

6. In the Solution Explorer, right-click the `wwwroot` folder and choose Add and New Item. In the Add New Item dialog box, select the JavaScript File item. Enter **worker.js** for the file name, as shown in Figure 5-5.

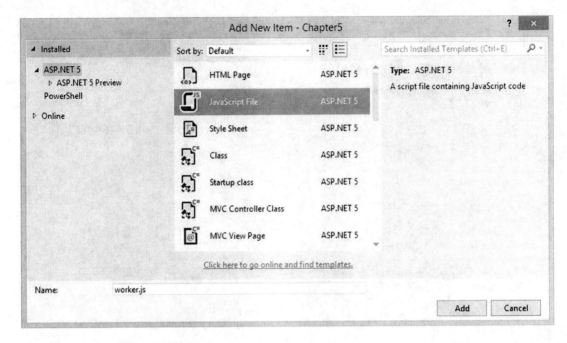

Figure 5-5. *Adding the worker.js file*

7. For the contents of this file, enter the following code. This is the implementation of the worker. It handles both the onconnect event (when the worker is first created) and the onmessage event (when a message is sent to the worker). The implementation simply echoes the message back to the caller.

```
/* This file implements the web worker */

// This event is fired when the web worker is started
onconnect = sendResponse("The worker has started");

// This event is fired when a message is received
onmessage = function (event) {
        sendResponse("Msg received: " + event.data);
}

// Sends a message to the main thread
function sendResponse(message) {
        postMessage(message);
}
```

8. Using the same instructions, add a `controlWorker.js` file in the `wwwroot` folder.

9. Enter the code shown in Listing 5-3 for its implementation. I will explain this in more detail later in the chapter.

Listing 5-3. The controlWorker.js Implementation

```
/* This file contains functions used to
   communicate with the web worker */

var myWorker;

function createWorker() {
    if (typeof(Worker) !== "undefined") {
        var log = document.querySelector("#output");
        log.value += "Starting worker process… ";

        myWorker = new Worker("worker.js");

        log.value += "Adding listener… ";
        myWorker.onmessage = function(event){
            log.value += event.data + "\n";
        }

        log.value += "Done!\n";
    }
    else {
        alert("Your browser does not support web workers");
    }
}

function sendWorkerMessage(){
    if (myWorker !== null) {
        var log = document.querySelector("#output");
        log.value += "Sending message… ";

        var message = document.querySelector("#message");
        myWorker.postMessage(message.value);

        log.value += "Done!\n";
    }
}

function closeWorker(){
    if (myWorker !== null) {
        var log = document.querySelector("#output");
        log.value += "Closing worker… ";

        myWorker.terminate;
        myWorker = null;

        log.value += "Done!\n";
    }
}
```

10. Press F5 to debug the application. Click the Create Worker button and then click the Send button. Modify the message and try clicking the Send Message button again. Finally, click the Close Worker button. The text area should look like Figure 5-6.

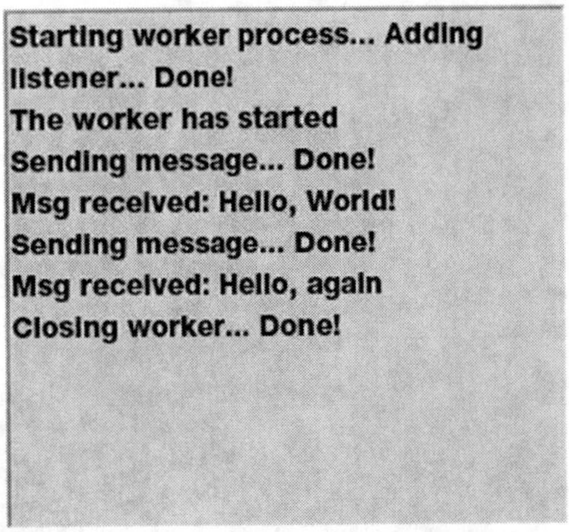

Starting worker process... Adding listener... Done!
The worker has started
Sending message... Done!
Msg received: Hello, World!
Sending message... Done!
Msg received: Hello, again
Closing worker... Done!

Figure 5-6. The message log

The controlWorker.js file contains three functions that provide the implementation for the three buttons on the form. It first declares a myWorker variable, which holds a reference to the dedicated web worker, and then implements the following functions:

- createWorker(): This function first checks to see whether the browser supports web workers by seeing whether the Worker class is defined. If not, an alert is raised. It then creates an instance of the Worker class, saving its reference in the myWorker variable. The worker implementation is passed to its constructor by referencing the worker.js script file. It then implements the onmessage event handler that adds the incoming message to the output field.

- sendWorkerMessage(): This simply calls the worker's postMessage() method, passing in the text specified in the message field. Notice it is using the querySelector() method that I explained earlier in this chapter.

- closeWorker(): This calls the worker's terminate() method and sets the myWorker variable to null. The worker is closed immediately without any ability to perform any cleanup operations.

▪ **Tip** In the same way that you added an onmessage event handler, you can also create an onerror event handler to respond to errors from the worker. The web worker can report errors by using the throw function.

With this simple implementation you can see how easy it is to create a worker and use messages to communicate with it.

Creating a Shared Worker

A shared web worker allows you to create a worker and then reuse it from other pages. There are a couple of advantages to using shared workers. The most obvious one is that multiple pages can share the same thread instead of having to create a new worker thread for every page. The other, which I'll explain later, is to share state information across pages.

■ **Caution**   IE 11 supports dedicated web workers but does not support shared workers.

Now you'll create a shared worker, which is implemented in a JavaScript file. The concept is essentially the same, but the communication is done a little differently. You'll add a few more buttons to the web page and implement a new set of JavaScript functions to communicate with the shared worker.

EXERCISE 5-2. CREATING A SHARED WORKER

1. Open the Index.cshtml file and add the following script reference in the head element after the previous reference:

    ```
    <script type="text/javascript" src="~/controlSharedWorker.js"></script>
    ```

2. Add the code shown in bold in Listing 5-4 to the form element. This will add another set of buttons to control the shared worker.

    Listing 5-4. The Additional Buttons in Index.cshtml

    ```
    <form id="control" method="post" action="">
        <input id="create" type="button" class="button" value="Create Worker"
               onclick="createWorker()"> <br>
        <input id="send" type="button" class="button" value="Send Message"
               onclick="sendWorkerMessage()">
        <input id="message" type="text" class="text" value="Hello, World!"><br>
        <input id="kill" type="button" class="button" value="Close Worker"
               onclick="closeWorker()">
        <br><br>
        <input id="createS" type="button" class="button" value="Create Shared"
               onclick="createSharedWorker()"> <br>
        <input id="sendS" type="button" class="button" value="Send Shared Msg"
               onclick="sendSharedWorkerMessage()">
        <input id="messageS" type="text" class="text" value="Hello, World!"><br>
        <input id="killS" type="button" class="button" value="Close Shared"
               onclick="closeSharedWorker()">
    </form>
    ```

3. From the Solution Explorer, add another file to the wwwroot folder named sharedWorker.js and enter the code shown in Listing 5-5. This is the implementation of the shared worker.

Listing 5-5. The sharedWorker.js Implementation

```
/* This file implements the shared web worker */
var clients = 0;

onconnect = function(event) {
    var port = event.ports[0];
    clients++;

    /* Attach the event listener */
    port.addEventListener("message", function(event){
        sendResponse(event.target, "Msg received: " + event.data);
    }, false);

    port.start();

    sendResponse(port, "You are client # " + clients + "\n");
}

function sendResponse(senderPort, message) {
    senderPort.postMessage( message);
}
```

4. Add another file in the wwwroot folder named controlSharedWorker.js and enter the implementation shown in Listing 5-6. I will explain this code later.

Listing 5-6. The controlSharedWorker.js Implementation

```
/* This file contains functions used to
   communicate with the web worker */

var mySharedWorker;

function createSharedWorker() {
    if (typeof(SharedWorker) !== "undefined") {
        var log = document.querySelector("#output");
        log.value += "Starting shared worker process… ";

        mySharedWorker = new SharedWorker("sharedWorker.js");

        log.value += "Adding listener… ";
        mySharedWorker.port.addEventListener("message", function(event){
            log.value += event.data + "\n";
        }, false);

        mySharedWorker.port.start();
```

```
                log.value += "Done!\n";
            }
            else {
                alert("Your browser does not support shared web workers");
            }
        }
    }

    function sendSharedWorkerMessage(){
        if (mySharedWorker !== null) {
            var log = document.querySelector("#output");
            log.value += "Sending message… ";

            var message = document.querySelector("#messageS");
            mySharedWorker.port.postMessage(message.value);

            log.value += "Done!\n";
        }
    }

    function closeSharedWorker(){
        if (mySharedWorker !== null) {
            var log = document.querySelector("#output");
            log.value += "Closing worker… ";

            mySharedWorker.port.terminate;
            mySharedWorker = null;

            log.value += "Done!\n";
        }
    }
```

5. Press F5 to debug the application. Create a shared worker and send a message to it. It should work just like the previous exercise.

6. Leaving the browser tab running, create a new tab and enter the same URL as the first tab. This will open the same page in a second tab. Create a shared worker from the second tab. Then click the Send Shared Message button to test the connection. Notice the message says that you are the second client, as demonstrated in Figure 5-7.

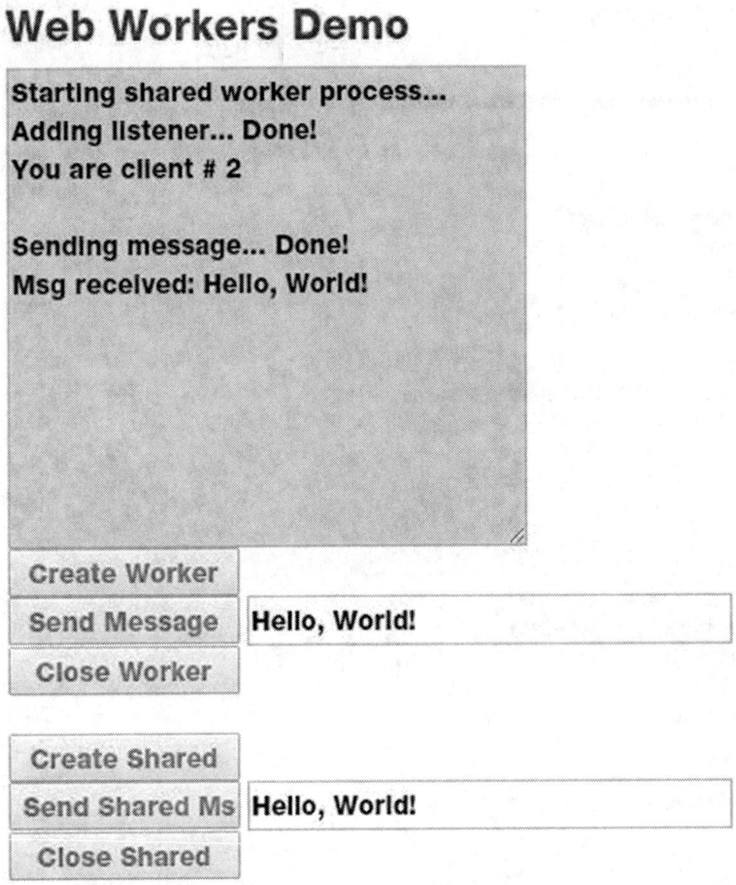

Web Workers Demo

Starting shared worker process...
Adding listener... Done!
You are client # 2

Sending message... Done!
Msg received: Hello, World!

Create Worker
Send Message	Hello, World!
Close Worker

Create Shared
Send Shared Ms	Hello, World!
Close Shared

Figure 5-7. Opening a second copy of the page

Messages go between the worker and the page that invoked the worker. Multiple pages can invoke a shared worker, but messages are not shared; each message is still between a single page and the worker. However, the data within the worker is shared and accessible from multiple pages.

Now let's look at how the shared worker was implemented. Just like the dedicated worker, it must handle the onconnect and onmessage events. However, you can't attach the ommessage handler directly to the worker; instead, you must access a port and attach to that. The onconnect event receives an event parameter, and you access the port by event.ports[0]. Once you have the port, you can attach the event handler to it. You use the port's addEventHandler() method. This takes two parameters. The first is the name of the event, message in this case. The second parameter is the function that will be called when the event is raised.

When sending a message, you must also use the port object. This port object is provided in the event.target property of the incoming message. Both this event handler and the onconnect event handler use the sendResponse() function passing in the port object.

The functions in the controlSharedWorker.js file are almost identical to their dedicated counterparts. However, they must also use the port object. The port is included in the event.

Notice in the sharedWorker.js file that the clients variable is declared and then incremented in the onconnect event handler. This is used to keep track of how many clients have connected to the shared worker. I added this just to demonstrate how this variable is global to all the clients attached to the worker. In fact, there is no per-port instance data; all data is global.

Also, when a message comes in, the event parameter includes the port that the response should be sent to. The worker doesn't "remember" the port for each client. It just does what it's instructed to do and returns a response on the specified port.

Client-Side Package Management

Visual Studio 2015 and ASP.NET 5 introduce a pretty significant shift in how client-side packaging is accomplished. NuGet is still around but has been relegated to server-side packages. On the client, you'll now use tools such as Bower, Grunt, Gulp, and Node Package Manager (NPM). Most of the basic functionality is preconfigured for you by the project templates. You won't need to deal with any of this to implement the examples in this book. However, I wanted to give you an overview of what each of these tools do and how they work. Let's start by looking at the projects files that were created for you.

Configuration: IConfiguration

If you take a look at the Solution Explorer, you might find yourself asking, "Where's the web.config file?" If you look near the end of the file list, you'll see a config.json file, which is where you'll find configuration settings such as connection strings. Configuration data can be stored in either JSON, XML, or INI files, and you can have many configuration files.

Take a look at the Startup.cs file. It defines an IConfiguration member and a constructor that defines the files to be loaded.

```
public Startup(IHostingEnvironment env)
{
    // Setup configuration sources.
    var configuration = new Configuration()
        .AddJsonFile("config.json")
        .AddJsonFile($"config.{env.EnvironmentName}.json", optional: true);

    if (env.IsEnvironment("Development"))
    {
        // This reads the configuration keys from the secret store.
        // For more details on using the user secret store see
        // http://go.microsoft.com/fwlink/?LinkID=532709
        configuration.AddUserSecrets();
    }
    configuration.AddEnvironmentVariables();
    Configuration = configuration;
}

public IConfiguration Configuration { get; set; }
```

So, you can decide how you want the configuration data organized and what file format to use. The initial code that is generated by the project template loads data from the config.json file using the AddJsonFile() method. It also loads any environment variables that may be defined using the AddEnvironmentVariables() method.

Here's a good article that explains the new configuration model: http://blog.jsinh.in/asp-net-5-configuration-microsoft-framework-configurationmodel/#.VQ3TUvnF9Cg.

Static Files: wwwroot

The wwwroot folder is new with ASP.NET 5 and provides a place to put all of your static content such as CSS, JavaScript, images, and static HTML. The idea here is to make a clear distinction between content that is generated through server-side code and content that is simply provided to the browser as is.

This folder is known as the web root. This is roughly equivalent to the Content and Scripts folders that were used with previous version of MVC. These folders were at the same level in the Solution Explorer as Models, Views, and Controllers. Moving them up a level, consolidating them into one, and calling it the web root make it a little more obvious what should be in there.

Package Management: Bower

While NuGet has been a welcome friend of .NET developers, Bower has been popular for managing client-side dependencies. So, with ASP.NET 5, you'll use Bower to configure the client-side packages that are needed for your application. (You'll continue to use NuGet for server-side packages.) The client-side dependencies are listed in the bower.json file; Listing 5-7 shows the initial, template-generated file.

Listing 5-7. The bower.json Configuration File

```
{
    "name": "WebApplication",
    "private": true,
    "dependencies": {
        "bootstrap": "3.0.0",
        "jquery": "1.10.2",
        "jquery-validation": "1.11.1",
        "jquery-validation-unobtrusive": "3.2.2",
        "hammer.js": "2.0.4",
        "bootstrap-touch-carousel": "0.8.0"
    },
    "exportsOverride": {
    "bootstrap": {
      "js": "dist/js/*.*",
      "css": "dist/css/*.*",
      "fonts": "dist/fonts/*.*"
    },
    "bootstrap-touch-carousel": {
      "js": "dist/js/*.*",
      "css": "dist/css/*.*"
        },
      "jquery": {
      "": "jquery.{js,min.js,min.map}"
        },
```

```
    "jquery-validation": {
        "": "jquery.validate.js"
    },
    "jquery-validation-unobtrusive": {
      "": "jquery.validate.unobtrusive.{js,min.js}"
    },
    "hammer": {
      "": "hammer.{js,min.js}"
        }
    }
}
```

The nice thing about working with this file is the IntelliSense support. For example, open this file and go to the dependencies section. On the last line, where `bootstrap-touch-carousel` is defined, go to the end of the line, enter a comma, and hit Return. Then enter a quote and start typing a package name. Notice that the list of available packages is automatically shown as you type. Enter **"modernizr": "** and notice that the available version number is displayed for you, as shown in Figure 5-8.

Figure 5-8. Bower IntelliSense support r

Also notice the version semantics. The current stable version as of this writing is 2.8.3. These numbers specify the major version, minor version, and patch number, respectively. Prefixing a version with a carat symbol (^) indicates that the major version must match. For example, if ^2.8.3 was specified, any version equal to or greater than 2.8.3 would be used as long as the major version was 2. So, 2.8.5 or 2.9 would be used but not 3.1. The tilde symbol (~) indicates that both the major and minor versions must match. So, ~2.8.3 will use any path level of 2.8 greater or equal to 3; so, 2.8.5 would be used, but 2.9 would not. Omitting both of these indicates that the latest version should be used, as long as it is at least 2.8.3.

Build Tasks: Gulp

With all the client-side files that are needed in most web applications, acquiring, organizing, and preparing them can be a tedious task. You already looked at Bower as a great tool for managing dependencies. Gulp is another useful tool that allows you to automate build tasks. Gulp is a JavaScript-based framework that uses Node.js and the NPM.

One typical scenario for Gulp is to tell Bower to check for and download dependencies. In fact, the initial gulpfile.js, shown in Listing 5-8, does just that.

Listing 5-8. The Initial gulpfile.js File

```
/// <binding Clean='clean' />

var gulp = require("gulp"),
  rimraf = require("rimraf"),
  fs = require("fs");

eval("var project = " + fs.readFileSync("./project.json"));

var paths = {
  bower: "./bower_components/",
  lib: "./" + project.webroot + "/lib/"
};

gulp.task("clean", function (cb) {
  rimraf(paths.lib, cb);
});

gulp.task("copy", ["clean"], function () {
  var bower = {
    "bootstrap": "bootstrap/dist/**/*.{js,map,css,ttf,svg,woff,eot}",
    "bootstrap-touch-carousel": "bootstrap-touch-carousel/dist/**/*.{js,css}",
    "hammer.js": "hammer.js/hammer*.{js,map}",
    "jquery": "jquery/jquery*.{js,map}",
    "jquery-validation": "jquery-validation/jquery.validate.js",
    "jquery-validation-unobtrusive": "jquery-validation-unobtrusive/jquery.validate.
    unobtrusive.js"
  }

  for (var destinationDir in bower) {
    gulp.src(paths.bower + bower[destinationDir])
      .pipe(gulp.dest(paths.lib + destinationDir));
  }
});
```

Of course, there are many other tasks that you could do such as bundling and minifying your JavaScript or CSS files. Another example is precompiling a Less style sheet into a CSS file.

■ **Note**   In addition to Gulp, Grunt is used for client-side build automation. Grunt can perform the same types of tasks as Gulp but accomplishes this in a different way. Both Grunt and Gulp will likely be around for a while. If you're thinking about diving into one of these tools but not sure which one, here is a good article that describes the differences between Grunt and Gulp with some advice about which one you should consider using: `https://medium.com/@preslavrachev/gulp-vs-grunt-why-one-why-the-other-f5d3b398edc4`.

Summary

In this chapter, you tried a few useful techniques that you may likely use in many of your web projects.

- Query selectors take advantage of the same powerful CSS selectors in your JavaScript code.

- Web workers execute CPU-intensive or slow operations on a separate thread to improve overall responsiveness.

I also introduced some of the new client-side tools that are available for managing your web application. In Chapter 6, I'll show you how the HTML5 improvements can be used in creating mobile-friendly web applications.

CHAPTER 6

■ ■ ■

Mobile Web Applications

So far, we have looked only at desktop browsers; however, one of the really great aspects of HTML5 is how well it is supported on a wide variety of devices including mobile phone, tablets, and TVs. As of this writing, the Chrome and Opera platforms lead the pack with 523 and 489 points, respectively, as reported by Html5Test.com. But Amazon Silk, Firefox Mobile, Android, and BlackBerry are not far behind with 468, 456, 452, and 449 points, out of a possible score of 555.

On a mobile device you will use native applications as well as web applications. Native apps are developed for a specific mobile platform and installed on the device, or they are downloaded through the phone service. Native apps can often provide the best user experience because they can make maximum use of the device's specific hardware and OS features. However, web apps, in part because of the popularity of HTML5, are increasingly in demand as well. And they can be developed almost as easily as those used by desktop browsers.

Using Emulators

To see how your web site works on a mobile device, you can use a number of phone emulator applications. While these may not function exactly like the actual hardware, they provide a reasonable approximation. I'll show you how to install and use several of the more common utilities.

Using the Opera Mobile Emulator

Opera provides a free mobile emulator application, which you can download from `www.opera.com/developer/tools/mobile`. One thing that is particularly nice about this utility is that you can choose, from a pretty long list, which device you want to emulate. After you have installed this application, start it and you should see the launch window shown in Figure 6-1.

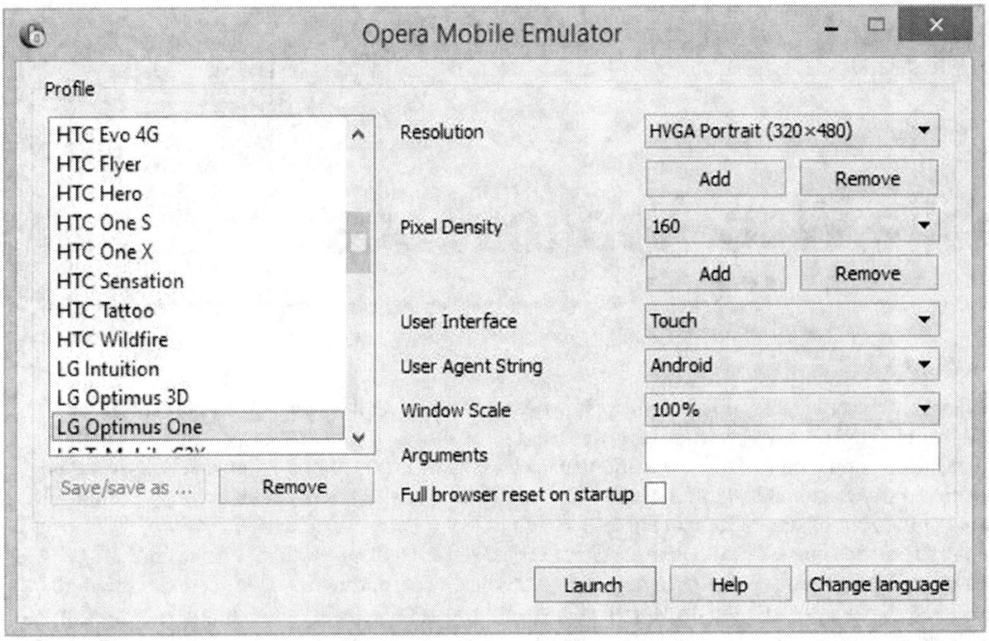

Figure 6-1. *The Opera emulator launch window*

When you select a device, the window displays the hardware details such as screen resolution. Select the LG Optimus One device and click the Launch button. With this emulator you can use either the device keypad or your desktop keyboard. Enter the URL of your site from Chapter 4, which should look like Figure 6-2.

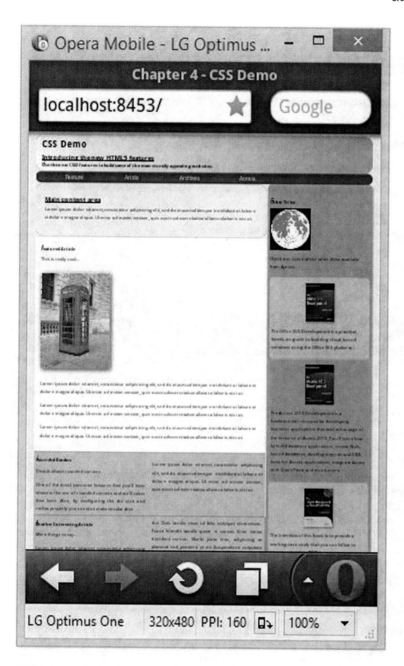

Figure 6-2. *Emulating the LG Optimus One device*

Notice that page is scaled to fit in the screen, which makes it mostly unreadable. You will deal with that later in the chapter. You can try some other devices such as the Nokia N800, which is shown in Figure 6-3. As you might expect, the larger form factors handle the page better.

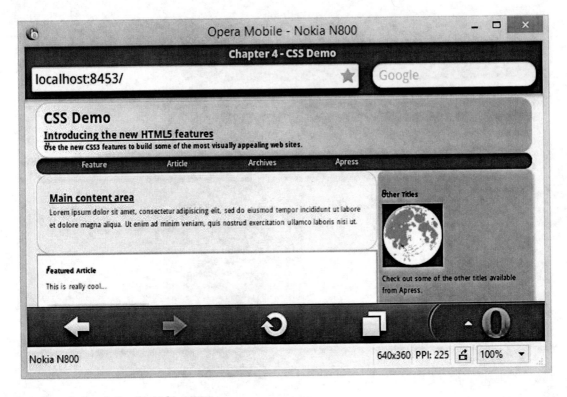

Figure 6-3. Emulating the Nokia N800

Installing Chrome Ripple

Emulating a mobile device on Chrome and Firefox requires a different approach by using add-ons to the desktop browser. When using the emulators, you are essentially using the desktop browser with some add-on functionality to simulate the device's form factor.

Start the Chrome desktop browser and click the Apps icon and select the Web Store app. In the search box, select the Extensions option and type **ripple emulator**. The results should look like Figure 6-4. Click the FREE button to install the extension.

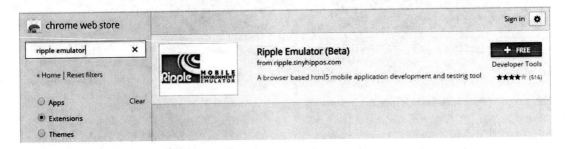

Figure 6-4. The Ripple emulator in the web store

Once you have installed the add-on, use the Chrome browser and enter the URL of the Chapter4 web site. In the top-right corner, there is a button, shown in Figure 6-5, which is used to start the emulator.

Figure 6-5. Launching Ripple

Click this button and then click the Enable button, as shown in Figure 6-6.

Figure 6-6. Enabling the Ripple emulator

This will display the current page using the emulator mode. The first time you start Ripple for a specific URL, you'll see the prompt shown in Figure 6-7. Click the BlackBerry 10 WebWorks button to choose this platform to emulate.

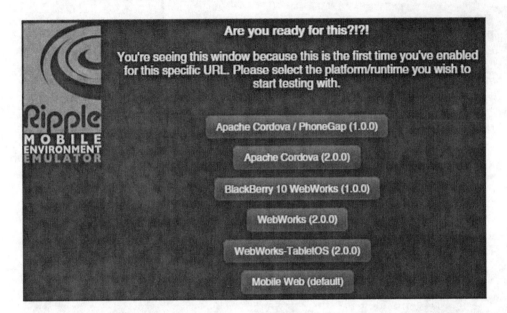

Figure 6-7. *Selecting the desired platform*

Your web page on the BlackBerry 10 device should look like Figure 6-8.

Figure 6-8. *The web page on the BlackBerry 10 device*

There are two small buttons at the top-left and top-right corners of the browser window with arrows on them. Use these to show/hide the option windows. For example, the one on the left, shown in Figure 6-9, allows you to change the device orientation or to choose a different platform to emulate. It also provides some technical details of the current device such as the screen resolution. The button on the right includes the Settings tab where you can switch between dark and light themes.

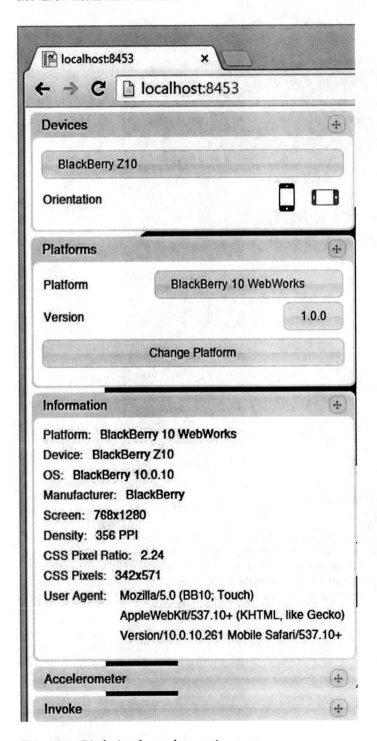

Figure 6-9. Displaying the emulator options

Emulating the Other Devices

To simulate your web site on an iPhone, using Chrome, go to this site: `http://iphone-emulator.org`. When the emulator is displayed, enter the URL of the Chapter4 site into the search box on the device. The site will look like Figure 6-10.

Figure 6-10. *Emulating the web page on an iPhone*

Notice the buttons at the top of the page that enable you to also emulate other devices such as the iPad and Android.

■ **Tip**   There are other emulators available; I've covered only a few. If you want to look into other options, try BrowserStack at `https://www.browserstack.com/list-of-browsers-and-platforms?product=live`. You can also check out the resources on ASP.net at `www.asp.net/mobile/device-simulators`.

Handling Form Factors

The biggest challenge when creating web applications that work well on mobile devices is handling the various form factors. On the larger devices you'll want to take advantage of the extra space while still making a reasonable appearance on the smaller ones. In the samples that I've shown you so far, the device either scaled the page to fit or cropped it. Neither approach is optimal.

There are three techniques that will help you improve how your site looks across all form factors.

- *Media queries*: This allows you to apply different styles based on attributes of the existing viewport. I will spend most the rest of this chapter demonstrating this.

- *Use a CSS flexbox layout*: This is similar to designing forms with Windows Presentation Foundation (WPF) that allows the browser to resize or move elements dynamically based on the window size. I will explain how this works, and you'll then use it to configure the navigation links.

- *Flexible images and videos*: This simply instructs the browser to stretch or shrink the image to fit the available space.

■ **Tip**   One of the things that the various emulators do is limit the window size based on the device characteristics. You can accomplish the same thing by simply resizing your browser window. For your initial testing, you can shrink the window and see how the layout responds. Then use the emulators for the final testing.

Understanding Media Queries

CSS 2.1 introduced the `media` keyword, allowing you to define a printer-friendly style sheet. For example, you can use something like this:

```
<link rel="stylesheet" type="text/css" href="screen.css" media="screen" />
<link rel="stylesheet" type="text/css" href="print.css" media="print" />
```

You can then define one style sheet for browsers (screen) and a different style sheet for the print version of your web page. Alternatively, you could embed media-specific style rules within a single style sheet. For example, this will change the font size when printed:

```
@media print
{
    h1, h2, h3
    {
        font-size: 14px;
    }
}
```

▒ **Tip** There are other media types that are supported including aural, braille, handheld, projection, tty, and tv. As you can see, the media type was initially used to represent the type of device that is rendering the page. Also, the all type is supported but is also implied if no media type is specified. Styles with the all type are applied for every device.

With CSS3, this has been enhanced significantly to allow you to query various attributes to determine the appropriate styles. For example, you can apply a style when the width of the windows is 600px or smaller like this:

```
@media (max-width:600px)
{
    h1
    {
        font-size: 12px;
    }
}
```

The features that can be selected in a media query are as follows:

- width
- height
- device-width
- device-height
- orientation
- aspect-ratio
- device-aspect-ratio
- color (0 if monochrome or number of bits used to specify a color)
- color-index (number of colors available)
- monochrome (0 if color, or number of bits for grayscale)
- resolution (specified in dpi or dpcm)
- scan (for TV, specifies scanning mode)
- grid (1 if a grid device such as TTY display, 0 if bitmap)

Most of these support min- and max- prefixes, which means you don't have to use a greater-than or lesser-than operator. For example, if you wanted a style for windows between 500px and 700px, inclusive, you would specify this as follows:

```
@media screen and (min-width: 500px) and (max-width: 700px)
```

Notice in this example I also included the screen media type. In this case, this style is ignored for all other types such as print.

■ **Tip** For a complete definition on each of these features, see the W3 specification at www.w3.org/TR/css3-mediaqueries/#media1.

Using Media Queries

There is a lot that you can do with media queries to dynamically style your web page. For example, you could use the color and monochrome features to apply more appropriate styles when displayed on a monochrome device. The color feature returns the number of colors supported, so (min-color: 2) will select all color devices. You can also use (orientation: portrait) and (orientation: landscape) to arrange the elements based on the device's orientation.

For this demonstration you will focus on the width of the window, but the same basic concept applies to the other features as well. As the width of the window shrinks, the styles will gradually adjust to accommodate the size while retaining as much of the original layout as possible.

A typical approach is to plan for three different styles: large, medium, and small. The large style is probably how the site is initially designed, as is the case with your Chapter4 site. There are sidebars and multiple columns of content. The medium style will keep the same basic layout but start to shrink areas as needed. A useful technique is to use relative sizing so as the window shrinks, each element gradually shrinks as well. The small style will be used for handheld devices, and you'll generally keep the layout to a single column. Since the page will tend to be longer now, links to bookmarks on the page become more important.

Modifying the Chapter4 Site

To demonstrate these techniques, you'll add some additional style rules to the site that you built in Chapter 4. You'll use media queries to selectively apply these styles based on the width of the window.

■ **Tip** The Chapter4 site was created using the WebMatrix application. However, the source code download provides this as both a WebMatrix project and a Visual Studio project. You'll find these in the Chapter4 folder. You can use whichever you prefer. The instructions will tell you how to modify the Default.cshtml file. If you're using Visual Studio, this will be the Index.cshtml file; the changes are identical in both files. I'm using the version that was also modified in Chapter 5 to set the internal links to green using JavaScript.

Open the Chapter4 project and run the application. We'll continue to use the Chrome browser, but most browsers will support the styling features that were demonstrated in this chapter. Try shrinking the width of the browser window. Notice that the page does not scale at all; the browser simply clips whatever does not fit in the window. That's your first clue that you have some work to do. Web pages should be fluid and adjust to the window size.

■ **Caution**   To make the changes easier to follow, you will simply append additional style rules to the end of your `style` tag. As I mentioned in Chapter 4, identical selectors will overwrite styles defined earlier in the file. However, it is important to use identical selectors. You can write a similar selector that will return the same elements, but if it is considered less specific, it won't override the previous style. For example, in this document, `nav a` will return the same elements as `nav ul li a`, but the latter is considered more specific and will be preferred over the former even if it is earlier in the file.

Configuring the Medium Layout

The current layout of your web page is based on a relatively large window such as a desktop browser. When designing a web page, you should also consider the appropriate layout for smaller devices. I suggest creating a separate design for small-resolution devices such as typical mobile devices. In this chapter, you'll use media queries to implement small, medium, and large configurations. However, the medium layout is often a compromise between small and large. Starting with a large layout and then designing the small layout usually works best.

Scrolling horizontally is not intuitive and should be avoided if at all possible. So if you have a narrow resolution, you should stack elements vertically. The `aside` element, for example, will need to go to the bottom of the page. You might consider eliminating the images or changing the font sizes.

Once you have a small layout in mind, you can gradually introduce these changes as the width shrinks. The approach I like to take is to gradually start shrinking the width of the browser window and see what breaks. Then make the corrections to deal with that and try shrinking it some more. With the small layout already designed, you'll know where you're going as you make adjustments in this iterative process.

Now you'll define the style for the medium and small layouts, starting with medium. On medium-sized devices, you'll use the same basic layout but just shrink some of the elements. For this site, medium will be defined as widths between 600px and 940px. The size of the web page is 940px, so if the window is wider than that, no adjustment is necessary. The 600px minimum size is somewhat arbitrary. I'll explain how I arrived at that figure later.

The medium layout needs a little adjustment. You'll use a simple trick of defining the elements with relative sizes. This allows them to automatically shrink or stretch as the window is resized. Open the `Default.cshtml` file and add the rules shown in Listing 6-1 to the existing `style` element. Add this after all the existing rules.

Listing 6-1. Defining the Medium Layout

```
@@media screen and (max-width: 940px)
{
    body
    {
        width: 100%;
    }

    aside
    {
        width: 30%;
    }

    nav ul li a
    {
        width: 100px;
    }
}
```

▓ **Note**　In the Razor syntax, an ampersand (@) is used to indicate that what follows it is code, not content. To include an ampersand in the context such as a media query, you'll need to use a double ampersand.

By setting the body width to 100,% it will automatically shrink to fit the window. It won't stretch past 940px, however, because this style is applied only when the width is smaller than that. The aside element is set to 30%. The current ratio (280px/940px) is approximately 30%. As you continue shrinking the window, the links in the nav element will eventually be clipped, so this style also reduces their width, moving them closer together.

Run the application and try shrinking the window. You should notice a nice fluid layout that adjusts to the window size, as shown in Figure 6-11.

CSS Demo

Introducing the new HTML5 features

Use the new CSS3 features to build some of the most visually appealing web sites.

Feature   Article   Archives   **Apress**

Main content area

Lorem ipsum dolor sit amet, consectetur adipisicing elit, sed do eiusmod tempor incididunt ut labore et dolore magna aliqua. Ut enim ad minim veniam, quis nostrud exercitation ullamco laboris nisi ut.

Other Titles

Featured Article

This is really cool...

Check out some of the other titles available from Apress.

Pro Office 365 Development

Pro Office 365 Development is a practical, hands-on guide to building cloud-based solutions using the Office 365 platform.

Lorem ipsum dolor sit amet, consectetur adipisicing elit, sed do eiusmod

Pro
Access 2010

Figure 6-11. Displaying the medium layout

Configuring the Small Layout

Eventually, however, the layout doesn't work well, as illustrated in Figure 6-12.

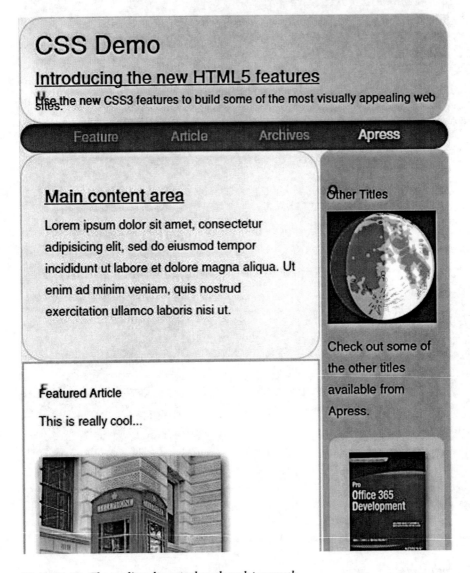

Figure 6-12. *The medium layout when shrunk too much*

There are several issues here that you'll address.

- The header text is wrapping to another line and overlapping.

- The text columns are too narrow; this size cannot adequately support three content columns.

The primary change that you'll make that will adjust the layout is to move the aside element to the bottom of the page rather than alongside the other content. As you resize the window, the other changes were gradual, but this change will cause a jump. The main content will go from 70% of the window size to 100%. You'll need to determine the appropriate width that should trigger the change. I choose 600px, but you can experiment with other values and see how the page works.

Enter the code in Listing 6-2 to the end of the existing style element.

Listing 6-2. Defining the Small Layout

```
@@media screen and (max-width: 600px)
{
    /* Move the aside to the bottom of the page */
    #contentArea, #MainContent, aside
    {
        display: block;
    }

    aside
    {
        width: 98%;
    }

    /* Use a single column for the article content */
    .otherContent
    {
        -webkit-column-count: 1;
        column-count: 1;
    }

    /* Fix the line spacing of the header */
    h2, h3
    {
        line-height:normal;
    }

    /* Force the intro element to stretch to fit the content */
    .intro
    {
        height: min-content;
    }
```

```
/* Move the book images to the left */
.book img
{
    float: left;
    margin-right:  10px;
    margin-bottom: 5px;
}

/* Make the book elements tall enough to fit the image */
.book
{
    min-height: 120px;
}
}
```

■ **Note**   The previous style that you added for the medium size also applies to the small style since both apply to widths less than 940px. The small style will define additional rules, but keep in mind the previous styles apply as well.

The small layout rules make the following adjustments:

- The aside element is moved to the bottom. This is done by undoing the table and cell attributes that you entered in Chapter 4 and then changing the width to be 98%. Previously, the #contentArea element had the display attribute set to table, and the #mainContent and aside elements were set to table-cell. By setting all three of these to block, the virtual table is removed.

- The content is displayed in two columns, and this will be reduced to a single column.

- Since the header text can now use more than one line, change the line height so the lines do not overlap.

- Force the intro section to stretch vertically to ensure all the content fits.

- Move the book images to the left and the corresponding text to the right.

- Ensure the book elements are large enough to fit the image.

Display the web page with these changes and resize the window. If you make the window narrow enough, the links will wrap, as shown in Figure 6-13.

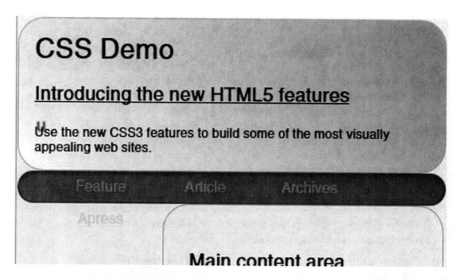

Figure 6-13. *The web page with a narrow window*

Using a Flexbox

When creating the style for a medium-sized window, you decreased the width of the links so they would fit in the smaller window. You could do that again so they still fit, but eventually you will need a better solution. What if you needed to add another link or two or if one of them was longer than the fixed width that you assigned? To resolve this issue, you'll use a flexible box, or *flexbox*. A flexbox allows you to define blocks of content that are automatically arranged based on the available space.

When working with the flexbox, you will need to configure the container as well as the items that are included in the container. These are sometime referred to as the *parent* and its *children*. For example, the nav tag in the document has the following content. The ul tag contains a series of li tags.

```
<nav>
    <ul>
        <li><a href="#feature">Feature</a></li>
        <li><a href="#other">Article</a></li>
        <li><a href="#another">Archives</a></li>
        <li><a href="http://www.apress.com" target="_blank">Apress</a></li>
    </ul>
</nav>
```

Configuring the Container

On the container element, ul in this case, you'll set the display attribute to flex to indicate that a flexbox should be used. You can then specify flow-direction, which is either row or column. With the direction set to row, the items are aligned horizontally, left to right; with column, they are stacked vertically, top to bottom. You could also add -reverse to reverse the order (right to left or bottom to top). These are the allowed values:

- row: Horizontally, left to right (this is the default value)

- row-reverse: Horizontally, right to left

- column: Vertically, top to bottom

- column-reverse: Vertically, bottom to top

Then you can specify the flex-wrap attribute, which determine what happens when the items do not fit into the allotted space. The following are the possible settings:

- nowrap: The content is displayed in a single row (or column) and clipped if necessary (this is the default value).

- wrap: The items wrap to the next row or column in the same direction.

- wrap-reverse: The items will wrap to the next row (or column) in reverse direction. For example, if the flow-direction is row (left to right), the second row will be from right to left.

Both flex-direction and flex-wrap can be combined into a single flex-flow attribute with the direction and wrap options included. For example, flex-flow: row wrap will align the items horizontally and enable wrapping to the next row.

■ **Note**   The direction specifies the main axis, horizontal or vertical. There are several attributes that you can use to configure the alignment; some affect the alignment along the main axis, and some apply to the minor axis. I will discuss these assuming the row direction is used. This is the most common, and it will be easier to follow using these terms. The CSS attributes and values are purposely generic, using words like *start*/*end* instead of *top*/*bottom* or *left*/*right*. If you're using the column direction, the attributes and values apply equally well, but the words to describe them will be different (for example, top-aligned instead of left-aligned).

The following attributes can be used to further configure the alignment of items:

- justify-content: Main axis, affects the horizontal spacing of items within a row

- align-items: Minor axis, affects the vertical alignment within a row

- align-content: Minor axis, affects the vertical spacing between rows

You can specify how you want the items justified along the main axis, which determines how any extra space should be allocated. The justify-content attribute supports the following options:

- flex-start: The default. The items are left justified (or top justified if using the column direction). All extra space is at the end.

- flex-end: The items are right-justified (or bottom-justified).

- center: The items are placed in the center, with extra space divided at the beginning and end.

- space-between: The first item is left aligned, the last item is right aligned, and the extra space is distributed over the spaces between the items.

- space-around: This is similar to space-between, except the extra space is also added before the first item and after the last item.

The align-items attribute specifies how items are aligned in the minor axis. For example, if the flow-direction is row, the justify-content attribute describes how the horizontal spacing is arranged. However, the align-items attribute specifies how items within the row are aligned vertically. If the items in the row have differing heights, you can choose to align the tops or the bottoms, for example. These are the available options:

- flex-start: The default. This aligns the tops.

- flex-end: This aligns the bottoms.

- center: This centers each item, with extra space evenly distributed between top and bottom.

- stretch: This stretches the item to the size of the largest item in the row.

- baseline: The items are aligned using their baseline.

▉ **Tip** The term *baseline* came from the print world where characters were aligned along a baseline. This is not necessarily the bottom of the text because of fonts with serifs as well as superscripts and subscripts. However, the baseline provides a visual guide to placing characters so the line appears straight. In CSS, this concept is even more complicated because we're not just dealing with text. If you want to delve into this subject, here is a good article: www.smashingmagazine.com/2012/12/17/css-baseline-the-good-the-bad-and-the-ugly.

If you have multiple rows of items, the align-content attribute specifies how the extra vertical spaced is placed around the rows. This supports the same options as justify-content: flex-start, flex-end, center, space-between, and space-around. It also supports the stretch option.

Configuring the Items

There are several attributes that can be applied to the child items that influence how they are aligned. You can assign a numeric value for the flex-grow and flex-shrink attributes. This indicates how much the item can grow or shrink relative to the other items. For example, items with a value of 2 will grow twice as much as items with a value of 1. Also, the flex-basis attribute is used to indicate the basis of an item's initial size. This is a numeric value that indicates the initial value to be used. If set to auto, which is the default value, this will be the actual width of the item.

You can also specify a numeric value for the order property. By default, items are displayed in the order that they appear in the HTML content. However, the order property, if used, will override this.

As I explained previously, the alignment along the minor axis is determined by the align-items attribute. However, this can be overridden on one or more items. If you have set align-items to flex-start, for example, this will align them along the top. You can override this for an individual item by setting its align-self attributes. This takes the same values as the align-items attribute.

■ **Note** You can find the complete specification at `www.w3.org/TR/css-flexbox-1`. As of this writing, this was in a Working Draft status. Some of these concepts are better understood with some visual examples. Here is a good article that demonstrates these techniques: `https://developer.mozilla.org/en-US/docs/Web/Guide/CSS/Flexible_boxes`.

Adjusting the Links

Now you'll modify your sample page to fix the link alignment using a flexbox. Add the following to the end of the `style` tag. This will configure the `ul` element to display the elements horizontally and to enable wrapping, if necessary. The links will also be left-justified. The width of the links is set to `auto` so it can accommodate long and short elements.

```
nav ul
{
    display: flex;
    flex-flow: row wrap;
    justify-content: flex-start;
}

nav ul li a
{
    width: auto;
}
```

You'll also need to fix the size of the `nav` element so it can grow, vertically, if the links need to be wrapped. The height is currently set to 30px. Change the `height` attribute to `min-height`, as shown in the following code. This will set the initial height to 30px but allow it to grow to fit the contents.

```
/* Make the radius half of the height */
nav
{
    min-height: 30px;
    border-radius:15px;
}
```

Save your changes and refresh the web page. Shrink the window as narrow as it will go. Even at this size, the page layout still looks good, as shown in Figure 6-14.

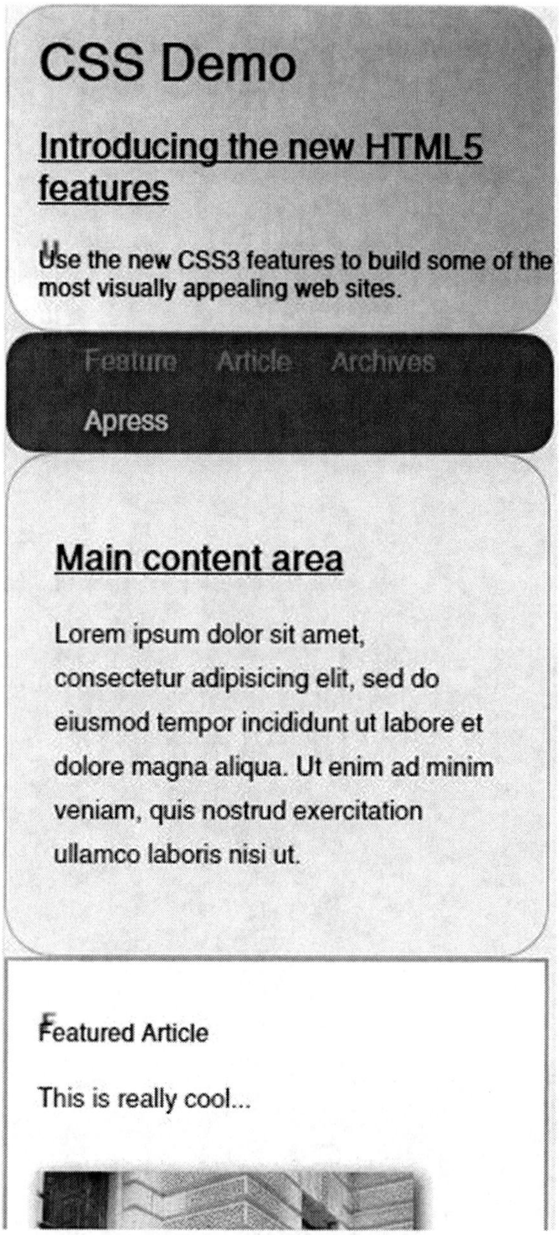

CSS Demo

Introducing the new HTML5 features

Use the new CSS3 features to build some of the most visually appealing web sites.

Feature   Article   Archives

Apress

Main content area

Lorem ipsum dolor sit amet, consectetur adipisicing elit, sed do eiusmod tempor incididunt ut labore et dolore magna aliqua. Ut enim ad minim veniam, quis nostrud exercitation ullamco laboris nisi ut.

Featured Article

This is really cool...

Figure 6-14. *The web page with its smallest size*

The flexbox works well when combined with media queries. One example of this is to configure the direction of the links to be vertical when the window width is small. Try entering this at the end of your style element to demonstrate this:

```
@@media screen and (max-width: 400px)
{
    nav ul
    {
        flex-direction: column;
    }
}
```

If you shrink the page small enough, the links be aligned vertically, as shown in Figure 6-15.

Figure 6-15. *Using vertical links*

Using Flexible Images

If you have large images, you may find them being clipped. To prevent that, set the max-width property to 100%. This will cause the images to be resized to fit the width of the container. This is not done inside a media query, and this format will be applied at all resolutions. For example, you can specify the following to configure the phone booth image:

```
#phone
{
    max-width: 100%;
    height: auto;
}
```

Setting the height to auto will change the height to maintain the existing aspect ratio. You can do the same thing with video elements using the following style rule:

```
.video embed, .video object, .video iframe
{
    width: 100%;
    height: auto;
}
```

Viewing the Page on a Mobile Device

For a final test, display the site using Chrome and enable the Ripple emulator as I showed you earlier. Select the PhoneGap platform. Your page should look like Figure 6-16.

Figure 6-16. *The web page as seen on the Ripple emulator*

Summary

In this chapter, I showed you how to install and use several mobile device emulators including the following:

- Opera Mobile Emulator
- Chrome Ripple add-on
- iPhone emulator

To handle the various form factors, media queries were used to selectively apply styles based on the window width. You implemented large, medium, and small layouts that scale cleanly as the window is resized. Also, by setting the width to 100%, you can auto-size images and video. Finally, you used a flexbox to dynamically arrange the navigation links.

PART III

■ ■ ■

Digging Deeper

CHAPTER 7

■ ■ ■

Supporting Older Browsers

Now you have this great-looking, HTML5-compliant web page that you created in Chapter 4. You want to show it off, so you send a link to a colleague who just happens to still use IE 8, and they see something like Figure 7-1.

CSS Demo

Introducing the new HTML5 features

Use the new CSS3 features to build some of the most visually appealing web sites.

- Feature
- Article
- Archives
- Apress

Main content area

Lorem ipsum dolor sit amet, consectetur adipisicing elit, sed do eiusmod tempor incididunt ut labore et dolore magna aliqua. Ut enim ad minim veniam, quis nostrud exercitation ullamco laboris nisi ut.

Featured Article

This is really cool...

Other Titles

Check out some of the other titles available from Apress.

Pro Office 365 Development is a practical, hands-on guide to building cloud-based solutions using the Office 365 platform.

Lorem ipsum dolor sit amet, consectetur adipisicing elit, sed do eiusmod tempor incididunt ut labore et dolore magna aliqua. Ut enim ad minim veniam, quis nostrud exercitation ullamco laboris nisi ut.

Figure 7-1. *The CSS demo as shown in IE 8*

The page looks awful and nothing like what you were expecting. You're certainly not going to win any prizes for it. Not to be deterred, you send the link to your boss, and things get worse. Your boss is using IE 7 and sees something like Figure 7-2.

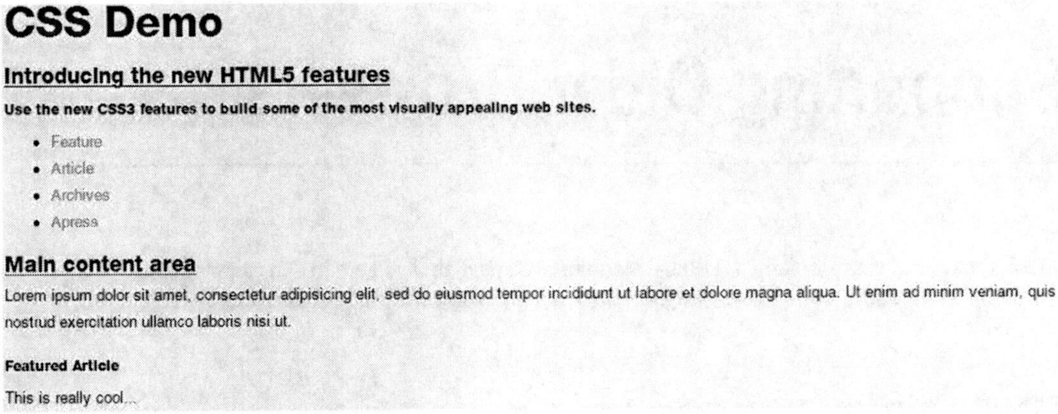

CSS Demo

Introducing the new HTML5 features

Use the new CSS3 features to build some of the most visually appealing web sites.

- Feature
- Article
- Archives
- Apress

Main content area

Lorem ipsum dolor sit amet, consectetur adipisicing elit, sed do eiusmod tempor incididunt ut labore et dolore magna aliqua. Ut enim ad minim veniam, quis nostrud exercitation ullamco laboris nisi ut.

Featured Article

This is really cool...

Figure 7-2. The CSS demo as shown in IE 7

The sidebar is no longer on the side but tacked on at the bottom of the page. Your boss begins wondering what you've been doing in all your spare time. You've just learned two important lessons, the hard way.

- Always control your demo environment; in this case, let them see the page on your browser.

- More importantly, test your web site on several different browsers.

In this chapter, I will show you some fairly simple techniques to get your page looking its best even with older browsers. You don't have to write much code because there is a lot of open source code that you can easily add to your site.

Making Some Simple Changes

There are a couple of really easy changes that will make the web page look much better. You'll start with those, and then later I'll show you some of the more involved solutions.

Emulating Older Browsers

To test your web page using some older versions of Internet Explorer, you'll use IE 11 in Emulator mode. After launching Internet Explorer, hit F12 to display the Developer Tools pane. By default, the browser will use "edge" mode, which is the latest version. To change this, click the Edge drop-down menu, as shown in Figure 7-3.

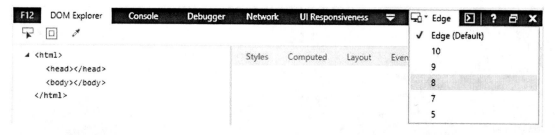

Figure 7-3. *Modifying the emulation mode*

For this chapter, use the same project you created in Chapter 4 (Visual Studio version), which you can download from www.apress.com.

Using Modernizr

When supporting older browsers, the first thing you should do is employ the Modernizr open source JavaScript library. This library performs two essential functions.

- Detects the current browser's available features and provides this information as queryable properties. For example, in your JavaScript, you can place conditional logic like this:

```
if (!Modernizr.cssanimations) {
    alert("Your browser does not support CSS animation");
}
```

- Provides shims to implement missing functionality. This includes the html5shim library that allows you to style your content using the new elements such as header, footer, nav, and aside.

■ **Tip** For more information, check out the Modernizr web site at http://modernizr.com.

So, let's add the Modernizr library to your page and see what happens! In Chapter 5 I briefly explained the Bower tool that is used as a client-side package manager. Now, you'll see it in action. Because this project was created using the Empty template, you'll need to install Bower. Go to the NuGet PackageManager from the Tools menu. Enter **bower** in the search box and select Bower as shown in Figure 7-4. Click the Install button to begin the install.

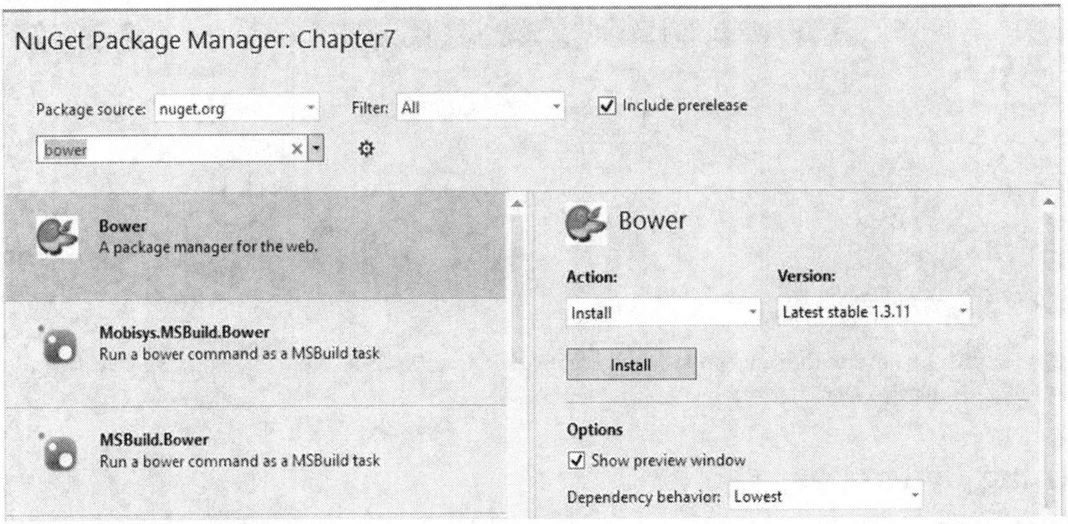

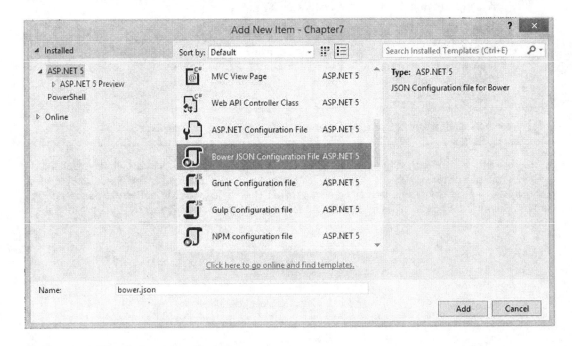

Figure 7-4. *Adding Bower to the project*

Now you'll also need to create the bower.json file. From the Solution Explorer, right-click the Chapter 7 project and select the Add and New Item links. Select the Bower JSON Configuration file option as shown in Figure 7-5. The file name should default to bower.json.

Figure 7-5. *Adding the bower.json file.*

Add the line shown in bold in the following code:

```
{
    "name": "Chapter7",
    "private": true,
    "dependencies": {
        "modernizr": "2.8.3"
    }
}
```

■ **Tip**   As I explained in Chapter 5, Visual Studio provides IntelliSense while you're editing this file. After selecting modernizr from the list and typing the colon, the current version will be displayed. As of this writing, it is 2.8.3. You should take whatever the latest version that is displayed by IntelliSense.

You can install Grunt or Gulp and setup a task to automatically update the Modernizr file and copy it to the wwwroot folder. For simplicity, you'll perform this manually. In the Solution Explorer, expand the Dependencies folder and right-click the Bower item. Select the Restore Packages link. This will force a download of the latest version.

In the Solution Explorer, right-click the wwwroot folder and select the Add and New Item links and enter the name **lib**. Then right-click the modernizr item in the Dependencies\Bower folder and select the Open in File Explorer link. This will open Windows Explorer in this location. You should see a modernizr.js file; copy this to the wwwroot\lib folder in the Solution Explorer.

With Modernizr now installed, you can include the Modernizer library in your page by adding this at the top of your Index.html file, just after the DOCTYPE tag:

```
<script  type="text/javascript" src="lib/modernizr.js"></script>
```

Display the page using Internet Explorer; then go to the Developer Tools pane and change the browser mode to IE 7, as I explained earlier. Your page should look like Figure 7-6.

CSS Demo

Introducing the new HTML5 features

Use the new CSS3 features to build some of the most visually appealing web sites.

| Feature | Article | Archives | Apress |

Main content area

Lorem ipsum dolor sit amet, consectetur adipisicing elit, sed do eiusmod tempor incididunt ut labore et dolore magna aliqua. Ut enim ad minim veniam, quis nostrud exercitation ullamco laboris nisi ut.

Featured Article

This is really cool...

Lorem ipsum dolor sit amet, consectetur adipisicing elit, sed do eiusmod tempor incididunt ut labore et dolore magna aliqua. Ut enim ad minim veniam, quis nostrud exercitation ullamco laboris nisi ut.

Figure 7-6. The demo page with Modernizr as viewed in IE 7

Notice that the border and background colors are now showing, which goes a long way to making the page look like it was originally intended. Also, the navigation links are arranged horizontally.

■ **Note** A *shim* is a thin object, often made of wood, that is used to fill a gap between two objects. In this context, the term refers to a relatively small piece of code that fills in the gap between a browser's current functionality and the full HTML5 specification. The term *shim* has been used in software development circles for a long time. The term *polyfill* was introduced for referring to a browser-related shim. So, in this context, the two terms are synonymous.

Adding More Polyfills

Now you're probably starting to feel a little better. By adding Modernizr, the page looks decent. However, upon closer inspection, there is a fairly long list of features that are not working, including the following:

- Tables
- Rounded corners
- Gradient background fills
- Striped articles
- Animation
- 3D transforms
- Multiple columns

Given a sufficient amount of patience and persistence (and, of course, time), you could probably implement all of these features so that your page looks the same in both IE 7 and the latest version of Chrome. However, I don't recommend you do that. Essentially, you should make sure your page works great on the latest HTML5-compliant browsers and works acceptably on older browsers. It doesn't have to work great on every browser. Consider the following:

- Most users are not going to view your site on a host of browsers and compare the experience of each. Your page does not need to look identical in every browser.
- If someone is using IE 7, they are used to bad-looking web sites. Implementing just a few of these polyfills will probably make your page stand out as one of the better sites they've visited.
- HTML5 is supposed to make your job as web developer easier. However, if you try to make every page work like native HTML5 on older browsers, you'll be spending far more time, not less.

For each feature that your page uses that is not natively supported by commonly used browsers, you have the following options:

- *Fail*: Simply display an error stating this browser does not support the necessary features and offer some suggested browsers to use. For example, the primary purpose of the sample site you created in Chapter 5 was to demonstrate how web workers are used. If the page is viewed by a browser that doesn't support web workers, there's no point trying to make the page work. Just fail!
- *Polyfill*: Implement an alternate solution to provide the needed feature. This can range from simple solutions to rather complex. For example, if a gradient fill is not supported, you could just use a solid color fill, or you could provide a shim and implement a gradient using JavaScript.
- *Ignore*: Just leave the feature unimplemented. For example, you could ignore rounded corners; in older browsers, they'll be square corners.

There are no hard-and-fast rules here; you'll need to decide on a case-by-case basis which features are important to you and how much time you're willing to spend making them work on older browsers. In the rest of this chapter, I will demonstrate some techniques to backfill some of these features using mostly open source shims that are publicly available. I don't want to leave you with the impression, however, that you have to backfill every feature. In fact, several of these features for this demo, including multicolumn support, 3D transforms, and animation will be ignored because they are relatively difficult or just not that important.

> ■ **Tip** There are a plethora of shims and polyfills available. This article provides a good reference if you're looking for something specific: `https://github.com/Modernizr/Modernizr/wiki/HTML5-Cross-Browser-Polyfills`. Keep in mind that these may not always work properly, so test them and keep what works. Also, combining various shims can create some interesting results because the side effects from one can break another one.

Displaying Tables

As you test your page in several browsers, note the features that are not working correctly and then prioritize them. In this case, the `aside` element should be alongside the main content, not at the end of the page. In my opinion, this is the most critical issue and should therefore be addressed first.

> ■ **Tip** Tables were first supported in IE 8. If you change the browser mode to IE 8, you'll see the sidebar is alongside the main content. So, table support is an issue only for IE 7 and older. You might consider simply ignoring the issue and explain that your site works best with IE 8 and newer. To see how many users that would affect, check out the latest browsers' stats at `www.w3schools.com/browsers/browsers_stats.asp`. According to these statistics, that's only about 0.1 percent of the total number of browsers in use. These statistics represent an overall usage; you may have a specific target audience that can have different characteristics.

To support tables in IE 7, you'll use a behavioral CSS extension, which allows you to embed a JavaScript in a style sheet. An extension is invoked by adding a rule like this:

```
header
{
    behavior: url(customBehavior.htc);
}
```

The implementation is provided in an HTML component (HTC) file with the `.htc` extension. There are a few things about using `.htc` files that you should be aware of.

- In general, you can open an HTML file in a browser without using IIS. For example, you could simply open the `Index.html` file with Internet Explorer (or any browser) and the page would work fine. However, `.htc` files are ignored if the page is not actually served up by a web server such as IIS or Apache.

- You may need to define the HTC content type on your web server. IIS and IIS Express both support this by default, but you may need to add this with Apache or other web servers.

- Even though the `.htc` file is typically referenced in a CSS file, the URL specified in the `behavior` attribute must be relative to the location of the HTML document that invoked the style sheet. If you put the `.htc` file in the `css` folder (with all the other style sheets), you'll need to reference it with a relative path, `css/customBehavior.htc`.

To display tables, you will use an open source HTC that can be downloaded from `http://tanalin.com/en/projects/display-table-htc`.

EXERCISE 7-1. SUPPORTING TABLES

1. In the Solution Explorer, right-click the wwwroot folder and select the Add and New Folder links. Enter the name **css**.

2. Download the latest .zip file from this site: http://tanalin.com/en/projects/ display-table-htc. (The latest file as of this writing is display-table. htc_2011-11-25.zip.) This file contains an uncompressed and a minimized version. Copy the display-table.htc file to the css folder in the Solution Explorer.

3. Open the Index.html and find the portion where the table is defined. Add the code shown in bold from Listing 7-1 to the existing style rules. This specifies a vendor-prefixed version of the display attribute and invokes the display-table.htc component.

Listing 7-1. Defining a New Table

```
/* Setup a table for the content and sidebar */
#contentArea
{
    display: table;
    -dt-display: table;
    behavior: url(css/display-table.htc);
}
#mainContent
{
    display: table-cell;
    -dt-display: table-cell;
    padding-right: 2px;
    behavior: url(css/display-table.htc);
}
aside
{
    display: table-cell;
    -dt-display: table-cell;
    width: 280px;
    behavior: url(css/display-table.htc);
}
```

4. Save your changes and view the Index.html page in Internet Explorer. Change the emulator mode to IE 7, and you should now see a table set up, as shown in Figure 7-7.

CSS Demo

Introducing the new HTML5 features

Use the new CSS3 features to build some of the most visually appealing web sites.

| Feature | Article | Archives | Apress |

Main content area

Lorem ipsum dolor sit amet, consectetur adipisicing elit, sed do eiusmod tempor incididunt ut labore et dolore magna aliqua. Ut enim ad minim veniam, quis nostrud exercitation ullamco laboris nisi ut.

Other Titles

Check out some of the other titles available from Apress.

Featured Article

This is really cool...

Pro Office 365 Development is a practical, hands-on guide to building cloud-based solutions using the Office 365 platform.

Figure 7-7. The table support added in IE 7

■ **Note** The `display-table.htc` file uses its own, nonstandard, vendor-specific prefix. So, you needed to add the `-dt-display` attribute. You can also ignore the warning that is generated because of this.

---

5. Now there's one more thing that needs to be fixed. You'll notice that the `aside` element is missing some styles such as `background-color` and `padding`. This is a side effect of the CSS extension. To create the table in your page, this code created real table elements for you such as `tr` and `td`. So, once the JavaScript runs, the `aside` element is removed and replaced with rows and cells. Since there is no `aside` element anymore, you can't use an element selector to style it. However, there is only one `aside` element in your source document, and it has the sidebar `id` attribute.

6. Close the browser.

7. Replace all `aside` selectors with `#sidebar`, including the one you just added. There are several places in the `Index.html` file that you'll need to change.

8. View the page again and change the emulator mode to IE 7. The sidebar should now have a background color, and there is also padding around the text.

Adding Rounded Corners

If the browser does not support rounded corners, you can easily add them thanks to a nifty jQuery plug-in written by Dave Methvin. In addition to rounded corners, this plug-in can also create a number of other patterns, which are displayed at http://jquery.malsup.com/corner. This is provided through an open source license so you can freely download and use it in your application.

You'll use this plug-in to implement rounded corners for the nav and footer elements. However, this should be done only if rounded corners are not supported natively. So, the first question is how do you know if the browser supports rounded corners? The answer again is Modernizer. Adding a statement like this will conditionally call the custom method:

```
if (!Modernizr.borderradius)
```

▥ **Tip**   I will show you another technique for rounding corners later in this chapter.

EXERCISE 7-2. ADDING ROUNDED CORNERS

1. Go to http://jquery.malsup.com/corner. Click the jquery.corner.js link near the top of the page. This will download the latest version. Save the file in your wwwroot\lib folder in the Solution Explorer.

▥ **Note**   This plug-in is not available through Bower, so you'll need to download and install this the old-fashioned way.

---

2. This function is based on jQuery, so you'll also need to reference that in your page. Open the bower.json file and add the lines shown in bold (don't forget to add the comma at the end of the previous line).

```
{
    "name": "Chapter7",
    "private": true,
    "dependencies": {
        "modernizr": "2.8.3",
        "jquery": "2.1.4",
        "jquery-validation-unobtrusive": "3.2.2"
    }
}
```

3. After saving the bower.json file, you should see a jquery item in the Dependencies\Bower folder. Like you did for Modernizr, right-click the jquery item and select the Open in File Explorer link. Go to the dist subfolder and copy the jquery.js file to the wwwroot\lib folder in the Solution Explorer.

4. In the same way, copy the `jquery.validation.unobtrusive.js` file to the `wwwroot\lib` folder.

5. Open the `Index.html` file and add these references near the top of the page, just after the Modernizr script:

```
<script type="text/javascript" src="lib/jquery.js"></script>
<script type="text/javascript" src="lib/jquery.corner.js"></script>
```

6. Now invoke this by adding this `script` element at the end of the `Index.html` file, after the footer element and just before the body closing tag.

```
<script type="text/javascript">
if (!Modernizr.borderradius) {
    $("nav").corner("15px");
    $("footer").corner("25px");
}
</script>
```

7. This code uses the jQuery selector to find the `nav` and `footer` elements and calls the `corner()` method specifying the radius.

8. Save your changes and view the page using Internet Explorer. Switch the emulator mode to IE 7, and your page should look like Figure 7-8.

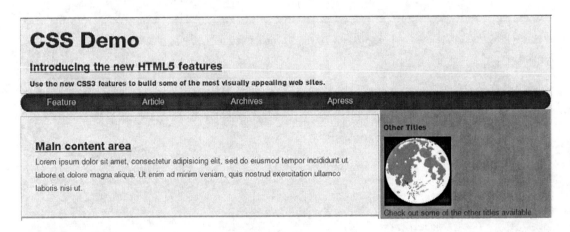

Figure 7-8. The demo page with rounded corners

Adding Gradients

Next, you'll add a gradient background to the intro section using another open source solution from PIE (progressive Internet Explorer). This is implemented as an HTC file just like the table support that you added earlier. Once you have downloaded the component, you simply invoke it using the behavior property of your style sheet rule.

EXERCISE 7-3. ADDING BACKGROUND GRADIENTS

1. Go to the `http://css3pie.com` site and click the Download button. This will download a `PIE-1.0.0.zip` file (you may see a different version number; just download the latest version).

2. There are several files inside this `.zip` file. Copy the `PIE.htc` file to your `wwwroot\css` folder.

3. From Solution Explorer, right-click the `wwwroot\css` folder and click the Add and Existing Item links. Navigate to the `css` folder and select the `PIE.htc` file.

4. Open the `Index.html` file and find where the rules for the `.intro` class are defined. Add the following lines shown in bold. This code will add another vendor-prefixed attribute (`-pie-`) and then invoke the PIE component using the `behavior` property.

```
/* Gradients */
.intro
{
    border: 1px solid #999999;
    text-align:left;
    margin-top: 6px;
    padding-left: 15px;
    border-radius:25px;
    background-image: linear-gradient(45deg, #ffffff, #6699cc);
    -pie-background: linear-gradient(45deg, #ffffff, #6699cc);
    behavior: url(css/PIE.htc);
}
```

5. Save your changes, view the page using Internet Explorer, and switch the emulator mode to IE 7. You should now have a linear gradient that looks just like the native gradient. You might have also noticed that the corners are rounded as well. The `PIE.htc` shim also supports rounded corners and took care of that for you.

■ **Note**   PIE is designed to backfill several CSS3 features, which are listed in this article: `http://css3pie.com/documentation/supported-css3-features`. It will attempt to address any of these features that are included in the element that references the `PIE.htc` shim. However, it does not do anything with features that are supported natively.

The page should now look like Figure 7-9.

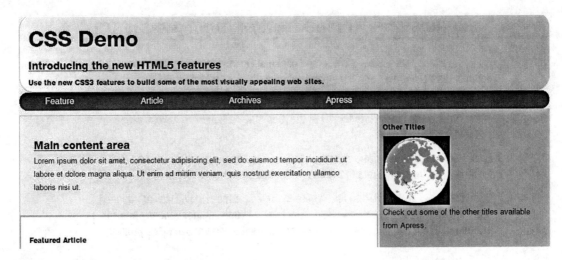

Figure 7-9. The demo page with a gradient background

Striping the Book List

Recall from Chapter 4 that the list of books was styled using an :nth-child selector so alternating elements would have a different background. In older browsers that do not support this, you can accomplish this the old-fashioned way, by iterating the list in JavaScript and changing the style on alternating elements.

The trick, however, is determining whether the :nth-child selector is available because Modernizr does not provide this. As of this writing, Modernizr is working on a version 3 beta that will include this ability. For more details, check out the list of features at http://v3.modernizr.com/download.

■ **Note**   The solution provided here is based on a post by Lea Verou. I had to adjust this to work with IE, however. For more details, check out the article at http://lea.verou.me/2011/07/detecting-css-selectors-support-my-jsconf-eu-talk/.

EXERCISE 7-4. STRIPING THE BOOK LIST

1. Open the Index.html file and add the following code to the script element at the top of the file:

```
function supportsSelector(selector) {
    var el = document.createElement('div');
    el.innerHTML = ['&shy;', '<style>', selector, '{}', '</style>'].join('');
    try
    {
        el = document.body.appendChild(el);
        var style = el.getElementsByTagName('style')[0],
            ret = !!(style.sheet.rules || style.sheet.cssRules)[0];
    }
```

```
        catch(e){
            ret = false;
        }
        document.body.removeChild(el);
        return ret;
    }
```

2. This code creates a new style element and adds the selector in question. It then checks to see whether it is actually there. If not, the selector is not supported. This is done in a try/catch block in case older browsers do not support either the style.sheet.rules or style.sheet.cssRules property.

3. Now with your handy supportsSelector() function, you can implement the manual striping technique. Add the following code to the script element at the bottom of the file after the existing function you added for the rounded corners:

```
if (!supportsSelector(":nth-child(2n+0)")) {
    var titles = document.getElementById("titles");
    var articles = titles.getElementsByTagName("article");
    for (var i = 0; i < articles.length; i++) {
        var title = articles[i];
        if (i % 2) {
            title.style.background = "#6699cc";
            title.style.border = "1px solid #c0c0c0";
        }
        else {
            title.style.background = "#c0c0c0";
            title.style.border = "1px solid #6699cc";
        }
    }
}
```

4. If the :nth-child selector is not supported, this code gets the #titles element using the getElementById() function. This is the section element that contains a series of article elements, one for each book. It then gets an array of child article elements using the getElementsByTagName() function. Note that this method is invoked on the titles object and not the document object. Once it has the array of elements, the code simply iterates the array, modifying the background and border properties.

5. Save your changes and view the page using the IE 7 emulation mode. The page should look like Figure 7-10.

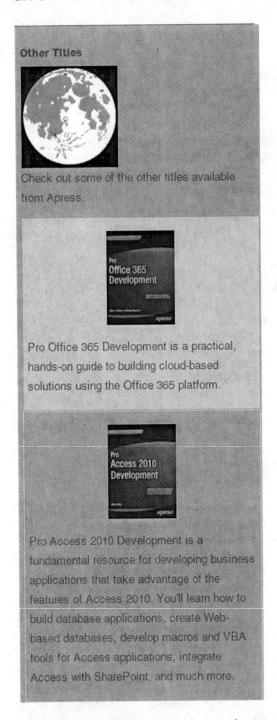

Figure 7-10. The aside element with manual striping

Hiding Unsupported Elements

As stated earlier in the chapter, for each unsupported feature you need to decide whether this is a deal-breaker and the page just needs to fail, whether you want to polyfill that feature, or whether you want to simply ignore it on older browsers. From the initial list of unsupported changes, there are three left that you have not implemented yet:

- CSS animation

- 3D transforms

- Multiple columns

You can fairly easily implement animation by using JavaScript to change the background image as a timer expires. That's the way it was normally done before we had CSS animation. Implementing a 3D transform in an older browser, however, just isn't going to work. I would categorize both of these as nice to have but not really worth the trouble, so we'll leave these features out if the browser doesn't support them.

The one feature that would be nice to emulate is the multiple-column support. There are shims available for this such as this one available from GitHub: https://github.com/gryzzly/CSS-Multi-column-Layout-Module-Polyfill/blob/master/index.html. Perhaps with enough time and patience you could get something to work, but this is one of those hard decisions. Is it worth the effort? In some unique circumstances, it might be, but in general you probably shouldn't spend 80 percent of your time on a nice-to-have feature that will affect only a few percent of the expected audience.

One thing you should consider, though, is hiding elements that aren't functional. The static picture of the moon isn't very interesting, for example, so you'll hide this element by setting its size to 0.

EXERCISE 7-5. HIDING ELEMENTS

1. Add the following code to the `script` element at the bottom of the `Index.html` file:

```
if (!Modernizr.cssanimations) {
    document.getElementById("moon").style.width = "0px";
    document.getElementById("moon").style.height = "0px";
}
```

2. This code simply shrinks the moon `div` if CSS animations are not supported. View the page in Internet Explorer and switch the emulator mode to IE 7. The final web page should look like Figure 7-11.

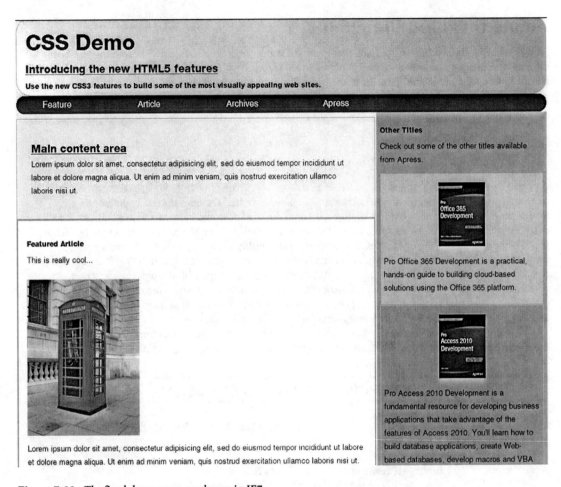

Figure 7-11. *The final demo page as shown in IE7*

3. Finally, after all this work, you should try the page in a browser that supports all these features to make sure it still looks great there. The final version in Chrome should look like Figure 7-12.

CSS Demo

Introducing the new HTML5 features

Use the new CSS3 features to build some of the most visually appealing web sites.

Feature	Article	Archives	Apress

Main content area

Lorem ipsum dolor sit amet, consectetur adipisicing elit, sed do eiusmod tempor incididunt ut labore et dolore magna aliqua. Ut enim ad minim veniam, quis nostrud exercitation ullamco laboris nisi ut.

Featured Article

This is really cool...

Lorem ipsum dolor sit amet, consectetur adipisicing elit, sed do eiusmod tempor incididunt ut labore et dolore magna aliqua. Ut enim ad minim veniam, quis nostrud exercitation ullamco laboris nisi ut.

Lorem ipsum dolor sit amet, consectetur adipisicing elit, sed do eiusmod tempor incididunt ut labore et dolore magna aliqua. Ut enim ad minim veniam, quis nostrud exercitation ullamco laboris nisi ut.

Lorem ipsum dolor sit amet, consectetur adipisicing elit, sed do eiusmod tempor incididunt ut labore et dolore magna aliqua. Ut enim ad minim veniam, quis nostrud exercitation ullamco laboris nisi ut.

Rounded Borders

Details about rounded corners

Other Titles

Check out some of the other titles available from Apress.

Pro Office 365 Development is a practical, hands-on guide to building cloud-based solutions using the Office 365 platform.

Pro Access 2010 Development is a fundamental resource for developing business applications that take advantage of the features of Access 2010. You'll learn how to build database applications, create Web-based databases, develop macros and VBA tools for Access applications, integrate Access with SharePoint, and much more.

radius properly you can also make circular divs

Lorem ipsum dolor sit amet, consectetur adipisicing elit, sed do eiusmod tempor incididunt ut labore et

Figure 7-12. The final demo page as shown in Chrome

■ **Tip** The source code download contains the complete Index.html file. Refer to this if there are any questions about exactly how or where a change should be made.

Summary

In this chapter, I showed you some techniques for making your web page look great even with older browsers that do not support the new HTML5 features. These techniques include the following:

- Using Modernizr for feature detection and basic element support
- Displaying tables
- Adding rounded corners
- Supporting gradient background images
- Manually striping a list
- Hiding unsupported elements

For every unsupported feature you'll need to decide the following:

- Whether the feature is critical to the page (and if so, the page should fail)
- Whether the feature can be easily polyfilled
- Whether the feature can be ignored

This is a bit of a balancing act because you want the page to look good in all browsers but you don't want to spend an excessive amount of time supporting every possible browser.

The final implementation of the demo page struck a good compromise. The site looks great and functions properly. While a few of the new HTML5 features are omitted, overall it's still a great site considering the browser support, and the additional work was minimal.

In the next chapter, I'll show you how to use the new `audio` and `video` elements that were introduced in HTML5.

CHAPTER 8

■ ■ ■

Audio and Video

In this chapter, I will demonstrate the new audio and video elements introduced with HTML5. The two elements are identical in terms of their attributes and the methods and events they support. I will spend most of the chapter discussing and demonstrating the audio element, but just keep in mind that everything I'm showing you applies to video as well. There are some exercises at the end of the chapter that will apply these same techniques to the video element so you can see this for yourself.

I will demonstrate how to add audio and video elements using the native controls provided by the browser. This approach makes embedding audio and video in your web site a trivial matter of adding some simple markup. If you want to write your own controls, however, this chapter will also demonstrate how to do that and to wire up all the events with JavaScript.

Because each browser supports different media formats, you might need to encode multiple versions of your media files. However, most major browsers now support the MP3 and MP4 formats, so this is becoming less of a concern. The audio and video elements can support multiple sources, so each browser can choose the appropriate version to use.

■ **Note** The video element supports three additional attributes (width, height, and poster) that the audio element doesn't. I will explain these later in the chapter.

Using the audio Element

I'll start with a pretty simple exercise of adding an audio element to a web page. Then you'll support multiple formats and try your site on various bowsers.

Creating the Sample Project

In this chapter, you'll create a web site project that you'll use to try the audio and video HTML5 elements. You'll create an empty web site now and then progressively add features to it throughout the chapter.

EXERCISE 8-1. ADDING AUDIO TO A PAGE

1. Start Visual Studio 2015 and click New Project. Select the ASP.NET Web Application project template and enter **Chapter8** for the name.

2. In the second dialog, select the ASP.NET 5 Empty project.

3. In Solution Explorer, right-click the wwwroot folder and click the Add and New Folder links. Enter the name **Media**.

4. You'll need an MP3 file to use as a sample audio clip. The file I'm using is copyrighted, so I can't include it with the source code. You should be able to find one on your computer or download one from the internet. You can also rip a CD through Windows Media Player and select MP3 as the format.

5. Drag the MP3 file from Windows Explorer to the wwwroot\Media folder in Visual Studio.

6. Now you'll add the web page that you'll be working on throughout this chapter. From Solution Explorer, right-click the wwwroot folder and click the Add and New Item links. In the Add New Item dialog, select HTML Page and enter the name **Index.html**, as shown in Figure 8-1.

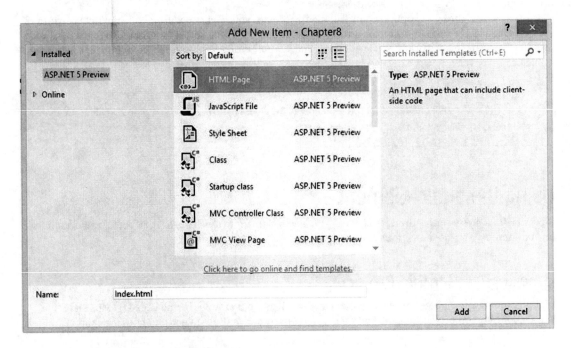

Figure 8-1. *Adding the Index.html page*

7. Open the Index.html file. In the empty body that was created by the file template, create a div element. Inside that div, enter **<audio src=**, and you should see a link that you can use to select the source from a file in your project. Select the Media folder and then your MP3 file, as shown in Figure 8-2.

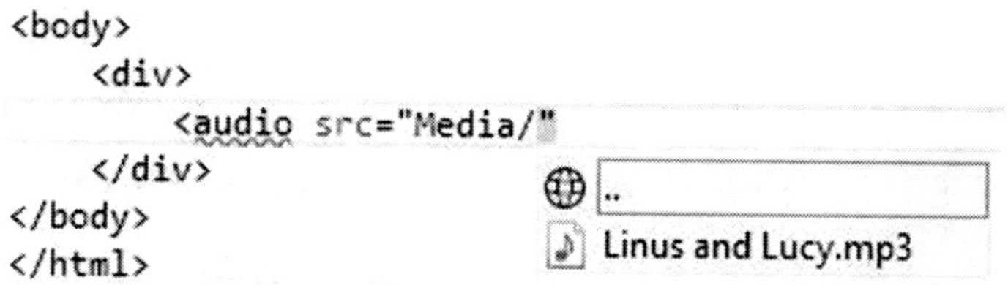

```
<body>
    <div>
        <audio src="Media/"
    </div>
</body>
</html>
```

⊕ [..]

♪ Linus and Lucy.mp3

Figure 8-2. *Using a link to select the source*

8. Add the autoplay attribute and close the audio element. Add text inside the audio element like this:

```
<body>
    <div>
        <audio src="Media/Linus and Lucy.mp3" autoplay>
            <p>HTML5 audio is not supported on your browser</p>
        </audio>
    </div>
</body>
```

9. Save your changes, make sure Internet Explorer is chosen as your default browser for debugging, and browse the Index.html page.

10. Open the Startup.cs file and comment out the implementation of the Configure() method.

11. Once the page has loaded, your audio clip should start playing. The page, however, will be blank.

12. Press F12 to open the Developer Tools pane, if not already opened. Change the browser mode to IE 8. The music will stop, and you'll see the "HTML5 audio is not supported on your browser" text displayed.

This first exercise demonstrated the basic use of the audio element. You simply enter the src attribute, which specifies the URL of the audio file. The content inside the audio element is used when the browser does not support the audio element. Since IE 8 does not support the audio element, the text included in the p tag is displayed instead. You can take advantage of this to simply display a message as you did here. However, you could use this to provide a link to download the file or use a plug-in to implement a fallback solution.

Using the Native Controls

In terms of the UI, there are basically three options:

- *No controls*: The audio plays, but there are no controls available to the user. The clip can be started automatically when the page is loaded using the autoplay attribute. You can also start, pause, and stop the audio clip using JavaScript.

- *Native controls*: The browser provides controls for the user to play, pause, and stop the audio clip and control the volume.

- *Custom controls*: The page provides custom controls that interact with the audio element through JavaScript.

191

To enable the native control, simply add the `controls` attribute like this:

```
<audio src="~/Media/Linus and Lucy.mp3" autoplay controls>
```

Save your changes and browse to your page, and the native controls should appear similar to Figure 8-3.

Figure 8-3. *Displaying the native audio controls in Internet Explorer*

In Opera and Chrome, the controls look like Figure 8-4.

Figure 8-4. *The audio controls in Opera*

In Firefox, the controls look like Figure 8-5.

Figure 8-5. *The audio controls in Firefox*

In Safari, the audio controls look like Figure 8-6.

Figure 8-6. *The audio control in Safari*

■ **Tip**   Safari on Windows requires that QuickTime be installed in order to support the `audio` element. You can download it from this site: `https://support.apple.com/kb/DL837?locale=en_US`. You may need to reboot your PC after installing QuickTime before Safari will be able to work.

As you can see, the controls are styled differently in each browser. With native controls you have little control over how the audio controls are displayed. You can change the width by setting the `style` attribute, which will stretch the progress bar. Extending the height beyond the normal height will only add white space on top of the control, as shown in Figure 8-7. In IE, decreasing the height, however, will shrink the control; in Chrome, it will clip it.

Figure 8-7. Extending the size of the native controls

Reviewing Browser Support

While all major browsers support the audio element, they don't all support the same audio formats. Until recently, browsers generally supported either MP3 or Vorbis, and you would need to provide both. However, most current browsers now support MP3, as well as MP4 for videos. HTML5 provides a way to supply multiple formats, if needed, to support older browsers.

▓ **Tip** Here's a handy page that tests browser support for the audio and video elements: http://hpr.dogphilosophy.net/test/. It also provides an overview of the support for various browsers.

The audio element allows you to specify multiple sources, and the browser will iterate through the sources until it finds one that it supports. Instead of using a src attribute, you'll provide one or more source elements within the audio element, like this:

```
<audio autoplay controls>
    <source src="Media/Linus and Lucy.ogg" />
    <source src="Media/Linus and Lucy.mp3" />
    <p>HTML5 audio is not supported on your browser</p>
</audio>
```

The browser will use the first source that it supports, so if it matters to you, you should list the preferred file first. For example, Chrome supports both MP3 and Vorbis formats. If you prefer that the MP3 file be used, you should list it before the .ogg file.

While just listing the sources like this will work, the browser must download the file and open it to see whether it is able to play it. That's not very efficient to download a fairly large file only to find out it can't be used. You should also include the type attribute, which specifies the type of resource this is. The browser can then determine whether the file is supported by looking at the markup. The type attribute specifies the MIME format like this:

```
<source src="Media/Linus and Lucy.ogg" type="audio/ogg" />
<source src="Media/Linus and Lucy.mp3" type="audio/mp3" />
```

You can also specify the codec in the type attribute like this:

```
<source src="Media/Linus and Lucy.ogg" type='audio/ogg; codecs="vorbis"' />
```

This will help the browser choose a compatible media file more efficiently, as I'll explain later in the chapter. Notice that the codecs values are included within double quotes, so you'll need to use single quotes around the type attribute value. Now you'll modify your web page so it will work on other browsers as well.

EXERCISE 8-2. ADDING MULTIPLE SOURCES

1. Create a Vorbis-encoded audio file of your sample audio clip that has the `.ogg` extension and copy this to the `wwwroot\Media` folder.

■ **Tip** I used a utility called XMedia Recode that you can download at `http://www.xmedia-recode.de/download.html`. You can use this utility to format both audio and video files. After you have installed this application, run it, click the Open File button in the ribbon, and select the MP3 file. On the Format tab, select the OGG format. Notice the File Extension option is automatically set to .ogg and the Codec option is set to Vorbis on the Audio tab. Click the "Add to queue" button in the ribbon. Select the Queue tab to see the job that has been defined to convert this file. At the bottom of the window you can specify the location that the new file should be saved in. Click the Browse button and navigate to the `Chapter8\Media` folder. Finally, click the Encode button to start the job. A dialog will be displayed to show the progress of the job.

---

2. In Solution Explorer, right-click the `Media` folder and click the Add and Existing Item links. Navigate to the `Chapter8\wwwroot\Media` folder and select the `.ogg` file that you just encoded.

3. In the `Index.html` file, replace the `audio` element with the following code (you'll need to adjust the actual file name to match yours):

```
<audio autoplay controls >
    <source src="Media/Linus and Lucy.ogg" type="audio/ogg" />
    <source src="Media/Linus and Lucy.mp3" type="audio/mp3" />
    <p>HTML5 audio is not supported on your browser</p>
</audio>
```

4. Save your changes and browse to your page. Open the page using several browsers and verify that the controls are displayed and the audio starts playing when the page is loaded.

Building Your Own Controls

All of the DOM elements and events are available in JavaScript, so it's a fairly straightforward process to create your own controls to work with the audio element. However, there are several facets that you'll need to control, so it's not a trivial exercise. There are three areas that you'll need to address:

- Play/Pause
- Displaying progress and fast-forwarding/rewinding
- Adjust volume/mute

You will need to respond to events from both the custom controls and the audio element. In this exercise, you'll start by adding all the necessary controls to the page. Then I'll show you how to implement the event handlers that are needed for each area. The input elements that you'll use to control the audio element are as follows:

- *Play/Pause button*: The label will toggle between "Play" and "Pause" depending on the state of the audio elements.

- *Seek*: This is a range control (introduced in Chapters 2 and 3) that will serve both to show the progress and allow the user to seek a specific location.

- *Duration*: This is a span element that displays both the current location and the total duration of the audio file.

- *Mute button*: The label will toggle between "Mute" and "Unmute."

- *Volume*: This is another range control that is used to specify the volume level.

The audio events that you'll provide handlers for include the following:

- onplay: Raised when the audio is started

- onpause: Raised when the audio is paused

- onended: Raised when the audio has completed

- ontimeupdate: Raised periodically as the audio clip is played

- ondurationchanged: Raised when the duration changes, which occurs when the file is loaded

- onvolumnechanged: Raised when the volume level changes or the mute property has changed

Adding the Custom Controls

You'll start by adding the custom controls and defining the event handlers that you'll need. Then I'll explain the JavaScript that you'll use to implement them.

EXERCISE 8-3. ADDING CUSTOM CONTROLS

1. Open the Index.html file and remove the controls attribute. This will cause the audio element to be hidden.

2. Add the following div after the audio element. This will include all the input elements that you'll need to control the audio.

```
<div id="audioControls">
  <input type="button" value="Play" id="play" onclick="togglePlay()" />
  <input type="range" id="audioSeek" onchange="seekAudio()" />
  <span id="duration"></span>
  <input type="button" id="mute" value="Mute" onclick="toggleMute()" />
  <input type="range" id="volume" min="0" max="1" step="any"
    onchange="setVolume()" />
</div>
```

3. Modify the `audio` element to add the necessary event handlers by adding the code shown in bold. This also defines the `id` attribute that you'll use to access the `audio` and `source` elements.

```
<audio id="audio" autoplay
    onplay="updatePlayPause()"
    onpause="updatePlayPause()"
    onended="endAudio()"
    ontimeupdate="updateSeek()"
    ondurationchange="setupSeek()"
    onvolumechange="updateMute()" >
    <source src="Media/Linus and Lucy.ogg" type="audio/ogg"
        id="oggSource" />
    <source src="Media/Linus and Lucy.mp3" type="audio/mp3"
        id="mp3Source" />
    <p>HTML5 audio is not supported on your browser</p>
</audio>
```

4. In Visual Studio, change the debug browser to use Opera. (You can also use Chrome if you prefer.) Save your changes and browse to your page. The page should look like Figure 8-8.

Figure 8-8. *The custom audio controls*

5. Close the browser and stop the debugger.

Implementing the Event Handlers

Now you're ready to implement the event handlers. I'll group these around the three main areas (play, seek, and volume) and explain one section at a time.

Supporting Play and Pause

Add the code shown in Listing 8-1 after the outer `div`, just before the end of the `body` element.

Listing 8-1. The Initial script Element

```
<script type="text/javascript">

var audio = document.getElementById("audio");

function setupSeek() {
    var seek = document.getElementById("audioSeek");
    seek.min = 0;
    seek.max = Math.round(audio.duration);
```

```
    seek.value = 0;
    var duration = document.getElementById("duration");
    duration.innerHTML = "0/" + Math.round(audio.duration);
}

function togglePlay() {
    if (audio.paused || audio.ended) {
        audio.play();
    }
    else {
        audio.pause();
    }
}

function updatePlayPause() {
    var play = document.getElementById("play");
    if (audio.paused || audio.ended) {
        play.value = "Play";
    }
    else {
        play.value = "Pause";
    }
}

function endAudio() {
    document.getElementById("play").value = "Play";
    document.getElementById("audioSeek").value = 0;
    document.getElementById("duration").innerHTML = "0/" + Math.round(audio.duration);
}
```

```
</script>
```

This code first declares the audio variable that references the audio element. Since this is used by most of the functions, it's more efficient to get it once and store it in a variable that all functions can access.

The first method, setupSeek(), is called in response to the ondurationchange event. When the page is first loaded, it doesn't know how long the audio clip is until the file is opened and the metadata is loaded. As soon as the metadata has been loaded, the duration can be determined, and the event is raised. The duration property is expressed in seconds. The setupSeek() function uses the duration property to set the max attribute of the audioSeek range control. It is also used to set the initial value of the span element. Notice that the Math.round() function is called to round this value to the nearest integer.

The togglePlay() method is called when the user clicks the Play button. If the current state of the audio element is paused or ended, it calls the play() function. Otherwise, it calls the pause() method. The updatePlayPause() method sets the label of the Play button. If the audio is currently playing, the text is changed to "Pause" since that will be the result if the button is clicked. Otherwise, the text is set to "Play."

■ **Tip**   The `togglePlay()` function responds to the Play button being clicked, and the `updatePlayPause()` function responds to the `audio` element being started or paused. When the button is clicked, the `togglePlay()` method will change the state of the `audio` element. This state change will raise either an `onplay` or `onpause` event, which are both handled by the `updatePlayPause()` function. This is done this way because it is possible that the audio can be played or paused through means other than clicking the Play button. For example, if you left the `controls` attribute, you would have both the native controls as well as the custom controls. Responding to the `onplay` and `onpause` events ensures the button label is always correct regardless of how the `audio` element is manipulated.

Finally, the `endAudio()` function is called when the audio has finished playing. This performs some synchronization including setting the button label and initializing the range and span controls.

Supporting Progress and Seek

Next, add the functions shown in Listing 8-2 to the same `script` element.

Listing 8-2. Functions to Support the range Control

```
function seekAudio() {
    var seek = document.getElementById("audioSeek");
    audio.currentTime = seek.value;
}

function updateSeek() {
    var seek = document.getElementById("audioSeek");
    seek.value = Math.round(audio.currentTime);
    var duration = document.getElementById("duration");
    duration.innerHTML = Math.round(audio.currentTime) + "/" + Math.round(audio.duration);
}
```

Just like with the Play button, there is one event handler, `seekAudio()`, that responds to the input element and a separate event handler, `updateSeek()`, that responds to the audio element. The `seekAudio()` function is called when the user moves the slider on the range control. It simply sets the `currentTime` property using the value selected by the range control.

The `updateSeek()` function is called when the `ontimeupdate` event is raised by the audio element. This updates the range control to reflect the current position within the file. It also updates the span control to show the actual position (in seconds). Again, the `currentTime` property is rounded to the nearest integer.

Controlling the Volume

The last set of functions is used to support both the volume control and the mute button. Add the code shown in Listing 8-3 to the same `script` element you have been using.

Listing 8-3. Controlling the Volume

```
function toggleMute() {
    audio.muted = !audio.muted;
}

function updateMute() {
    var mute = document.getElementById("mute");
    if (audio.muted) {
        mute.value = "Unmute";
    }
    else {
        mute.value = "Mute";
    }
}

function setVolume() {
    var volume = document.getElementById("volume");
    audio.volume = volume.value;
}
```

As its name suggests, the `toggleMute()` function toggles the `muted` property of the `audio` element. When this is changed, the onvolumechange event is raised by the `audio` element. The `updateMute()` function responds to that event and sets the button label according to the current value of the `muted` property. Again, doing it this way ensures the button label is correct.

Finally, the `setVolume()` function is called when the user moves the slider on the second range control. It sets the `volume` property of the `audio` element to whatever was selected on the range control.

▓ **Note**   The `volume` property has a value between 0 and 1. You could think of this as 0 percent and 100 percent. When you defined the `range` control, the `min` attribute was set to 0 and `max` was set to 1, so the scale is correct. You can simply set the `volume` property using the range value. If you want to display the actual value of the `volume` property, just convert it to a percentage.

Now you're ready to try your custom controls. Save your changes and browse to your page. The page should look similar to Figure 8-9.

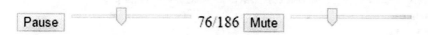

Figure 8-9. *The completed custom controls*

You did not provide any style rules, so the controls are displayed using default styles. But now you have access to the individual controls, so you can arrange and style them anyway you want (refer to Chapter 4 for using CSS styles).

Changing the Audio Source

In this example, the audio source was defined in the markup. However, you can easily control this using JavaScript. If you're using a single src attribute as you did initially, you just need to change this attribute to reference a different file. However, if you're using multiple source elements, you'll need to update all of these and then call the load() method.

To demonstrate this, when the clip has finished, you'll change the source to a second audio clip and play that one as well.

EXERCISE 8-4. CHANGING THE AUDIO SOURCE

1. Close the browser and stop the debugger.

2. Create another audio file in both .mp3 and .ogg formats and copy these to the wwwroot\Media folder.

3. In Solution Explorer, right-click the wwwroot\Media folder and click the Add and Existing Item links. Navigate to the Chapter8\wwwroot\Media folder and select both the .mp3 and .ogg files that you just encoded.

4. Open the Index.html file. At the top of the existing script element, declare the following variable. This will be used to keep track of how many songs were played.

    ```
    var songCount = 0;
    ```

5. Add the following code shown in bold to the endAudio() function. If the audio clip that just finished is the first one, the code will change the src attribute to reference the second file. The file is then loaded and played. (Note you'll need to change these file names to use the actual files that you included in your project.)

    ```
    function endAudio() {
        document.getElementById("play").value = "Play";
        document.getElementById("audioSeek").value = 0;
        document.getElementById("duration").innerHTML = "0/" +
          Math.round(audio.duration);

        if (++songCount < 2) {
          document.getElementById("oggSource").src = "Media/Sample.ogg";
          document.getElementById("mp3Source").src = "Media/Sample.mp3";
          audio.load();
          audio.play();
        }
    }
    ```

6. Save your changes and browse to your page. The initial song should start playing.

7. To save some time, fast-forward the clip to almost the end of the file and then wait for it to finish. The second file should automatically start playing. You should notice the span control was updated to show the duration of the second file.

Detecting Audio Support

You can programmatically determine whether a source is supported by the browser by calling the canPlayType() method on the audio element, passing in the type attribute. To demonstrate this, add the following code to the beginning of the script block, after the audio variable declaration:

```
var sources = audio.getElementsByTagName("source");
for (var i = 0; i < sources.length; i++) {
    alert("[" + sources[i].type + "] - " + audio.canPlayType(sources[i].type));
}
```

This code iterates through all the source elements and displays a pop-up indicating if the type is supported. Save your changes and try running this in Opera. You should see the results shown in Figures 8-10 and 8-11.

The page at localhost:43735 says:

[audio/mp3] - probably

OK

Figure 8-10. *The canPlayType( ) results for audio/mp3*

The page at localhost:43735 says:

[audio/ogg] - maybe

☐ Prevent this page from creating additional dialogs.

OK

Figure 8-11. *The canPlayType( ) results for audio/ogg*

How do you like that? You ask a yes or no question and get back a "probably" or "maybe" response. Well, as it turns out, the canPlayType() function does not return either "no" or "yes." Instead, it returns either "maybe," "probably," or a blank string. The blank string can be interpreted as a "no." Let's talk about "maybe" and "probably."

The source file is a container that provides metadata about the media in addition to the actual data. Specifying a MIME type like audio/ogg merely indicates the type of container but doesn't explicitly state how the data is encoded (what codec is used). If the browser supports that container type, canPlayType() returns "maybe." There's no evidence to indicate it is not supported but can't tell for certain that it is. If the container type is not supported, like audio/mp3, a blank string is returned (meaning it is not supported).

■ **Note**   A blank string is used to indicate "not supported" because in JavaScript, a blank string is a *falsy* value, whereas "no" is a *truthy* value. So, you can code if (canPlayType(type)) and only "maybe" and "probably" results will be selected.

"Probably" is as good as you'll get, with the canPlayType() method anyway; you don't ever get a "yes." Table 8-1 lists the possible responses.

Table 8-1. canPlayType( ) Method Responses

Codec	Container Supported	Container Not Supported
Undefined	"maybe"	Blank
Supported	"probably"	Blank
Not supported	Blank	Blank

Understanding Video Formats

As I said at the beginning of the chapter, the video element works just like the audio element, so everything you have learned so far also applies to video.

Reviewing Browser Support

A video file usually contains both audio and video, so all of the audio types and codecs that I covered earlier still apply. In addition, the video portion can be encoded in various ways. Fortunately, the industry seems to be narrowing down to three primary formats:

- *MP4 (*.mp4)*: Using H.264 video encoding and MP3 audio encoding

- *WebM (*.webm)*: Using VP8 video encoding and Vorbis audio encoding

- *Ogg (*.ogv)*: Using Theora video encoding and Vorbis audio encoding

Table 8-2 lists the formats that are currently supported by the major browsers.

Table 8-2. *Video/Audio Codec Support*

Browser	MP4	WebM	Ogg
IE 11	Yes	No	No
Firefox	Yes	Yes	Yes
Chrome	Yes	Yes	Yes
Safari	Yes	No	No
Opera	Yes	Yes	Yes

As you can see, the MP4 format has become the standard across all major browsers. However, as with audio, you can encode a video file in multiple formats and provide several sources so the browser can select one that it supports.

Downloading Sample Videos

For the remainder of this chapter, I'll be using a demo video that you can download from Microsoft using this site: `http://ie.microsoft.com/testdrive/graphics/videoformatsupport/default.html`. This is a trailer from the *Big Buck Bunny* movie. This site provides several versions of this video clip so you can see how various browsers display them.

Open this site using Internet Explorer. Right-click the H.264 baseline profile video and click the "Save video as" link. Browse to the `Chapter8\wwwroot\Media` folder and save the file as `BigBuckBunny.mp4`. Open the same site using Chrome or Opera and right-click the WebM version. Click the "Save video as" link and browse to the `Chapter8\wwwroot\Media` folder. Save this as `BigBuckBunny.webm`.

Using the video Element

Now that you have some video files to work with, you'll add a `video` element to your application. You'll add both sources like you did with the `audio` element. In the first exercise, you'll use the native controls and test the application in several browsers. Then, you'll add custom controls that are implemented just like the audio controls.

Adding Video to the Demo Page

Adding video is a simple matter of adding the media files to your project and then adding some simple markup to the page to play it.

EXERCISE 8-5. ADDING A VIDEO ELEMENT

1. In Solution Explorer, right-click the `wwwroot\Media` folder and click the Add and Existing Item links. Select both versions of the *Big Buck Bunny* video files.

2. In the `Index.html` file, remove the `autoplay` attribute from the `audio` element. You will autoplay the video, and removing this will keep them from both playing at the same time.

3. Add the following markup, just after the `div` that contains the audio controls:

```
<video id="video" autoplay controls loop>
    <source src="Media/BigBuckBunny.webm" type="video/webm" />
    <source src="Media/BigBuckBunny.mp4" type="video/mp4" />
    <p>HTML5 video is not supported on your browser</p>
</video>
```

4. Save your changes and browse to your page.

5. Try it in several browsers to make sure the video can be played in each.

For the `video` element, you included the `autoplay`, `controls`, and `loop` attributes. You already used the `autoplay` and `controls` attributes when working with the `audio` element. The `loop` attribute will cause the video to start over at the beginning when it finishes. This is also supported by the `audio` element.

■ **Tip**　The `canPlayType()` method that you used earlier on audio sources can also be used on video files. It works the same way, either returning a blank string indicating the file is not supported or returning a "maybe" or "probably" result.

Adding Custom Video Controls

Now you'll add custom controls for the `video` element just like you did for the `audio` element.

EXERCISE 8-6. ADDING CUSTOM VIDEO CONTROLS

1. Modify the markup in the `Index.html` file by replacing the `video` element with this:

```
<video id="video"
    onplay="updatePlayPauseVideo()"
    onpause="updatePlayPauseVideo()"
    onended="endVideo()"
    ontimeupdate="updateSeekVideo()"
    ondurationchange="setupSeekVideo()"
    onvolumechange="updateMuteVideo()">
    <source src="Media/BigBuckBunny.webm" type="video/webm" />
```

```
    <source src="Media/BigBuckBunny.mp4" type="video/mp4" />
    <p>HTML5 video is not supported on your browser</p>
</video>
```

2. Add a new `div` after the `video` element and enter the following markup for it:

```
<div id="videoControls">
    <input type="button" value="Play" id="playVideo"
onclick="togglePlayVideo()" />
    <input type="range" id="videoSeek" onchange="seekVideo()" />
    <span id="durationVideo"></span>
    <input type="button" id="muteVideo" value="Mute"
onclick="toggleMuteVideo()" />
    <input type="range" id="volumeVideo" min="0" max="1" step="any"
        onchange="setVolumeVideo()" />
</div>
```

3. Add a new `script` element using the code shown in Listing 8-4. This code is identical to the script used for the `audio` element except it uses the `video` element and the video controls.

Listing 8-4. The JavaScript Functions for the Video Controls

```
<script type="text/javascript">
var video = document.getElementById("video");

function setupSeekVideo() {
    var seek = document.getElementById("videoSeek");
    seek.min = 0;
    seek.max = Math.round(video.duration);
    seek.value = 0;
    var duration = document.getElementById("durationVideo");
    duration.innerHTML = "0/" + Math.round(video.duration);
}

function togglePlayVideo() {
    if (video.paused || video.ended) {
        video.play();
    }
    else {
        video.pause();
    }
}

function updatePlayPauseVideo() {
    var play = document.getElementById("playVideo");
    if (video.paused || video.ended) {
        play.value = "Play";
    }
    else {
        play.value = "Pause";
    }
}
```

```
function endVideo() {
    document.getElementById("playVideo").value = "Play";
    document.getElementById("videoSeek").value = 0;
    document.getElementById("durationVideo").innerHTML = "0/"
        + Math.round(video.duration);
}

function seekVideo() {
    var seek = document.getElementById("videoSeek");
    video.currentTime = seek.value;
}

function updateSeekVideo() {
    var seek = document.getElementById("videoSeek");
    seek.value = Math.round(video.currentTime);
    var duration = document.getElementById("durationVideo");
    duration.innerHTML = Math.round(video.currentTime) + "/"
        + Math.round(video.duration);
}

function toggleMuteVideo() {
    video.muted = !video.muted;
}

function updateMuteVideo() {
    var mute = document.getElementById("muteVideo");
    if (video.muted) {
        mute.value = "Unmute";
    }
    else {
        mute.value = "Mute";
    }
}

function setVolumeVideo() {
    var volume = document.getElementById("volumeVideo");
    video.volume = volume.value;
}

</script>
```

4. This code is almost identical to the code you added earlier to support the custom audio controls. Save your changes.

5. Select Opera as the debug browser and browse to your page. Try the video controls, which should look like Figure 8-12.

Figure 8-12. *The video element and controls*

Adding a Poster

The poster attribute is supported by the video element (but not the audio element). Before the video is started, you can use the poster attribute to specify the image that is displayed. If this is not specified, the browser will usually open the video and display the first frame. To add a poster, just include the image in your project and reference it in the poster attribute.

There's one thing to be careful about, however. If you define a poster, the initial size of the video element will be the size of the poster image. If this is not the same as the video, the size will change when the video starts playing. You should either ensure the image is the same size or explicitly size the video element, which will stretch (or shrink) the poster image to fit.

EXERCISE 8-7. ADDING A POSTER IMAGE

1. Download an image file to use as the poster image. You can find images from this site:
    http://wiki.creativecommons.org/Case_Studies/Blender_Foundation. Save
    the picture in the Chapter8\wwwroot\Media folder and name it **BBB_Poster.png**.

2. In Solution Explorer, right-click the wwwroot\Media folder and click the Add and
    Existing Item links. Browse to the Chapter8\wwwroot\Media folder and select the
    BBB_Poster.png image.

3. Modify the markup of the video element by adding the poster, width, and height attributes shown in bold.

    ```
    <video id="video" poster="Media/BBB_Poster.png" width="852"
    height="480"
    ```

4. Save your changes and browse to your page. You should now see the poster image until the video is started, as shown in Figure 8-13.

Figure 8-13. *The video element showing the poster image*

Summary

In this chapter, you created a simple web page that demonstrates the features of the audio and video elements. Browsers have standardized on the MP3 format for audio and MP4 for video. However, additional support can achieved by supplying the media files in multiple formats so browsers can use the one that it supports. This is pretty easy to do and fairly efficient since the browser can usually determine from the markup which file to download.

I showed you how to create your own controls for playing, pausing, and seeking within your audio and video files. By wiring up some simple JavaScript event handlers, making a custom media player becomes a straightforward exercise.

In the next chapter, I'll demonstrate how to take advantage of Scalable Vector Graphics (SVG) in HTML5.

CHAPTER 9

■ ■ ■

Scalable Vector Graphics

In this chapter, I'll show you how to use Scalable Vector Graphics (SVG) in an HTML5 web application using Visual Studio, ASP.NET MVC, and SQL Server. There are a lot of really cool things that you can do with SVG. I've picked out a fun demonstration that can be easily applied to many business applications. But first, let me give you an introduction to what SVG is.

Most people think of a graphic element as some form of bitmap, with an array of rows and columns of pixels, and each pixel is assigned a specific color. In contrast, however, vector graphics express an image as a collection of formulas. For example, draw a circle with a center at point x, y and a radius r. More complex images are defined as a collection of graphic elements including circles, lines, and paths. While the rendering engine will ultimately determine the specific pixels that need to be set, the image definition is based on a formula. This fundamental difference provides two significant advantages to using vector graphics.

First, as its name suggests, vector graphics are scalable. If you want to expand the size of the image, the rendering engine simply recalculates the formula based on the new size and there is no loss of clarity. If you zoom in on a bitmap image, you'll quickly start to see graininess and the image becomes blurry.

Second, each element in the image can be manipulated independently. If there are several circles in the image, for example, you can highlight one by simply changing the color of that image. Since vector graphics are formula based, you can easily adjust the formula to modify the image. What makes this particularly useful is that these elements can be styled using CSS, employing the powerful selectors and formatting capabilities that I showed you in Chapter 4.

Introducing SVG

You'll begin by creating a page that uses simple geometric shapes to draw a picture. Then you'll apply styles to these shapes using CSS. I'll show you how to save these markup elements in an .svg image file. This image file can be used just like other image files such as .jpg and .png files.

Creating the Sample Project

You'll first need to create a Visual Studio project. This will use a different project template than you used in previous chapters. For one of the exercises in this chapter you will need to connect to a SQL Server database. Instead of wiring this up manually, you'll use the Web Site template, which does most of this for you.

EXERCISE 9-1. CREATING THE VISUAL STUDIO PROJECT

1. Start Visual Studio 2015. In the Start Page, click the New Project link.

2. In the New project dialog box, select the ASP.NET Web Application template. Enter the project name **Chapter9** and select a location for this project.

3. In the next dialog box, select the ASP.NET 5 Web Site template and make sure the "Host in the cloud" check box is not selected. Click the OK button, and the project will be created (this may take a minute).

4. Right-click the Views\Home folder and click the Add and New Item links. In the Add New Item dialog box, select the MVC View Page template, enter the name **Snowman.cshtml**, and click the Add button.

Adding Some Simple Shapes

To demonstrate how an svg element works, you'll add some simple shapes such as circles, rectangles, and lines. Most images can be expressed as a collection of geometrical shapes, as I will demonstrate here.

EXERCISE 9-2. ADDING A SNOWMAN

1. Replace the initial contents of the Snowman.cshtml file with the following:

```
<svg xmlns:svg="http://www.w3.org/2000/svg" version="1.2"
    width="100px" height="230px"
    xmlns="http://www.w3.org/2000/svg"
    xmlns:xlink="http://www.w3.org/1999/xlink">
</svg>
```

▪ **Note** The width and height attributes define the element's intrinsic dimensions. In IE 9, you can omit these and the page will render correctly based on the actual space used. With other browsers, if the width and height are not specified, the image will be clipped to some default size.

---

2. Inside the svg element, add the following elements. These are just simple shapes, mostly circle elements with a rectangle (rect), line, and polygon.

```
<circle class="body" cx="50" cy="171" r="40" />
<circle class="body" cx="50" cy="103" r="30" />
<circle class="body" cx="50" cy="50" r="25" />
<line class="hat" x1="30" y1="25" x2="70" y2="25" />
<rect class="hat" x="40" y="10" width="20" height="15" />
<circle class="button" cx="50" cy="82" r="4" />
<circle class="button" cx="50" cy="100" r="4" />
<circle class="button" cx="50" cy="118" r="4" />
<circle class="eye" cx="42" cy="42" r="4" />
```

```
<circle class="eye" cx="58" cy="42" r="4" />
<polygon class="nose" points="45,60 45,50 60,55" />
```

A circle is expressed as a center point, cx and cy, and a radius, r. A line is specified as a beginning point, x1 and y1, and an endpoint, x2 and y2. A rectangle (rect) element is described by the top-left corner location, x and y, a width, and a height. A polygon is defined by a set of points in the form of x1,y1 x2,y2 x3,y3. You can specify any number of points. It is rendered by drawing a line segment between each of these points and a line segment from the last point, back to the first point.

3. Open the HomeController.cs file (in the Controllers folder) and add the following action. This will allow you to navigate to the new view.

```
public IActionResult Snowman()
{
    return View("~/Views/Home/Snowman.cshtml");
}
```

4. Save your changes and press F5 to view the application. To get to the new page, add /Home/Snowman to the URL. The page should look like Figure 9-1 (you will also see the ASP.NET default header and footer on your page).

Figure 9-1. *The initial SVG image without styling*

Adding Styles

The default style for these elements is a solid black fill, and because some of these shapes are on top of each other, several are not currently visible. Notice that you assigned a class attribute to each element. Now you'll apply styles for these elements using the class attribute. Add the code shown in Listing 9-1 inside the svg element, just before the elements you added earlier.

Listing 9-1. Adding SVG Styles

```css
<style type="text/css" >
    .body
    {
        fill: white;
        stroke: gray;
        stroke-width: 1px;
    }

    .hat
    {
        fill: black;
        stroke: black;
        stroke-width: 3px;
    }

    .button
    {
        fill: black;
    }

    .eye
    {
        fill: black;
    }

    .nose
    {
        fill: orange;
    }
</style>
```

Save these changes and refresh the browser to view the updated web page, which should look like Figure 9-2.

Figure 9-2. *The SVG images with styling applied*

Using SVG Image Files

In addition to embedding an svg element, you can save this as a stand-alone image file with an .svg extension. This file can then be used just like other graphic images. I'll show you how to create a stand-alone SVG image and then use it on a page.

Creating an SVG Image

I'll first show you how to create a stand-alone .svg file and then use it as a background image. This will also demonstrate the scalability of SVG images.

EXERCISE 9-3. CREATING AN SVG IMAGE

1. From the wwwroot\images folder, click the New and File links. In the Add New Item dialog box, select Text File, enter the name **snowman.svg**, and click the Add button.

2. Enter the following markup instructions:

   ```
   <?xml version="1.0" standalone="no"?>
   <!DOCTYPE svg PUBLIC "-//W3C//DTD SVG 1.2//EN"
   "http://www.w3.org/Graphics/SVG/1.2/DTD/svg12.dtd">
   ```

3. Copy and paste the entire svg element from the Snowman.cshtml file, including the style element to the new text file.

4. Click the Save button.

5. To test your image, from Solution Explorer, right-click the snowman.svg file and click the "Open with" link. Then select Internet Explorer in the Open With dialog box. This should launch a browser and display the snowman image.

Using an SVG Background

Now you have an image file that you can use just like other images. To demonstrate this, you'll add a div element to your page and use the snowman.svg file as the background image. You'll also adjust the div size so you can see how the image looks when resized.

EXERCISE 9-4. ADDING A BACKGROUND IMAGE

1. In the Snowman.cshtml file, add the following code after the svg element:

   ```
   <div id="container"></div>
   ```

2. This simply defines a div element. Now you'll use CSS to configure it. Add the following style element before the svg element:

   ```
   <style type="text/css">
     #container {
       height: 800px;
       width: 350px;
       background-image: url("../images/snowman.svg");
       background-size: contain;
     }
   </style>
   ```

3. Press F5 to debug your application. In addition to the small image, you should also see a larger version of your image, as shown in Figure 9-3. Notice that there is no loss of image quality when expanding the size of the image.

Figure 9-3. The page with the snowman background

Creating an Interactive Map

Drawing pictures of snowmen may be fun, but let's move on to some more practical uses of SVG. You will create a map of the United States with each state represented by a separate SVG *path* element, which I'll explain later. You'll store the path definitions in a SQL Server database. I'll show you how to access the database using a model class and then display it using a view definition. Once you have the map displayed, I'll show you some CSS tricks to style the map using both static and dynamic styles. Finally, you'll add some animation to add a little flair to your web page.

Using Path Elements

The path element is the most versatile of all SVG elements. It is a collection of "move to," "line to,"and various "curve to" commands. The shape is drawn by following the path commands. Each command starts from the current position and either moves to a new position or draws a line to the next position. Here's an example:

- Move to 25, 50.

- Draw a line to 50, 50.

- Draw a line to 50, 25.

- Draw an arc to 25, 50.

This is expressed as follows:

```
<path d="M25,50 L50,50 L50,25 A25,25 0 0,0 25,50 z" />
```

The "move to" and "line to" commands are pretty straightforward. The "arc to" command, as well as all the other curve commands, is more complicated because you need to provide additional control points that describe how the curve should be drawn. Each command uses a single letter, as shown in Table 9-1.

Table 9-1. *The Available Path Commands*

Command	Abbr.	Description
Move to	M	Moves to the specified position
Line to	L	Draws a line to the specified position
Horizontal line to	H	Draws a horizontal line to the specified x coordinate
Vertical line to	V	Draws a vertical line to the specified y coordinate
Arc to	A	Draws an arc to the specified position
Curve to	C	Draws a cubic Bezier curve
Shorthand curve to	S	Draws a simplified cubic Bezier curve
Quadratic curve to	Q	Draws a quadratic Bezier curve
Shorthand quadratic curve to	T	Draws a simplified quadratic Bezier curve
Close path	Z	Closes the figure by drawing a line to the starting position

For each of these commands, an uppercase letter is used when absolute coordinates are used. You can also specify relative coordinates and use a lowercase letter to indicate the values are relative to the current position. For more information about constructing a path element, see the article at http://www.w3.org/TR/SVG/paths.html#PathData.

As you can probably envision, drawing a complex shape like the state of Alaska will take a lot of commands. You won't want to edit this by hand. Fortunately, there are tools available to help build a path definition. For example, a free web-based tool is available at http://code.google.com/p/svg-edit. Just for grins, Listing 9-2 shows the path element for Alaska.

Listing 9-2. The Path Element Definition for Alaska

```
<path d="M 158.07671,453.67502 L 157.75339,539.03215 L 159.36999,540.00211 L
162.44156,540.16377 L 163.8965,539.03215 L 166.48308,539.03215 L 166.64475,541.94205 L
173.59618,548.73182 L 174.08117,551.3184 L 177.47605,549.37846 L 178.1227,549.2168 L
178.44602,546.14524 L 179.90096,544.52863 L 181.0326,544.36697 L 182.97253,542.91201 L
186.04409,545.01361 L 186.69074,547.92352 L 188.63067,549.05514 L 189.7623,551.48006 L
193.64218,553.25833 L 197.03706,559.2398 L 199.78529,563.11966 L 202.04855,565.86791 L
203.50351,569.58611 L 208.515,571.36439 L 213.68817,573.46598 L 214.65813,577.83084 L
215.14311,580.9024 L 214.17315,584.29729 L 212.39487,586.56054 L 210.77826,585.75224 L
209.32331,582.68067 L 206.57507,581.22573 L 204.7968,580.09409 L 203.98849,580.9024 L
205.44344,583.65065 L 205.6051,587.36885 L 204.47347,587.85383 L 202.53354,585.9139 L
200.43195,584.62061 L 200.91693,586.23722 L 202.21021,588.0155 L 201.40191,588.8238 C
201.40191,588.8238 200.59361,588.50048 200.10863,587.85383 C 199.62363,587.20719
198.00703,584.45895 198.00703,584.45895 L 197.03706,582.19569 C 197.03706,582.19569
196.71374,583.48898 196.06709,583.16565 C 195.42044,582.84233 194.7738,581.71071
194.7738,581.71071 L 196.55207,579.77077 L 195.09712,578.31582 L 195.09712,573.30432 L
194.28882,573.30432 L 193.48052,576.6992 L 192.34888,577.1842 L 191.37892,573.46598 L
190.73227,569.74777 L 189.92396,569.26279 L 190.24729,574.92094 L 190.24729,576.05256 L
188.79233,574.75928 L 185.23579,568.77781 L 183.13419,568.29283 L 182.48755,564.57462 L
180.87094,561.66472 L 179.25432,560.53308 L 179.25432,558.26983 L 181.35592,556.97654 L
180.87094,556.65322 L 178.28436,557.29986 L 174.88947,554.87495 L 172.30289,551.96504 L
167.45306,549.37846 L 163.41152,546.79188 L 164.70482,543.55866 L 164.70482,541.94205 L
162.92654,543.55866 L 160.01664,544.69029 L 156.29843,543.55866 L 150.64028,541.13375 L
145.14381,541.13375 L 144.49717,541.61873 L 138.03072,537.73885 L 135.92912,537.41553 L
133.18088,531.59573 L 129.62433,531.91905 L 126.06778,533.374 L 126.55277,537.90052 L
127.68439,534.99062 L 128.65437,535.31394 L 127.19941,539.67879 L 130.43263,536.93055 L
131.07928,538.54716 L 127.19941,542.91201 L 125.90612,542.58869 L 125.42114,540.64875 L
124.12785,539.84045 L 122.83456,540.97208 L 120.08632,539.19381 L 117.01475,541.29541 L
115.23649,543.397 L 111.8416,545.4986 L 107.15342,545.33693 L 106.66844,543.23534 L
110.38664,542.58869 L 110.38664,541.29541 L 108.12338,540.64875 L 109.09336,538.22384 L
111.35661,534.34397 L 111.35661,532.5657 L 111.51827,531.75739 L 115.88313,529.49413 L
116.85309,530.78742 L 119.60134,530.78742 L 118.30805,528.20085 L 114.58983,527.87752 L
109.57834,530.62576 L 107.15342,534.02064 L 105.37515,536.60723 L 104.24352,538.87049 L
100.04033,540.32543 L 96.96876,542.91201 L 96.645439,544.52863 L 98.908696,545.4986 L
99.717009,547.60018 L 96.96876,550.83341 L 90.502321,555.03661 L 82.742574,559.2398 L
80.640977,560.37142 L 75.306159,561.50306 L 69.971333,563.76631 L 71.749608,565.0596 L
70.294654,566.51455 L 69.809672,567.64618 L 67.061434,566.67621 L 63.828214,566.83787 L
63.019902,569.10113 L 62.049939,569.10113 L 62.37326,566.67621 L 58.816709,567.96951 L
55.90681,568.93947 L 52.511924,567.64618 L 49.602023,569.58611 L 46.368799,569.58611 L
44.267202,570.87941 L 42.65059,571.68771 L 40.548995,571.36439 L 37.962415,570.23276 L
35.699158,570.87941 L 34.729191,571.84937 L 33.112578,570.71775 L 33.112578,568.77781 L
36.184142,567.48452 L 42.488929,568.13117 L 46.853782,566.51455 L 48.955378,564.41296 L
51.86528,563.76631 L 53.643553,562.958 L 56.391794,563.11966 L 58.008406,564.41296 L
58.978369,564.08964 L 61.241626,561.3414 L 64.313196,560.37142 L 67.708076,559.72478 L
69.00137,559.40146 L 69.648012,559.88644 L 70.456324,559.88644 L 71.749608,556.16823 L
75.791141,554.71329 L 77.731077,550.99508 L 79.994336,546.46856 L 81.610951,545.01361 L
81.934272,542.42703 L 80.317657,543.72032 L 76.922764,544.36697 L 76.276122,541.94205 L
74.982838,541.61873 L 74.012865,542.58869 L 73.851205,545.4986 L 72.39625,545.33693 L
70.941306,539.51713 L 69.648012,540.81041 L 68.516388,540.32543 L 68.193068,538.3855 L
64.151535,538.54716 L 62.049939,539.67879 L 59.463361,539.35547 L 60.918305,537.90052 L
61.403286,535.31394 L 60.756645,533.374 L 62.211599,532.40404 L 63.504883,532.24238 L
```

```
62.858241,530.4641 L 62.858241,526.09925 L 61.888278,525.12928 L 61.079966,526.58423 L
54.936843,526.58423 L 53.481892,525.29094 L 52.835247,521.41108 L 50.733651,517.85452 L
50.733651,516.88456 L 52.835247,516.07625 L 52.996908,513.97465 L 54.128536,512.84303 L
53.320231,512.35805 L 52.026941,512.84303 L 50.895313,510.09479 L 51.86528,505.08328 L
56.391794,501.85007 L 58.978369,500.23345 L 60.918305,496.51525 L 63.666554,495.22195 L
66.253132,496.35359 L 66.576453,498.77851 L 69.00137,498.45517 L 72.23459,496.03026 L
73.851205,496.67691 L 74.821167,497.32355 L 76.437782,497.32355 L 78.701041,496.03026 L
79.509354,491.6654 C 79.509354,491.6654 79.832675,488.75551 80.479317,488.27052 C
81.125959,487.78554 81.44928,487.30056 81.44928,487.30056 L 80.317657,485.36062 L
77.731077,486.16893 L 74.497847,486.97723 L 72.557911,486.49225 L 69.00137,484.71397 L
63.989875,484.55231 L 60.433324,480.83411 L 60.918305,476.95424 L 61.564957,474.52932 L
59.463361,472.75105 L 57.523423,469.03283 L 58.008406,468.22453 L 64.798177,467.73955 L
66.899773,467.73955 L 67.869736,468.70951 L 68.516388,468.70951 L 68.354728,467.0929 L
72.23459,466.44626 L 74.821167,466.76958 L 76.276122,467.90121 L 74.821167,470.00281 L
74.336186,471.45775 L 77.084435,473.07437 L 82.095932,474.85264 L 83.874208,473.88268 L
81.610951,469.51783 L 80.640977,466.2846 L 81.610951,465.47629 L 78.21606,463.53636 L
77.731077,462.40472 L 78.21606,460.78812 L 77.407756,456.90825 L 74.497847,452.22007 L
72.072929,448.01688 L 74.982838,446.07694 L 78.21606,446.07694 L 79.994336,446.72359 L
84.197528,446.56193 L 87.915733,443.00539 L 89.047366,439.93382 L 92.765578,437.5089 L
94.382182,438.47887 L 97.130421,437.83222 L 100.84863,435.73062 L 101.98027,435.56896 L
102.95023,436.37728 L 107.47674,436.21561 L 110.22498,433.14405 L 111.35661,433.14405 L
114.91316,435.56896 L 116.85309,437.67056 L 116.36811,438.80219 L 117.01475,439.93382 L
118.63137,438.31721 L 122.51124,438.64053 L 122.83456,442.35873 L 124.7745,443.81369 L
131.88759,444.46033 L 138.19238,448.66352 L 139.64732,447.69356 L 144.82049,450.28014 L
146.92208,449.6335 L 148.86202,448.82518 L 153.71185,450.76512 L 158.07671,453.67502 z M
42.973913,482.61238 L 45.075509,487.9472 L 44.913847,488.91717 L 42.003945,488.59384 L
40.225672,484.55231 L 38.447399,483.09737 L 36.02248,483.09737 L 35.86082,480.51078 L
37.639093,478.08586 L 38.770722,480.51078 L 40.225672,481.96573 L 42.973913,482.61238 z M
40.387333,516.07625 L 44.105542,516.88456 L 47.823749,517.85452 L 48.632056,518.8245 L
47.015444,522.5427 L 43.94388,522.38104 L 40.548995,518.8245 L 40.387333,516.07625 z M
19.694697,502.01173 L 20.826327,504.5983 L 21.957955,506.21492 L 20.826327,507.02322 L
18.72473,503.95166 L 18.72473,502.01173 L 19.694697,502.01173 z M 5.9534943,575.0826 L
9.3483796,572.81934 L 12.743265,571.84937 L 15.329845,572.17269 L 15.814828,573.7893 L
17.754763,574.27429 L 19.694697,572.33436 L 19.371375,570.71775 L 22.119616,570.0711 L
25.029518,572.65768 L 23.897889,574.43595 L 19.533037,575.56758 L 16.784795,575.0826 L
13.066588,573.95097 L 8.7017347,575.40592 L 7.0851227,575.72924 L 5.9534943,575.0826 z M
54.936843,570.55609 L 56.553455,572.49602 L 58.655048,570.87941 L 57.2001,569.58611 L
54.936843,570.55609 z M 57.846745,573.62764 L 58.978369,571.36439 L 61.079966,571.68771 L
60.271663,573.62764 L 57.846745,573.62764 z M 81.44928,571.68771 L 82.904234,573.46598 L
83.874208,572.33436 L 83.065895,570.39442 L 81.44928,571.68771 z M 90.17899,559.2398 L
91.310623,565.0596 L 94.220522,565.86791 L 99.232017,562.958 L 103.59687,560.37142 L
101.98027,557.94651 L 102.46525,555.52159 L 100.36365,556.81488 L 97.453752,556.00657 L
99.070357,554.87495 L 101.01029,555.68325 L 104.89016,553.90497 L 105.37515,552.45003 L
102.95023,551.64172 L 103.75853,549.70178 L 101.01029,551.64172 L 96.322118,555.19827 L
91.472284,558.10817 L 90.17899,559.2398 z M 132.53423,539.35547 L 134.95915,537.90052 L
133.98918,536.12224 L 132.21091,537.09221 L 132.53423,539.35547 z" />
```

■ **Tip**   This data, as well as the data for all the other states, was downloaded from
http://en.wikipedia.org/wiki/File:Blank_US_Map.svg. You can find a lot of similar material by going to
http://commons.wikimedia.org and entering **svg map** in the search criteria.

Implementing the Initial Map

You'll start by creating the initial map without any styles applied. The actual path elements will be stored in a SQL database. You will create the database, add a State table, and store the path definitions. You'll then create a model using Entity Framework to provide the state data. Finally, you'll create a new view that will display the map and then provide a link to access it.

Creating the Database

The path elements can be quite long and are static (the shape of Alaska is not likely to change any time soon), so they can be stored in a database and retrieved by .NET when needed to render the page. The MVC project template that you used is already configured for a database connection. You'll need to create the State table and populate it with the appropriate path definitions.

EXERCISE 9-5. CREATING THE STATE TABLE

1. The database used by .NET is not actually created until the first time it is accessed. The easiest way to create the database is to register yourself. Press F5 to debug the application. Click the Register link in the header and enter a username and password.

2. Once the registration is done, you can close the browser window, which will also stop the debugger.

3. Start SQL Server Management Studio (SSMS). In the Connect to Server dialog box, enter the server name as **(LocalDB)\MSSQLLocalDB** and use Windows authentication, as shown in Figure 9-4. Click the Connect button to open the database.

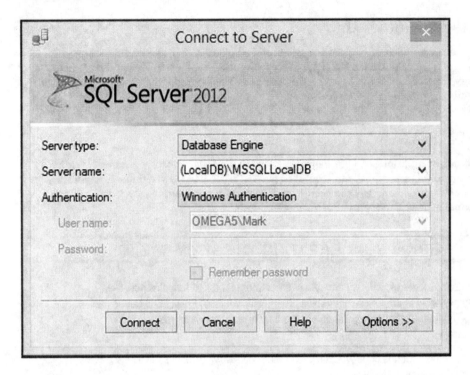

Figure 9-4. Connecting to SQL Server

4. After connecting, you should see the database in Object Explorer, as shown in Figure 9-5.

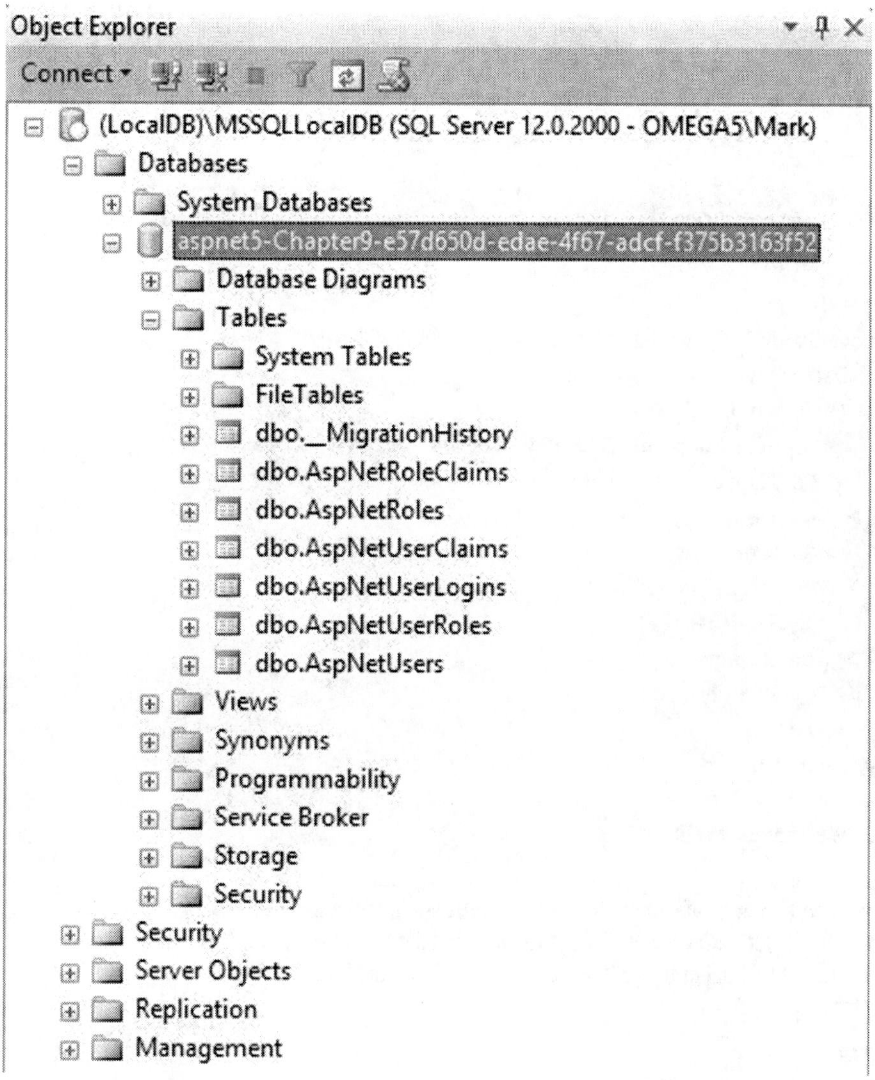

Figure 9-5. *The database contents*

5. If you don't have SQL Server Management Studio, you can access the database through Visual Studio. From the View menu, click the SQL Server Object Explorer link. You can then navigate to your database, as shown in Figure 9-6.

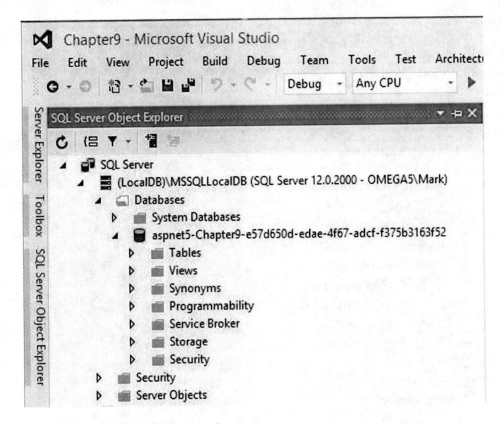

Figure 9-6. *Selecting the Chapter9 database*

6. In the download that is available at www.apress.com, you'll find a States.sql file in the Chapter9 folder. Open this file in SSMS and click the Execute button. This will create the State table using the following script and then populate it with a record for each state:

```
CREATE TABLE State(
  Id int identity  NOT NULL,
  StateCode nchar(10) NOT NULL,
  StateName nvarchar(50) NOT NULL,
  Path ntext NULL,
 CONSTRAINT PK_State PRIMARY KEY CLUSTERED
 (
  Id ASC
)WITH (PAD_INDEX = OFF, STATISTICS_NORECOMPUTE = OFF, IGNORE_DUP_KEY
  = OFF,
 ALLOW_ROW_LOCKS = ON, ALLOW_PAGE_LOCKS = ON) ON [PRIMARY]
) ON [PRIMARY] TEXTIMAGE_ON [PRIMARY]
```

7. To verify the data was loaded correctly, open another query window using the New Query button. After connecting, select the Chapter9 database and execute this query:

```
select * from State
```

8. You should see results similar to Figure 9-7.

	Id	StateCode	StateName	Path	
	Results	Messages			
1	1	HI	Hawaii	M 233.08751,519.30948 L 235.02744,515.75293 L 237.2907,515.42961 L 237.61402,516.2...	
2	2	AK	Alaska	M 158.07671,453.67502 L 157.75339,539.03215 L 159.36999,540.00211 L 162.44156,540....	
3	3	FL	Florida	M 759.8167,439.1428 L 762.08236,446.4614 L 765.81206,456.20366 L 771.14685,465.579...	
4	4	NH	New Hampshire	M 880.79902,142.42476 L 881.66802,141.34826 L 882.75824,138.05724 L 880.21516,137....	
5	5	VT	Vermont	M 844.48416,154.05791 L 844.80086,148.71228 L 841.91015,137.92811 L 841.26351,137....	
6	6	ME	Maine	M 922.83976,78.830719 L 924.77969,80.932305 L 927.04294,84.650496 L 927.04294,86.5...	
7	7	RI	Rhode Island	M 874.07001,178.89536 L 870.37422,163.93937 L 876.6435,162.09423 L 878.83463,164.0...	
8	8	NY	New York	M 830.37944,188.7456 L 829.24781,187.77564 L 826.66123,187.61398 L 824.39799,185.6...	
9	9	PA	Pennsylvania	M 825.1237,224.69205 L 826.43212,224.42105 L 828.76165,223.1678 L 829.97353,220.68...	
10	10	NJ	New Jersey	M 829.67942,188.46016 L 827.35687,191.19443 L 827.35687,194.26599 L 825.41693,197....	

Figure 9-7. *The contents of the State table*

▪ **Tip** If you're using Visual Studio instead of SSMS, you can right-click the database in Server Explorer and click the New Query link. Then select the Chapter9 database in the query window.

Creating the Model

Creating a model that uses a SQL table is a pretty simple task. You'll use the Entity Framework to create a model class that provides data from the specified table.

EXERCISE 9-6. CREATING AN ENTITY FRAMEWORK MODEL

1. From Solution Explorer, right-click the Models folder and click the Add and New Item links. In the Add New Item dialog box, select the Class template and enter **State.cs** for the name.

2. Add the following using statements at the top of the file:

```
using System.ComponentModel.DataAnnotations;
using Microsoft.Data.Entity;
```

3. Add the following properties to the State class. These will map to the columns in the State table that you just created.

```
[Key] public int Id { get; set; }
public string StateCode { get; set; }
```

```
public string StateName { get; set; }
public string Path { get; set; }
```

4. Add the following class in this same State.cs file, after the State class definition. This class configures the Entity Framework so it can create a State class for each record in the State table.

```
public class StateDbContext : ApplicationDbContext
{
    public DbSet<State> States { get; set; }

    protected override void OnConfiguring(DbContextOptionsBuilder
     options)
    {
        options.UseSqlServer(Startup.Configuration
          .Get("Data:DefaultConnection:ConnectionString"));
        base.OnConfiguring(options);
    }
}
```

5. Open the Startup.cs class and add the static attribute to the Configuration property, as shown here in bold:

    public **static** IConfiguration Configuration { get; set; }

6. You now have a model that you can use to provide the state details for the map. Rebuild the project. This will make the model available for linking to a view.

Creating the Map View

With a model already defined, you'll now create the view that will display the model elements.

EXERCISE 9-7. CREATING THE MAP VIEW

1. Right-click the Views\Home folder and click the Add and New Items links.

2. In the Add New Item dialog box, select the MVC View Page template, enter the name **Map.cshtml**, and click the Add button.

3. Replace the entire contents with the following. This will set up the view to use the State model and enable the code to access its properties.

    ```
    @model IEnumerable<Chapter9.Models.State>
    @using Chapter9.Models
    ```

4. Add the following code, which defines an svg element just like you did earlier. It then uses a foreach loop to create a path element for each State defined in the model. Notice that it is storing the StateCode column in the id attribute and the StateName column in the class attribute.

```
<svg xmlns:svg="http://www.w3.org/2000/svg" version="1.2"
  width="959" height="593" id="map">

  @foreach (State s in Model)
  {
    <path id="@s.StateCode.Trim()" class="@s.StateName.Trim()"
        d="@s.Path" />
  }
</svg>
```

5. Now you'll need to implement a controller action that will display the map view. Open the HomeController.cs class and add the following namespace:

   ```
   using Chapter9.Models;
   ```

6. Then add the following method to the HomeController class. This executes a query to extract all the records from the State table and provide it to the view.

   ```
   public ActionResult Map()
   {
       StateDbContext DC = new StateDbContext();
       var states = from s in DC.States select s;

       return View(states);
   }
   ```

7. Now you'll add a link that will display the map page. Go to the _Layout.cshtml file in the Views\Shared folder and add the following line after the existing asp-action statements:

   ```
   <li><a asp-controller="Home" asp-action="Map">Map</a></li>
   ```

8. Press F5 to build and run the application. Click the Map link. You should see a map of the United States, and all of the states are filled with the default color (black).

Styling the State Elements

Now that all the mechanical work is done, you can have some fun styling the path elements. As I demonstrated earlier with the snowman image, each element can be styled using a special style sheet. You can also style them dynamically using JavaScript. I will show you how to use solid-color fills, gradients, and background images to format each element.

Using Basic Fill Colors

▓ **Note**   Throughout this chapter you will be using colors to style each state differently. In the print version of this book, some of these colors might not display well when converted to grayscale. You will want to work through the exercise or download the project, to see the results of the styles being applied.

You'll start by adding some simple fill rules. Using a simple element selector, you'll set the stroke color to black and the fill color to khaki. Then, to add some variety and to demonstrate using attribute selectors, you'll change the fill color based on the state code. The id attribute contains the two-letter state code, and the class attribute contains the state name. Using the first letter of the id attribute, you'll set the fill color as follows:

- A: Red
- N: Yellow
- M: Green
- C: Blue
- O: Purple
- I: Orange

Enter the style element shown in Listing 9-3 inside the svg element before the foreach loop.

Listing 9-3. Adding Basic Fill Definitions

```
<style type="text/css" >
    path
    {
    stroke: black;
    fill: khaki;
    }

    path[id^="A"]
    {
        fill: red;
    }
    path[id^="N"]
    {
        fill: yellow;
    }
    path[id^="M"]
    {
        fill: green;
    }
    path[id^="C"]
    {
    fill: blue;
    }
    path[id^="O"]
    {
        fill: purple;
    }
    path[id^="I"]
    {
    fill: orange;
    }
</style>
```

Refresh your browser, and the map should now look like Figure 9-8.

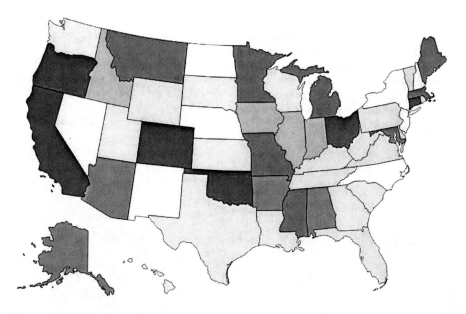

Figure 9-8. *The map with some basic styling*

As you're moving the mouse around the map, it would be nice to highlight the state that the mouse is currently pointing to. Add the following rule to the style element after the existing rules:

```
path:hover
{
    opacity: .5;
}
```

Using Gradient Fills

You can use gradient fills with SVG elements, but they are implemented differently than typical HTML elements. You first have to define the gradient and then reference it using a URL.

Add the following defs element inside the svg element but before the style element:

```
<defs>
    <linearGradient id="blueGradient"
                    x1="0%"  y1="0%"
                    x2="100%"  y2="100%"
                    spreadMethod="pad">
        <stop offset="0%"    stop-color="#ffffff" stop-opacity="1"/>
        <stop offset="50%" stop-color="#6699cc" stop-opacity="1"/>
        <stop offset="100%" stop-color="#4466aa" stop-opacity="1"/>
    </linearGradient>
</defs>
```

The defs element is used to define something that can be referred to later in the document. It doesn't do anything until it is actually referenced. Here you are defining a linearGradient element and giving it the id blueGradient. You will reference it using the id attribute.

The attributes are different from the gradients you used in Chapter 4 but accomplish basically the same thing. The x1, y1, x2, and y2 attributes define a vector that specifies the direction of the gradient. In this case, it will start from the top-left corner and go to the bottom-right corner. This specifies three color values that define the gradient color at the beginning, midpoint, and end.

Now add the following path rule at the end of the style element. This will use the new gradient for the state of Wyoming.

```
path[id="WY"]
{
    fill: url(#blueGradient);
}
```

Refresh the browser, and you should see a gradient fill for Wyoming, as shown in Figure 9-9.

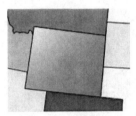

Figure 9-9. *Using a gradient fill*

Using a Background Image

You can also use an image file for the shape background. You will need to first define this as a pattern in the defs element and then reference it just like you did with the gradient. For this exercise you'll use an image of the state flag of Texas and make this the background for that state.

EXERCISE 9-8. USING A BACKGROUND IMAGE

1. In the source code download for Chapter 9 there is a TX_Flag.jpg file; copy this to the wwwroot\images folder in Solution Explorer.

2. Add the following code to the defs element to define the background image. This specifies that the pattern should use the TX_Flag.jpg image file and stretch it to 377 x 226 pixels. This will make it large enough to cover the path element without needing to repeat.

   ```
   <pattern id="TXflag" patternUnits="objectBoundingBox" width="1"
       height="1">
     <image xlink:href="~/images/TX_Flag.jpg" x="0" y="0"
       width="377" height="226" />
   </pattern>
   ```

---

3. Add the following path rule, which will use the new pattern for the state of Texas.

```
path[id="TX"]
{
    fill: url(#TXflag);
}
```

4. Save your changes and refresh the browser. You should see the background image, as shown in Figure 9-10.

Figure 9-10. *Using a background image*

Since this is a chapter on SVG, I felt a little funny about using a bitmap image. You can see the degraded image quality when the image is stretched. The state flag of Texas is one of the easiest to draw with SVG, but I wanted to demonstrate that bitmapped images can be used within an SVG definition. But just for the record, Listing 9-4 shows the flag expressed in SVG (this was downloaded from the same Wikimedia Commons site I mentioned earlier and reformatted slightly).

Listing 9-4. The Texas State Flag in SVG

```
<rect width="1080" height="720" fill="#fff"/>
<rect y="360" width="1080" height="360" fill="#bf0a30"/>
<rect width="360" height="720" fill="#002868"/>
<g transform="translate(180,360)" fill="#fff">
    <g id="c">
        <path id="t" d="M 0,-135 v 135 h 67.5"
              transform="rotate(18 0,-135)"/>
        <use xlink:href="#t" transform="scale(-1,1)"/>
    </g>
    <use xlink:href="#c" transform="rotate(72)"/>
    <use xlink:href="#c" transform="rotate(144)"/>
    <use xlink:href="#c" transform="rotate(216)"/>
    <use xlink:href="#c" transform="rotate(288)"/>
</g>
```

Notice that the group element, g, is used to define a single path. This is rotated with five different angles to create a five-pointed star.

Altering Styles with JavaScript

One of the primary uses of this kind of application is to dynamically style each element based on some external data. For example, you might want to highlight states where you have sales locations. Or perhaps you want to set the colors based on some type of demographics such as population. So far you have used only static styles, but you can just as easily set the styles using JavaScript.

In this example, you will first set the fill attribute on all path elements to khaki using JavaScript. This will replace the CSS property that sets the default color. This code will then set the fill color of the path element for Virginia. In a real application, you would normally define the style based on external data.

This exercise will also show you how to use JavaScript to respond to the onmouseover and onmouseout events. You will replace the path:hover rule and accomplish this using these event handlers.

EXERCISE 9-9. ADJUSTING STYLES USING JAVASCRIPT

1. Add the following script element in the map.cshtml file, just before the defs element:

```
<script type="text/javascript">
  function adjustStates() {
    var paths = document.getElementsByTagName("path");
    for (var i = 0; i < paths.length; i++) {
      paths[i].setAttributeNS(null, "fill", "khaki");
    }

    var path = document.getElementById("VA");
    path.setAttributeNS(null, "fill", "teal");
  }
</script>
```

2. In the svg element, add the onload attribute using the code shown in bold:

```
<svg xmlns:svg="http://www.w3.org/2000/svg" version="1.2"
    width="959" height="593" id="map" onload="adjustStates()" >
```

3. In the style element, remove the default khaki fill like this:

```
path
{
stroke: black;
/*fill: khaki; */
}
```

4. Refresh the browser, and Virginia should no longer use the default color, as shown in Figure 9-11.

Figure 9-11. *Virginia styled with JavaScript*

5. Now you'll also use JavaScript to implement the hover style. You can use the
    event.target property to get the path element that triggered the event. You can
    then determine the state code by accessing its id attribute. Add the following
    methods to the existing script element:

```
function hoverState(e) {
  var event = e || window.event;
  var state = event.target.getAttributeNS(null, "id");
  var path = document.getElementById(state);
  path.setAttributeNS(null, "fill-opacity", "0.5");
}

function unhoverState(e) {
  var event = e || window.event;
  var state = event.target.getAttributeNS(null, "id");
  var path = document.getElementById(state);
  path.setAttributeNS(null, "fill-opacity", "1.0");
}
```

6. Then bind the mouseover and mouseout event handlers by adding the code shown
    in bold to the adjustStates() function. This uses the addEventListener()
    method to bind hoverState() and unhoverState() event handlers to each path
    element.

```
function adjustStates() {
  var paths = document.getElementsByTagName("path");
  for (var i = 0; i < paths.length; i++) {
    paths[i].setAttributeNS(null, "fill", "khaki");

    paths[i].addEventListener("mouseover", hoverState, true);
    paths[i].addEventListener("mouseout", unhoverState, true);
  }

  var path = document.getElementById("VA");
  path.setAttributeNS(null, "fill", "teal");
}
```

▪ **Caution**   In Internet Explorer, the `event` object is not passed to the event handler. Instead, it is made available through the global `window.event` property. The event handlers can be coded to work with either model by setting the event variable like this: `var event = e || window.event`. This will use the object passed in, if available, and if not, it will use the global `window.event` object. For this to work, however, you must register the event handlers by using the `addEventListener()` method. You cannot simply set the `onmouseover` attribute.

---

7. Remove the `path:hover` style rule like this:

```
/*path:hover
{
   opacity: .5;
}*/
```

8. Save your changes and refresh the browser. As you move the mouse around, the states should highlight just like they did with the `path:hover` style.

Adding Animation

A typical application of a map like this will allow the user to select a region and have something happen as a result of that selection. The page will display some information based on the item that was selected. To demonstrate that, you'll add some animation when the user clicks a state. This example will be using 3D transforms and Opera, so I'll be using the `-webkit-` vendor prefix.

The CSS animation that I showed you in Chapter 4 does not work on SVG elements. Instead, you'll implement the animation using JavaScript. When a state is selected, you'll first make a copy of the selected element. Then you'll use a timer to gradually change its rotation angle. You need to make a copy so that as the image rotates it doesn't leave a hole in the map. Also, the new element will be on top of all the others, so you don't have to worry about it being hidden by the other elements.

Once the copy of the element has completed its animation, you'll remove it from the document. Then you'll display an alert showing the state code and state name of the `path` that was selected.

EXERCISE 9-10. ADDING ANIMATION

1. Because this uses a 3D transform, you'll need to set some of the transform properties on the `path` elements. Add the following rule to the `style` element:

```
path
{
   -webkit-perspective: 200px;
   -webkit-transform-style: preserve-3d;
}
```

2. Then add the code shown in Listing 9-5 to the `script` element.

Listing 9-5. Adding Function to Support Animation

```
// Setup some global variables
var timer;
var stateCode;
var stateName;
var animate;
var angle;

function selectState(e) {
    var event = e || window.event;

    // Get the state code and state name
    stateCode = event.target.getAttributeNS(null, "id");
    stateName = event.target.getAttributeNS(null, "class");

    // Get the selected path element and then make a copy of it
    var path = document.getElementById(stateCode);
    animate = path.cloneNode(false);

    // Set some display properties and add the copy to the document
    animate.setAttributeNS(null, "fill-opacity", "1.0");
    animate.setAttributeNS(null, "stroke-width", "3");
    document.getElementById("map").appendChild(animate);

    angle = 0;

    // Setup a timer to run every 10 msec
    timer = setInterval(function () { animateState(); }, 10);
}

function animateState() {
    angle += 1;

    // If we've rotated 360 degress, stop the timer, destroy the copy
    // of the element, and show an alert
    if (angle > 360) {
        clearInterval(timer);
        animate.setAttributeNS(null, "visibility", "hidden");
        var old = document.getElementById("map").removeChild(animate);

        alert(stateCode + " - " + stateName);

        return;
    }

    // Change the image rotation
    animate.style.webkitTransform = "rotateY(" + Math.round(angle) + "deg)";
}
```

The selectState() function gets the state code and state name from the selected path element. It then gets the path element and uses its cloneNode() method to make a copy of it. Because the mouse is currently over the selected path, it will have the opacity set to 50 percent. So, this code changes the opacity of the copy to 100 percent. It also sets the stroke width to give this element a wider border. The copy is then added to the document, and a timer is started to cause the animation.

Every ten milliseconds, the animateState() function is called, which increments the angle and redraws the image. If the rotation has reached 360 degrees, this method cancels the timer and removes the copy of the path element. It also raises an alert to display the state code and state name.

3. Add another event handler by adding the code shown in bold to the adjustStates() function. This will call the selectState() method when the user clicks a path element.

```
function adjustStates() {
  var paths = document.getElementsByTagName("path");
  for (var i = 0; i < paths.length; i++) {
    paths[i].setAttributeNS(null, "fill", "khaki");

    paths[i].addEventListener("mouseover", hoverState, true);
    paths[i].addEventListener("mouseout", unhoverState, true);
    paths[i].addEventListener("click", selectState, true);
  }

  var path = document.getElementById("VA");
  path.setAttributeNS(null, "fill", "teal");
}
```

4. Change the debug browser to Opera. Press F5 to start the application and go to the map page. Click a state and you should see it fly off the page, as shown in Figure 9-12.

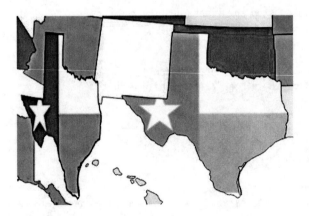

Figure 9-12. *Animating the selected state*

5. The image will then fly back into place, and an alert will appear, as shown in Figure 9-13.

The page at localhost:6986 says:

TX - Texas

OK

Figure 9-13. *The alert showing the name of the selected state*

Summary

In this chapter, I introduced SVG with a couple of fairly simple applications. An SVG image consists of multiple elements, which can be simple elements such as lines, circles, and rectangles or more complex options such as polygons and paths. The key feature of SVG is that each individual element can be styled independently both statically and dynamically. This enables much greater control and interaction. Also, because the image is based on an expression, the images can be scaled without affecting the image quality.

In the exercises in this chapter, you did the following:

- Designed an image using simple geometric shapes
- Created a stand-alone .svg image file
- Displayed a map as a collection of path elements
- Implemented animation on an SVG element

You also used Entity Framework to implement a model class that accesses a SQL Server database and then designed a view that creates an SVG image using the model elements.

In the next chapter, I'll show you how to use the canvas element to construct graphical elements in HTML5.

CHAPTER 10

Canvas

In this chapter I'll show how to use the canvas element in HTML5 to create some fun graphics. As you'll see, it is very different from SVG, which you explored in the previous chapter. I will discuss the differences in more detail later, but the main thing you'll notice is that canvas is completely implemented in JavaScript. The only part that is in the markup is a simple element definition like this:

```
<canvas id="myCanvas" width="400" height="400">
    Canvas is not supported on this browser
</canvas>
```

Instead, you'll define the content by calling the various drawing methods using JavaScript. Just like with the audio and video elements, the markup within the canvas element is used when the browser does not support canvas. You can use this to provide the appropriate fallback content.

Through the exercises in the chapter, you will create three different canvas implementations that, collectively, will demonstrate the capability of canvas. You will create the following:

- A chess board with moving chess pieces

- A simple model of the solar system

- A page that demonstrates the various ways shapes can be composited

Of course, you can use your imagination to apply these principles in any number of fun and compelling graphical applications.

Creating a Chess Board

In the first application you'll draw a chess board, which is just a series of squares with alternating colors. I'll show you how to use a gradient to make the board a little more interesting. You'll use image files to draw the chess pieces in the appropriate squares. Finally, you'll apply a little bit of animation to move the pieces around the board. This will give you a good sense of how basic drawing techniques are used before getting into more advanced topics.

Creating the Visual Studio Project

You'll start by creating a Visual Studio project using the same empty template that you have used in previous chapters.

EXERCISE 10-1. CREATING THE VISUAL STUDIO PROJECT

1. Start Visual Studio 2015. In the Start Page, click the New Project link.

2. In the New project dialog box, select the ASP.NET Web Application template. Enter the project name **Chapter10** and select a location for this project.

3. In the next dialog box, select the ASP.NET 5 Empty template. Click the OK button and the project will be created.

4. Open the Startup.cs file and comment out the implementation for the Configure() method like this:

    ```
    public void Configure(IApplicationBuilder app)
    {
        //app.Run(async (context) =>
        //{
        //    await context.Response.WriteAsync("Hello World!");
        //});
    }
    ```

5. In Solution Explorer, right-click the wwwroot folder and click the Add and New Item links. In the Add New Item dialog box, select the HTML Page template, enter the name **Index.html**, and click the Add button.

The canvas element is appropriately named because it provides an area that you can use to draw on. When you create a canvas element, you define its size using the height and width attributes. You can specify other attributes through markup or CSS to specify the margin, padding, and border. These attributes affect where the element is positioned within the page. However, you cannot modify any of the content within the element. The canvas element itself simply defines a blank area on which you can create your masterpiece.

When you create a canvas element in HTML, you will generally assign an id attribute so you can access it in JavaScript using the getElementById() method. You don't have to; you can access it using the getElementsByTagName() method or use the new query selectors I described in Chapter 5.

Once you have the canvas element, you'll then get its drawing context by calling getContext(). You must specify which context to use. The context specifies a set of API functions and drawing capabilities. The only one that is generally available is 2d, and we will be using that exclusively in this chapter.

■ **Note**   The other possible context is not 3d as you might expect; it's WebGL or, in some browsers, experimental-webgl. This is not quite ready for prime time and it is very different from the 2d context.

Drawing Rectangles

Unlike SVG, the only shape that you can draw directly is a rectangle. You can draw more complex shapes using paths, which I'll explain later. There are three methods that you can use to draw rectangles.

*   clearRect(): Clears the specified rectangle
*   strokeRect(): Draws a border around the specified rectangle with no fill
*   fillRect(): Draws a filled-in rectangle

Each of these methods takes four parameters. The first two define the x and y coordinates of the top-left corner of the rectangle. The last two parameters specify the width and height, respectively. The drawing context has the strokeStyle and fillStyle properties that control how the border or fill will be drawn. You set these before drawing the rectangle. Once set, all subsequent shapes are drawn with these properties until you change the properties.

■ **Tip**   Just like SVG, in canvas, the top-left corner of the canvas element has the x and y coordinates of 0, 0.

To demonstrate drawing rectangles, you'll start by drawing the chessboard, which contains eight rows of eight squares each.

EXERCISE 10-2. DRAWING A SIMPLE CHESSBOARD

1. Add a canvas to the index.html page by inserting the following markup in the blank body that was created by the template:

```
<canvas id="board" width ="600" height ="600">
    Not supported
</canvas>
```

2. Then add a script element after the canvas element but still inside the body element using the code shown in Listing 10-1.

    Listing 10-1. Drawing a Simple Chessboard

```
<script id="chess board" type="text/javascript">
    // Get the canvas context
    var chessCanvas = document.getElementById("board");
    var chessContext = chessCanvas.getContext("2d");

    drawBoard();

    // Draw the chess board
    function drawBoard() {

        chessContext.clearRect(0, 0, 600, 600);

        chessContext.fillStyle = "red";
        chessContext.strokeStyle = "red";

        // Draw the alternating squares
        for (var x = 0; x < 8; x++) {
            for (var y = 0; y < 8; y++) {
                if ((x + y) % 2) {
                    chessContext.fillRect(75 * x, 75 * y, 75, 75);
                }
            }
        }
```

239

```
                  // Add a border around the entire board
                  chessContext.strokeRect(0, 0, 600, 600);
            }
      </script>
```

3. Save your changes and press F5 to start the application. The page should look like Figure 10-1.

Figure 10-1. *The initial chessboard*

The drawBoard() function first clears the area on which it will be drawing. It then uses nested for loops to draw the squares. The fillStyle and strokeStyle attributes are both set to red; by default these are both black. Notice that it draws only the red squares. Since the entire area was cleared first, any area not drawn on will be white. This code uses nested for loops to iterate through the eight rows and eight columns. The red squares are the ones where the sum of the row and the column is odd. For even-numbered rows (0, 2, 4, and 6), the odd columns (1, 3, 5, and 7) will be red. For odd-numbered rows, the even-numbered columns will be red. To clean up the edge squares, a red border is drawn around the entire board.

Using Gradients

You can also use a gradient to fill a shape instead of a solid color. To do that, you must first create a gradient object using the drawing context's createLinearGradient() method. This method takes four parameters, which are the x and y coordinates of the beginning and ending points of the gradient. This allows you to specify whether the gradient should go from top to bottom, left to right, or corner to corner. The gradient is computed across the entire canvas. You cannot define gradients for individual elements.

You must then define the color stops. Each color stop defines a position along the gradient and a color. At a minimum, you'll need color stops at 0 and 1, which define the beginning and ending colors. You can also add color stops in between these if you want to control the transition. For example, if you want to define the color at the halfway point, use 0.5.

Finally, you'll use this gradient to specify the fillStyle property. To try it, add the following code shown in bold:

```
function drawBoard() {

    chessContext.clearRect(0, 0, 600, 600);

    var gradient = chessContext.createLinearGradient(0, 600, 600, 0);
    gradient.addColorStop(0.0, "#D50005");
    gradient.addColorStop(0.5, "#E27883");
    gradient.addColorStop(1.0, "#FFDDDD");

    chessContext.fillStyle = gradient;
    chessContext.strokeStyle = "red";
```

Save your changes and press F5 to start the application. The page should now look like Figure 10-2. Notice that the color transitions across the canvas, not across each square.

Figure 10-2. The board using a gradient fill

Using Images

Now you're ready to add the chess pieces, which will be drawn using image files. It is really easy to add an image to a canvas. You create an Image object, set its src property as the location of the image file, and then call the drawing context's drawImage() method like this:

```
var myImage = new Image();
myImage.src = "images/sample.jpg";
context.drawImage(myImage, 0,0, 50, 100);
```

The first parameter of the drawImage() method specifies the image that will be drawn. This can be an Image object, as I've shown here. Alternatively, you can also specify an img, video, or canvas element that is already on the page. The next two parameters specify the x and y locations of the top-left corner of the image. The fourth and fifth parameters are optional and specify the width and height, respectively, that the image will be scaled to fit into. If you don't specify these parameters, the image will be drawn using its intrinsic size.

The drawImage() method also allows you to supply four additional parameters. These are used to specify only the portion of the image that should be displayed on the canvas. These additional parameters include an x coordinate and a y coordinate that specify the top-left corner, as well as a width and height to define the specified portion. Use the last four parameters if you want only a portion of the image to be drawn. If these are omitted, the entire image will be displayed.

In this application you will be drawing 32 pieces using 12 different images. Also, later in this chapter you will be adding code to move the pieces around. To facilitate this, you'll add some structure to your application. You will define a class that will store attributes about a chess piece such as the image to use and its location on the board. Then you'll implement a generic drawing function that uses the details from these attributes.

EXERCISE 10-3. DRAWING CHESS PIECES

1. In Solution Explorer, right-click the wwwroot folder and click the Add and New Folder links. Enter **images** for the folder name.

2. The images for the chess pieces are included in the source code download file. You'll find these in the Chapter10\Images folder. Drag all 12 files to the wwwroot\images folder in Solution Explorer.

3. Add the variable declarations shown in bold in Listing 10-2 to your script element. This will define a variable to reference an Image object for each of the 12 image files. It will also define an array that you will be using to store the 32 chess pieces.

Listing 10-2. Defining the Image Variables

```
<script type="text/javascript">
    // Get the canvas context
    var chessCanvas = document.getElementById("board");
    var chessContext = chessCanvas.getContext("2d");

    // Define the chess piece images
    var imgPawn = new Image();
    var imgRook = new Image();
    var imgKnight = new Image();
    var imgBishop = new Image();
    var imgQueen = new Image();
    var imgKing = new Image();
    var imgPawnW = new Image();
    var imgRookW = new Image();
    var imgKnightW = new Image();
    var imgBishopW = new Image();
    var imgQueenW = new Image();
    var imgKingW = new Image();

    // Define an array to store 32 pieces
    var pieces = new Array(32);

    drawBoard();
```

4. Add the `loadImages()` function, shown in Listing 10-3, to your `script` element after the existing `drawBoard()` function.

   Listing 10-3. Loading the Image Files

```
function loadImages() {
    imgPawn.src = "images/pawn.png";
    imgRook.src = "images/rook.png";
    imgKnight.src = "images/knight.png";
    imgBishop.src = "images/bishop.png";
    imgQueen.src = "images/queen.png";
    imgKing.src = "images/king.png";
    imgPawnW.src = "images/wpawn.png";
    imgRookW.src = "images/wrook.png";
    imgKnightW.src = "images/wknight.png";
    imgBishopW.src = "images/wbishop.png";
    imgQueenW.src = "images/wqueen.png";
    imgKingW.src = "images/wking.png";
}
```

5. Now you're ready to define the chess pieces. You'll use a class definition that will store the attributes needed to draw the chess piece. The `image` property contains a reference to the appropriate `Image` object. The `x` and `y` properties specify the square that the piece is in, from 0 to 7, left to right and top to bottom. The `height` and `width` properties indicate the size of the image, which will vary depending on the type of piece. The `killed` property is used to indicate whether the piece has been captured. Captured images are not displayed. Add the following code to the end of the `script` element:

```
// Define a class to store the piece properties
function ChessPiece() {
    this.image = null;
    this.x = 0;
    this.y = 0;
    this.height = 0;
    this.width = 0;
    this.killed = false;
}
```

6. Add the code shown in Listing 10-4 to the end of your `script` element. This implements the `drawPiece()` function that draws a single chess piece based on the class properties. Finally, it provides a `drawAllPieces()` function that will draw each of the pieces defined in the array.

Listing 10-4. Drawing the Chess Pieces

```
// Draw a chess piece
function drawPiece(p) {
    if (!p.killed)
        chessContext.drawImage(p.image,
                               (75 - p.width) / 2 + (75 * p.x),
                               73 - p.height + (75 * p.y),
                               p.width,
                               p.height);
}

// Draw all of the chess pieces
function drawAllPieces() {
    for (var i = 0; i < 32; i++) {
        if (pieces[i] != null) {
            drawPiece(pieces[i]);
        }
    }
}
```

7. Now you need to create 32 instances of the ChessPiece class and specify all of the appropriate properties. Add the createPieces() function shown in Listing 10-5. This function creates the instances of the ChessPiece class, storing them in the pieces array, and sets the properties of each one.

■ **Tip**   Since this is rather long and tedious, I made this function available in the source code download as a separate file. If you prefer, instead of typing the function from Listing 10-5, you can find the createPieces.js file in the Chapter10 folder and drag this to the wwwroot folder in Solution Explorer. Then add this reference in the head section:

```
<script type="text/javascript" src="createPieces.js"></script>
```

Listing 10-5. Implementing the createPieces() Function

```
function createPieces() {
    var piece;

    // Black pawns
    for (var i = 0; i < 8; i++) {
        piece = new ChessPiece();
        piece.image = imgPawn,
        piece.x = i;
        piece.y = 1;
        piece.height = 50;
        piece.width = 28;

        pieces[i] = piece;
    }
```

```
// Black rooks
piece = new ChessPiece();
piece.image = imgRook;
piece.x = 0;
piece.y = 0;
piece.height = 60;
piece.width = 36;
pieces[8] = piece;

piece = new ChessPiece();
piece.image = imgRook;
piece.x = 7;
piece.y = 0;
piece.height = 60;
piece.width = 36;
pieces[9] = piece;

// Black knights
piece = new ChessPiece();
piece.image = imgKnight;
piece.x = 1;
piece.y = 0;
piece.height = 60;
piece.width = 36;
pieces[10] = piece;

piece = new ChessPiece();
piece.image = imgKnight;
piece.x = 6;
piece.y = 0;
piece.height = 60;
piece.width = 36;
pieces[11] = piece;

// Black bishops
piece = new ChessPiece();
piece.image = imgBishop;
piece.x = 2;
piece.y = 0;
piece.height = 65;
piece.width = 30;
pieces[12] = piece;

piece = new ChessPiece();
piece.image = imgBishop;
piece.x = 5;
piece.y = 0;
piece.height = 65;
piece.width = 30;
pieces[13] = piece;
```

```
// Black queen
piece = new ChessPiece();
piece.image = imgQueen;
piece.x = 3;
piece.y = 0;
piece.height = 70;
piece.width = 32;
pieces[14] = piece;

// Black king
piece = new ChessPiece();
piece.image = imgKing;
piece.x = 4;
piece.y = 0;
piece.height = 70;
piece.width = 28;
pieces[15] = piece;

// White pawns
for (var i = 0; i < 8; i++) {
    piece = new ChessPiece();
    piece.image = imgPawnW,
    piece.x = i;
    piece.y = 6;
    piece.height = 50;
    piece.width = 28;

    pieces[16 + i] = piece;
}

// White rooks
piece = new ChessPiece();
piece.image = imgRookW;
piece.x = 0;
piece.y = 7;
piece.height = 60;
piece.width = 36;
pieces[24] = piece;

piece = new ChessPiece();
piece.image = imgRookW;
piece.x = 7;
piece.y = 7;
piece.height = 60;
piece.width = 36;
pieces[25] = piece;

// White knights
piece = new ChessPiece();
piece.image = imgKnightW;
piece.x = 1;
```

```
        piece.y = 7;
        piece.height = 60;
        piece.width = 36;
        pieces[26] = piece;

        piece = new ChessPiece();
        piece.image = imgKnightW;
        piece.x = 6;
        piece.y = 7;
        piece.height = 60;
        piece.width = 36;
        pieces[27] = piece;

        // White bishops
        piece = new ChessPiece();
        piece.image = imgBishopW;
        piece.x = 2;
        piece.y = 7;
        piece.height = 65;
        piece.width = 30;
        pieces[28] = piece;

        piece = new ChessPiece();
        piece.image = imgBishopW;
        piece.x = 5;
        piece.y = 7;
        piece.height = 65;
        piece.width = 30;
        pieces[29] = piece;

        // White queen
        piece = new ChessPiece();
        piece.image = imgQueenW;
        piece.x = 3;
        piece.y = 7;
        piece.height = 70;
        piece.width = 32;
        pieces[30] = piece;

        // White king
        piece = new ChessPiece();
        piece.image = imgKingW;
        piece.x = 4;
        piece.y = 7;
        piece.height = 70;
        piece.width = 28;
        pieces[31] = piece;
}
```

8. Modify the `drawBoard()` function to also call `drawAllPieces()` after the board has been drawn.

    ```
    // Add a border around the entire board
    chessContext.strokeRect(0, 0, 600, 600);

    drawAllPieces();
    }
    ```

9. Finally, replace the call to `drawBoard()` function in the main script with the code shown in bold. This will call the `loadImages()` and `createPieces()` functions and wait 300ms before calling `drawBoard()`.

    ```
    // Define an array to store 32 pieces
    var pieces = new Array(32);

    loadImages();
    createPieces();

    setTimeout(drawBoard, 300);

    // Draw the chess board
    function drawBoard() {
    ```

10. Save your changes and press F5 to start the application. You should now see the chess pieces, as shown in Figure 10-3.

Figure 10-3. *The chess board with the pieces displayed*

■ **Note**   When you create an Image object and set its src property, the specified image file is downloaded asynchronously. It's possible that the file has not been loaded before the drawImage() function is called. If this happens, the image is not displayed. The 300ms delay is a simple solution to this problem. You could implement the onload event handler for each Image object, which is called when the image has been loaded. This is a bit complicated since you'll need to wait for all 12 images to be loaded.

Adding Simple Animation

To demonstrate simple animation using canvas, you'll move the pieces around. The function that draws each piece computes the location based on the square that the piece is in. To move a piece, you just need to update the x or y property and then redraw it.

When you redraw a piece in its new location, it is still visible in the old location as well. Also, if you were to capture a piece by moving a piece in the same square as another, you would end up with two pieces in the same square. You could implement some complex logic to clear the square and redraw a red or white square before moving the piece. However, for this demonstration, you will simply clear the entire canvas and redraw the board and all of the pieces.

To implement the automation, you'll create a makeNextMove() function. This will adjust the x and y positions of a chess piece and then redraw the board and all of the pieces. You'll use the setInterval() function to call this repeatedly so the pieces will move in succession.

EXERCISE 10-4. ANIMATING THE CHESS PIECES

1. Add the following variables shown in bold near the beginning of the script element:

    ```
    // Define an array to store 32 pieces
    var pieces = new Array(32);
    var moveNumber = -1;
    var timer;

    loadImages();
    ```

2. Implement the makeNextMove() function shown in Listing 10-6. This code "moves" a piece by adjusting its x and y properties. It keeps track of the move number and uses this to adjust the appropriate piece. The seventh move captures a piece and sets its killed property. Since this ends the animation, the seventh move also uses the clearTimer() function so no more timer events will occur. After each move, the board and all the pieces are redrawn. After the seventh move, this function also uses the fillText() method, which is used to write text to the canvas.

Listing 10-6. The makeNextMove Implementation

```
function makeNextMove() {
    function inner() {
        if (moveNumber === 1) {
            pieces[20].y--;()
        }
        if (moveNumber === 2) {
            pieces[4].y += 2;
        }
        if (moveNumber === 3) {
            pieces[29].y = 4;
            pieces[29].x = 2;
        }
        if (moveNumber === 4) {
            pieces[6].y++;
        }
        if (moveNumber === 5) {
            pieces[30].x = 5;
            pieces[30].y = 5;
        }
```

```
            if (moveNumber === 6) {
                pieces[7].y++;
            }
            if (moveNumber === 7) {
                pieces[30].x = 5;
                pieces[30].y = 1;
                pieces[5].killed = true;
                clearInterval(timer);
            }

            moveNumber++;

            drawBoard();
            drawAllPieces();

            if (moveNumber > 7) {
                chessContext.font = "30pt Arial";
                chessContext.fillStyle = "black";
                chessContext.fillText("Checkmate!", 200, 220);
            }
        }
    }

    return inner;
}
```

3. Add the following code to the end of the main script, just before the `drawBoard()` function definition. This will call the `makeNextMove()` function every two seconds.

```
timer = setInterval(makeNextMove(), 2000);
```

4. Save your changes and press F5 to start the application. After a series of moves, the page should look like Figure 10-4.

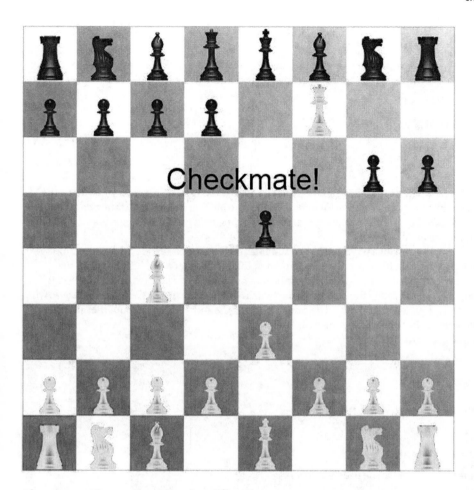

Figure 10-4. *The completed chess board( )*

■ **Caution** The makeNextMove( ) function uses an often misunderstood feature of JavaScript called *closure*. This function defines another function called inner( ), which does the actual work. The inner( ) function is then returned. The makeNextMove( ) function will be called by the window object when the timer expires. However, all of the variables that it uses, such as the array of chess pieces, will be out of scope. The inner( ) function will be able to access these variables, so this works around the scope issue. For more information about closures, see this article: http://stackoverflow.com/questions/111102/how-do-javascript-closures-work.

Modeling the Solar System

For the next canvas you'll draw a moving model of the solar system. For the sake of time, you'll show only the earth, sun, and moon. This implementation will take advantage of these two important features of canvas:

- Paths
- Transformations

Using Paths

As I mentioned earlier, the only simple shape that canvas supports is the rectangle, which you used in the previous example. For all other shapes you must define a path. The basic approach to defining paths in canvas is similar to SVG. You use a move command to set the starting point and then some combination of line and curve commands to draw a shape.

In canvas, you always start with a beginPath() command. After calling the desired drawing commands, the path is completed by calling either stroke() to draw an outline of the shape or fill() to fill in the shape. The shape is not actually drawn to the canvas until either stroke() or fill() is called. If you call beginPath() again, before completing the current shape (with a call to stroke() or fill()), the canvas will ignore the previous uncompleted commands. The same strokeStyle and fillStyle properties that you used with rectangles also define the color of the path.

The actual drawing commands are as follows:

- moveTo()
- lineTo()
- arcTo()
- bezierCurveTo()
- quadraticCurveTo()

In addition, these functions can be used for drawing:

- closePath(): This performs a lineTo() command from the current position to the starting position to close in the shape. If you use the fill() command, the closePath() function is automatically called if you're not currently at the starting position.

- arc(): This draws an arc at the specified location; you don't have to move there first. However, this is still treated as a path; you need to first call beginPath(), and the arc is not actually drawn until you call either stroke() or fill().

Drawing Arcs

The arc() command is one that you'll likely use a lot and will be important in this example. The arc() command takes the following parameters:

arc(x, y, radius, start, end, counterclockwise)

The first two parameters specify the x and y coordinates of the center point. The third parameter specifies the radius. The fourth and fifth parameters determine the starting and ending points of the arc. These are specified as an angle from the x-axis. The 0° angle is the right side of the circle; a 90° angle would be the bottom edge of the circle. The angles are specified in radians, however, not degrees.

Unless you're drawing a full circle, the direction of the arc is important. For example, if you drew an arc from 0° to 90°, the arc would be 1/4 of a circle, from the right side to the bottom. However, using the same end points but drawing in a counterclockwise direction, that arc would be 3/4 of the circle. The final parameter, if true, indicates that the arc should be draw in a counterclockwise direction. This parameter is optional. If you don't specify it, it will draw the arc in a clockwise direction.

Using Transformations

At first, transformations in canvas may seem a bit confusing, but they can be quite helpful once you understand how they work. First, transformations have no effect on what has already been drawn on the canvas. Instead, transformations modify the grid system that will be used to draw subsequent shapes. I will demonstrate three types of transformations in this chapter.

- Translating
- Rotating
- Scaling

As I mentioned earlier, a canvas element uses a grid system where the origin is at the top-left corner of the canvas. So, a point at 100, 50 will be 100 pixels to the right and 50 pixels down from that corner. Transformations simply adjust the grid system. For example, the following command will shift the origin 100 pixels to the right and 50 pixels down:

```
context.translate (100, 50);
```

This is illustrated in Figure 10-5.

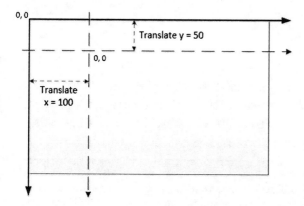

Figure 10-5. *Translating the context origin*

Now when you move to 10, 20, since this is relative to the new origin, the actual position (relative to the canvas), will be 110, 70. You might be wondering why you would want to do this. Well, suppose you were drawing a picture of the U.S. flag, which has 50 stars on it. A five-pointed star is a fairly complex shape to draw, which will require a number of drawing commands. Once you have drawn the first star, you'll need to repeat the process 49 more times, each time using different values.

By simply translating the context to the right a little, you can repeat the same commands using the same values. But now the star will be in a different location. Granted, you could accomplish the same thing by creating a drawStar() function that accepted x, y parameters. Then call this 50 times, passing in different values. However, once you get used to using transformation, you will find this easier, especially with the other types such as rotation.

The rotate transformation doesn't move the origin; instead, it rotates the x- and y-axes by the specified amount. A positive amount is used for a clockwise rotation, and a negative value is used to rotate counterclockwise. Figure 10-6 demonstrates how a rotate transformation works.

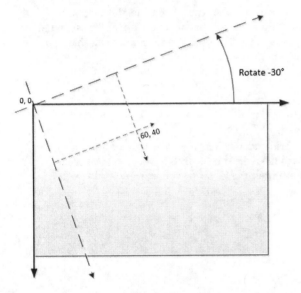

Figure 10-6. *Rotating the drawing context's grid*

▓ **Note**   I indicated the rotation angle as 30° since that is what most people are familiar with. However, the rotate() command expects the value in radians. If your geometry is a little rusty, a full circle is 360° or 2π radians. In JavaScript, you can use the Math.PI property to get the value of π (Pi). For example, 30° is 1/12 of a full circle, so you can write this as (Math.PI*2/12). In general, radians are calculated as degrees * (Math.PI/180).

You can use multiple transformations. For example, you can translate the origin and then rotate the x- or y-axis. You can also rotate the grid some more and translate again. Each transformation is always relative to the current position and orientation.

Saving the Context State

The state of a drawing context includes the various properties such as fillStyle and strokeStyle that you have already used. It also includes the accumulation of all transformations that have been applied. If you start using multiple transformations, getting back to the original state may be difficult. Fortunately, the drawing context provides the ability to save and then restore the state of the context.

The current state is saved by calling the save() function. Saving the state pushes the current state onto a stack. Calling the restore() function pops the most recently saved state off the stack and makes that the current state. This is illustrated in Figure 10-7.

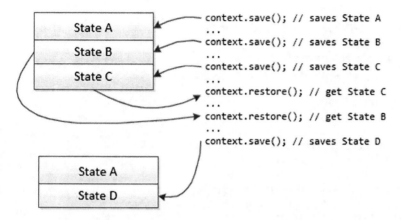

Figure 10-7. *Saving and restoring the drawing context state*

You should generally save the state before doing any transformations, especially complex ones. When you have finished drawing whatever elements needed the transformation, you can restore the state to the way it was. Remember, changing the state by setting the fillStyle or performing a transformation does not affect what has already been drawn.

Drawing the Solar System

With these features at your disposal, let's draw a simple model of the solar system.

EXERCISE 10-5. MODELING THE SOLAR SYSTEM

1. Open the index.html file and add the canvas element shown in bold just after the existing canvas element.

```
<div>
    <canvas id="board" width ="600" height ="600">
        Not supported
    </canvas>
    <canvas id="solarSystem" width="450" height="400">
        Not supported
    </canvas>
</div>
```

2. Add a new `script` element in the body element just after the existing `script` element using the code shown in Listing 10-7.

Listing 10-7. Initial Solar System Implementation

```
<script id="solar system" type="text/javascript">

    var ss = document.getElementById('solarSystem')
    var ssContext = ss.getContext('2d');

    setInterval(animateSS, 100);

    function animateSS() {
        var ss = document.getElementById('solarSystem')
        var ssContext = ss.getContext('2d');

        // Clear the canvas and draw the background
        ssContext.clearRect(0, 0, 450, 400);
        ssContext.fillStyle = "#2F1D92";
        ssContext.fillRect(0, 0, 450, 400);

        ssContext.save();

        // Draw the sun
        ssContext.translate(220, 200);
        ssContext.fillStyle = "yellow";
        ssContext.beginPath();
        ssContext.arc(0, 0, 15, 0, Math.PI * 2, true);
        ssContext.fill();

        // Draw the earth orbit
        ssContext.strokeStyle = "black";
        ssContext.beginPath();
        ssContext.arc(0, 0, 150, 0, Math.PI * 2);
        ssContext.stroke();

        ssContext.restore()
    }
</script>
```

■ **Tip** In Visual Studio, you can collapse an HTML element in the editor. Since you're done with the previous script element, you can collapse it, which will make it easier to see the new element that you'll be working on. While you don't need to set the id attribute of a script element, if you do, it will be displayed when the element is collapsed, as demonstrated in Figure 10-8. This will make it easier to manage pages with multiple script elements.

```
<!DOCTYPE html>
<html>
<head>...</head>
<body>
    <canvas id="board" width="600" height="600">
        Not supported
    </canvas>
    <canvas id="solarSystem" width="450" height="400">
        Not supported
    </canvas>

    <script id="chess board">...</script>

    <script id="solar system" type="text/javascript">

    var ss = document.getElementById('solarSystem')
    var ssContext = ss.getContext('2d');

    setInterval(animateSS, 100);
```

Figure 10-8. *Collapsing the script element*

3. This code gets the canvas element and then obtains the 2d drawing context, just like the previous example. It then uses the setInterval() function to call the animateSS() function every 100 milliseconds. The animateSS() function is what does the real work. It clears the entire area and then fills it with dark blue. The rest of the code relies on transformations, so it first saves the drawing context and then restores it when finished.

4. This animateSS() function uses the translate() function to move the origin to the approximate midpoint of the canvas. The sun and the earth orbits are drawn using the arc() function. Notice the center point for both is 0, 0 since the context's origin is now in the middle of the canvas. Also, notice the start angle is 0 and the end angle is specified as Math.PI 2. In radians, this is a full circle or 360°. The arc for the sun is filled in, and the orbit is not.

5. Press F5 to start the application. So far, the drawing is not very interesting; it's a sun with an orbit drawn around it, as shown in Figure 10-9.

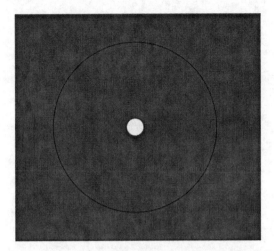

Figure 10-9. *The initial solar system drawing*

6. Now you'll draw the earth and animate it around the orbit. Normally the earth will revolve around the sun once every 365.24 days, but we'll speed this up a bit and complete the trip in 60 seconds. To determine where to put the earth each time the canvas is redrawn, you must calculate the number of seconds. The amount of rotation per second is calculated as Math.PI * 2 / 60. Multiply this value by the number of seconds to determine the angle where the earth should be.

7. Add the code from Listing 10-8 that is shown in bold. This code uses the rotate function to rotate the drawing context the appropriate angle. Since the arc for the earth orbit is 150px, this code then uses the translate function to move the context 150 pixels to the right so the earth can be drawn at the adjusted 0,0 coordinate. Notice that this is combining two separate transforms, one to rotate based the earth position in its orbit and one to translate the appropriate distance from the sun. The earth is then drawn using a filled arc with a center point of 0,0, the new origin of the context.

Listing 10-8. Drawing the Earth

```
// Draw the earth orbit
ssContext.strokeStyle = "black";
ssContext.beginPath();
ssContext.arc(0, 0, 150, 0, Math.PI * 2);
ssContext.stroke();

// Compute the current time in seconds (use the milliseconds
// to allow for fractional parts).
var now = new Date();
var seconds = ((now.getSeconds() * 1000) + now.getMilliseconds()) / 1000;


//------------------------------------------------
// Earth
//------------------------------------------------
```

```
// Rotate the context once every 60 seconds
var anglePerSecond = ((Math.PI * 2) / 60);
ssContext.rotate(anglePerSecond * seconds);
ssContext.translate(150, 0);

// Draw the earth
ssContext.fillStyle = "green";
ssContext.beginPath();
ssContext.arc(0, 0, 10, 0, Math.PI * 2, true);
ssContext.fill();

ssContext.restore()
```

8. Save your changes and press F5 to start the application. Now you should see the earth make its way around the sun, as shown in Figure 10-10.

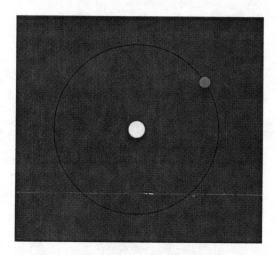

Figure 10-10. *Adding the earth to the drawing*

9. Now you'll show the moon revolving around the earth, which will demonstrate the real power of using transformations. The specific position of the moon is based on two moving objects. While it's certainly possible to compute this using some complex formulas (scientists have been doing this for centuries) with transformations, you don't have to. The drawing context was rotated the appropriate angle based on current time (number of seconds). It was then translated by the radius of the orbit, so the earth is now at the origin of the context. It doesn't really matter where the earth is; you can simply draw the moon relative to the current origin.

10. You will now draw the moon just like you drew the earth. Instead of the origin being at the sun and rotating the earth around the sun, the origin is on the earth, and you'll rotate the moon around the earth. The moon will rotate around the earth approximately once each month; in other words, it will complete about 12 revolutions for each earth orbit. So, you'll need to rotate 12 times faster. The anglePerSecond is now computed as 12 * ((Math.PI * 2) / 60). Add the code shown in bold in Listing 10-9.

Listing 10-9. Drawing the Moon

```
// Draw the earth
ssContext.fillStyle = "green";
ssContext.beginPath();
ssContext.arc(0, -0, 10, 0, Math.PI * 2, true);
ssContext.fill();

//------------------------------------------------
// Moon
//------------------------------------------------
// Rotate the context 12 times for every earth revolution
anglePerSecond = 12 * ((Math.PI * 2) / 60);
ssContext.rotate(anglePerSecond * seconds);
ssContext.translate(0, 35);

// draw the moon
ssContext.fillStyle = "white";
ssContext.beginPath();
ssContext.arc(0, 0, 5, 0, Math.PI * 2, true);
ssContext.fill();

ssContext.restore()
```

■ **Note** There are about 12.368 lunar months per solar year. You can make your model more accurate by using this figure instead of 12 in the preceding code.

11. Save your changes and press F5 to start the application. You should now see the moon rotating around the earth, as shown in Figure 10-11.

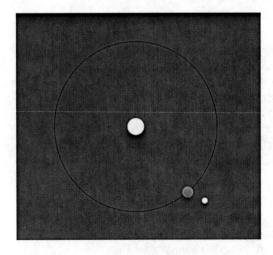

Figure 10-11. Including the moon

Applying Scaling

Before you finish this model, there's one minor correction that you'll make. The earth's orbit is not actually a perfect circle. This attribute is known as *eccentricity*. (If you're curious about orbital eccentricity, check out the article at http://en.wikipedia.org/wiki/Orbital_eccentricity.) To model this in your drawing, you'll stretch the orbit, making it a little bit wider than it is tall. To do this, you'll use scaling.

The scale() function performs the third type of transformation. This function takes two parameters that specify the scaling along the x- and y-axes. A scale factor of 1 is the normal scale. A factor less than 1 will compress the drawing, and a factor greater than 1 will stretch it. While the imperfection in the earth's orbit is extremely slight, you'll exaggerate it here and use a scale factor of 1.1 for the x-axis.

Add the following code shown in bold just before the earth orbit is drawn:

```
// Draw the earth orbit
ssContext.scale(1.1, 1);
ssContext.strokeStyle = "black";
```

Press F5 to start the application, which should look like Figure 10-12.

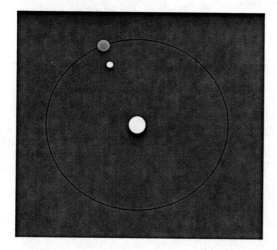

Figure 10-12. *Adding scaling*

You now have a slightly out-of-shape orbit. By simply changing the scale factor, all the various drawing elements were adjusted proportionally. Also, after restoring the context, the scaling is restored to normal so subsequent elements are drawn correctly.

■ **Note** The alignment in Figure 10-12 demonstrates a solar eclipse, where the moon passes between the earth and the sun, casting a shadow over the earth.

Clipping a Canvas

I want to cover one more feature related to paths. Earlier I said that after you call beginPath() and then the desired drawing functions, you can call either stroke() or fill(). There is one more function you can call as well: clip(). The clip() function will use the path that you just defined and will not allow anything to be drawn outside of that path. This doesn't affect what has already been drawn, but any future shapes will be restricted to the clipping area defined by this path.

To demonstrate this, you'll go back to the chess board example and define a clipping path using an arc. Go to the board script element and add the code shown in bold to the drawBoard() function.

```
var gradient = chessContext.createLinearGradient(0, 600, 600, 0);
gradient.addColorStop(0, "#D50005");
gradient.addColorStop(0.5, "#E27883");
gradient.addColorStop(1, "#FFDDDD");

// Clip the path
chessContext.beginPath();
chessContext.arc(300, 300, 300, 0, (Math.PI * 2), true);
chessContext.clip();

chessContext.fillStyle = gradient;
chessContext.strokeStyle = "red";

// Draw the alternating squares
```

This defines a circle on the board, and anything outside of that circle will not be visible. Press F5 to start the application, which should look like Figure 10-13.

Figure 10-13. *The chess board with a clipping path*

■ **Note**   If you define the clipping path after the board is drawn, the entire board will be drawn, but the pieces will be cropped, so any part that is outside the clipping area will be hidden.

Understanding Compositing

With all the shapes you have drawn so far, the one drawn last overlaid, or hid, whatever preceded it. This behavior is referred to as *compositing*. The default behavior, called *source-over*, is to draw the current shape on top of whatever may already be on the canvas, as you've seen. The compositing terminology uses *source* to refer to the shape being drawn and *destination* as the result of what was previously drawn. In addition to source-over, there are 11 other behaviors that you can configure using the globalCompositeOperation property. These are best explained by seeing a sample of each.

In this exercise, you will overlap a red square with a blue circle. You will do this 12 times, each time using a different value for the globalCompositeOperation property. To make this work correctly, you'll create 12 canvas elements, drawing the same elements on each.

EXERCISE 10-6. EXPLORING COMPOSITING

1. In the main div element, comment out the board and solarSystem canvas elements and create 12 new canvas elements using the code shown in Listing 10-10.

Listing 10-10. Creating 12 canvas Elements

```
<div>
    <div>
        <canvas id="composting1" width="120" height="120"></canvas>
        <br />source-over
    </div>
    <div>
        <canvas id="composting2" width="120" height="120"></canvas>
        <br />destination-over
    </div>
    <div>
        <canvas id="composting3" width="120" height="120"></canvas>
        <br />source-in
    </div>
    <div>
        <canvas id="composting4" width="120" height="120"></canvas>
        <br />destination-in
    </div>
    <div>
        <canvas id="composting5" width="120" height="120"></canvas>
        <br />source-out
    </div>
    <div>
        <canvas id="composting6" width="120" height="120"></canvas>
        <br />destination-out
    </div>
    <div>
        <canvas id="composting7" width="120" height="120"></canvas>
        <br />source-atop
    </div>
    <div>
        <canvas id="composting8" width="120" height="120"></canvas>
        <br />destination-atop
    </div>
    <div>
        <canvas id="composting9" width="120" height="120"></canvas>
        <br />xor
    </div>
    <div>
        <canvas id="composting10" width="120" height="120"></canvas>
        <br />copy
    </div>
```

```
<div>
    <canvas id="composting11" width="120" height="120"></canvas>
    <br />lighter
</div>
<div>
    <canvas id="composting12" width="120" height="120"></canvas>
    <br />darker
</div>

<!--<canvas id="board" width ="600" height ="600">
    Not supported
</canvas>
<canvas id="solarSystem" width="450" height="400">
    Not supported
</canvas> -->
</div>
```

2. Add the following `style` element in the `head` section. This will format the `canvas` elements into three columns so you can see all 12 examples on one screen.

```
<style>
    body div
    {
        -webkit-column-count: 3;
        column-count: 3;
    }

</style
```

3. Comment out the chessboard and solar system `script` elements. (Since the canvas elements are no longer on the page, the scripts will fail.)

4. Add the `script` element shown in Listing 10-11 to the `body` element, just after the existing `script` elements.

Listing 10-11. Drawing the Compositing Canvases

```
<script id="compositing" type="text/javascript">
    for (var i = 1; i <= 12; i++) {
        var c = document.getElementById("composting" + i);
        var cContext = c.getContext("2d");

        cContext.fillStyle = "red";
        cContext.fillRect(10, 20, 80, 80);

        switch (i) {
            case 1: cContext.globalCompositeOperation = "source-over"; break;
            case 2: cContext.globalCompositeOperation = "destination-over"; break;
            case 3: cContext.globalCompositeOperation = "source-in"; break;
            case 4: cContext.globalCompositeOperation = "destination-in"; break;
            case 5: cContext.globalCompositeOperation = "source-out"; break;
```

```
                        case 6: cContext.globalCompositeOperation = "destination-out"; break;
                        case 7: cContext.globalCompositeOperation = "source-atop"; break;
                        case 8: cContext.globalCompositeOperation = "destination-atop"; break;
                        case 9: cContext.globalCompositeOperation = "xor"; break;
                        case 10: cContext.globalCompositeOperation = "copy"; break;
                        case 11: cContext.globalCompositeOperation = "lighter"; break;
                        case 12: cContext.globalCompositeOperation = "darker"; break;
                    }

                    cContext.fillStyle = "blue";
                    cContext.beginPath();
                    cContext.arc(65, 75, 40, 0, (Math.PI * 2), true);
                    cContext.fill();
                }
            </script>
```

5. This code uses a for loop to process all 12 canvas elements. It gets the corresponding element and then obtains its drawing context. It adds a red square and then sets the globalCompositeOperation property. Finally, it adds a blue circle, which is offset slightly from the position of the square.

6. Change the debugging browser to use Chrome because this supports all of the compositing options.

■ **Note**   All of the browsers support all of these options, except darker. Chrome is the only browser, as of this writing, that supports darker correctly.

---

7. Save your changes and press F5 to start the application. The web page should look like Figure 10-14.

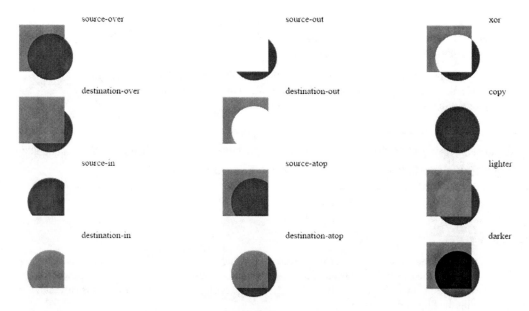

Figure 10-14. *Demonstrating the compositing options*

The compositing options are as follows:

- `source-over`: This is the default operation. The source element (the element being added) is drawn on top of the destination (whatever is already in this location).

- `destination-over`: This is the opposite of `source-over`, where the source element is added underneath the existing elements.

- `source-in`: Only the portion of the source object that is also in a destination element is displayed. Note that none of the destination element is displayed; it is being used like a clipping shape.

- `destination-in`: Only the portion of the destination object that is also in the source element is displayed.

- `source-out`: Only the portion of the source element that does not overlap the destination element is displayed.

- `destination-out`: Only the portion of the destination element that does not overlap the source element is displayed.

- `source-atop`: The source is displayed on top of the destination element, but the entire shape is clipped by the destination element.

- `destination-atop`: The source is displayed beneath the destination element, but the entire shape is clipped by the source element.

- `xor`: Only the portions of the source and destination elements that do not overlap are displayed.

- `copy`: The name is misleading. This draws the source elements and clears everything else.

- `lighter`: This draws both the source and destination elements, and the overlapping area is displayed in a lighter color. The actual color is determined by adding the color values of the source and destination elements.

- `darker`: This draws both the source and destination elements, and the overlapping area is displayed in a darker color. The actual color is determined by subtracting the color values of the source and destination elements.

■ **Tip**   Some of the names of these compositing options may not be very intuitive. I suggest that you keep this figure handy to refer to later in case you don't remember what copy does, for example.

Summary

In this chapter, you used the canvas element to create some graphical web pages. You used rectangles and paths to draw shapes on the canvas. You also included images on your canvas. One of the really powerful features of canvas is the ability to apply transformations. The appropriate use of transformations can really simplify some complex drawing applications.

Canvas is fundamentally different from SVG. In SVG, each shape is a separate DOM node. This provides two important features that you cannot do with canvas:

- Attach event handlers to individual shapes.

- Individual shapes can be manipulated. A good example of this is defining the :hover pseudo-rule, which allows the shape's attributes to be changed when the mouse is hovered over it.

In contrast to SVG, canvas is pixel based, which means it is resolution dependent. Notice that all of the drawing commands used pixel locations or sizes. When you draw a shape on a canvas element, the pixels of that canvas are adjusted as appropriate and all that is remembered is the resulting pixel content.

Canvas will tend to be more efficient because of its raw pixel manipulation. SVG, on the other hand, must perform a lot of rendering (and rerendering). However, larger images with less dense content, such as maps, will generally perform better in SVG.

PART IV

Advanced Features

■ ■ ■

CHAPTER 11

Indexed DB

As browser technology has evolved, providing more and more functionality on the client device, the need to store and manipulate data locally has increased as well. To address this need, two competing technologies have emerged.

- *Web SQL*: A SQL engine hosted within the browser
- *Indexed DB*: An API for storing and retrieving objects using keys and indices

---

■ **Note**   In November 2010, the W3C Working Group decided to stop work on Web SQL, and it is no longer part of the HTML5 specifications. Several browsers still support it, however, but its adoption as a cross-platform standard is unlikely.

This chapter will demonstrate how to use Indexed DB to store and use data on the client. If you are used to working with SQL databases, I will warn you, this is not a SQL database. It is quite powerful and useful once you get the hang of it, but you'll need to adjust your perspective and set aside your SQL experience as you work through this chapter.

To explore the capabilities of Indexed DB, you will rewrite the chessboard application that you created using canvas in Chapter 10. As I explain each of the exercises, I will not go into much detail about canvas; however, refer to Chapter 10 if you need more information. Your new version of the application will create object stores to define the positions of each piece and then manipulate this data as the pieces are moved.

Introducing Indexed DB

Before I get started with the detailed demonstration, there are a few key points that I think will help you better understand how Indexed DB works. Like other databases, the data is placed in a persistent data store. In this case, it's on the local hard drive. The data is permanent.

I will explain each of these entities in more detail, but I will first introduce them and their relationships. A database consists of *object stores*. Each object store is a collection of objects, with each object identified by a unique key. An object store can have one or more indices. Each *index* provides an alternate way of identifying the key to an object store. This is illustrated in Figure 11-1.

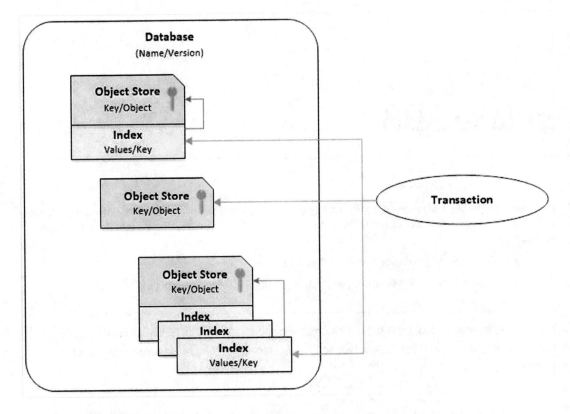

Figure 11-1. The database entities

Object stores are accessed through a *transaction* object. When creating the transaction, you must define its scope. This indicates which object stores it will reference and whether it will be reading or writing data to the database.

Using Object Stores

The primary storage unit is called an *object store*. This is aptly named because they are simply a collection of objects that are referenced by a key. You can think of this as a set of name-value pairs, the value being an object with a set of properties. You can use an *in-line* key, where one of the object properties serves as the key. For example, if the object has an id property with unique values, you can use that as the in-line key. If you use *out-of-line* keys, then you will specify a key when adding an object to the store. Alternatively, you can use a *key generator*, where the object store will assign incremental key values for you. The following code demonstrates these alternatives:

```
// Using an inline key
var typeStore = db.createObjectStore("pieceType", { keyPath: "id" });
typeStore.add(pieceType);

// Using an out-of-line key
var sampleStore = db.createObjectStore("sample", { });
sampleStore.add(sample, 5);
```

```
// Using a key generator
var pieceStore = db.createObjectStore("piece", { autoIncrement: true });
pieceStore.add(piece);
```

As its name implies, you can also create an index on an object store; in fact, you can create as many indices as you want. An index enables you to find a specific object or collection of objects quickly. An index is a collection of name-value pairs, where the value is a key into the object store. For example, if you have a customer object store and want to search by last name, you can create an index on the lastName property of the object. The database will automatically create an entry in the index for each object in the store. This entry will contain the last name and the corresponding key to that object. The following code demonstrates how to use an index:

```
// Create an index on the lastName property
customerStore.createIndex("lastName", "id", { unique: true });
```

```
// Get the index
var index = customerStore.index("lastName");
index.get(lastName).onsuccess = function();        // get the object
index.getKey(lastName).onsuccess = function();  // get the key
```

The second parameter to the createIndex() function, id in this case, specifies the key path. This tells the database engine how to extract the key from an object. For inline keys, this is the name of the property used to define the unique key.

Indexed DB does not support relationships between object stores. You can't enforce a foreign key relationship, for example. You can certainly use foreign keys, where a property in one object store is a key into another, as I will demonstrate later. However, the database does not enforce this constraint. Also, you can't perform joins between object stores.

Defining the Database

When you open a database, you need to implement three event handlers.

- onsuccess: The database is opened; do something with it.
- onerror: An error occurred, likely an access issue.
- onupgradeneeded: The database needs to be created or upgraded.

When opening a database, if it doesn't exist, it will be created automatically; however, the onupgradeneeded event will be raised. You must implement an event handler for this event, which will create object stores and populate them with any default data. This is the only place where you are allowed to alter the database structure. The important thing to remember is that the onupgradeneeded event is fired before the onsuccess event.

The open() call also specifies a version number. If this is not the current version, the onupgradeneeded event is raised in this scenario also. Your event handler needs to handle altering the structure to match the version requested by the caller. You can query the database's current version like this:

```
var request = dbEng.open("Sample", 2); // get version 2

request.onupgradeneeded = function (event) {
    alert("Configuring database - current version is " + e.oldVersion +
          ", requested version is " + e.newVersion);
}
```

Based on the current version, the code may need to perform different actions.

Processing Asynchronously

A key aspect of Indexed DB that may take some getting used to is its asynchronous processing; almost all database operations are done asynchronously. The general pattern is to call a method to perform a database operation such as opening a database or retrieving a set of records (objects). This will return a request object. You must then implement the onsuccess and onerror event handlers for that request object. If the request was successful, the onsuccess handler is called, and the result of the method call is passed through the event object.

For complex processing that requires several database calls, you'll need to be careful to nest the event handlers and consider when they are executed. For example, if you needed to make three database requests, your code might look like this:

```
var request = dbCall1()
request.onsuccess = function (e1) {
    f1(e1.target.result);

    dbCall2().onsuccess = function (e2) {
        f3(e2.target.result, e1.target.result);

        dbCall3().onsuccess = function (e3) {
            f5(e3.target.result, e2.target.result, e1.target.result);
        }

        f4(e2.target.result);
    }

    f2(e1.target.result);
}

request.onerror = function(e) {
    alert("The call failed")
}
```

This code calls dbCall1(), dbCall2(), and dbCall3(), in that order, and they will be processed sequentially. In other words, dbCall2() will not start until dbCall1() has completed, and only if it was successful. Each call provides an onsuccess event handler, which makes the next call. If the first call fails, an alert is raised. What may be unexpected is the order that the nondatabase calls are executed. The database calls return immediately, and the event handler is called later, when the operation has completed. As soon as the call to dbCall2() is made, the function returns, and f2() will be executed. Later, the dbCall2() completes, its event handler is called, and f3() is executed.

■ **Tip** The onerror event is bubbled up the hierarchy. For example, an error that occurs on the request object, if not handled, will be raised on the transaction object. If not handled there, it will be raised on the database object. In many cases, you can use just a single event handler at the database level and handle all the errors there.

Because of the nesting approach, the event handler has access to the event object from previous calls. For this reason, you should use unique names for the event parameter. This will avoid ambiguity. Also, notice the use of closure to access these event objects. As I mentioned, f2() is called before f3(), so the event handler for dbCall1(), which defines the e1 parameter, has completed and is no longer in scope by the time the event handler for dbCall2() is executed. The closure feature of JavaScript allows the subsequent event handlers to access this object. This is important because if you need to access all three object stores to complete an operation, you will need to wait until all three have completed and then access all three results.

▓ **Tip** To avoid closure, you could extract the properties that you need from the first two database calls and store them in local variables (declared prior to the dbCall1() call). Then in the f5() call, you can use these variables instead of the e1 and e2 event objects. This is just a matter of preference because either approach will work fine.

Using Transactions

All data access, both reading and writing, is done within a transaction, so you must first create a transaction object. When the transaction is created, you specify its scope, which is defined by the object stores it will access. You also specify the mode (read-only or read-write). You can then obtain an object store from the transaction and get or put data from/into the store like this:

```
var xact = db.transaction(["piece", "pieceType"], "readwrite");
var pieceStore = xact.objectStore("piece");
```

For read-write transactions, the data changes are not committed until the transaction completes. The interesting question to ask is "when does a transaction complete?" A transaction is complete when there are no more outstanding requests for it. Remember, everything is request-based. You make a request and then implement an event handler to do something when it finishes. If that event handler issues another request on that transaction, then the transaction stays alive. This is another important reason for nesting the event handlers. If you end an event handler without issuing another request, the transaction will complete, and all changes are committed. If you try to use the transaction after that, you will get a TRANSACTION_INACTIVE_ERR error.

Another thing to remember is that read-write transactions cannot have overlapping scopes. If you create a read-write transaction, you can create a second one as long as they don't both include some of the same object stores. If they have overlapping scopes, you must wait for the first transaction to complete before creating the second one. Read-only transactions, however, can have overlapping scopes.

Creating the Application

You'll start by creating a chessboard using canvas and configuring images for the chess pieces like you did in the previous chapter.

Creating the Visual Studio Project

You'll start by creating a Visual Studio project using the same Empty template that you used in previous chapters.

EXERCISE 11-1. CREATING THE VISUAL STUDIO PROJECT

1. Start Visual Studio 2015. From the Start Page, click the New Project link.

2. In the New project dialog box, select the ASP.NET Web Application template. Enter the project name **Chapter11** and select a location for this project.

3. In the next dialog box, select the ASP.NET 5 Empty template and click the OK button to create the project.

4. Open the Startup.cs file and comment out the implementation for the Configure() method like this:

```
public void Configure(IApplicationBuilder app)
{
    //app.Run(async (context) =>
    //{
    //    await context.Response.WriteAsync("Hello World!");
    //});
}
```

5. In Solution Explorer, right-click the wwwroot folder and click the Add and New Item links. In the Add New Item dialog box, select the HTML Page template, enter the name **Index.html**, and click the Add button.

6. In the Index.html file, in the empty body element that was created, add the following markup:

```
<div>
    <canvas id="board" width ="600" height ="600">
        Not supported
    </canvas>
</div>
```

7. In Solution Explorer, right-click the wwwroot folder and click the Add and New Folder links. Enter **images** for the folder name.

8. The images for the chess pieces are included in the source code download file. These are the same images used in Chapter 10. You'll find these in the Chapter10\ Images folder. Drag all 12 files to the images folder in Solution Explorer.

Creating the Canvas

Now you'll design the canvas element using JavaScript. The initial design will just draw an empty board, and you'll add the chess pieces later. Refer to Chapter 10 for more explanation about working with a canvas element. Add a script element after the div element but inside the body element using the code from Listing 11-1.

Listing 11-1. Designing the Initial Canvas

```
<script>
    // Get the canvas context
    var chessCanvas = document.getElementById("board");
    var chessContext = chessCanvas.getContext("2d");

    drawBoard();

    function drawBoard() {
        chessContext.clearRect(0, 0, 600, 600);

        var gradient = chessContext.createLinearGradient(0, 600, 600, 0);
        gradient.addColorStop(0, "#D50005");
        gradient.addColorStop(0.5, "#E27883");
        gradient.addColorStop(1, "#FFDDDD");

        chessContext.fillStyle = gradient;
        chessContext.strokeStyle = "red";

        // Draw the alternating squares
        for (var x = 0; x < 8; x++) {
            for (var y = 0; y < 8; y++) {
                if ((x + y) % 2) {
                    chessContext.fillRect(75 * x, 75 * y, 75, 75);
                }
            }
        }

        // Add a border around the entire board
        chessContext.strokeRect(0, 0, 600, 600);
    }
</script>
```

Press F5 to start the application, which should look like Figure 11-2.

Figure 11-2. *The initial (blank) chessboard*

Configuring the Images

You will be using image files to represent the chess pieces. Before adding them to the canvas, you'll need to create an Image object for each one and specify its src attribute. You'll also put these into an array to make it easier to programmatically select the desired image. Add the code shown in Listing 11-2 to the beginning of the script element that you just created, before the existing code.

Listing 11-2. Adding the Image Objects

```
// Define the chess piece images
var imgPawn = new Image();
var imgRook = new Image();
var imgKnight = new Image();
var imgBishop = new Image();
var imgQueen = new Image();
var imgKing = new Image();
var imgPawnW = new Image();
var imgRookW = new Image();
var imgKnightW = new Image();
var imgBishopW = new Image();
var imgQueenW = new Image();
var imgKingW = new Image();

// Specify the source for each image
imgPawn.src = "images/pawn.png";
imgRook.src = "images/rook.png";
imgKnight.src = "images/knight.png";
imgBishop.src = "images/bishop.png";
```

```
imgQueen.src = "images/queen.png";
imgKing.src = "images/king.png";
imgPawnW.src = "images/wpawn.png";
imgRookW.src = "images/wrook.png";
imgKnightW.src = "images/wknight.png";
imgBishopW.src = "images/wbishop.png";
imgQueenW.src = "images/wqueen.png";
imgKingW.src = "images/wking.png";

// Define an array of Image objects
var images = [
        imgPawn ,
        imgRook ,
        imgKnight ,
        imgBishop ,
        imgQueen ,
        imgKing ,
        imgPawnW ,
        imgRookW ,
        imgKnightW ,
        imgBishopW ,
        imgQueenW ,
        imgKingW
];
```

Creating the Database

Now you're ready to create and use a local Indexed DB database to configure and display the chess pieces. Initially, the data will be loaded from static data, and you will simply display the starting position. Later you will animate the pieces by updating their location in the object store.

Declaring the Static Data

You will need to populate the database with some data. For this application, you will just declare the data as a static array and copy it to the object store. For other applications, this could be downloaded from a server or entered from user input. Add the declarations shown in Listing 11-3 to the script element, just after the image variables.

Listing 11-3. Declaring the Static Data

```
var pieceTypes = [
    { name: "pawn", height: "50", width: "28", blackImage: 0, whiteImage: 6 },
    { name: "rook", height: "60", width: "36", blackImage: 1, whiteImage: 7 },
    { name: "knight", height: "60", width: "36", blackImage: 2, whiteImage: 8 },
    { name: "bishop", height: "65", width: "30", blackImage: 3, whiteImage: 9 },
    { name: "queen", height: "70", width: "32", blackImage: 4, whiteImage: 10 },
    { name: "king", height: "70", width: "28", blackImage: 5, whiteImage: 11 }
];
```

```
var pieces = [
    { type: "pawn", color: "white", row: 6, column: 0, pos: "a2", killed: false },
    { type: "pawn", color: "white", row: 6, column: 1, pos: "b2", killed: false },
    { type: "pawn", color: "white", row: 6, column: 2, pos: "c2", killed: false },
    { type: "pawn", color: "white", row: 6, column: 3, pos: "d2", killed: false },
    { type: "pawn", color: "white", row: 6, column: 4, pos: "e2", killed: false },
    { type: "pawn", color: "white", row: 6, column: 5, pos: "f2", killed: false },
    { type: "pawn", color: "white", row: 6, column: 6, pos: "g2", killed: false },
    { type: "pawn", color: "white", row: 6, column: 7, pos: "h2", killed: false },
    { type: "rook", color: "white", row: 7, column: 0, pos: "a1", killed: false },
    { type: "rook", color: "white", row: 7, column: 7, pos: "h1", killed: false },
    { type: "knight", color: "white", row: 7, column: 1, pos: "b12", killed: false },
    { type: "knight", color: "white", row: 7, column: 6, pos: "g1", killed: false },
    { type: "bishop", color: "white", row: 7, column: 2, pos: "c1", killed: false },
    { type: "bishop", color: "white", row: 7, column: 5, pos: "f1", killed: false },
    { type: "queen", color: "white", row: 7, column: 3, pos: "d1", killed: false },
    { type: "king", color: "white", row: 7, column: 4, pos: "e1", killed: false },
    { type: "pawn", color: "black", row: 1, column: 0, pos: "a7", killed: false },
    { type: "pawn", color: "black", row: 1, column: 1, pos: "b7", killed: false },
    { type: "pawn", color: "black", row: 1, column: 2, pos: "c7", killed: false },
    { type: "pawn", color: "black", row: 1, column: 3, pos: "d7", killed: false },
    { type: "pawn", color: "black", row: 1, column: 4, pos: "e7", killed: false },
    { type: "pawn", color: "black", row: 1, column: 5, pos: "f7", killed: false },
    { type: "pawn", color: "black", row: 1, column: 6, pos: "g7", killed: false },
    { type: "pawn", color: "black", row: 1, column: 7, pos: "h7", killed: false },
    { type: "rook", color: "black", row: 0, column: 0, pos: "a8", killed: false },
    { type: "rook", color: "black", row: 0, column: 7, pos: "h8", killed: false },
    { type: "knight", color: "black", row: 0, column: 1, pos: "b8", killed: false },
    { type: "knight", color: "black", row: 0, column: 6, pos: "g8", killed: false },
    { type: "bishop", color: "black", row: 0, column: 2, pos: "c8", killed: false },
    { type: "bishop", color: "black", row: 0, column: 5, pos: "f8", killed: false },
    { type: "queen", color: "black", row: 0, column: 3, pos: "d8", killed: false },
    { type: "king", color: "black", row: 0, column: 4, pos: "e8", killed: false }
];
```

The pieceTypes[] array defines the properties needed to display each piece such as height and width. It also specifies the corresponding index in the images[] array for both the black and white images. The pieces[] array contains the same details used in the previous chapter such as row and column and defines the starting position for each of the 32 pieces.

Opening the Database

Add the code shown in Listing 11-4 to the script object, just after the call to drawBoard() (and before the implementation of the drawBoard() function).

Listing 11-4. Opening the Database

```
var dbEng = window.indexedDB ||
        window.webkitIndexedDB || // Chrome
        window.mozIndexedDB ||    // Firefox
        window.msIndexedDB;       // IE
```

```
var db;   // This is a handle to the database

if (!dbEng)
    alert("IndexedDB is not supported on this browser");
else {
    var request = dbEng.open("Chess", 1);

    request.onsuccess = function (event) {
        db = event.target.result;
    }

    request.onerror = function (event) {
        alert("Please allow the browser to open the database");
    }

    request.onupgradeneeded = function (event) {
        configureDatabase(event);
    }
}
```

If you can't access the indexedDB object, then the browser does not support it. For this demo you can simply use alert() to notify the user and stop further processing.

This code then uses the indexedDB object to open the Chess database, specifying that version 1 should be used. The open() method returns an IDBOpenDBRequest object, as I described earlier. You will attach three event handlers for this request.

- onsuccess: This event handler simply saves the reference to the database. You will add more logic here later. Notice that the database is obtained from the event.target.result property, which is how all results are returned.

- onerror: The primary reason that the browser fails to open a database is that the browser has the IndexedDB feature blocked. This can be disabled for security reasons. In this case, the user is prompted to allow access. Alternatively, you could choose to display the error message instead.

- onupgradeneeded: This is raised if the database does not exist or if the specified version is not the current version. This calls the configureDatabase() function, which you'll implement now.

Defining the Database Structure

Add the code shown in Listing 11-5 to implement the configureDatabase() function.

Listing 11-5. Defining the Database Structure

```
function configureDatabase(e) {
    alert("Configuring database - current version is " + e.oldVersion +
            ", requested version is " + e.newVersion);

    db = e.currentTarget.result;

    // Remove all existing data stores
    var storeList = db.objectStoreNames;
```

```
for (var i = 0; i < storeList.length; i++) {
    db.deleteObjectStore(storeList[i]);
}

// Store the piece types
var typeStore = db.createObjectStore
    ("pieceType", { keyPath: "name" });

for (var i in pieceTypes){
    typeStore.add(pieceTypes[i]);
}

// Create the piece data store (you'll add
// the data later)
var pieceStore = db.createObjectStore
    ("piece", { autoIncrement: true });

pieceStore.createIndex
    ("piecePosition", "pos", { unique: true });
}
```

■ **Caution**　The `configureDatabase()` function will be called if the database does not exist or if it is not the current version. For version changes, you can get the current version by using the `db.version` property and then make the necessary adjustments. Also, the `event` object passed to the `onupgradeneeded` event handler will have the `e.oldVersion` and `e.newVersion` properties. To simplify things in this project, you'll simply remove all object stores and rebuild the database from scratch. This will wipe out all existing data. That is fine for this example, but in most cases you'll need to preserve the data where possible.

The `objectStoreNames` property of the database object contains a list of the names of all the object stores that have been created. To remove all the existing object stores, each of the names in this list is passed to the `deleteObjectStore()` method.

Initially, you'll create two data stores using the `createObjectStore()` method.

- `pieceType`: Contains an object for each type of piece such as pawn, rook, or king

- `piece`: Contains an object for each piece, 16 black and 16 white

Specifying the Object Key

When creating an object store, you must specify a name for the store when calling the `createObjectStore()` method. You can also specify one or more optional parameters. Only two are supported.

- keypath: This is specified as a collection of property names. If you're using a single property, you can specify this as a string rather than a collection of strings. This defines the object property (or properties) that will be used as the key. If no keypath is specified, the key must be defined out-of-line using a key generator or providing the key as explained later in this section.

- autoIncrement: If true, this indicates that the keys are sequentially assigned by the object store.

Every object in a store must have a unique key. There are three ways to specify the key.

- Use the keypath parameter to specify one or more properties that define a unique key. As objects are added, the keypath is used to generate a key based on the object's properties.

- Use a key generator. If autoIncrement is specified, the object store will assign a key based on an internal counter.

- Provide the key value when adding the object. If you don't specify a key path or use a key generator, you must supply a key when adding an object to a store.

For the pieceType store you'll use a keypath. The name property will specify the type such as pawn or knight. This will be a unique value for each object. This is also the value that will be used to retrieve an object, so this is a perfect candidate for a key path. After creating the object store, the data from the pieceTypes[] array is then copied to the pieceType store.

▤ **Note** While in the onupgradeneeded event handler, data can be added to an object store without explicitly creating a transaction. There is an implicit transaction created in response to the onupgradeneeded event.

Creating an Index

For the piece store there is no natural key available in the pieces data, so you'll use a key generator. It will generate unique keys, but the keys will have no real meaning; they're just a synthetic key used to satisfy the unique constraint. Initially when you're drawing the board, you'll retrieve all of the objects, so you don't need to know what the key is.

Later you'll need to retrieve a piece so you can move it. You will find the desired piece based on its position on the board. To facilitate that, you'll add an index to the store based on the pos property. Since no two pieces can occupy the same space, the pos property can be used as a unique index. By specifying this as a unique index, you will get an error if you try to insert an object with the same position as an existing object.

▤ **Caution** Since the pos property is unique, you might be tempted to use it as the key. However, since you will be moving pieces, their position will change, and it's considered a poor design pattern to use a key that changes often. For Indexed DB, this is especially problematic since you can't actually change a key; you must delete the current object and then add it with the new key.

When creating an index, you must specify a keypath like this:

```
pieceStore.createIndex
    ("piecePosition", "pos", { unique: true });
```

In this case, the pos property is the keypath for this index. The keypath may include more than one property, in which case the index will be based on the combination of the selected properties. When an object store has an index, the index is automatically populated when an object is added to the store.

Resetting the Board

You created the piece object store but have not populated it yet. You'll do that in a separate function. To understand why, let me explain the database life cycle. The first time the web page is displayed, the database is opened, and since it doesn't exist, a new database will be created. This happens because the onupgradeneeded event is raised, and you implemented this event handler to create the object stores. When the page is displayed again (or simply refreshed), this step will be skipped since the database already exists.

Later, when you start moving the pieces around as well as deleting them, you'll want to move them back to their initial position when the page is reloaded. You can use this method to do that. You'll now add a resetBoard() function to the script using the following code. This will be called not when the database is created but when the page is loaded.

```
function resetBoard() {

    var xact = db.transaction(["piece"], "readwrite");
    var pieceStore = xact.objectStore("piece");
    var request = pieceStore.clear();
    request.onsuccess = function(event) {
        for (var i in pieces) {
            pieceStore.put(pieces[i]);
        }
}}
```

This code creates a transaction using the read-write mode and specifies only the piece object store since that is the only one you'll need to access. Then the piece store is obtained from the transaction. The clear() method is used to delete all the objects from the store. Finally, all the objects in the pieces[] array are copied to the object store.

Now add the following code shown in bold to the onsuccess event handler. This will call the resetBoard() function after the database has been opened. ()

▮ **Note** The onupgradeneeded event is raised, and its event handler must complete before the onsuccess event is raised. This ensures that the database has been properly configured before it is used.

```
var request = dbEng.open("Chess", 1);

request.onsuccess = function (event) {
    db = event.target.result;

    // Add the pieces to the board
    resetBoard();
}
```

■ **Tip** In the `resetBoard()` function, you called the `put()` method (repeatedly, 32 times). However, you did not get any response objects or implement any event handlers. This code appears to be working synchronously. Actually, these calls are processed asynchronously, and a response object is returned in both cases, but the return value was ignored. You could implement both `onsuccess` and `onerror` event handlers for these requests. In this case, you cheated a little. Since you don't need the result value like you would when retrieving data, you don't have to handle the `onsuccess` event. Because these calls are within a transaction, subsequent use of these object stores by a different transaction will be blocked until the updates are complete.

Drawing the Pieces

So far you have opened the database, configuring the object stores, if necessary. You have also populated the piece store with the initial positions. Now you're ready to draw the pieces. To do that you'll implement a `drawAllPieces()` function to iterate through all of the pieces and a `drawPiece()` function to display a single image. These functions will be similar to the functions you created in Chapter 10 with the same names. However, the data for these functions will be retrieved from the new database.

The `drawAllPieces()` function will use a cursor to process all the objects in the `piece` object store. For each piece, this will extract the necessary properties and pass them to the `drawPiece()` function. The `drawPiece()` function must then access the `pieceType` store to obtain the type properties such as `height` and `width` and display the image in the appropriate location.

Using a Cursor

When retrieving data from an object store, if you want to retrieve a single record using its key, use the `get()` method, which I will describe next. You can also select one or more objects using an index, and I will explain that later in this chapter. To get all the pieces, you'll need to access the entire object store, which you'll do using a cursor.

After creating the transaction and obtaining the object store, you'll call its `openCursor()` method. This returns an `IDBRequest` object, and you'll need to provide an `onsuccess` event handler for it. When the event fires, it provides the first object only. You can obtain the next object by calling the `continue()` method. To demonstrate this, add the function shown in Listing 11-6 to the `script` element.

Listing 11-6. Drawing the Pieces

```
function drawAllPieces() {

    var xact = db.transaction(["piece", "pieceType"]);

    var pieceStore = xact.objectStore("piece");
    var cursor = pieceStore.openCursor();
    cursor.onsuccess = function (event) {
        var item = event.target.result;
```

```
        if (item) {
            if (!item.value.killed) {
                drawPiece(item.value.type,
                          item.value.color,
                          item.value.row,
                          item.value.column,
                          xact);
            }
            item.continue();
        }
    }
}
```

This code creates a transaction that will use both the piece and pieceType object stores. The mode is not specified, and the default value is readonly. It then gets the piece object store and calls its openCursor() method. The onsuccess event handler gets the first object from the event object (using event.target.result). If the piece has not been captured, the drawPiece() function is called to display it, which you'll implement next. I'll explain the killed property later. You pass in all the properties that it will need such as type, color, row, and column. You'll also pass in the transaction object so the drawPiece() function can use the same transaction to access the pieceType store.

Calling the continue() method will cause the same event to be raised again, this time supplying the next object in the event.target.result property. If there are no more objects, the result property will be null. This is how you'll know all the objects have been processed.

The openCursor() method provides some basic capabilities to filter the objects that are returned. If no parameters are supplied, it will return all the objects in the store. You can specify a key range using one of the following:

- IDBKeyRange.only(): Specifies a single value and only records that match are returned.

- IDBKeyRange.lowerBound(): Returns only key values greater than the value specified. By default this is inclusive, so it will also return objects with keys that have an exact match as well, but you can change this to only return values that are greater.

- IDBKeyRange.upperBound(): Works just like lowerBound() except it returns values less than or equal to the value specified. I will demonstrate this later in the chapter.

- IDBKeyRange.bound(): Allows you to specify both a lower and upper bound. You can also indicate whether either of these values is inclusive. The default value for these is false, meaning not inclusive.

You can also pass a second parameter to the openCursor() function to specify the direction that the records are returned. The supported values for this are defined in the IDBCursorDirection enum. The possible values are as follows:

- next: Returns the next record in increasing key order (this is the default value)

- prev: Returns the previous record

- nextunique: Returns the next record that has a different key; this ignores duplicate keys

- prevunique: Returns the previous record, ignoring duplicate keys

The following example will return objects where the key is greater than 3 and less than or equal to 7 and return them in descending order. The last two parameters when creating the key range indicate that the lower bound is not inclusive but the upper bound is. When opening the cursor, the second parameter specifies the reverse direction should be used.

```
var keyRange = IDBKeyRange.bound(3, 7, false, true);
store.openCursor(keyRange, IDBCursorDirection.prev);
```

Retrieving a Single Object

Now you'll implement the drawPiece() function that will draw a single piece on the board. It must first access the pieceType object store to get the image details. In this case, you'll retrieve a single object using its key. The key to the pieceType object store is the type property. Add the function shown in Listing 11-7 to the script element.

Listing 11-7. Drawing a Single Piece

```
function drawPiece(type, color, row, column, xact) {

    var typeStore = xact.objectStore("pieceType");
    var request = typeStore.get(type);
    request.onsuccess = function (event) {
        var img;

        if (color === "black") {
            img = images[event.target.result.blackImage];
        }
        else {
            img = images[event.target.result.whiteImage];
        }

        chessContext.drawImage(img,
                    (75 - event.target.result.width) / 2 + (75 * column),
                    73 - event.target.result.height + (75 * row),
                    event.target.result.width,
                    event.target.result.height);
    }
}
```

This code uses the same transaction object, which is passed in. It obtains the pieceType object store and then calls its get() method. The onsuccess event handler gets the necessary properties and calls the canvas drawImage() method. Refer to Chapter 10 for more information about drawing images on a canvas.

Now add the call to drawAllPieces() in the onsuccess event handler for the open() call by adding the code shown in bold.

```
request.onsuccess = function (event) {
    db = event.target.result;

    // Add the pieces to the board
    resetBoard();
```

```
    // Draw the pieces in their initial positions
    drawAllPieces();
}
```

Testing the Application

Now you're ready to test the application, which will display the initial starting positions. Press F5 to start the application. You should see an alert letting you know that the database is being configured, as shown in Figure 11-3.

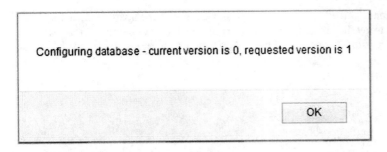

Figure 11-3. *The alert showing the database is being configured*

When you run this application again, this configuration will not be necessary. The chessboard should look like Figure 11-4.

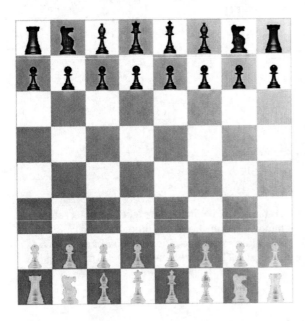

Figure 11-4. *The completed chessboard with static positions*

▓ **Tip**   If you want to remove the database from your machine, you can find the folder where they are stored and delete the corresponding subfolder. On my machine, the path is C:\Users\Mark\AppData\Roaming\ Mozilla\Firefox\Profiles\p1i1rsab.default\storage\default. In this folder there is a subfolder for each database. The subfolder name includes the protocol (http), domain name, and port, if applicable. For my application, this is http+++localhost+25519. Delete this folder and restart the browser. The page should reconfigure the database since it must create a new one.

Moving the Pieces

Now you're ready to animate the board by moving the pieces. You'll use the same canned moves that were used in Chapter 10. A piece can be moved by simply updating its position and then redrawing the board. There is one complication, however; if a move captures a piece, you need to remove it from the board. For now, you'll simply delete the object from the store, but I'll show you a better way at the end of the chapter.

Defining the Moves

Since you're so database savvy now, you'll store the moves in the database as well. A move is defined by the starting and ending positions. For example, "move the piece at e2 to e3." You'll number these moves from 1 to 7 so they will be applied in the correct order. You'll need a new object store to hold the move details. To do that, you'll need to specify a new version, which will raise the onupgradeneeded event. Then you'll add logic the configureDatabase() function to create the new store.

EXERCISE 11-2. ADDING THE MOVES STORE

1. Add the following code to the script element just after the existing static data definitions for the pieceTypes and pieces arrays:

```
var moves = [
    { id: 1, start: "e2", end: "e3" },
    { id: 2, start: "e7", end: "e5" },
    { id: 3, start: "f1", end: "c4" },
    { id: 4, start: "h7", end: "h6" },
    { id: 5, start: "d1", end: "f3" },
    { id: 6, start: "g7", end: "g6" },
    { id: 7, start: "f3", end: "f7" }
];
```

2. Add the following code shown in bold to the end of the configureDatabase() function. This will create and populate the move store when the database is configured.

```
pieceStore.createIndex
    ("piecePosition", "pos", { unique: true });

// Store the moves
var moveStore = db.createObjectStore
    ("move", { keyPath: "id" });

for (var i in moves) {
    moveStore.add(moves[i]);
}
```

3. On the open() call, change the version to **2** as shown in bold. This will cause the onupgradeneeded event to be raised the next time the page is loaded.

```
if (!dbEng)
    alert("IndexedDB is not supported on this browser");
else {
    var request = dbEng.open("Chess", 2);
```

■ **Caution**   In this example, the configureDatabase() function simply removes all the existing data stores and then re-creates them. You could do this because you didn't need to be concerned about maintaining any of the existing data; it was reloaded using canned values. In many scenarios you will not be able to do that. Instead, you'll need to make specific changes based on the current version. For example, if version 5 is requested and the current version is 2, you'll need to add the version 3 changes and then the version 4 changes and finally the version 5 changes. Keep this in mind when planning your structure changes.

Converting the Position

The objects in the piece store have the row, column, and pos properties. The row and column properties follow the same convention that was used in Chapter 10, where the top-left square is at 0,0. That is consistent with how canvas works and simplifies the drawPiece() implementation. In contrast, the pos property uses the notation widely used in chess where the columns (files) go from *a* to *h* as you move left to right. The rows (ranks) go from 1 to 8 as you move from the bottom of the board to the top. Thus, a1 is the bottom-left square.

Before you get into the heavy work of moving the pieces, you'll create a function that will convert the pos property into row and column properties. When a piece is moved to e3, for example, you'll need to convert e3 into the corresponding row and column coordinates, which would be 5 (row) and 4 (column). Add the function shown in Listing 11-8 to the end of the existing script element.

Listing 11-8. Implementing the computeRowColumn() Function

```
function computeRowColumn(oStart, end) {
    oStart.pos = end;
    switch (end.substring(0, 1)) {
        case "a": oStart.column = 0; break;
        case "b": oStart.column = 1; break;
        case "c": oStart.column = 2; break;
        case "d": oStart.column = 3; break;
        case "e": oStart.column = 4; break;
        case "f": oStart.column = 5; break;
        case "g": oStart.column = 6; break;
        case "h": oStart.column = 7; break;
    }

    oStart.row = 8 - parseInt(end.substr(1, 1));
}
```

The oStart parameter is the object from the piece store that was found at the starting position (e2 in our example). The end parameter is the ending position, e3, which is copied to the pos property since this will be the piece's new position.

This code then uses a switch statement to convert the a – h file notation into a 0 – 7 coordinate. This is then stored in the column property. The row property is computed by taking the last digit from the position and subtracting it from 8.

Making a Move

Just like you did in Chapter 10, you'll use a timer to make the next move every two seconds. You'll need a timer variable so you can clear the timer when the animation is done. You'll also need to keep track of the current move. Add the two variables shown in bold to the script element just before the drawBoard() method is called.

```
// Get the canvas context
var chessCanvas = document.getElementById("board");
var chessContext = chessCanvas.getContext("2d");()

var moveNumber = 1;
var timer;

drawBoard();
```

Moving a piece will require making up to five database calls:

1. Get the next object from the move store (this defines the start and end positions).

2. Get the object at the start position.

3. Get the object at the end position (there will be one only if the move is capturing a piece).

4. Remove the object at the end position (this step will be needed only on some moves).

5. Update the object at the start position (to move it to the end position).

These calls will all be made using the same transaction. As I demonstrated at the beginning of the chapter, you'll need to nest the onsuccess event handlers for each of these calls. Add the makeNextMove() function shown in Listing 11-9 to the end of the script element.

Listing 11-9. Implementing the makeNextMove() Function

```
function makeNextMove() {

    var xact = db.transaction(["move", "piece"], "readwrite");
    var moveStore = xact.objectStore("move");

    moveStore.get(moveNumber).onsuccess = function (e1) {
        var startPos = e1.target.result.start;
        var endPos = e1.target.result.end;
        var startKey = null;
        var oStart = null;

        var pieceStore = xact.objectStore("piece");
        var index = pieceStore.index("piecePosition");

        index.getKey(startPos).onsuccess = function (e2) {
            startKey = e2.target.result;
            index.get(startPos).onsuccess = function (e3) {
                oStart = e3.target.result;

                // If there is a piece at the ending location, we'll
                // need to update it to prevent a duplicate pos index
                removePiece(endPos, oStart, startKey, pieceStore);
            }
        }
    }
}
```

This function creates a transaction that will access both the move and piece stores. The mode is set to readwrite because the objects in the piece store will be modified. It then gets the move store and calls its get() method specifying the current move, which is the key to the table. This will return a single object, and the start and end positions are extracted from the result in the onsuccess event handler.

■ **Tip**   Notice that this code doesn't explicitly define a request variable. Instead, the onsuccess event handler is attached directly to the database call. In the previous examples, I declared a request variable and then attached the event handler to it to help you see what was happening. However, attaching the event handler directly to the method accomplishes the same thing but simplifies the code a little.

Obtaining the Object Key

For the piece store, you used a key generator, so the key is not part of the object. The code in the makeNextMove() function will use the index based on the pos property to retrieve the object at the start position (and also at the end position if there is a piece there). To update or delete an object, you will need its key.

When retrieving the piece object at the start position, this code first gets the piece store from the transaction. It then gets the piecePosition index from the store. To get the key value, you'll need to call index.getKey() method, which returns the key for the requested start position. This is stored in the startKey variable.

To get the desired object, you'll call the index.get() method passing in the position to search for. This returns the object at the requested start position and stores it in the oStart variable.

In both cases, the data is returned in the result property. Again, the event handlers that process the results are nested.

With the necessary data obtained, the removePiece() method is called, passing in the following parameters:

- end: The ending position of the piece being moved

- oStart: An object representing the piece being moved

- startID: The key to the oStart object

- pieceStore : The piece store that will be used to perform the update

Performing the Update

Now you'll implement the removePiece() function. This is perhaps misnamed since it will remove a piece only when necessary. Add the following code to the end of the script element to implement the removePiece() function:

```
function removePiece(endPos, oStart, startKey, pieceStore) {
    var index = pieceStore.index("piecePosition");
    index.getKey(endPos).onsuccess = function (e4) {
        var endKey = e4.target.result;
        if (endKey) {
            pieceStore.delete(endKey).onsuccess = function (e5) {
                movePiece(oStart, startKey, endPos, pieceStore)
            }
        }
        else
            movePiece(oStart, startKey, endPos, pieceStore);
    }
}
```

This code gets the key at the ending position. If there is a piece there, it calls the delete() method to remove it and then calls the movePiece() function in the onsuccess handler for the delete() method. Notice that it does not retrieve the object; only the key is needed to perform the delete. If there is no piece there, it just calls the movePiece() function. When calling the movePiece() function, all the data it needs is passed to it including the object, its key, the end position, and the object store that it will use.

Now you'll implement the movePiece() function that will finally perform the actual update. To update an object, you call the put() method. Unlike the add() method that you used earlier to add the pieces, the put() method requires both the object and the key. If there is no object with the specified key, the object will be added. Add the movePiece() method shown in Listing 11-10 to the end of the script element.

Listing 11-10. Implementing the movePiece() Function

```
function movePiece(oStart, startID, end, pieceStore) {

    computeRowColumn(oStart, end);

    var startUpdateReq = pieceStore.put(oStart, startID);
    startUpdateReq.onsuccess = function (event) {

        moveNumber++;

        drawBoard();
        drawAllPieces();

        if (moveNumber > 7) {
            clearInterval(timer);
            chessContext.font = "30pt Arial";
            chessContext.fillStyle = "black";
            chessContext.fillText("Checkmate!", 200, 220);
        }
    }
}
```

This code first computes the row and column properties using the computeRowColumn() function that you created earlier. It then updates the object. In the onsuccess event handler, it increments the moveNumber variable and draws the board and all of the pieces using the existing functions. Finally, if this is the last move, the timer is cleared and the "Checkmate!" text is drawn on the canvas.

Starting the Animation

The last step is to start the timer that will cause the makeNextMove() function to be called. You'll do this in the onsuccess event handler for the open() call. Add the code shown in bold:

```
var request = dbEng.open("Chess", 2);

request.onsuccess = function (event) {
    db = event.target.result;

    // Add the pieces to the board
    resetBoard();

    // Draw the pieces in their initial positions
    drawAllPieces();

    // Start the animation
    timer = setInterval(makeNextMove, 2000);
}
```

Save your changes and press F5 to start the application. You should see the alert letting you know that the database is being configured since you changed the database version. After a series of moves, you should see the completed board shown in Figure 11-5.

Figure 11-5. The completed chessboard

Tracking the Captured Pieces

When capturing a piece, you simply deleted the object, and that works since the piece doesn't need to be displayed. However, if your application wants to keep track of the pieces that were captured, you might want to keep the object in the store. Now I'll show you how to change this to update the object instead of deleting it. I also show you how to query this store to list the pieces that have been captured.

The first step is to change the removePiece() function. Instead of deleting the object at the end position, you'll update it and set the killed property. You'll also need to change the pos property since there is a unique index on this. Since the piece is not displayed, the position can be anything. To ensure it is unique, you'll prefix its unique ID with an x. Also, by prefixing these with an x, you'll be able to query for them, as I'll explain later.

Comment out the delete() call and add the code shown in bold:

```
function removePiece(end, oStart, startID, pieceStore) {
    var index = pieceStore.index("piecePosition");
    index.getKey(end).onsuccess = function (e4) {
        var endID = e4.target.result;
        if (endID) {
            //pieceStore.delete (endID).onsuccess = function (e5) {
            //    movePiece(oStart, startID, pieceStore)
            //}

            index.get(endPos).onsuccess = function (e5) {
                oEnd = e5.target.result;
                oEnd.pos = 'x' + endKey;
                oEnd.killed = true;
```

```
                pieceStore.put(oEnd, endKey).onsuccess = function (e6) {
                    movePiece(oStart, startKey, endPos, pieceStore)
                }
            }
        }
        else
            movePiece(oStart, startID, end, pieceStore);
    }
}
```

Now add the following code to the end of the script element to implement the displayCapturedPieces() function:

```
function displayCapturedPieces() {
    var xact = db.transaction(["piece"]);
    var textOut = "";

    var pieceStore = xact.objectStore("piece");
    var index = pieceStore.index("piecePosition");

    var keyRange = IDBKeyRange.lowerBound("x");
    var cursor = index.openCursor(keyRange);

    cursor.onsuccess = function (event) {
        var item = event.target.result;
        if (item) {
            textOut += " - " + item.value.color + " " +
                            item.value.type + "\r\n";
            item.continue();
        }
        else if (textOut.length > 0)
            alert("The following pieces were captured:\r\n" + textOut);
    }
}
```

This code creates a read-only transaction using only the piece store. It then gets the store and its piecePosition index. It defines a key range using a lower bound of x. This will only return objects that begin with *x* or greater. Since the pieces on the board will have a position that starts with *a* through *h,* these will be excluded. The code then iterates through the cursor and concatenates the piece details into a text string. The result is displayed using an alert() function.

■ **Caution**   Be aware that the string comparisons in the key range are case sensitive. If you had used an uppercase *X,* this would not have worked since a lowercase *a* comes after an uppercase *X.* The W3C specification provides some details on how comparisons are supposed to work. For details, see the article at www.w3.org/TR/IndexedDB/#key-construct.

Now you'll need to call this function after the animation is completed. Add the following line of code to the makeNextMove() function after the "Checkmate!" text is displayed:

```
displayCapturedPieces();
```

Save your changes and press F5 to start the application. After the animation has finished, you should see the alert shown in Figure 11-6.

The following pieces were captured:
- black pawn

OK

Figure 11-6. *Listing the captured pieces*

Summary

In this chapter, you took a crash course in Indexed DB. Through a fairly simple application, you utilized most of the capabilities of this new technology. Probably the biggest challenge is to get used to the asynchronous processing. The sample application provides lots of examples of nesting successive calls through the onsuccess event handler. The following are some of the key concepts to remember:

- Create the database and create its structure by responding to the onupgradeneeded event handler when the database is opened. Use the version to force an upgrade, if necessary.

- Objects in a store must have a unique key, which can be defined either by a key path for in-line keys or by a key generator for out-of-line keys. You can also supply the key manually when the object is added, but that's not generally a practical solution.

- All data access (read and write) must be done through a transaction object. When creating the transaction, you must specify the scope, which is the list of object stores that it will use as well as the type of access that is required.

- You can add one or more indices to an object store. Each index maps a key path in the object to the object's key.

- Use a cursor to process multiple objects in an object store. The objects that are selected can be filtered by specifying a key range.

- Add an object to the object store and update it later.

- Retrieve an object from an object store.

- Delete an object from an object store by specifying the object's key.

- Obtain the key for an object by using the getKey() method of the index.

- Use the put() method of an object store to add or update an object. The put() method requires both the objects and the key. This will add the object if the specified key is not found.

There is a lot that you can do with Indexed DB. Because the data is on the client, you avoid round-trips to the server.

CHAPTER 12

■ ■ ■

Geolocation and Mapping

This chapter will demonstrate two technologies that provide powerful features that enable you to easily create some useful web sites. Geolocation provides a standardized API that is used to determine the client's location. Mapping technology adds the ability to display this location on a map along with other points of interest. Together, these form a platform that has many useful applications.

In this chapter, you'll use the geolocation API to find your current position. The accuracy of that position will vary greatly depending on available hardware and the environment. However, HTML5 defines a standard API that is used on all devices so you can provide device-independent solutions.

Just knowing your location in terms of latitude and longitude is not very helpful. To put this data to use, you'll use the Bing Maps API to display that location on a map. Then you can map additional points of interest and see them in relation to your current location.

Understanding Geolocation

While not technically part of the HTML5 specification, the WC3 has defined a standard API for accessing geolocation information, which is supported by all major current browser versions. The technology that determines the location, however, varies greatly depending on the device capabilities and the client's environment.

Surveying Geolocation Technologies

Several technologies can be used to determine the current location, including the following:

- *Global positioning system (GPS)*: GPS communicates with satellites to determine the current location with extremely high accuracy, particularly in rural areas. Tall buildings in an urban area can affect the accuracy, but in most cases GPS provides good results. The biggest limitation is that this doesn't work indoors well. To use GPS, the device must have specific GPS hardware, but this is becoming increasingly common on mobile devices.

- *Wi-Fi positioning*: Wi-Fi networks have a relatively short range and systems such as Skyhook Wireless maintain a large database of Wi-Fi networks and their locations. Simply being connected to a Wi-Fi network will give a pretty good idea of where you are. Often, however, you may be within range of multiple networks, and the system can use triangulation to determine the location with even greater accuracy. Of course, this requires that you have a device that is Wi-Fi enabled, and it doesn't work in rural areas where there are no Wi-Fi networks.

- *Cell tower triangulation*: This uses the same principle as Wi-Fi positioning except it uses cellular telephone towers. It is not as accurate, however, because a cell tower has a much larger range. Since all cell phones will have the ability to communicate with cell towers, this technology has a broad application.

- *IP block*: Every device that connects to the Internet will have an IP address, which is usually provided by the ISP. Each ISP will have a block of IP addresses that it can use, which are typically assigned by geographical location. So, the IP address with which you connect to the Internet can provide a general location, usually a metropolitan area. There are several factors, however, that can yield incorrect results, such as NAT'ed addresses.

Each of these technologies has different hardware requirements and provide varying levels of accuracy. With the geolocation specification, you can easily request the current location from the browser and let it determine the best way to supply that based on the current hardware and access to external sources including satellites, cell towers, and Wi-Fi networks.

Using Geolocation Data

Most people think of geolocation as a device that provides turn-by-turn directions, but that is only one application of this technology. Of course, this requires precise location that can be obtained only through GPS. However, even when the current location is far less accurate, your web site can still make valuable use of this information. Even if the location is determined only by the IP address, this will usually be sufficient to set the default language, for example. You may need to allow the end user to override this, but most of your audience will see the initial page in their native language.

When retrieving the current location, the geolocation service also returns the estimated accuracy. Your application should use this to determine the features that will be provided. Suppose, for example, that you're creating a web page for the U.S. Postal Service that shows where the nearest post offices are. If the current location is known with high accuracy, the web page can show a map and indicate the current location as well as the nearby post offices. In addition, it could provide the estimated driving time to each.

However, if the location is known with lesser accuracy, the page could display a map that shows where the post offices are in that general area. Presumably, the user will know where they are and can use this information to determine the best location to use. However, if the accuracy is poor, the page should prompt for a ZIP code and then display the nearest post offices based on the user input. So, depending on the accuracy, the application can gracefully degrade the functionality.

Using the Geolocation API

To demonstrate how to use the geolocation API, you'll create a simple web page that calls the API to determine your current location. Initially, this data will be displayed on the web page as text. Later you'll display this location on a map.

Creating the Visual Studio Project

You'll start by creating a Visual Studio project using the same Empty template that you used in previous chapters.

EXERCISE 12-1. CREATING THE VISUAL STUDIO PROJECT

1. Start Visual Studio 2015 and click the New Project link from the Start page.

2. In the New project dialog box, select the ASP.NET Web Application template. Select a location for this project and enter the project name **Chapter12**.

3. In the next dialog box, select the ASP.NET 5 Empty template. Click the OK button and the project will be created.

4. Open the Startup.cs file and comment out the implementation of the Configure() method as you did in previous projects.

5. Right-click the new wwwroot folder and click the Add and New Item links. In the Add New Item dialog box, select the HTML page, enter the name **Index.html**, and click the Add button.

6. In the Index.html file, add the following div element inside the empty body that was created:

```
<div style="width:800px; height:50px;">
    <span id="lbl"> </span>
</div>
```

Using the Geolocation Object

The geolocation API is provided by the geolocation object, which you can access through the navigator object like this:

```
navigator.geolocation
```

If a falsy value is returned such as null or undefined, then geolocation is not supported on the current browser. You can check for support using code like this:

```
if (!navigator.geolocation) {
    alert("Geolocation is not supported");
}
else
    // do something with geolocation
```

To get the current location, use the getCurrentPosition() function, which takes three parameters:

- A callback function that is executed when the call is successful

- An error callback function that is called when an error occurs

- A PositionOptions collection that contains zero or more options

The last two parameters can be omitted. The following options are supported:

- maximumAge: The browser can cache previous positions and return this without actually trying to determine the location. However, the maximumAge attribute specifies how long (in milliseconds) a previous position can be reused without re-querying the current location.

- timeout: The timeout attribute specifies how long the browser should wait for a response from the geolocation object. This is also expressed in milliseconds.

- enableHighAccuracy: This is just a hint to the browser. If you don't need greater accuracy for a particular purpose, setting this to false may yield a faster response or use less power, which is a consideration for mobile devices.

If the call was successful, the position is passed to the callback function that was specified. The Position object includes a coords object that contains the following required properties:

- latitude (specified in degrees)
- longitude (specified in degrees)
- accuracy (specified in meters)

In addition, the following optional properties may be provided depending on the environment and the available hardware. If these are not supported, they will be set to null. (The optional properties are typically available only when GPS is used.)

- altitude (specified in meters)
- altitudeAccuracy (specified in meters)
- heading (specified in degrees; north = 0, west = 90, and so on)
- speed (specified in meters/second, NaN if stationary)

These properties can be obtained by the callback function like this:

```
function successCallback(pos) {
    var lat = pos.coords.latitude;
    var long = pos.coords.longitude;
    var accuracy =  pos.coords.accuracy + " meters";
}
```

If the call was not successful, the PositionError object is passed to the error callback function. This object includes a code property and a message property. The error code will have one of three possible values.

- 1: PERMISSION_DENIED
- 2: POSITION_UNAVAILABLE
- 3: TIMEOUT

▓ **Caution**   Your application will get the location and simply display it (and later map it). However, your script could easily pass this information back to the server, which is a potential privacy issue. Since the browser cannot control what the client does with this information, for privacy reasons the browser may block the access to the geolocation object. In this case, the PERMISSION_DENIED error code is returned. I will demonstrate this later.

If the client is moving and you want to continuously monitor the current location, you could call the getCurrentLocation() function repeatedly using a setInterval() function. To simplify this, the geolocation object includes a watchPosition() function. This takes the same three parameters as the getCurrentLocation() function (success callback, error callback, and options). The callback function is then invoked whenever the position changes. The watchPosition() function returns a timer handle. You can pass this handle to the clearWatch() function when you want to stop monitoring the position like this:

```
var handle = geolocation.watchPosition(callback);
...
geolocation.clearWatch(handle);
```

Displaying the Location

Now you'll add code to your application to get the current location and display it. The web page has a span element with an id of lbl. You'll get the geolocation object and call its getCurrentLocation() function. Both the success and error callback functions will display the appropriate results in the span element.

```
EXERCISE 12-2. DISPLAYING THE LOCATION
```

1.   Add the script element shown in Listing 12-1 to the end of the body element.

Listing 12-1.   Displaying the Location

```
<script type="text/javascript">

    var lbl = document.getElementById("lbl");

    if (navigator.geolocation) {
        navigator.geolocation
            .getCurrentPosition(showLocation,
                                errorHandler,
                                {
                                    maximumAge: 100,
                                    timeout: 6000,
                                    enableHighAccuracy: true
                                });
    }
    else {
        alert("Geolocation not suported");
    }
```

```
function showLocation(pos) {
    lbl.innerHTML =
        "Your latitude: " + pos.coords.latitude +
        " and longitude: " + pos.coords.longitude +
        " (Accuracy of: " +  pos.coords.accuracy + " meters)";

}

function errorHandler(e) {
    if (e.code === 1) { // PERMISSION_DENIED
        lbl.innerHTML = "Permission denied. - " + e.message;
    } else if (e.code === 2) { //POSITION_UNAVAILABLE
        lbl.innerHTML = "Make sure your network connection is active and " +
            "try this again. - " + e.message;
    } else if (e.code === 3) { //TIMEOUT
        lbl.innerHTML = "A timeout ocurred; try again. - " + e.message;
    }
}

</script>
```

2. Press F5 to start the application. The first time a site tries to access the geolocation object, you will get a prompt like the one shown in Figure 12-1.

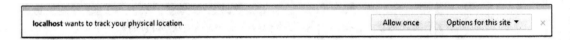

Figure 12-1. *Prompting for geolocation access*

■ **Note** I'm using IE 11 for this demonstration. If you're using a different browser, this prompt may work a little differently.

---

3. To test the error handler, expand the "Options for this site" drop-down and select the "Always deny and don't tell me" option. The page should display an error message like the one shown in Figure 12-2.

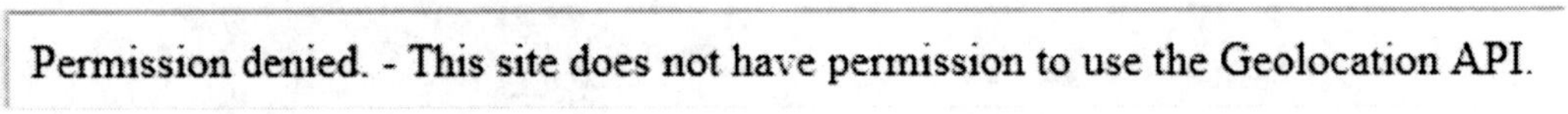

Permission denied. - This site does not have permission to use the Geolocation API.

Figure 12-2. *Displaying the access denied error*

4. Once you have set this option, IE will no longer prompt you anymore but will always deny the access. To clear this, select the Tools menu and then select Internet Options. In the middle of the Privacy tab there are options to control the geolocation access. Click the Clear Sites button shown in Figure 12-3.

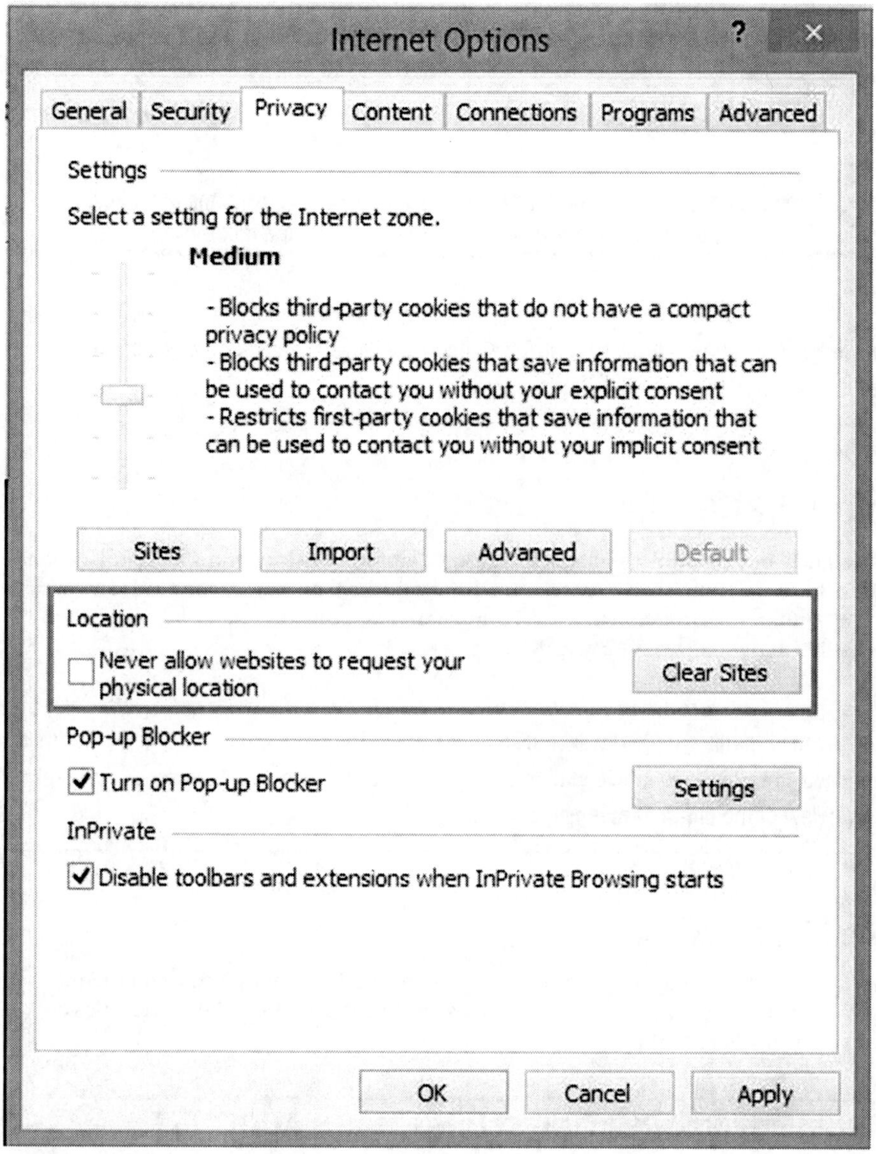

Figure 12-3. *Clearing the site access choices*

5. Click the OK button to close this dialog box. Refresh the web page. It should now prompt you again. This time select the "Always allow" option. Your current location should be displayed as shown in Figure 12-4.

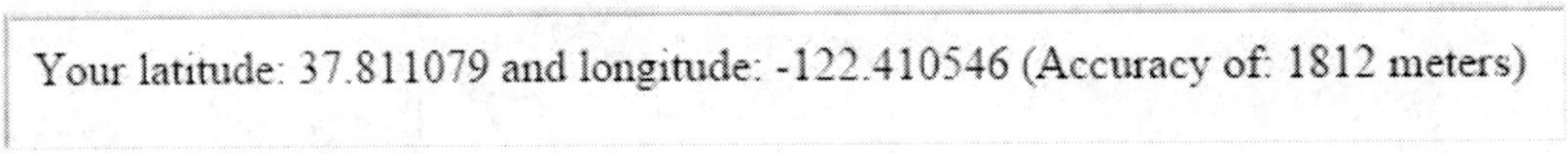

Your latitude: 37.811079 and longitude: -122.410546 (Accuracy of: 1812 meters)

Figure 12-4. *Displaying the current location*

I'm using a normal LAN-connected machine without cell or GPS support, so it is using the IP address to determine the location. Consequently, the accuracy estimate is 1.8km (just over a mile).

■ **Note** Geolocation works on all current browsers. However, if you try this application on an older browser such as IE 8, you'll see the alert that geolocation is not supported.

Using Mapping Platforms

Simply displaying the latitude and longitude is not interesting (or helpful). However, showing your location relative to other points of interest is much more useful. And displaying them on a map with roads and other reference points can really put this information to work. Fortunately, mapping technology has become so sophisticated and accessible that this is really easy to do.

■ **Note** For the demonstration in this chapter I will be using Bing Maps. There are other mapping platforms available. If you're interested, check out the article at http://en.wikipedia.org/wiki/Comparison_of_web_ map_services for an overview of the different mapping services.

Creating a Bing Maps Account

To use Bing Maps, you'll need to first set up an account, which is free for developers. Once your account is created, you'll receive a key that you'll need to include when accessing the mapping API. I will take you through the process of setting up an account.

EXERCISE 12-3. CREATING A BING MAPS ACCOUNT

1. Go to the Bing Maps site at this address: www.microsoft.com/maps/create-a-bing-maps-key.aspx.

2. You need to get a key that will allow you to access the mapping API. Go to the Basic Key tab. A free, basic key is fine for working through these exercises. Click the Get the Basic Key link near the bottom of the page.

3. In the next page, you'll need to log in with a Windows Live ID. If you don't have one, click the Create button to create an account.

4. Once you have signed in, you should see the "Create account" page shown in Figure 12-5.

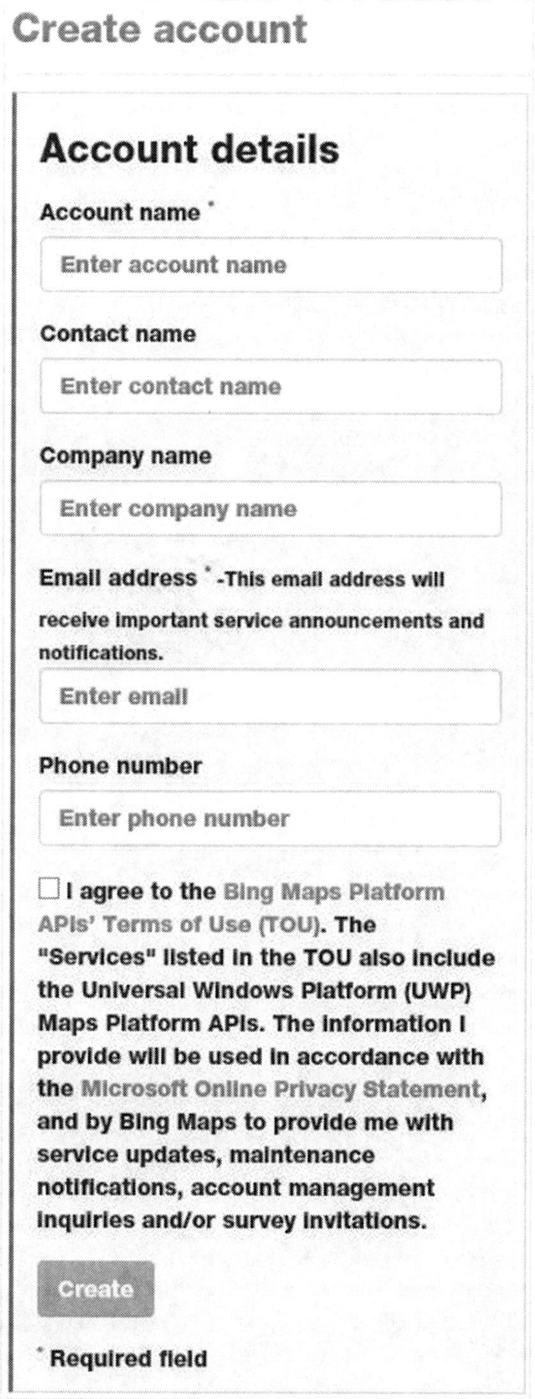

Create account

Account details

Account name *

Enter account name

Contact name

Enter contact name

Company name

Enter company name

Email address * -This email address will receive important service announcements and notifications.

Enter email

Phone number

Enter phone number

☐ **I agree to the** Bing Maps Platform APIs' Terms of Use (TOU). **The "Services" listed in the TOU also include the Universal Windows Platform (UWP) Maps Platform APIs. The information I provide will be used in accordance with the** Microsoft Online Privacy Statement, **and by Bing Maps to provide me with service updates, maintenance notifications, account management inquiries and/or survey invitations.**

Create

* **Required field**

Figure 12-5. *The "Create account" page*

5. Enter an account name. This is just for you to identify it if you have multiple accounts; *Testing* is fine. The e-mail address should default in from your Windows Live account. Make sure you select the check box agreeing to the terms of use. Click the Save button to create the account.

6. From the My account menu, select the "Create or view keys" link. You probably won't have any existing keys shown. Click the link to create a new key.

7. In the "Create key" page, enter an application name such as **HTML5 Test**. For the URL, enter **http://localhost** and select Dev/Test for the application type, as shown in Figure 12-6. Enter the characters that are displayed at the bottom of the form and click the Submit button.

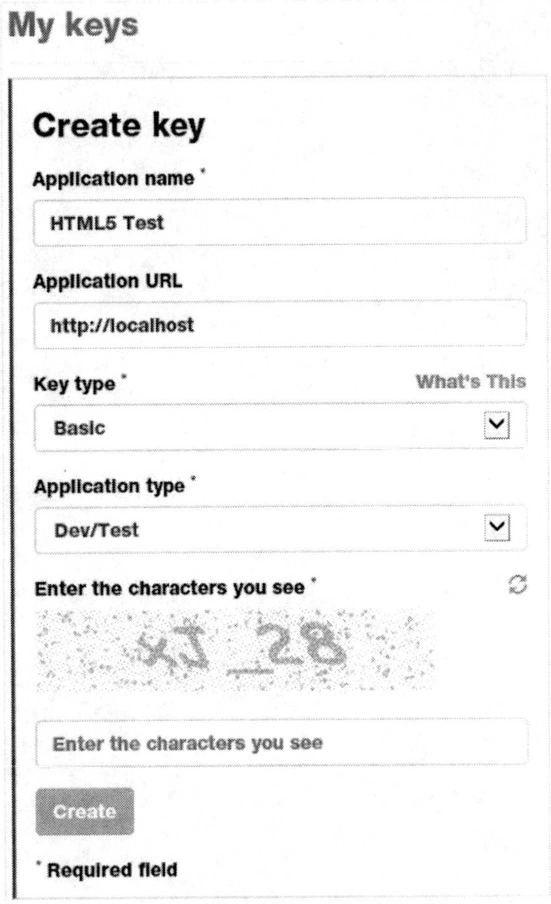

My keys

Create key

Application name *

    HTML5 Test

Application URL

    http://localhost

Key type *   What's This

    Basic   ⌄

Application type *

    Dev/Test   ⌄

Enter the characters you see *   ⟳

    XJ_28

    Enter the characters you see

    Create

* **Required field**

Figure 12-6. Creating a key

> ■ **Note** Bing Maps monitors the use of your key. However, since you're not actually deploying this to a public-facing web site, this is not really applicable. If you are developing a commercial application, you can use a free key for development purposes, but you will need to purchase a key for the live web site.

8. After the key has been generated, you should see it displayed on the page. Save this because you will need it later.

Adding a Map

Now you'll add a map to your web page. You'll first add a div to the page that will contain the map. You'll also need to add a reference to the Ajax script that is used to manipulate the map. Then you'll display the map, centering it on your current location.

EXERCISE 12-4. ADDING A MAP

---

1. Add the code shown in bold to the body element, which will add the div that the map will be displayed in.

```
<body>
    <div style="width:800px; height:50px;">
        <span id="lbl"> </span>
    </div>
    <div id="map" style="width:800px; height:600px;">

    </div>
```

2. Add the following reference inside the head element. This will enable your page to call the map API.

```
<script
    type="text/javascript"
    src="http://ecn.dev.virtualearth.net/mapcontrol/mapcontrol.ashx?v=7.0">
</script>
```

3. Add the following declaration at the top of the existing script element (inside the body element). This will store a reference to the map object.

```
var map = null;
```

4. Modify the showLocation() function, adding the code shown in bold in Listing 12-2. Enter your Bing Maps key where is says <use your key here>. The key should be enclosed in double quotes.

Listing 12-2. The Modified showLocation() Function

```
function showLocation(pos) {
    lbl.innerHTML =
        "Your latitude: " + pos.coords.latitude +
        " and longitude: " + pos.coords.longitude +
        " (Accuracy of: " +  pos.coords.accuracy + " meters)";

    // Save the current location
    var lat = pos.coords.latitude;
    var long = pos.coords.longitude;

    // Create the map
    map = new Microsoft.Maps.Map(document.getElementById("map"),
        { credentials:
            "<use your key here>" });

    // Center it on the current location
    map.setView({ zoom: 18, center: new Microsoft.Maps.Location(lat, long) });
}
```

5. Press F5 to start the application. Depending on your location, your page should look like Figure 12-7. Notice the controls at the top-left corner of the page. You can use this to zoom in or out and pan in any direction. The Automatic mode will switch to the satellite view if the map is zoomed in sufficiently.

Figure 12-7. Displaying the initial map

When calling the setView() function to specify the center location, this code also set the zoom to 18. Depending on your application, you may not want to zoom in that far initially. Try this code using 15 or 16 to see how that looks. Of course, the user can also adjust the zoom once the map is displayed.

Adding Pushpins

Now you'll display some pushpins on the map. To add a pushpin, you first create a Pushpin object, specifying its location. Then add it to the map's entities collection. First, you will add a default pushpin at the current location. Later, you'll add custom pushpins to indicate points of interest.

Add the following code shown in bold to the end of the showLocation() function:

```
// Center it on the current location
map.setView({ zoom: 18, center: new Microsoft.Maps.Location(lat, long) });

// Mark the current location
var pushpin = new Microsoft.Maps.Pushpin
    (new Microsoft.Maps.Location(lat, long), null);
map.entities.push(pushpin);
```

The lat and long variables contain the same values used to center the map. Press F5 to start the application. You should see a pushpin indicating the current location, as shown in Figure 12-8.

Figure 12-8. *Adding a pushpin in the current location*

One of the most common uses of maps in a web page is to show where there are nearby locations. For example, you might have multiple store locations, and you'll want to show where each one is. Or perhaps you are in a police department and want to map out where certain crimes have been committed. You could have a public transit system and want to show where all the bus or train stops are.

Each of these scenarios is basically the same; you have a collection of locations that you want to show on a map. You can add as many locations as you want. For each, just create a Pushpin object and add it to the entities collection. If you have more than one location, you should make the pushpins look different so the user can easily distinguish between them.

For this demonstration, you will indicate where there are nearby restrooms. Instead of a standard pushpin, you will use an image with a familiar restroom icon. Normally you would query the server to get a list of locations based on the where the client is. However, to simplify this exercise, these will be hard-coded.

■ **Caution**   I am hard-coding the location of the restrooms, which are probably nowhere near where your current location is. You can either provide different restroom locations that are near you or simply override your current location to match mine. This will be consistent with the restroom locations.

EXERCISE 12-5. ADDING CUSTOM PUSHPINS

1. In Solution Explorer, right-click the wwwroot folder project and click the Add and New Folder links. Enter the name **images**.

2. The source code download contains a restroom.gif image file. Drag this onto the wwwroot\images folder in Solution Explorer.

3. Add the following declaration at the top of the existing script element. This defines the locations of the restrooms.

```
var restrooms = [
    { lat: 37.810079, long: -122.410806 },
    { lat: 37.809079, long: -122.410206 },
    { lat: 37.811279, long: -122.410446 }
];
```

4. Add the following code to the showLocation() function just before creating the map object. This will override your current location to be near where the restrooms are.

```
// Override these for testing purposes
lat = 37.811079;
long = -122.410546;
```

5. Add the following functions to the end of the script element. The markRestrooms() function iterates through this array, calling the markRestroom() function for each. The markRestroom() function adds a single pushpin. This first creates an options collection that defines the image file to use as well as the size of the image. This is passed in when creating the Pushpin object.

```
function markRestrooms() {
    for (var i in restrooms) {
        markRestroom(restrooms[i].lat, restrooms[i].long);
    }
}

function markRestroom(lat, long) {
    var pushpinOptions = { icon: '/images/restroom.gif', width: 35, height: 35 };
    var pushpin = new Microsoft.Maps.Pushpin
        (new Microsoft.Maps.Location(lat, long), pushpinOptions);
    map.entities.push(pushpin); ()
}
```

6. Add this function call at the end of the showLocation() function to display the
    additional pushpins:

    ```
    // Display the restroom locations
    markRestrooms();
    ```

7. Press F5 to debug the application. You should now see pushpins where the
    restrooms are located, as shown in Figure 12-9.

Figure 12-9. *Adding the restroom pushpins()*

▓ **Caution** This is purely fictional data. If you happen to be at San Francisco's Pier 39 while reading this book, don't use this map to try to find a restroom.

There is a lot more that you can do with the mapping API. For example, you can display directions for getting to a selected point of interest. You can even display where the traffic is currently heavy. Check out the interactive SDK at `www.bingmapsportal.com/isdk/ajaxv7`. You can try each feature, and the corresponding JavaScript code is displayed underneath the map.

Summary

In this chapter, you combined the features of geolocation with Bing Maps to create a really useful web site. Geolocation requests are processed asynchronously. After getting the `geolocation` object, you call its `getCurrentPosition()` function and specify the success and error callback functions. The `Position` object is passed to the callback function when the location has been retrieved. It contains the latitude, longitude, and estimated accuracy. If the client has GPS capability, the `Position` object will also include the altitude, speed, and direction.

Mapping platforms such as Bing Maps are really easy to use and integrate into your web page. In this application, you displayed the map and centered in on the current location. You also added pushpins to show where the nearby restrooms are.

CHAPTER 13

■ ■ ■

WebSockets

As I explained in Chapter 1, the web application pulls data from a web server. The client initiates the transfer by sending a request to the server. The response is then rendered in the browser. All web application design is based on this request-response paradigm. However, websocket technology opens up a whole new world, allowing server-initiated communication with client applications.

Socket technology is not new. Sockets have been used for decades as an effective protocol for point-to-point communication between applications. The exciting news, however, is that the W3C has included a WebSocket API specification as part of the HTML5 umbrella. With a standard protocol defined and compatible browsers becoming available, you can expect to see more and more web applications taking advantage of this technology.

In this chapter you will build a solution that uses WebSockets to implement a multisession chat application that enables an agent to chat with several customers at the same time. This solution will include a WebSocket server hosted in a console app that you will create using C# .NET. To do this, you'll need to understand the WebSocket protocols, so I will first explain this technology and then show you how to create your own custom server. You will then implement both the agent and customer client applications utilizing the native WebSocket support in HTML5.

■ **Caution** As of this writing, the W3C specification was still in draft and changes are likely. It is perhaps a bit premature to jump into this wholeheartedly. However, since this is such a promising part of the HTML5 specification, I wanted to introduce you to WebSockets. Just be aware that things can change. You can check out the current status of the W3C specification at http://dev.w3.org/html5/websockets. All major current browsers support WebSockets.

Understanding WebSockets

Sockets provide a mechanism for two-way transmissions between applications, including peer-to-peer communication. WebSockets, as I will explain in this chapter, are a specific implementation of sockets that enable a web application to communicate with a web server. Figure 13-1 illustrates the messages passed between the browser and server. After a series of handshaking messages that establish the connection, both sides can send messages to each other.

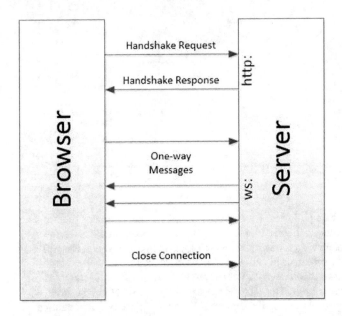

Figure 13-1. *The WebSockets messages*

■ **Tip** While WebSockets do not provide peer-to-peer communication, as you'll see later in this chapter, the server can be implemented to route messages from one client to another. Client A can send a message to the server, which is simply forwarded to Client B. This emulates peer-to-peer messaging while providing control of the routing.

Completing a Handshake

There is a fair amount of handshaking and protocol manipulation that is required to make WebSockets work. Fortunately, the browser implements the client-side protocol for you, making it really easy to write applications that use WebSockets. The handshaking messages use the HTTP protocol. Once the connection has been established, the subsequent messages are sent using the WebSocket protocol.

■ **Note** Several protocol versions have been proposed and implemented by various browsers. The current version (as of this writing) is version 13, which all of the major browsers support. You can review the specification of the version 13 protocol at https://tools.ietf.org/html/rfc6455.

The process starts when the browser sends a handshake request to the server. The handshake request will consist of multiple lines of text that will be similar to this:

```
GET /chat HTTP/1.1
Upgrade: websocket
Connection: Upgrade
```

```
Host: localhost:8100
Origin: http://localhost:29781
Sec-WebSocket-Key: <request key>
Sec-WebSocket-Version: 13
```

The request includes information about the address of the client and the protocol that it supports. You can see in this example that 13 is specified for Sec-WebSocket-Version. A request key is generated by the browser and will be different each time a connection request is made.

In return, the server will return a response like this:

```
HTTP/1.1 101 Switching Protocols
Upgrade: websocket
Connection: Upgrade
Sec-WebSocket-Accept: <response key>
```

The response key is generated by the server and is based on the request key that was specified. I will explain the algorithm for this later in the chapter.

Building WebSocket Frames

Once the handshaking is complete and the protocols have been negotiated, messages can be exchanged between the client and the server. These messages are sent using the WebSocket protocol. Messages are always one-way; no response is required. Of course, you can send a response, but that is just another one-way message in the opposite direction. Both endpoints are always listening for messages.

A message is sent as a frame. The frame consists of a series of bytes that indicate how the message should be processed. The remainder of the message contains the actual data being sent, which is often referred to as the payload. Figure 13-2 shows the layout of the frame.

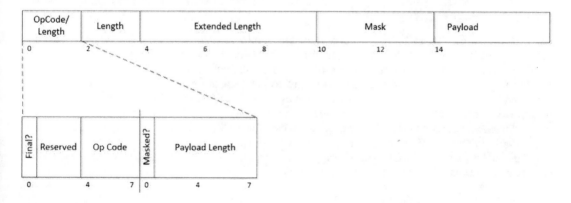

Figure 13-2. The WebSocket frame

The initial portion of the frame consists of up to 14 bytes. The first two bytes will be used on all frames. The first bit indicates whether this is the final frame. A message can be transmitted in multiple frames, and this bit should be set on the last frame to signal the message is complete. The next three bits are reserved for future use. The last half of the first byte contains an opcode that specifies what type of message this is. The values 0x3–0x7 and 0xB–0xF are reserved for future control frames, but the following values are currently defined:

- 0x0 indicates this is a continuation frame.

- 0x1 specifies the payload contains text.

- 0x2 indicates a binary payload.

- 0x8 indicates the connection is being closed.

- 0x9 specifies the message is a ping.

- 0xA specifies the message is a pong.

The first bit of the second byte indicates that masking is used. I will describe masking later. The remainder of the byte specifies the payload length. For payloads less than 126 bytes, the length is specified here. However, if the length is between 126 and 32,183, the length is set to 126, and the actual length is provided in the next two bytes. For messages longer than that, the length is set to 127, and the actual length is specified in the next eight bytes. So, depending on how long the message is, the frame will contain between 0 and 8 extra bytes.

The next four bytes contain the masking key. This is omitted if masking is not used. After that comes the actual payload.

For a simple, unmasked message containing the text *Hello*, the frame would contain the following bytes:

```
0x81, 0x05, 0x48, 0x65, 0x6c, 0x6c, 0x6f
```

The first byte, 0x81, in binary is 10000001. The first bit is set indicating this is the final frame, and the last bit is set to indicate the payload contains text. The next byte specifies a payload length of five characters, which follow immediately. The remaining five bytes contain the *H, e, l, l,* and *o* characters.

Unmasking a Frame

For security reasons, all frames from the client should be masked. *Masking* is a simple encoding scheme that uses a masking key that is different with each frame. The browser will take care of this for you; however, the server will need to unmask the data. Frames sent to the client should not be masked.

The masking key is provided in the four bytes directly following the length. The masking key is randomly generated by the client. To unmask the data, for each byte in the payload, the XOR operator is applied to the byte and the corresponding byte in the masking key. The first payload byte is XOR'ed with the first byte of the masking key, the second byte is XOR'ed with the second byte of the mask, and so on. The fifth byte is the XOR'ed with the first byte of the mask.

This can be done with the following C# expression. This assumes that payload[ ] contains an array of masked data and mask[ ] contains the 4-byte masking key.

```
for (int i = 0; i < length; i++)
{
    payload[i] = (byte)(payload[i] ^ masks[i % 4]);
}
```

The i % 4 expression gets the appropriate masking byte, and the ^ operator performs the XOR operation. After processing all of the bytes, the payload[ ] array will contain the unmasked data.

WebSocket Servers

To use WebSockets, you will need to provide an application that will implement the server-side protocol. I will show you how to build your own using .NET and hosted in a console application. As you are probably expecting, there is a bit of bit and byte manipulation necessary (no pun intended).

■ **Note**   There are a number of open source WebSocket server implementations. This article provides links to several of these that you might want to consider for future reference: `http://stackoverflow.com/questions/1530023/do-i-need-a-server-to-use-html5s-websockets`. These are implemented on various platforms including JavaScript and PHP. Many of them support multiple protocols.

To create a WebSocket server, you will first implement the following capabilities:

- Connection handshaking
- Listening for messages
- Decoding WebSocket frames
- Building and sending a message frame

Once the basic infrastructure is complete, you'll then provide the custom server features needed for your application. After all, the whole point of WebSockets is to allow the server to communicate with the client.

Designing the Agent Chat Application

In this chapter, you'll build a server and two client applications that will allow agents to chat with multiple clients simultaneously. An agent will log in and connect to the server using the agent web application, letting the server know that the agent is ready to accept chat sessions. The agent application will be designed to handle up to four simultaneous chat sessions. Clients can then use the client web application to connect to the server. Each client is routed to an available agent, and the chat session is started. From this point, the server is just forwarding messages between the client and the agent. Figure 13-3 describes this communication.

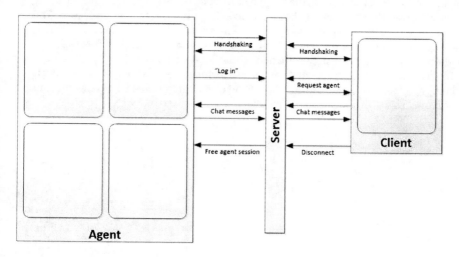

Figure 13-3. The WebSocket communication

To connect as an agent, the system will want to provide some authentication to ensure only authorized users can respond to clients. To simulate that, the agent application will use the standard ASP.NET web form that provides a login capability. You'll then add a custom chat page that will allow the agent to respond to four simultaneous chat sessions. However, anyone should be able to connect as a client so you'll use the Empty template that you've used in previous chapters.

Both applications will connect to the WebSocket server using the normal handshaking protocol. Once connected, the agent will send a message to the server that includes their name. This will signal the server that a new agent has come online. The agent's connection will be saved in a collection for future use.

The client application will also send a message to the server after the connection has been established, specifying the name of the client. The server will then find the first available agent that has an open chat session and send a message to that agent, providing the client's name. The agent page will then save the client's name on the page. At the same time, the server will send a message to the client, letting them know that an agent has been assigned to them.

At this point both the client and agent can send a message to the server, which is forwarded to the other application. Since the agent application can have four active sessions, the server will prefix the message with the client number so the agent application will know which session to update.

If the client disconnects, the server will send a message to the agent letting them know that. The agent application will then clear the corresponding chat session. If the agent disconnects, all the clients with active sessions with that agent are also notified and instructed to attempt a re-connect.

Creating a Simple Application

In this section you'll build a WebSocket server that handles the basic message protocols and test it using a simple web client. Initially, the server will just echo the message back to the client. You'll later add the functionality needed by the chat application. For this exercise, the server will be hosted in a console application.

Creating a WebSocket Server

To implement the WebSocket server, you will create a WsServer class. This class creates a socket that it uses to listen for new connections. When a connection is received, it creates another socket for that connection and performs the handshaking that I described earlier. If the handshaking is successful, it creates an instance of a WsConnection class that will manage the client connection.

The WsConnection class uses the new socket to listen for incoming messages on that connection. This class invokes the ReadMessage() method to process an incoming message. This handles all of the frame decoding and unmasking that may be required. The WsConnection class also provides a SendMessage() method that will send a message to the client at the other end of the connection.

The WsConnection class provides two events that are raised if handlers are provided. The first event is raised when an incoming message has been received. The second event is raised when the connection has been closed. The WsServer class will provide the event handlers for these events.

EXERCISE 13-1. CREATING A SIMPLE WEBSOCKET SERVER

1. Start Visual Studio 2015 and create a new project named **WsServer**. Select the Console Application template from the Windows category. Change the solution name to **Chapter13**, as shown in Figure 13-4.

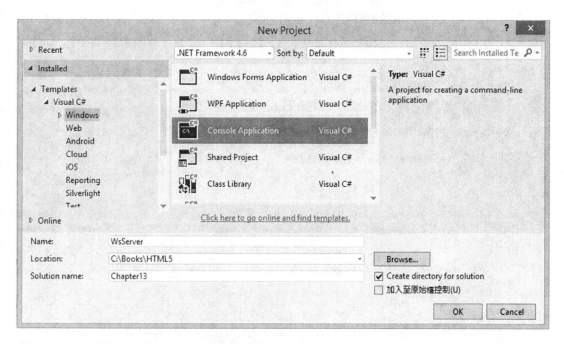

Figure 13-4. *Creating a console application project*

2. In Solution Explorer, right-click the WsServer project and click the Add and Class links. Enter **WsServer.cs** for the class name.

3. Enter the code shown in Listing 13-1 for the initial implementation of this class.

    Listing 13-1. Implementing the WsServer Class

    ```
    using System;
    using System.Collections.Generic;
    using System.Text;

    using System.Net;
    using System.Net.Sockets;
    using System.IO;
    using System.Security.Cryptography;
    ```

```
namespace WsServer
{
    public class WsServer
    {
        #region Members

        // This socket listens for new connections
        Socket _listener;

        // Configurable port # that is passed in the constructor
        int _port;

        // List of connections
        List<WsConnection> _unknown;

        #endregion Members

        public WsServer(int port)
        {
            _port = port;

            // This is a list of active connections
            _unknown = new List<WsConnection>();
        }

        public void StartSocketServer()
        {
            try
            {
                // Create a socket that will listen for messages
                _listener = new Socket(AddressFamily.InterNetwork,
                                       SocketType.Stream,
                                       ProtocolType.IP);

                // Create and bind the endpoint
                IPEndPoint ip = new IPEndPoint(IPAddress.Loopback, _port);
                _listener.Bind(ip);

                // Listen for new connections - the OnConnect() method
                // will be invoked to handle them
                _listener.Listen(100);
                _listener.BeginAccept(new AsyncCallback(OnConnect), null);
            }
            catch (Exception ex)
            {
            }
        }

        void MessageReceived(WsConnection sender, MessageReceivedEventArgs e)
        {
            string msg = e.Message;
            sender.SendMessage("echo: " + msg);
        }
```

```
            void Disconnected(WsConnection sender, EventArgs e)
            {
                _unknown.Remove(sender);
            }
        }
    }
```

The StartSocketServer() method is called to put the server to work. It creates a Socket object and configures it using the specified port. This method is hard-coded to use the localhost address. Once the end point is configured, the Socket object's BeginAccept() method is called. This will invoke the specified callback method (OnConnect) when a new connection is received. The OnConnect() function is called asynchronously. You'll later provide its implementation, which will call the EndAccept() function to tie up the loose ends. The MessageReceived() event handler simply writes the input message to the console and echoes the message back to the client. The WsConnection object that manages this connection is passed to the event handler. This code uses its SendMessage() method to send an echo back. The Disconnected() event handler removes this connection from its active list and displays a message to the console window.

4. Add the PerformHandshake() method using the code shown in Listing 13-2.

Listing 13-2. Implementing the Handshaking Protocol

```
private void PerformHandshake(Socket s)
{
    using (NetworkStream stream = new NetworkStream(s))
    using (StreamReader reader = new StreamReader(stream))
    using (StreamWriter writer = new StreamWriter(stream))
    {
        string key = "";

        // Read the input data using the stream reader, one line
        // at a time until all lines have been processed. The only
        // item that we need to get is the request key.
        string input = "Empty";
        while (!string.IsNullOrWhiteSpace(input))
        {
            input = reader.ReadLine();

            if (input != null &&
                input.Length > 18 &&
                input.Substring(0, 18) == "Sec-WebSocket-Key:")
                // Save the request key
                key = input.Substring(19);
        }
        // This guid is used to generate the response key
        const String keyGuid = "258EAFA5-E914-47DA-95CA-C5AB0DC85B11";
        string webSocketAccept;

        // The response key in generated by concatenating the request
        // key and the special guid. The result is then encrypted.
        string ret = key + keyGuid;
        SHA1 sha = new SHA1CryptoServiceProvider();
        byte[] sha1Hash = sha.ComputeHash(Encoding.UTF8.GetBytes(ret));
        webSocketAccept = Convert.ToBase64String(sha1Hash);
```

```
                     // Send handshake response to the client using the
                     // stream writer
                     writer.WriteLine("HTTP/1.1 101 Switching Protocols");
                     writer.WriteLine("Upgrade: websocket");
                     writer.WriteLine("Connection: Upgrade");
                     writer.WriteLine("Sec-WebSocket-Accept: " + webSocketAccept);
                     writer.WriteLine("");
              }
       }
```

The PerformHandshake() method creates a NetworkStream object passing in the Socket object to its constructor. This is the new socket that was created for this connection. It uses a StreamReader object to read the incoming data and later uses a StreamWriter to send data back. By creating these inside nested using statements, you won't have to worry about disposing them. Keep in mind that the handshaking is done using the HTTP protocol, so the act of reading and sending data does not use the WebSocket frames.

The StreamReader object is used to read the input, one line at a time. You don't need any of this data because, for this exercise, you're assuming the correct protocol is being requested. In a more general case, however, you may need to support multiple protocols, so you will need to read and interpret what is being sent in. You will need the request key, however, so this is extracted from the appropriate input line.

The response key is then concatenated with a special guid value. This is documented in the version 13 specification (https://tools.ietf.org/html/rfc6455). The resulting string is then hashed using the SHA1 algorithm. Finally, the StreamWriter object is used to send the response, including the generated key.

    5.   Add the OnConnect() event handler using the code in Listing 13-3.

Listing 13-3. Implementing the OnConnect() Event Handler

```
private void OnConnect(IAsyncResult asyn)
{
       // create a new socket for the connection
       Socket socket = _listener.EndAccept(asyn);

       // Perform the necessary handshaking
       PerformHandshake(socket);

       // Create a WsConnection object for this connection
       WsConnection client = new WsConnection(socket);
       _unknown.Add(client);

       // Wire-up the event handlers
       client.MessageReceived += new MessageReceivedEventHandler(MessageReceived);
       client.Disconnected += new WsDisconnectedEventHandler(Disconnected);

       // Listen for more connections
       _listener.BeginAccept(new AsyncCallback(OnConnect), null);
}
```

The OnConnect() method gets a new Socket for this connection by calling the EndAccept() method. It calls the PerformHandshake() method and creates a WsConnection class, which you will implement next. It then connects the event handlers so the WsServer object will be notified when a message is received or the connection is closed. Finally, BeginAccept() is called again to listen for more connections.

6. In Solution Explorer, right-click the WsServer project and click the Add and Class
links. Enter **WsConnection.cs** for the class name.

7. Enter the code shown in Listing 13-4 as the initial implementation for this class.

Listing 13-4. Implementing the WsConnection Class

```
using System;
using System.Text;

using System.Net.Sockets;

namespace WsServer
{
    // This class defines the data that is passed to the MessageReceived
    // event handler
    public class MessageReceivedEventArgs
    {
        public string Message { get; private set; }
        public int DataLength { get; private set; }
        public MessageReceivedEventArgs(string msg, int len)
        {
            DataLength = len;
            Message = msg;
        }
    }

    // Define the event handler delegates
    public delegate void MessageReceivedEventHandler
        (WsConnection sender, MessageReceivedEventArgs e);

    public delegate void WsDisconnectedEventHandler
        (WsConnection sender, EventArgs e);

    public class WsConnection : IDisposable
    {
        #region Members

        public Socket _mySocket;
        protected byte[] _inputBuffer;
        protected StringBuilder _inputString;

        // Define the events that are available
        public event MessageReceivedEventHandler MessageReceived;
        public event WsDisconnectedEventHandler Disconnected;

        #endregion Members

        public WsConnection(Socket s)
        {
            _mySocket = s;
            _inputBuffer = new byte[255];
            _inputString = new StringBuilder();
```

```
                        // Begin listening - the ReadMessage() method will be
                        // invoked when a message is received.
                        _mySocket.BeginReceive(_inputBuffer,
                                            0,
                                            _inputBuffer.Length,
                                            0,
                                            ReadMessage,
                                            null);
            }

            protected void OnMessageReceived(string msg)
            {
                // When a message is received, call the event handler if
                // one has been specified
                if (MessageReceived != null)
                    MessageReceived(this, new MessageReceivedEventArgs(msg, msg.
Length));
            }

            public void Dispose()
            {
                _mySocket.Close();
            }
        }
    }
```

The WsConnection class has three class members.

- **_mySocket:** The Socket object created for this connection. This is instantiated by the WsServer class and passed into the constructor.

- **_inputBuffer:** This is a byte array that holds the raw frame data. This is populated by the Socket object.

- **_inputString:** This is a StringBuilder object that contains the incoming message after it has been processed.

The WsConnection class supports two events that notify when important events occur.

- **MessageReceived:** Raised when a message has been received

- **WsDisconnected:** Raised when the socket has disconnected

The MessageReceived event uses a MessageReceivedEventArgs class to provide the received message to the event handler. The WsConnection class also implements the Dispose() method, which simply closes the socket associated with this connection.

The WsConnection class has two primary methods, which you'll implement now. These methods implement the WebSocket frame protocol.

- ReadMessage()

- SendMessage()

8. Add the ReadMessage() method using the code shown in Listing 13-5.

Listing 13-5. Implementing the ReadMessage() Method

```
protected void ReadMessage(IAsyncResult msg)
{
    int sizeOfReceivedData = _mySocket.EndReceive(msg);
    if (sizeOfReceivedData > 0)
    {
        // Get the data provided in the first 2 bytes
        bool final = (_inputBuffer[0] & 0x80) > 0 ? true : false;
        bool masked = (_inputBuffer[1] & 0x80) > 0 ? true : false;
        int dataLength = _inputBuffer[1] & 0x7F;

        int actualLength;
        int dataIndex = 0;
        byte[] length = new byte[8];
        byte[] masks = new byte[4];

        // Depending on the initial data length, get the actual length
        // and the maskingkey from the appropriate bytes.
        if (dataLength == 126)
        {
            dataIndex = 4;
            Array.Copy(_inputBuffer, 2, length, 0, 2);
            actualLength = BitConverter.ToInt16(length, 0);

            if (masked)
                Array.Copy(_inputBuffer, 4, masks, 0, 4);
        }
        else if (dataLength == 127)
        {
            dataIndex = 10;
            Array.Copy(_inputBuffer, 2, length, 0, 8);
            actualLength = (int)BitConverter.ToInt64(length, 0);
            if (masked)
                Array.Copy(_inputBuffer, 10, masks, 0, 4);
        }
        else
        {
            dataIndex = 2;
            actualLength = dataLength;
            if (masked)
                Array.Copy(_inputBuffer, 2, masks, 0, 4);
        }

        // If a mask is supplied, skip another 4 bytes
        if (masked)
            dataIndex += 4;

        // Get the actual data in the payload array
        byte[] payload = new byte[actualLength];
        Array.Copy(_inputBuffer, dataIndex, payload, 0, dataLength);
```

```
                    // Unmask the data, if necessary
                    if (masked)
                    {
                        for (int i = 0; i < actualLength; i++)
                        {
                            payload[i] = (byte)(payload[i] ^ masks[i % 4]);
                        }
                    }

                    // Copy the data into the input string and empty the buffer
                    _inputString.Append(Encoding.UTF8
                        .GetString(payload, 0, (int)actualLength));
                    Array.Clear(_inputBuffer, 0, _inputBuffer.Length);

                    // If this is the final frame, raise an event and clear the input
                    if (final)
                    {
                        // Do something with the data
                        OnMessageReceived(_inputString.ToString());

                        // Clear the input string
                        _inputString.Clear();
                    }

                    // Listen for more messages
                    try
                    {
                        _mySocket.BeginReceive(_inputBuffer,
                                               0,
                                               _inputBuffer.Length,
                                               0,
                                               ReadMessage,
                                               null);
                    }
                    catch (Exception ex)
                    {
                    }
                }
                // If we were not able to read the message, assume that
                // the socket is closed
                else
                {
                }
            }
```

ReadMessage() processes a single incoming frame. It looks at the first two bytes to determine where the length is specified and whether masking is used. It then gets the actual length and extracts the mask. Finally, the data is unmasked. The raw data for the frame is placed in the _inputBuffer byte array by the Socket object. The processed data is stored in the _inputString member. Both of these are class members. The processed data from each frame is appended to the _inputString member. When the final frame has been processed, the entire string is passed to the OnMessageReceived() method. This allows for a single message to be transmitted in multiple frames. The OnMessageReceived() method simply invokes the event handler, if defined.

9. Add the SendMessage() method using the code in Listing 13-6.

Listing 13-6. Implementing the SendMessage() Method

```
public void SendMessage(string msg)
{
    if (_mySocket.Connected)
    {
        // Create the output buffer
        Int64 dataLength = msg.Length;
        int dataStart = 0;
        byte[] dataOut = new byte[dataLength + 10];

        // Build the frame data - depending on the length, it can
        // be passed one of three ways
        dataOut[0] = 0x81;

        // Store the length in the 2nd byte
        if (dataLength < 256)
        {
            dataOut[1] = (byte)dataLength;
            dataStart = 2;
        }
        // Store the length in the 3rd and 4th bytes
        else if (dataLength < UInt16.MaxValue)
        {
            dataOut[1] = 0xFE;
            dataOut[2] = (byte)(dataLength & 0x00FF);
            dataOut[3] = (byte)(dataLength & 0xFF00);
            dataStart = 4;
        }
        // Store the length in bytes 3 - 9
        else
        {
            dataOut[1] = 0xFF;
            for (int i = 0; i < 8; i++)
                dataOut[i + 2] = (byte)((dataLength >> (i * 8)) & 0x000000FF);
            dataStart = 10;
        }

        // Encode the data and store it in the output buffer
        byte[] data = Encoding.UTF8.GetBytes(msg);
        Array.Copy(data, 0, dataOut, dataStart, dataLength);
```

```
                // Send the message
                try
                {
                    _mySocket.Send(dataOut,
                                (int)(dataLength + dataStart),
                                SocketFlags.None);
                }
                catch (Exception ex)
                {
                    // If we get an error, assume the socket has been disconnected
                    if (Disconnected != null)
                        Disconnected(this, EventArgs.Empty);
                }
            }
        }
```

The SendMessage() method constructs the frame header and then appends the actual text being sent. It then uses the Send() method of the Socket object to send this frame to the client.

10. With these classes implemented, you can now implement the main Program class. Add the following code to the Main() method:

```
// Create the WsServer, specifying the server's address
WsServer server = new WsServer(8300);

// Start the server
server.StartSocketServer();

// Keep running until the Enter key is pressed
string input = Console.ReadLine();
```

This code creates the WsServer class and calls the StartSocketServer() method. It calls the Console.ReadLine() method, which will wait until the Enter key is pressed.

Creating a Web Application

With a basic server implementation you're now ready to create a web application that will use it. You will create a project using the ASP.NET 5 Empty template that you used in previous chapters. You will later modify this application to use it as the client web page.

EXERCISE 13-2. CREATING A SIMPLE CLIENT

1. In Solution Explorer, right-click the Chapter13 solution and then click the Add and New Project links.

2. In the Add New Project dialog box, select the ASP.NET Web Application template. Enter the project name **Client**.

3. In the next dialog box, select the ASP.NET 5 Empty template. Click the OK button, and the project will be created.

4. Open the `Startup.cs` file and comment out the implementation of the `Configure()` method as you have in previous projects.

5. Right-click the new `wwwroot` folder and click the Add and New Item links. In the Add New Item dialog box, select the HTML Page, enter the name **Index.html**, and click the Add button.

6. In the `Index.html` file, replace the body element with the following markup:

```
<body onload="connect();">
    <div>
        <pre id="output"></pre>
        <input type="text" id="input" value="" />
        <input type="submit" id="sendMsg" value="Send Message"
                onclick="send();" />
    </div>
</body>
```

7. This creates a `pre` element that will be used to display messages that are received as well as other debugging messages. This also defines a text box for entering the message text and a button to send it. The onload event will call the `connect()` function that you will implement next.

8. Now you're ready to implement the JavaScript that will communicate with your WebSocket server. The browser takes care of the protocol and frame manipulation, so the client side is pretty easy. Add the `script` element shown in Listing 13-7 to the `head` element.

Listing 13-7. The Client-Side JavaScript

```
<script type="text/javascript">
    var ws; // This is our socket

    function connect() {

        output("Connecting to host...");
        try {
            ws = new WebSocket("ws://localhost:8300/chat");
        } catch (e) {
            output(e);
        }
        ws.onopen = function () {
            output("connected... ");
        };

        ws.onmessage = function (e) {
            output(e.data);
        };
```

```
            ws.onclose = function () {
                output("Connection closed");
            };
        };

        function send() {
            var input = document.getElementById("input");

            try {
                ws.send(input.value);
            } catch (e) {
                output(e);
            }
        }

        function output(msg) {
            var o = document.getElementById("output");
            o.innerHTML = o.innerHTML + "<p>" + msg + "</p>";
        };

    </script>
```

The onload event in the body element calls the connect() function. The connect() function creates a WebSocket object and wires up the onOpen, onMessage, and onClose() event handlers. When the Send Message button is clicked, the send() function is invoked. This gets the message from the text box and calls the WebSocket's send() function. The output() function simply add the specified text to the pre element.

Testing the Initial Project

You now have a basic server application and a simple client. You'll test this now to make sure the WebSocket is working properly before adding the custom features.

EXERCISE 13-3. TESTING THE INITIAL APPLICATION

1.   In Solution Explorer, right-click the Chapter13 solution and click the Set StartUp Projects link.

2.   In the dialog box, select the "Multiple startup projects" radio button. For both the WsServer and Client projects, change Action to Start. Also, use the arrows to the right of the project list so the WsServer project is started first, as shown in Figure 13-5. Click the OK button to save these options.

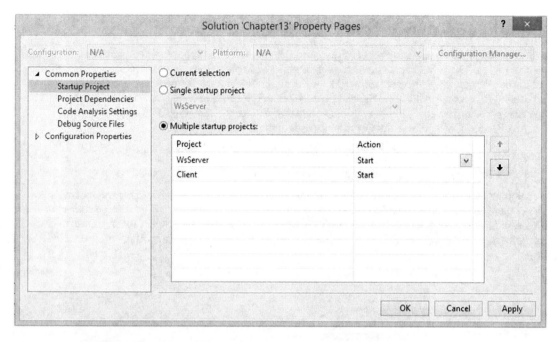

Figure 13-5. *Setting the startup projects*

3. Press F5 to start both the console application that hosts the WebSocket server and the client web page. The web page will show the "Connecting to host..." text and then "connected...."

4. Enter some text in the input box and click the Send Message button. You should see this text display in the console window; it will also be echoed on the client page, as shown in Figure 13-6.

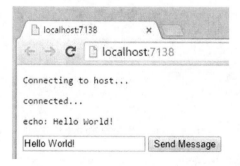

Figure 13-6. *The initial client web page*

Enhancing the WebSocket Server

The solution you have developed so far implements the WebSocket protocol and demonstrates how data is passed between the server and client. However, using a WebSocket server that merely echoes the message back is not very useful. This server must manage the communication with both clients and agents. When a client sends a message to the server it will be forwarded to the appropriate agent. When the agent sends a response (back to the server), the server must route that back to the corresponding client.

To do this, you will implement two more classes in the WsServer project.

- WsAgentConnection manages the communication with an agent application.

- WsClientConnection manages the communication with a client application.

Both of these classes will use an instance of the WsConnection class to send and receive messages. The WsAgentConnection class will reference up to four instances of the WsClientConnection class that represent the four clients the agent is currently chatting with. The WsClientConnection must also have a reference to the WsAgentConnection object that represents the agent supporting this client, as described in Figure 13-7.

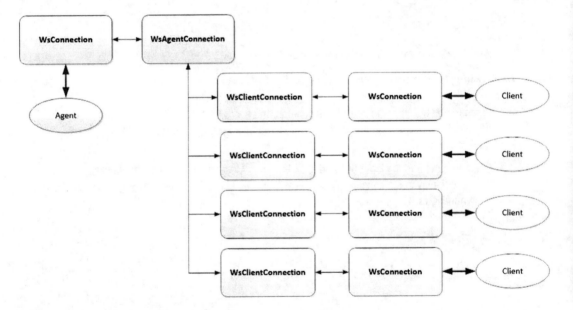

Figure 13-7. *The internal server classes*

When the server first receives a connection, it doesn't yet know whether it is a client or an agent. It will create a WsConnection object that will listen for messages. Both applications will be coded to immediately send a message to the server identifying both the type of application (client or agent) and also the agent's or client's name. When this message is received, the server will then create either a WsAgentConnection object or a WsClientConnection object and add this to either the agent or client list.

If this is a client, the server will find an available agent and perform the necessary linkages between the WsAgentConnection and WsClientConnection objects. The server will also send a response to the client letting them know the name of the agent that they will be working with. If this is an agent, a WsAgentConnection is created and added to the agent list so it is available to respond to new clients.

When the WsConnection object is first created, its MessageReceived and Disconnected events are handled by the WsServer object. The server will need to process the incoming message that identifies the client or agent. However, once the specialized class is created (WsAgentConnection or WsClientConnection), this class will need to handle these events. To do this, the WsServer object must remove the event handlers and then associate the event handlers from the new class. The specialized classes will both reraise the Disconnected event, which the WsServer object will handle.

Adding the WsAgentConnection Class

In Solution Explorer, right-click the WsServer project and click the Add and Class links. Enter **WsAgentConnection.cs** for the class name. Enter the code shown in Listing 13-8 as the implementation for this class.

Listing 13-8. Implementing the WsAgentConnection Class

```
using System;
using System.Collections.Generic;

namespace WsServer
{
    public delegate void WsDisconnectedAgentEventHandler
        (WsAgentConnection sender, EventArgs e);

    public class WsAgentConnection : IDisposable
    {
        public WsConnection _connection;
        public string _name;
        public Dictionary<int, WsClientConnection> _clients;

        public event WsDisconnectedAgentEventHandler AgentDisconnected;

        public WsAgentConnection(WsConnection conn, string name)
        {
            _connection = conn;
            _name = name;

            // Initialize our client list
            _clients = new Dictionary<int, WsClientConnection>();
            for (int i=1; i <= 4; i++)
            {
                _clients.Add(i, null);
            }
        }

        public void MessageReceived(WsConnection sender,
                                    MessageReceivedEventArgs e)
        {
            if (e.Message.Length >= 1)
            {
                if (e.Message[0] == '\u0003')
                {
```

```
                    if (AgentDisconnected != null)
                        AgentDisconnected(this, EventArgs.Empty);
                }

                else if (e.Message.Length > 1)
                {
                    string s = e.Message.Substring(0, 1);
                    int i = 0;
                    if (int.TryParse(s, out i))
                    {
                        WsClientConnection client = _clients[i];
                        if (client != null)
                        {
                            client.SendMessage(e.Message.Substring(2));
                        }
                    }
                }
            }
        }

        public void SendMessage(string msg)
        {
            if (_connection != null)
                _connection.SendMessage(msg);
        }

        public void Disconnected(WsConnection sender, EventArgs e)
        {
            if (AgentDisconnected != null)
                AgentDisconnected(this, EventArgs.Empty);
        }

        public void Dispose()
        {
            if (_connection != null)
                _connection.Dispose();
        }
    }
}
```

The WsAgentConnection class uses a Dictionary to store the client connections. The key will be an integer (1–4), which will be important to the agent application so it knows which chat window to update. The constructor creates all four entries, setting the WsConnection reference to null. A null reference indicates that there is no client actively communicating in this window. The constructor also receives the associated WsConnection object. This is saved in the _connection member and is used to send a message to the agent application.

When the web page closes its socket, a close frame is sent to the server to indicate that the connection is being closed. The first character is represented as \u0003. Additional data may follow this to specify the reason. If this character is found, the AgentDisconnected() event handler is invoked to perform the necessary cleanup. The MessageReceived() method checks for this message in the first character like this:

```
if (e.Message[0] == '\u0003')
```

When an agent sends a message to the server, it is prefixed with a number (1–4) indicating which client this should be forwarded to. The `MessageReceived()` event handler strips this off and then finds the corresponding `WsClientConnection` object in the `Dictionary`. The remainder of the message is then forwarded to the client using the `WsClientConnection` object's `SendMessage()` method.

The `SendMessage()` method simply calls the `SendMessage()` of the `WsConnection` object associated with this agent. The `Disconnected()` event handler raises the `AgentDisconnected` event, which will be handled by the `WsServer` class.

Adding the WsClientConnection Class

In Solution Explorer, right-click the WsServer project and click the Add and Class links. Enter **WsClientConnection.cs** for the class name. Enter the code shown in Listing 13-9 as the implementation for this class.

Listing 13-9. Implementing the WsClientConnection Class

```
using System;

namespace WsServer
{
    public delegate void WsDisconnectedClientEventHandler
        (WsClientConnection sender, EventArgs e);

    public class WsClientConnection : IDisposable
    {
        public WsConnection _connection;
        public string _name;
        public WsAgentConnection _agent;
        public int _clientID;

        public event WsDisconnectedClientEventHandler ClientDisconnected;

        public WsClientConnection(WsConnection conn,
                                  WsAgentConnection agent,
                                  int id,
                                  string name)
        {
            _connection = conn;
            _agent = agent;
            _clientID = id;
            _name = name;
        }

        public void MessageReceived(WsConnection sender,
                                    MessageReceivedEventArgs e)
        {
            if (_agent != null && e.Message.Length > 0)
            {
                if (e.Message[0] == '\u0003')
                {
                    if (ClientDisconnected != null)
                        ClientDisconnected(this, EventArgs.Empty);
                }
```

341

```
            else
                _agent.SendMessage(_clientID.ToString() + ": " + e.Message);
        }
    }

    public void SendMessage(string msg)
    {
        if (_connection != null)
            _connection.SendMessage(msg);
    }

    public void Disconnected(WsConnection sender, EventArgs e)
    {
        if (ClientDisconnected != null)
            ClientDisconnected(this, EventArgs.Empty);
    }

    public void Dispose()
    {
        if (_connection != null)
            _connection.Dispose();
    }
  }
}
```

The WsClientConnection class is similar to the WsAgentConnection class. Instead of a Dictionary of associated clients, it has a single reference to the WsAgentConnection object. This represents the agent that the client is chatting with. The constructor supplies the underlying WsConnection object, the associated WsAgentConection object, and the ID by which this client is known. This is used to prefix the message that is forwarded to the agent. The MessageReceived() method also uses the \u0003 character to see whether the socket is closing.

Enhancing the WsServer Class

Open the WsServer.cs file and add the code shown in bold. This creates the collections that will store the agent and client objects.

```
#region Members

// This socket listens for new connections
Socket _listener;

// Configurable port # that is passed in the constructor
int _port;

// List of connections
List<WsConnection> _unknown;

List<WsAgentConnection> _agents;
List<WsClientConnection> _clients;
```

```
#endregion Members

public WsServer(int port)
{
    _port = port;

    // This is a list of active connections
    _unknown = new List<WsConnection>();
    _agents = new List<WsAgentConnection>();
    _clients = new List<WsClientConnection>();
}
```

In the WsServer class, replace the MessageReceived() event handler with the code shown in Listing 13-10.

Listing 13-10. The Revised MessageReceived() Event Handler

```
void MessageReceived(WsConnection sender, MessageReceivedEventArgs e)
{
    string msg = e.Message;
    if (e.DataLength > 14 && (msg.Substring(0, 14) == "[Agent SignOn:"))
    {
        // This is an agent signing on
        string name = msg.Substring(14, e.DataLength - 15);
        WsAgentConnection agent = new WsAgentConnection(sender, name);

        // Re-wire the event handlers
        sender.Disconnected -= Disconnected;
        sender.MessageReceived -= MessageReceived;
        sender.Disconnected += agent.Disconnected;
        sender.MessageReceived += agent.MessageReceived;

        agent.AgentDisconnected +=
            new WsDisconnectedAgentEventHandler(AgentDisconnected);

        // Move this socket to the agent list
        _unknown.Remove(sender);
        _agents.Add(agent);

        // Send a response
        agent.SendMessage("Welcome, " + name);
    }
    else if (e.DataLength > 15 &&
            (msg.Substring(0, 15) == "[Client SignOn:"))
    {
        // This is a client requesting assistance
        string name = msg.Substring(15, e.DataLength - 16);

        // Find an agent
        WsAgentConnection agent = null;
        int clientID = 0;
        foreach (WsAgentConnection a in _agents)
```

```csharp
        {
            foreach (KeyValuePair<int, WsClientConnection> d in a._clients)
            {
                if (d.Value == null)
                {
                    agent = a;
                    clientID = d.Key;
                    break;
                }
            }
            if (agent != null)
                break;
        }

        if (agent != null)
        {
            WsClientConnection client =
                new WsClientConnection(sender, agent, clientID, name);

            // Re-wire the event handlers
            sender.Disconnected -= Disconnected;
            sender.MessageReceived -= MessageReceived;
            sender.Disconnected += client.Disconnected;
            sender.MessageReceived += client.MessageReceived;

            client.ClientDisconnected +=
                new WsDisconnectedClientEventHandler(ClientDisconnected);

            // Add this to the agent list
            _unknown.Remove(sender);
            _clients.Add(client);

            agent._clients[clientID] = client;

            // Send a message to the agent
            agent.SendMessage("[ClientName:" + clientID.ToString() +
                            name + "]");

            // Send a response
            client.SendMessage("Hello! My name is " + agent._name +
                ". How may I help you?");
        }
        else
        {
            // There are no agents available
            sender.SendMessage("There are no agents currently available;" +
                "please try again later");

            sender.Dispose();
        }
    }
}
```

As I explained earlier, the first message that is sent by both the client and agent applications is a sign-on message that includes their name. This will be formatted like one of these. Any other message will be ignored.

- Agent = "[Agent SignOn:<agent name>]"

- Client = "[Client SignOn:<client name>]"

The MessageReceived() event handler checks to see whether the incoming message is one of these. For an agent sign-on, the name is extracted from the message. It then creates a WsAgentConnection class and sets its _name property. The MessageReceived and Disconnected events from the WsConnection object are currently mapped to the WsServer event handler. This mapping is removed, and instead these events are mapped to the WsAgentConnection object's event handers. Also, the WsAgentConnection class defines an AgentDisconnected event, which is mapped to a new event handler that you will implement later. The WsConnection object is removed from the _unknown list, and the WsAgentConnection object is added to the _agents list. Finally, a welcome message is sent to the agent application.

When a client sign-on is received, similar processing is done to create the WsClientConnection object and rewire the event handlers. In addition, the code looks for an available agent. This iterates through the _agents list and for each agent looks for a Dictionary entry with a null WsClientConnection reference. The search stops when the first null entry is found.

■ **Tip** You might want to improve this search to load balance between available agents. As this is currently implemented, the first agent will handle the first four clients while the other agents are idle. The search could iterate through the agents looking for the one with the fewest active clients and send the new client to them.

If an available agent was found, the WsAgentConnection object and the Dictionary key are passed to the WsClientConnection object constructor. Also, the WsClientConnection object is stored in the available Dictionary entry. A message is sent to the agent application letting them know that a new client has been assigned to them. Finally, a message is sent to the client application letting the client know which agent will be assisting them. If there are no available agents, a message indicating that is sent to the client application.

Add the event handlers shown in Listing 13-11 to the WsServer class.

Listing 13-11. Adding the Additional Event Handlers

```
void ClientDisconnected(WsClientConnection sender, EventArgs e)
{
    if (sender._agent != null)
    {
        sender._agent._clients[sender._clientID] = null;
        sender._agent.SendMessage("[ClientClose:" +
            sender._clientID.ToString() + "]");
    }
    _clients.Remove(sender);
    sender.Dispose();
}
```

```
void AgentDisconnected(WsAgentConnection sender, EventArgs e)
{
    foreach (KeyValuePair<int, WsClientConnection> d in sender._clients)
    {
        if (d.Value != null)
        {
            _clients.Remove(d.Value);
            d.Value.SendMessage
                ("The agent has been disconnected; please reconnect");
        }
    }
    _agents.Remove(sender);
    sender.Dispose();
}
```

These event handlers are invoked when the client or agent application is closed or otherwise disconnected. In addition to removing the connection from the appropriate list, a message is sent to the other end of the conversation so proper cleanup can be performed. If an agent is disconnected, all of the clients that were connected to it need to be notified.

Creating the Agent Application

Now you'll create the agent application that will be used by the agents responding to client requests. This will support up to four simultaneous chat sessions.

Creating the Agent Project

The Agent application will start with the ASP.NET web site template. This provides the ability to register and log in to the site, simulating the authentication that an agent would normally use.

EXERCISE 13-4. CREATING THE AGENT PROJECT

1. From Solution Explorer, right-click the Chapter13 solution and click the Add and New Project links.

2. In the Add New Project dialog box, select the ASP.NET Web Application template and enter the name **Agent**. Click the OK button to continue.

3. In the next dialog box, select the ASP.NET 5 Web Site template and click the OK button. This template provides a login form that the agents will use to authenticate.

4. You will create a separate web page that supports the chat sessions. In Solution Explorer, right-click the Views\Home folder and click the Add and New Item links.

5. In the Add New Item dialog box, select the MVC View Page template, enter the name **Chat.cshtml**, and click the Add button to create the view.

---

6. In the Controllers folder, open the HomeController.cs file. Add the following method to the HomeController class:

```
public IActionResult Chat()
{
    ViewBag.Message = "Respond to chat";

    return View();
}
```

7. In the Views\Shared folder, open the _Layout.cshtml file. Inside the body element you'll see three li tags containing an asp-action property. These tags create the navigation links on the home page. Add the following line to this section to create a new navigation link to the new chat page:

```
<li><a asp-controller="Home" asp-action="Chat">Chat</a></li>
```

Implementing the Chat Web Page

Now you'll implement the chat page. This will support four separate chat sessions. You'll first add the markup for the elements that you'll need and then apply a style element to make the page look better. Then you'll add JavaScript to access the WebSocket and communicate with the WebSocket server that you created.

EXERCISE 13-5. IMPLEMENTING THE CHAT PAGE
---

1. Open the Chat.cshtml file and replace the entire contents with the markup shown in Listing 13-12.

Listing 13-12. Adding the Page Markup

```
<head>
</head>
<body onload="connect();">
    <div class="agent">
        <div>
        <p id="agentName">@User.Identity.Name</p>
        <pre id="output"></pre>
        </div>
        <div id="div1" class="client">
            <p id="client1" class="clientName">unassigned</p>
            <div id="chat1" class="chat">

            </div>
            <input type="text" id="input1" class="input" value="" />
            <input type="submit" value="Send" onclick="send('1');" />
        </div>
```

```
        <div id="div2" class="client">
            <p id="client2" class="clientName">unassigned</p>
            <div id="chat2" class="chat">

            </div>
            <input type="text" id="input2" class="input" value="" />
            <input type="submit" value="Send" onclick="send('2');" />
        </div>
        <div id="div3" class="client">
            <p id="client3" class="clientName">unassigned</p>
            <div id="chat3" class="chat">

            </div>
            <input type="text" id="input3" class="input" value="" />
            <input type="submit" value="Send" onclick="send('3');" />
        </div>
        <div id="div4" class="client">
            <p id="client4" class="clientName">unassigned</p>
            <div id="chat4" class="chat">

            </div>
            <input type="text" id="input4" class="input" value="" />
            <input type="submit" value="Send" onclick="send('4');" />
        </div>
    </div>
</body>
```

At the top of the body element, there is a p element with the value of @User.Indentity.Name. This is Razor syntax that will display the agent's name here. Since the agent will be logged in, the web page already knows their name.

This page will use a div element for each of the chat windows. Inside this there is an empty div element that will contain the messages that are sent back and forth. Inside the outer div there is p element that will hold the client's name, which is currently set to unassigned. There is also a text box that is used to enter the message and a button to send it.

1. To improve the layout of the form, add the style element shown in Listing 13-13 inside the head element.

Listing 13-13. Adding the style Element

```
<style>
    body
    {
        background: #f0f0f0;
        width: 900px;
    }
    .agent
    {
        display:block;
        float:right;
    }
```

```
    .client
    {
        display: block;
        float: left;
        width: 400px;
        height: 385px;
        border: 2px solid #6699cc;
        border-radius: 5px;
        background-color: white;
    }
    .chat
    {
        height: 300px;
        font-size: smaller;
        line-height: 12px;
        overflow-y: scroll;
    }
    .input
    {
        width:330px;
    }
    .clientName
    {
        height: 20px;
        width: 380px;
        text-align: center;
        font-size: 15px;
        font-weight: bold;
    }
</style>
```

2. Now you'll add the JavaScript code that will make all of this work. Add the `script` element shown in Listing 13-14 to the head element.

Listing 13-14. The JavaScript Implementation

```
<script type="text/javascript">

    var ws; // This is our socket

    function connect() {

        output("Connecting to host...");
        try {
            ws = new WebSocket("ws://localhost:8300/chat");
        } catch (e) {
            output(e);
        }
```

```javascript
    ws.onopen = function () {
        output("connected... ");

        // Send the Agent sign-on message
        var p = document.getElementById("agentName");
        ws.send("[Agent SignOn:" + p.innerHTML + "]");
    };

    ws.onmessage = function (e) {
        displayMsg(e.data);
    };

    ws.onclose = function () {
        output("Connection closed");
    };
};

// Send the input text to the server
function send(i) {
    var input = document.getElementById("input" + i);

    try {
        ws.send(i + ":" + input.value);
        var o = document.getElementById("chat" + i);
        o.innerHTML = o.innerHTML + "<p><b>Me:</b>" + input.value + "</p>";
        input.value = "";
    } catch (e) {
        output(e);
    }
}

// Add text to the debug area
function output(msg) {
    var o = document.getElementById("output");
    o.innerHTML = o.innerHTML + "<p>" + msg + "</p>";
};

// Handle a received message
function displayMsg(msg) {
    var i = msg.substring(0, 1);
    var cmd = msg.substring(0, 12);

    // For the initial message from the server, save the client's name
    if (cmd === "[ClientName:") {
        displayClientName(msg.substring(12));
    }

    // If the client has disconnected, clear the chat window
    else if (cmd === "[ClientClose") {
        resetClient(msg.substring(13,14));
    }
```

```
    // Display the message in the debug area is not formatted properly
    else if (i != "1" && i != "2" && i != "3" && i != "4") {
        output(msg)
    }

    // Display the message in the chat window
    else {
        var o = document.getElementById("chat" + i);
        o.innerHTML = o.innerHTML + "<p><b>Client:</b>" +
            msg.substring(3, msg.length) + "</p>";
    }
};

// Display the client's name in the chat window
function displayClientName(msg) {
    var i = msg.substring(0, 1);
    var o = document.getElementById("client" + i);
    o.innerHTML = msg.substring(1, msg.length - 1);
}

// Clear the chat window so it can be reused for another client
function resetClient(i) {
    // Clear the client's name
    var o = document.getElementById("client" + i);
    o.innerHTML = "unassigned";

    // Remove the chat messages
    var o2 = document.getElementById("chat" + i);
    while (o2.hasChildNodes()) {
        o2.removeChild(o2.firstChild);
    }
}
</script>
```

Just like the earlier web page that you implemented, the onload event calls the connect() function, which wires up the onopen, onmessage, and onclose event handlers. In this case, the onopen event handler sends the agent sign-on message to the server. The onmessage event handler calls the displayMsg() function. This has special logic to interpret the message. The server will send the client's name when the client is assigned and will send a message when the client has disconnected. These special cases are processed by the displayClientName() and resetClient() functions, respectively. For all other messages, the first character is expected to be 1–4, indicating which window this is for. Using this, the appropriate div element is obtained, and the message is added to it. The message is prefixed with the *Client:* text.

The send() function that is called when the Send button is clicked takes a parameter that indicates which window is sending the message. It uses this to get the appropriate input element and also to prefix the message so the server will know which client this is for. It also displays the text in the div element after prefixing it with the *Me:* text. This is done so the chat window contains both incoming and outgoing messages.

The resetClient() function changes the client name back to unassigned. It also iterates through the div, removing all of the p tags that were added.

Testing the Agent Application

Before you complete the development, let's test the form to make sure it looks good. In Solution Explorer, right-click the Agent project and click the Debug and "Start new instance" links. This should launch the browser and display the home page. Click the Register link at the top of the page and enter your e-mail address and a password, as shown in Figure 13-8.

Register.

Create a new account.

Email

markc@thecreativepeople.com

Password

•••••••••

Confirm password

•••••••••

Register

Figure 13-8. Registering the user

■ **Tip**　The next time you open this site, you'll use the Log In link instead of the Register link. When you log in, if you select the Remember Me check box, it will automatically log you in when the application is started.

Notice also the Chat link that you added in the page header. Click this link to open the chat page, which should look like Figure 13-9.

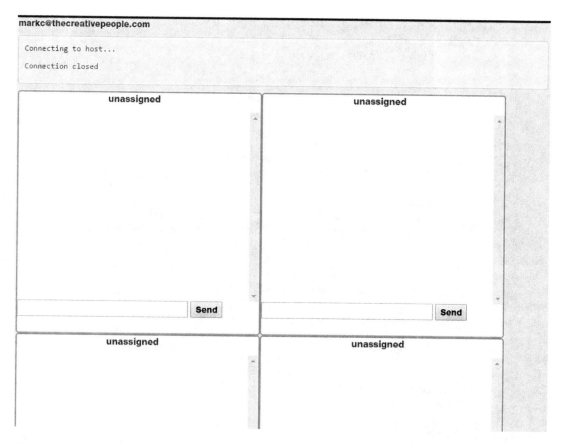

Figure 13-9. *The new chat page*

Because the server is not running, the connection could not be established, and the "Connection closed" message is displayed. Close the window and stop the debugger.

Implementing the Client Application

You created the Client project earlier in the chapter to test the initial server implementation. Now you'll modify the Index.html file to function as the client side of the chat solution.

EXERCISE 13-6. CREATING THE CLIENT APPLICATION

---

1. Open the Index.html file in the Client project.

2. Replace the body element with the following markup. This adds a div element that contains a text box for the client's name and a submit button. A second div implements the actual chat window. It includes a div that will display the chat messages, a text box for entering a new message, and a submit button that will send it.

```
<body>
    <div>
        <p>Enter your name to begin chat</p>
            <input type="text" id="name" class="input" value="" />
            <input type="submit" id="connect"
                value="Chat now..." onclick="connect();" />
        <pre id="output"></pre>
    </div>
    <div id="div1" class="client">
        <p id="client1" class="clientName"></p>
        <div id="chat1" class="chat">

        </div>
            <input type="text" id="input" class="input" value="" />
            <input type="submit" value="Send" class="send" onclick="send();" />
    </div>
</body>
```

3. Add the style element shown in Listing 13-15 to the head element.

Listing 13-15. Defining the CSS Styles

```
<style>
    body
    {
        background: #f0f0f0;
        width: 450px;
    }
    .client
    {
        display: block;
        float: left;
        width: 400px;
        height: 345px;
        border: 2px solid #6699cc;
        border-radius: 5px;
        background-color: white;
    }
    .chat
    {
        height: 300px;
        font-size: smaller;
        line-height: 12px;
        overflow-y: scroll;
    }
    .input
    {
        width:330px;
    }
</style>
```

4. Replace the existing `script` element with the code shown in Listing 13-16.

Listing 13-16. Adding the JavaScript

```
<script type="text/javascript">

    var ws; // This is our socket

    function connect() {

        output("Connecting to host...");
        try {
            ws = new WebSocket("ws://localhost:8300/chat");
        } catch (e) {
            output(e);
        }
        ws.onopen = function () {
            output("connected... ");
            var p = document.getElementById("name");
            ws.send("[Client SignOn:" + p.value + "]");
        };

        ws.onmessage = function (e) {
            displayMsg(e.data);
        };

        ws.onclose = function () {
            output("Connection closed");
        };
    };

    function send() {
        var input = document.getElementById("input");

        try {
            ws.send(input.value);
            var o = document.getElementById("chat1");
            o.innerHTML = o.innerHTML + "<p><b>Me:</b>" + input.value + "</p>";
            input.value = "";
        } catch (e) {
            output(e);
        }
    }

    function output(msg) {
        var o = document.getElementById("output");
        o.innerHTML = o.innerHTML + "<p>" + msg + "</p>";
    };
```

```
    function displayMsg(msg) {
        var o = document.getElementById("chat1");
        o.innerHTML = o.innerHTML + "<p><b>Agent:</b>" + msg + "</p>";
    };

</script>
```

This code is similar to the JavaScript on the Agent application. The connect() function gets a WebSocket and sends the initial sign-on message and then wires up the onmessage and onclose event handlers. The send() function sends the text that was entered to the server and echoes it on the page. The displayMsg() function is the event handler for processing incoming messages from the server, which are displayed on the page.

Adding Logging

You'll now add logging to the socket server. This will help you better understand what is happening behind the scenes and can be useful in debugging your solution. I'll show you how to use Log4Net to easily integrate logging in your server-side applications.

Installing Log4Net

You'll use NuGet to install the Log4Net package and add it to the WsServer project. From the Tools menu in Visual Studio, click the NuGet Package Manager and Manage NuGet Packages for Solution links. In the NuGet Package Manager, enter **log4net** in the search box. Then select the log4net package and select only the WsServer project, as shown in Figure 13-10; click the Install button.

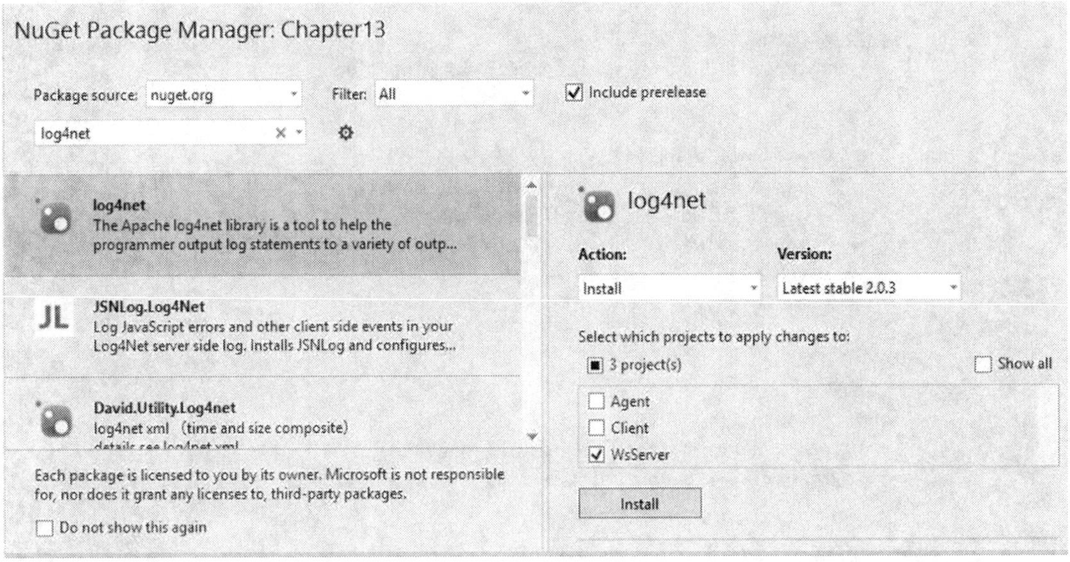

Figure 13-10. *Selecting the log4net package*

The confirmation window shown in Figure 13-11 will be displayed. Click the OK button to continue.

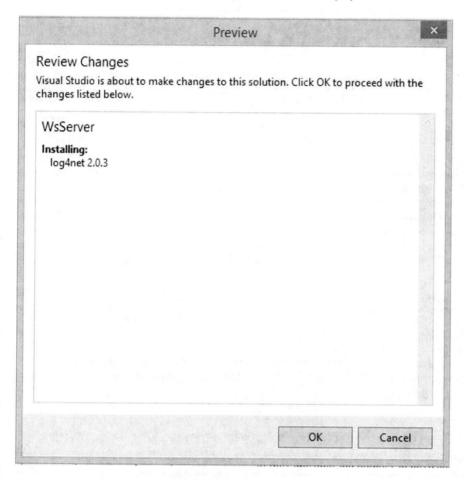

Figure 13-11. *Confirming the installation*

Configuring Log4Net

Log4Net is configured through the app.config file. This allows you the ability to change what is logged without changing the application. For example, you can set this to log only error messages. If you then need to later debug an issue, you can change the logging level to get more information in the logs.

Open the app.config file in the WsServer project. Replace the entire contents with the code shown in Listing 13-17.

Listing 13-17. The app.config Settings

```
<?xml version="1.0" encoding="utf-8" ?>
<configuration>
  <configSections>
    <section name="log4net"
             type="log4net.Config.Log4NetConfigurationSectionHandler, log4net"/>
  </configSections>
```

```
<startup>
  <supportedRuntime version="v4.0" sku=".NETFramework,Version=v4.6" />
</startup>

<log4net xmlns="urn:log4net">
  <root>
    <level value="DEBUG"/>
    <appender-ref ref="RollingFileAppender"/>
  </root>

  <appender name="RollingFileAppender" type="log4net.Appender.RollingFileAppender">
    <file value="WsServer.log" />
    <appendToFile value="true" />
    <rollingStyle value="Size" />
    <maxSizeRollBackups value="5" />
    <maximumFileSize value="10MB" />
    <staticLogFileName value="true" />
    <layout type="log4net.Layout.PatternLayout">
      <conversionPattern value="%date [%thread] %level %logger - %message%newline" />
    </layout>
  </appender>
</log4net>
```

```
</configuration>
```

You'll need to define a config section where your Log4Net entries will go. The settings shown here are some basic settings to create a rolling log file named WsServer.log. The logging level is set to DEBUG so all of your log statements will be saved in the log.

■ **Note** There is a lot that you can do with Log4Net. If you're interested in learning more about this utility, I suggest you start with this article by Tim Corey: www.codeproject.com/Articles/140911/log-net-Tutorial.

Adding Log Statements

The real work in adding logging is to put code in the right places to save useful pieces of information. You should have an idea of what parts of the code are more likely to fail and which events are most meaningful to capture. Avoid logging inside of a loop because that could generate a lot of log entries that are not really helpful. For the socket server you'll want to know when a socket is created or closed and when messages are sent or received. You'll also want to know when errors occur.

You'll need to reference Log4Net somewhere in your assembly. This is done only once per assembly. Open the Program.cs file and add the line shown in bold:

```
using System;
using System.Collections.Generic;
using System.Linq;
using System.Text;
using System.Threading.Tasks;
```

```
[assembly: log4net.Config.XmlConfigurator(Watch = true)]
```

```
namespace WsServer
```

Now, you'll add a logger in each class that will be using Log4Net. This will create a static member in the class that you will later use to generate some log entries. Add the following code shown in bold to the WsServer class:

```
public class WsServer
{
    private static readonly log4net.ILog log = log4net.LogManager.GetLogger
        (System.Reflection.MethodBase.GetCurrentMethod().DeclaringType);

    #region Members
```

Add the same line in the WsConnection class.

There are several places that you should add logging statements. The method you use, such as Debug, Info, or Error, will determine the logging level. You can then control which level to log in the app.config file. I'm using the ...Format() method, such as InfoFormat(), which works like the string.Format() method. You could also use the basic methods like Info() where you must pass in a string that is already formatted.

EXERCISE 13-7. ADD LOGGING TO THE WSSERVER CLASS

1. In the WsServer class, add the Error statement inside the catch block of the StartSocketServer() method.

```
catch (Exception ex)
{
    log.ErrorFormat("Listener failed, handle = {0}: {1}",
        _listener.Handle, ex.Message);
}
```

2. Add a Debug statement at the beginning of the MessageReceived() handler.

```
void MessageReceived(WsConnection sender, MessageReceivedEventArgs e)
{
    string msg = e.Message;

    log.Debug("Message received: " + msg);
```

3. Add an Info statement just before sending a message to the agent.

```
log.InfoFormat("Socket attached to agent {0}, handle = {1}",
    name, sender._mySocket.Handle.ToString());

// Send a response
agent.SendMessage("Welcome, " + name);
```

4. Add another just before attaching the client to the selected agent.

```
if (agent != null)
{
    WsClientConnection client =
        new WsClientConnection(sender, agent, clientID, name);

    log.InfoFormat("Client {0} assigned to agent {1}", name, agent._name);

    // Re-wire the event handlers
```

5. Add an Info statement inside the Disconnected() handler.

```
void Disconnected(WsConnection sender, EventArgs e)
{
    log.InfoFormat("Unattached socket disconnected, handle = {0}",
        sender._mySocket.Handle.ToString());

    _unknown.Remove(sender);
}
```

6. Add an Info statement inside the OnConnect() method.

```
// Perform the necessary handshaking
PerformHandshake(socket);

log.InfoFormat("New socket created, handle = {0}",
    socket.Handle.ToString());

// Create a WsConnection object for this connection
```

7. Add an Info statement inside the ClientDisconnected() handler.

```
void ClientDisconnected(WsClientConnection sender, EventArgs e)
{
    log.InfoFormat("Client {0}, socket disconnected, handle = {1}",
        sender._name, sender._connection._mySocket.Handle.ToString());

    if (sender._agent != null)
```

8. Add a similar statement inside the AgentDisconnected() handler.

```
void AgentDisconnected(WsAgentConnection sender, EventArgs e)
{
    log.InfoFormat("Agent {0} socket disconnected, handle = {1}",
        sender._name, sender._connection._mySocket.Handle.ToString());

    foreach (KeyValuePair<int, WsClientConnection> d in sender._clients)
```

EXERCISE 13-8. ADD LOGGING TO THE WSCONNECTION CLASS

1. Add a Debug statement inside the Dispose() method.

```
public void Dispose()
{
    log.DebugFormat("Socket closing, handle {0}", _mySocket.Handle);

    _mySocket.Close();
}
```

2. At the end of the ReadMessage() function, add an Error statement inside the catch block.

```
catch (Exception ex)
{
    log.ErrorFormat("ReceiveMessage failed, handle {0}, {1}",
        _mySocket.Handle, ex.Message);
}
```

3. Add an Error statement inside the else block.

```
// If we were not able to read the message, assume that
// the socket is closed
else
{
    log.ErrorFormat("ReceiveMessage failed, handle {0}", _mySocket.Handle);
}
```

4. Finally, add an Error statement inside the catch block in the SendMessage() method.

```
catch (Exception ex)
{
    log.ErrorFormat("SendMessage failed, handle = {0}: {1}", _mySocket.Handle,
        ex.Message);

    // If we get an error, assume the socket has been disconnected
    if (Disconnected != null)
        Disconnected(this, EventArgs.Empty);
}
```

Testing the Solution

Earlier in the chapter, you set up the WsServer and Client projects to both start when debugging. Now you'll need to add the Agent application as well. Then you will debug all three applications at the same time.

Testing the Messaging

Start by testing the basic socket communication, making sure that each message is being displayed in the correct window. You'll need to launch an additional client page to test simultaneous clients.

EXERCISE 13-9. TESTING THE SOLUTION

1. Right-click the Chapter13 solution and click the Set StartUp Projects link. In the dialog box, change the action for the Agent application to Start. Also move this down to be the second project loaded. Click the OK button to save these changes.

2. Press F5 to debug the applications. You should see the console app as well as two browser windows. Go to the agent page. If not already logged in, log in now. You should have to register only once. After that, you just log in. If you selected the "Remember me" check box, you should be logged in automatically.

3. Click the Chat link, which should display the new chat page, and show that you are connected to the server.

4. Go to the Client page, enter a name, and click the "Chat now" button. You should get a response in the chat window, as illustrated in Figure 13-12.

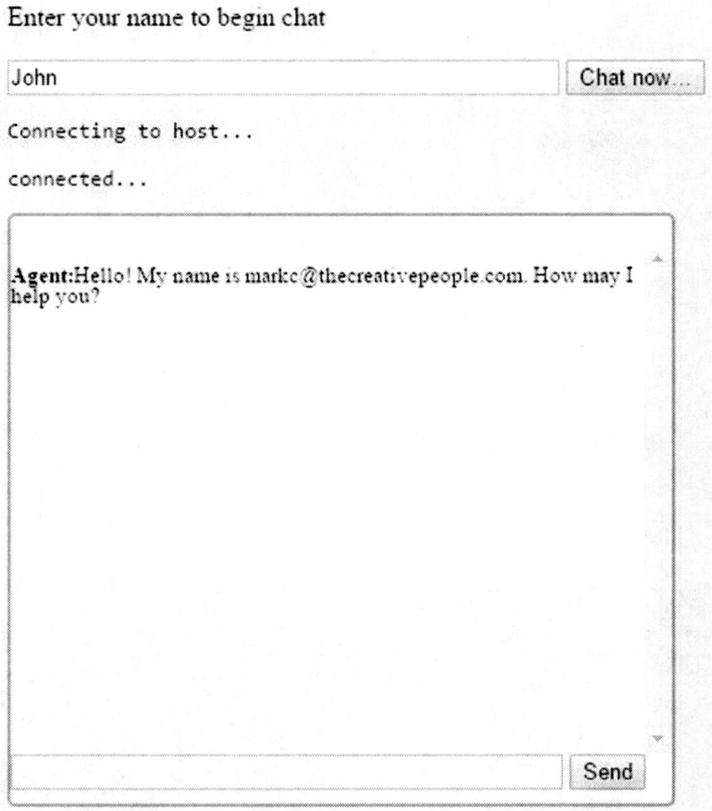

CHAPTER 13 ■ WEBSOCKETS

Enter your name to begin chat

| John | Chat now... |

Connecting to host...

connected...

> **Agent:**Hello! My name is markc@thecreativepeople.com. How may I help you?
>
> | | Send |

Figure 13-12. The client web application

5. Enter a message and send it. From the Agent page, enter a response and send it. You should see all of the messages displayed in the client's chat window.

6. Create another copy of the client page and enter a different name. Enter a message and send it.

7. Go to the Agent window and you should see messages in two windows, as shown in Figure 13-13.

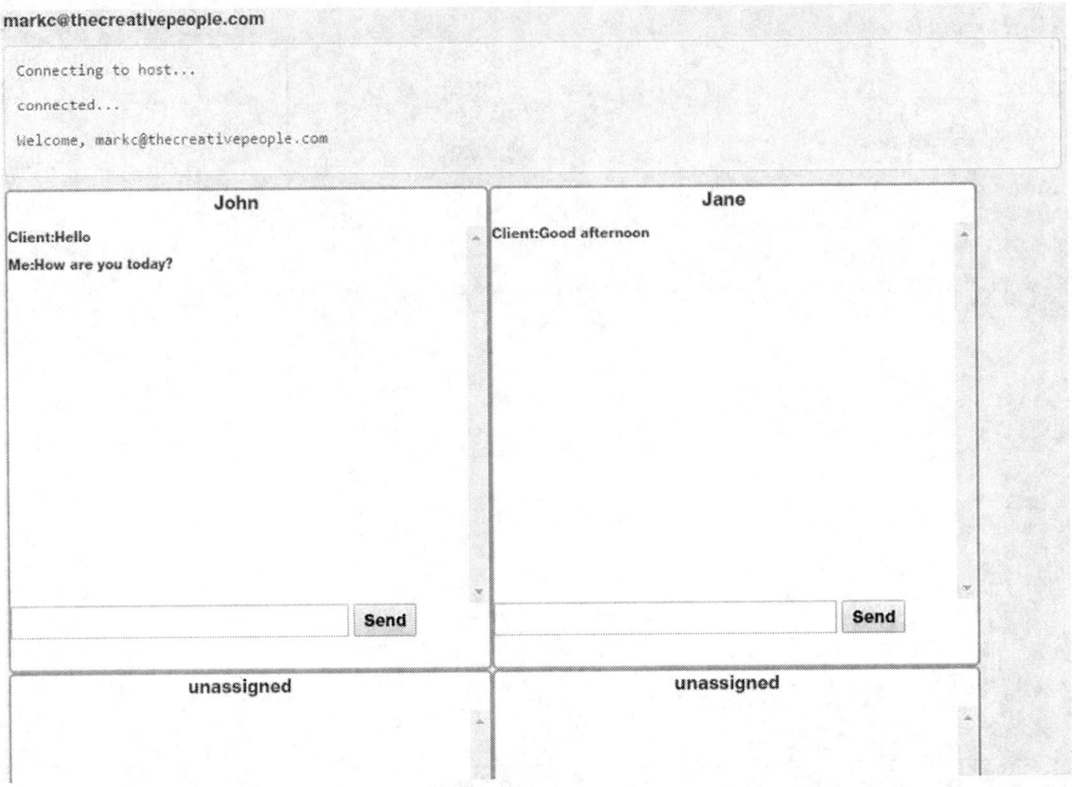

markc@thecreativepeople.com

```
Connecting to host...
connected...
Welcome, markc@thecreativepeople.com
```

John	Jane
Client:Hello Me:How are you today?	Client:Good afternoon
Send	Send
unassigned	unassigned

Figure 13-13. *The Agent page with multiple sessions*

Testing Disconnects

For a final test, you'll close some of the web pages and verify the other pages respond correctly. You'll also attempt to reconnect to a previous client.

With the agent and two client windows still open, close the first client window. Go to the agent page, and you should see that first window has been cleared and set to unassigned. However, the second client is still attached.

Now close the agent window. Go to the client window, and you should see a message indicating the agent has disconnected, as shown in Figure 13-14.

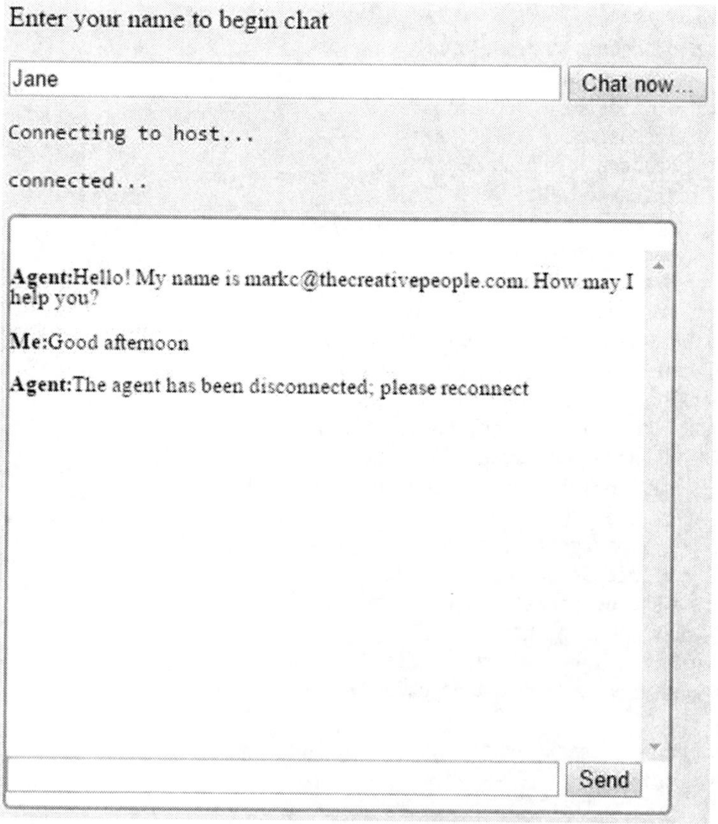

Enter your name to begin chat

| Jane | Chat now... |

Connecting to host...

connected...

Agent: Hello! My name is markc@thecreativepeople.com. How may I help you?

Me: Good afternoon

Agent: The agent has been disconnected; please reconnect

| | Send |

Figure 13-14. *A client window with a disconnected agent*

Now open a new tab and open the agent page by typing in the URL, which will be similar to http://localhost:7778/Home/Chat. You will probably have a different port number. Go back to the client page and click the "Chat now" button. You should then be reconnected to the agent. Close the client and agent windows and stop the debugger.

Open the WsServer.log file that was created by Log4Net, which you'll find in the WsServer\bin\Debug folder. It should look similar to the entries shown in Listing 13-18.

Listing 13-18. The WsServer.log File

```
INFO WsServer.WsServer - New socket created, handle = 1284
DEBUG WsServer.WsServer - Message received: [Agent SignOn:markc@.com]
INFO WsServer.WsServer - Socket attached to agent markc@.com, handle = 1284
INFO WsServer.WsServer - New socket created, handle = 1316
DEBUG WsServer.WsServer - Message received: [Client SignOn:John]
INFO WsServer.WsServer - Client John assigned to agent markc@thecreativepeople.com
INFO WsServer.WsServer - New socket created, handle = 1356
DEBUG WsServer.WsServer - Message received: [Client SignOn:Jane]
INFO WsServer.WsServer - Client Jane assigned to agent markc@thecreativepeople.com
INFO WsServer.WsServer - Client John, socket disconnected, handle = 1316
DEBUG WsServer.WsConnection - Socket closing, handle 1316
```

```
ERROR WsServer.WsConnection - ReceiveMessage failed, handle 1316,
                            Cannot access a disposed object.
INFO WsServer.WsServer - Agent markc@.com socket disconnected, handle = 1284
DEBUG WsServer.WsConnection - Socket closing, handle 1284
ERROR WsServer.WsConnection - ReceiveMessage failed, handle 1284,
                            Cannot access a disposed object.
INFO WsServer.WsServer - New socket created, handle = 732
DEBUG WsServer.WsServer - Message received: [Agent SignOn:markc@.com]
INFO WsServer.WsServer - Socket attached to agent markc@.com, handle = 732
INFO WsServer.WsServer - New socket created, handle = 1344
DEBUG WsServer.WsServer - Message received: [Client SignOn:Jane]
INFO WsServer.WsServer - Client Jane assigned to agent markc@.com
INFO WsServer.WsServer - Client Jane, socket disconnected, handle = 1356
DEBUG WsServer.WsConnection - Socket closing, handle 1356
ERROR WsServer.WsConnection - ReceiveMessage failed, handle 1356,
                            Cannot access a disposed object.
INFO WsServer.WsServer - Client Jane, socket disconnected, handle = 1344
DEBUG WsServer.WsConnection - Socket closing, handle 1344
ERROR WsServer.WsConnection - ReceiveMessage failed, handle 1344,
                            Cannot access a disposed object.
INFO WsServer.WsServer - Agent markc@.com socket disconnected, handle = 732
DEBUG WsServer.WsConnection - Socket closing, handle 732
ERROR WsServer.WsConnection - ReceiveMessage failed, handle 732,
                            Cannot access a disposed object.
```

This provides a good summary of how each socket was created and the messages that are sent back and forth.

Summary

In this relatively brief introduction to WebSockets, you created a simple chat system that allows an agent to chat with multiple clients simultaneously. While the server implementation was pretty involved, the client side was fairly simple. After creating the WebSocket object, specifying the location of the WebSocket server, you just wire up event handlers to be notified when the connection is established, when a message is received, and when the connection has been closed.

In this demo, you created a stand-alone application, but in many cases you'll simply add the chat capability to your existing web application. For example, you might ask the user if they want assistance with the page they are viewing, and if they do, this simple code will allow them to chat right from that page.

The server sides require a bit of protocol handling. First, the server receives handshaking messages using http. The request key is obtained and used to generate the response key. The entire response is then sent back to the client. The actual messages are sent using the ws protocol, which includes a frame header. Messages from the client are masked, which require logic in the server to unmask it. Messages from the server are not masked.

The demo application provides a chat capability. This is only one possible use of WebSockets. They can also be used any time the server needs to communication with the client. Keep in mind, however, that the client must initiate the connection with the server.

■ ■ ■

CHAPTER 14

Drag and Drop

The ability to select an element and drag it to another location is an excellent example of a natural user experience. I can still remember the early Apple computers where you could delete a file by dragging it onto a trash can icon. This action, and hundreds more like it, is a key component of user experiences found on desktop applications. Web applications, however, have lagged far behind in this arena. With the drag-and-drop (DnD) API in HTML5, you'll find web applications rapidly catching up.

In this chapter, you'll build a web application that implements a checkers game, using the DnD API to move the pieces around the board. I will first explain the concepts and how a DnD application is structured. Then I'll dive into the code, demonstrating the various aspects. I'll finish up with some advanced features including dragging between browser windows.

Understanding Drag and Drop

Before I get into building an application, I want to explain the basic concepts of the DnD API. This will help you put this in context as you start to write code. I will first explain the events that are raised; it is important to know when each is raised and on which object. Then you'll look at the dataTransfer object, which you'll use to pass information from the object being dragged to each of the events and eventually to the drop action. You can also use this to configure various aspects of the dragging operation. Finally, I'll show you how to make objects draggable.

Handling Events

As with its desktop counterpart, DnD is an event-based API. As the user selects an item, moves it, and drops it, events are raised, allowing the application to control and respond to these actions. To effectively use this API, you'll need to know when these events are raised and on which element they are raised. At first, this may seem confusing, but it's pretty straightforward once you see this in perspective.

In a DnD operation, two elements are involved:

- The element that is being dragged, sometimes referred to as the *source*

- The element being dropped on, usually called the *target*

You can think of this as the source being an arrow that is being dropped onto a target, as illustrated in Figure 14-1.

- dragstart
- drag
- dragend

- dragenter
- dragover
- dragleave
- drop

Figure 14-1. *The source and target elements*

During a DnD operation, events are fired on both elements, and I've indicated which events are raised on each. On the source element, the dragstart, drag, and dragend events are comparable to the mousedown, mousemove, and mouseup events in a Windows application. When you click an element and start to move the mouse, the dragstart event is raised. This is immediately followed by the drag event, and the drag event is also repeatedly raised with each move of the mouse. Finally, the dragend event is raised when the mouse button is released.

The events on the target element are a little more interesting. As the mouse is moved around the page, when it enters the area defined by an element, the dragenter event is raised on that element. As the mouse continues to move, the dragover event is raised on the target element. If the mouse moves outside of that element, the dragleave event is fired on the target element. Presumably, the mouse is now on a different element, and a dragenter event is raised on that element. However, if the mouse button is released while over the target element, instead of a dragleave event, the drop event will be raised.

Now let's walk through a typical scenario and see the order of these events. This is illustrated in Table 14-1.

Table 14-1. *Sequence of Events*

Element	Event	Notes
Source	dragstart	Raised when the mouse is clicked and starts to move
Source	drag	Raised with each mouse move
Target	dragenter	Raised when the mouse enters the target element's space
Target	dragover	Raised with each mouse move when the pointer is over the target
Source	drag	Continues to be raised as the mouse moves
Target	dragleave	Raised when the mouse is moved past the current target
Target	dragenter	Raised when mouse moves to a new target element
Target	drop	Raised when the mouse button is released
Source	dragend	Ends the drag-and-drop operation

Now that you understand the events that are used, you can implement a DnD operation by providing appropriate handlers for each of these events.

Using the Data Transfer Object

There is one more DnD concept that you should understand. Simply dragging an element around a page is not all that useful; what you're really after is the data associated with the element. In the example I gave earlier with dragging a file to the trash can, seeing the icon swallowed up by the trash may be fun to watch, but the ultimate goal is to delete the file. In this case, you're passing a file specification to the recycle bin so it can perform the requested action in the file system.

Storing Data

In the DnD API, the dataTransfer object is used to store the data associated with the operation. The dataTransfer object is usually initialized in the dragstart event handler. Recall that this event is raised on the source element. The event handler can access the data from the source element and store it in the dataTransfer object. This is then provided to all of the other event handlers so they can use it in their specific processing. Ultimately, this is used by the drop event handler to take the appropriate action on this data.

The dataTransfer object is provided as a property of the event object that is passed to each of the event handlers. You use the setData() method to store data in the dataTransfer object. To indicate the type of data, an appropriate MIME type needs to be supplied as well. For example, to add some simple text, call the method like this:

```
e.dataTransfer.setData("text", "Hello, World!");
```

To access this data in a subsequent event, such as the drop event, use the getData() method like this:

```
var msg = e.dataTransfer.getData("text");
```

You'll need to use the same MIME type when retrieving the data as was used when the data was stored.

■ **Caution**   Not all browsers recognize all MIME types. In this example, you might expect text/plain to be used. This works fine in Firefox and Opera but is not supported in Chrome or IE. However, if you use just text, this will work on all of these browsers.

Using Drop Effects

Another purpose for the dataTransfer object is to provide feedback to the user as to the action that will occur when the item is dropped. This is called the *drop effect*, and there are four possible values.

- copy: The selected element will be copied in the target location.
- move: The selected element will be moved to the target location.
- link: A link to the selected item will be created in the target location.
- none: The drop operation is not allowed.

When you start dragging an item, the cursor will change to indicate the drop effect that will occur when the item is dropped on the target. This is standard Windows UI, and you can try this on most applications. For example, using the text editor in Visual Studio, select some text and then start dragging it. You should see the cursor change to either a move cursor or a "not allowed" cursor depending on where you trying to move it to. If you hold down the Ctrl key before moving it, you should see the copy cursor instead of the move cursor.

In the dragstart event handler, you can specify the drop effects that are allowed based on the source element that is selected. You can specify more than one allowed effect by simply concatenating them (for example, copyMove) or specify all effects like this:

```
e.dataTransfer.effectAllowed = "all"; // "copy", "link", "move", "copyLink", "linkMove",
"copyMove"
```

Then, in the dragover event, you'll specify the drop effect that will occur if the source element is dropped there. If that drop effect is one of the allowed effects, the cursor will change to indicate that drop effect. If that effect is not allowed, however, the cursor will use the "not allowed" icon. If this is not a valid location to accept the drop, set the drop effect to none like this:

```
if (validLocation) {
    e.dataTransfer.dropEffect = "move";
}
else {
    e.dataTransfer.dropEffect = "none";
}
```

Enabling Draggable Elements

So, now you know you can disable the drop event on an element by setting the drop effect to none in the dragover event. But how do you control which elements can be dragged to start with? The answer is simple: just set the draggable attribute in the markup for the element. For example, to create a div that can be dragged, enter the markup like this:

```
<div id="myDiv" draggable="true">
    <p>This div is draggable</p>
</div>
```

By default, images and links are draggable. Go to google.com and try dragging the Google logo. You should see a somewhat muted copy of this image being dragged as you move the cursor.

If you drag this image onto a Firefox browser window, Firefox will navigate to this image. You've just seen drag and drop in action. Because using drag and drop is such a natural way of working, browsers try to accommodate this out of the box as best they can. For example, if you drag some text from a text editor that appears to be a URL onto a browser, it will try to navigate to that address. If you drag an image file onto a browser, it will either navigate to it or download it.

Sometimes the default action can cause issues with your custom code. I will show you in Exercise 14-3 how to disable this.

■ **Note** For more information on the DnD API, check out the W3C specification at
http://dev.w3.org/html5/spec/single-page.html#dnd.

Creating the Checkers Application

To demonstrate the DnD API, you'll create a web application that displays a typical checkers board of alternating red-and-white squares. You'll use image files to represent the checkers and display them in their initial starting position. Then you'll create event handlers that will allow you to move a piece to a different square. Finally, you'll add logic to disable illegal moves.

■ **Tip** Throughout this chapter you will be adding and modifying code in this project as you add features to the application. If there is any question about where each change should be made, the final code is listed in Appendix C, and it is also available with the source download.

Creating the Project

You'll first need to create a Visual Studio project that is similar to ones you created previously. This will use the Web Site ASP.NET 5 project template.

EXERCISE 14-1. CREATING THE VISUAL STUDIO PROJECT

1. Start Visual Studio 2015. In the Start Page, click the New Project link.

2. In the New project dialog box, select the ASP.NET Web Application template. Enter the project name **Chapter14** and select a location for this project.

3. In the next dialog box, select the ASP.NET 5 Web Site template. Click the OK button to create the project.

4. In Solution Explorer, right-click the Views\Home folder and click the Add and New Item links. In the Add New Item dialog box, select MVC View Page, enter the name **Checkers.cshtml**, and click the Add button.

5. Open the HomeController.cs file in the Controllers folder. Add the following code at the end of the class. This will display the new Checkers view.

    ```
    public IActionResult Checkers()
    {
        return View();
    }
    ```

6. The source code download for this chapter includes an Images folder with five images. Copy all five images to the wwwroot\images folder in Solution Explorer.

Drawing the Checkers Board

To draw the board, you'll use a separate div element for each square. You'll need eight rows with eight div elements each. Fortunately, this is pretty easy to do using a couple of nested for loops and the Razor syntax.

■ **Note** In Chapter 10 you drew a chess board using a canvas element. However, that won't work for this application because you need separate DOM elements for each square. You might be tempted to use SVG to create the board since each rect element is a separate DOM element; however, the SVG elements do not support the DnD API.

EXERCISE 14-2. DRAWING THE BOARD

1. Replace the default implementation of the Checkers.cshtml with the code shown in Listing 14-1.

Listing 14-1. The Initial Checkers.cshtml Implementation

```
<head>
</head>
<body>
    <div class="board">
        @for (int y = 0; y < 8; y++)
        {
            for (int x = 0; x < 8; x++)
            {
                string id = x.ToString() + y.ToString();
                string css;
                if ((x + y) % 2 == 0)
                {
                    css = "bwhite";
                }
                else
                {
                    css = "bblack";
                }
                <text>
                <div id="@id" class="@css" draggable="false">

                </div>
                </text>
            }
        }
    </div>
</body>
```

2. This code uses two nested `for` loops to create the `div` elements. Inside the second for loop, the `id` variable is computed by concatenating the x and y variables. The `css` variable alternates between `bwhite` and `bblack`. For even-numbered rows, the even columns are black, and the odd columns are white. This reverses for odd-numbered rows. The `draggable` attribute is set to false because we don't want squares being dragged, only pieces.

3. Now you'll need to add some style rules to set the size and color of each square. Add the `style` element shown in Listing 14-2 inside the `head` element.

Listing 14-2. Adding the CSS Styles

```
<style type="text/css" >
    .board
    {
        width: 400px;
        height: 400px;
        margin-top: 20px;
    }
    .bblack
    {
        background-color: #b93030;
        border-color: #b93030;
        border-width: 1px;
        border-style: solid;
        width: 48px;
        height: 48px;
        float: left;
        margin: 0px;
        padding: 0px;
    }
    .bwhite
    {
        background-color: #f7f7f7;
        border-color: #b93030;
        border-width: 1px;
        border-style: solid;
        width: 48px;
        height: 48px;
        float: left;
        margin: 0px;
        padding: 0px;
    }
</style>
```

4. Press F5 to preview this page, which should look like Figure 14-2. You didn't provide a link to get to the Checkers page. To navigate to your page, add **/Home/Checkers** to the URL in the browser.

Figure 14-2. *The initial board*

5. Now you'll add the checkers by including an `img` element inside the appropriate `div` elements. Add the code shown in bold in Listing 14-3.

Listing 14-3. Adding the Images

```
<text>
<div id="@id" class="@css" draggable="false">
    @if ((x + y) % 2 != 0 && y != 3 && y != 4)
    {
        string imgSrc;
        string pid;
        if (y < 3)
        {
            imgSrc = "../images/WhitePiece.png";
            pid = "w" + id;
        }
        else
        {
            imgSrc = "../images/BlackPiece.png";
            pid = "b" + id;
        }
        <text>
        <img id="@pid" src="@imgSrc" draggable="true" class="piece" >
        </text>
    }
</div>
</text>
```

6. To determine the appropriate squares, the first rule is that checkers are only on the black (or red in this case) squares. So, the code uses the same $(x + y) \% 2 \mathrel{!}= 0$ logic that was used to compute the css variable. Then, checkers are placed only on the top three and bottom three rows, so the code excludes rows 3 and 4. If the row is less than 3, this will add a white checker and use a black checker for the other rows. The code computes the id for the img element by prefixing the id of the square with either w or b. Notice that the draggable attribute is set to true.

7. The class attribute for the img elements was set to piece. Now add the following rule to the existing style element, which will add padding so the checker will be centered in the square.

```
.piece
{
    margin-left: 4px;
    margin-top: 4px;
}
```

8. Press F5 to start the application, and you should now see the checkers, as demonstrated in Figure 14-3.

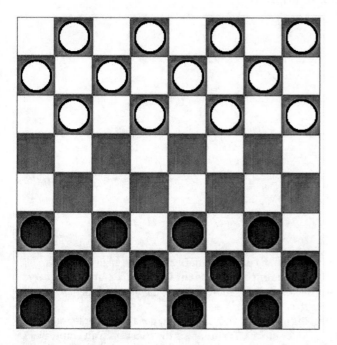

Figure 14-3. *The initial checker board with checkers*

Adding Drag-and-Drop Support

The img elements were added with the draggable attribute so you should be able to select one and drag it. However, you'll notice that none of the squares will accept the drop and the cursor shows the "not allowed" icon. If you want to try some default browser functionality, try dragging an image to address bar; the browser will navigate to the image's URL. You will now add code that will enable a drop so you can start moving the pieces. Then you'll refine this code to ensure that only legal moves are allowed.

Allowing a Drop

You have draggable elements, and all you need to complete a drag-and-drop operation is an element that will accept a drop. To do that, you'll need an event handler for the dragover event that sets the drop effect. By default the effectAllowed property is set to all so setting the drop effect to move, copy, or link will all be valid settings. To try this, add a script element at the end of the body element and add the code shown in Listing 14-4.

Listing 14-4. The Initial Event Implementation

```
<script type="text/javascript">
    // Get all the black squares
    var squares = document.querySelectorAll('.bblack');
    var i = 0;
    while (i < squares.length) {
        var s = squares[i++];
        // Add the event listeners
        s.addEventListener('dragover', dragOver, false);
    }

    // Handle the dragover event
    function dragOver(e) {
        if (e.preventDefault) {
            e.preventDefault();
        }

        e.dataTransfer.dropEffect = "move";
    }
</script>
```

This code uses the querySelectorAll() function that I described in Chapter 5 to get all of the black squares. It then iterates through the collection that is returned and adds an event handler for the dragover event. The dragover() function calls the preventDefault() function to cancel the browser's default action. It then gets the dataTransfer object and sets the dropEffect property to move.

Press F5 to run the application and try dragging a checker. You should now get a move cursor on all the black squares but a "not allowed" cursor on the white squares. Try dropping the checker on an empty black square. Since you have not yet implemented a drop event handler, the browser will execute its default drop action. Depending on the browser, this may navigate to the image file.

Performing the Custom Drop Action

The default action is not what you're looking for here, so you'll need to implement the drop event hander and provide your own logic. The drop event handler is where all the real work happens. This is where the file is deleted if it's a trash can. For this application, the drop action will create a new img element at the target location and remove the previous image.

To implement the drop, you'll also need to provide the dragstart event handler. In the dragstart event handler, you will store the id of the img element that is being dragged in the dataTransfer object. This will be used by the drop event handler so it will know which element to remove.

EXERCISE 14-3. IMPLEMENTING THE DROP

1. Add the following function to the existing script element, which will be used as the dragstart event handler. This code gets the id of the source element (remember the dragstart event is raised on the source element), which is the selected checker image. This id is stored in the dataTransfer object. This function also specifies that the allowed effects should be move since you'll be moving this image.

```
function dragStart(e) {
    e.dataTransfer.effectAllowed = "move";
    e.dataTransfer.setData("text", e.target.id);
}
```

2. To provide the drop event handler, add the code shown in Listing 14-5.

Listing 14-5. Implementing the Drop Event Handler

```
function drop(e) {
    // Prevent the event from being raised on the parent element
    if (e.stopPropagation) {
        e.stopPropagation();
    }

    // Stop the browsers default action
    if (e.preventDefault) {
        e.preventDefault();
    }

    // Get the img element that is being dragged
    var droppedID = e.dataTransfer.getData("text");
    var droppedPiece = document.getElementById(droppedID);

    // Create a new img on the target location
    var newPiece = document.createElement("img");
    newPiece.src = droppedPiece.src;
    newPiece.id = droppedPiece.id.substr(0, 1) + e.target.id;
    newPiece.draggable = true;
```

```
        newPiece.classList.add("piece");
        newPiece.addEventListener("dragstart", dragStart, false);
        e.target.appendChild(newPiece);

        // Remove the previous image
        droppedPiece.parentNode.removeChild(droppedPiece);
    }
```

3. This code first calls the `stopPropagation()` function to keep this event from bubbling up to the parent element. It also calls `preventDefault()` to cancel the browser's default action. It then gets the `id` from the `dataTransfer` object and uses this to access the `img` element. This function then creates a new `img` element and sets all the necessary properties and adds the necessary event handlers. As I explained, the drop event is raised on the target element, which is the element being dropped on. The `id` for the new `img` element is computed using the `id` of the new location, which is obtained from the `target` property of the `event` object. The ID prefix (b or w) is copied from the existing `img` element. Finally, this code removes the existing `img` element.

4. Now you'll need to wire up the event handlers. To do that, add the following code shown in bold near the beginning of the `script` element:

```
var squares = document.querySelectorAll('.bblack');
var i = 0;
while (i < squares.length) {
    var s = squares[i++];
    // Add the event listeners
    s.addEventListener('dragover', dragOver, false);
    s.addEventListener('drop', drop, false);
}

i = 0;
var pieces = document.querySelectorAll('img');
while (i < pieces.length) {
    var p = pieces[i++];
    p.addEventListener('dragstart', dragStart, false);
}
```

5. The `drop` event handler is added to the squares since these are the target elements. The `dragstart` event must be added to the `img` elements. This code gets all of the `img` elements using the `querySelectorAll()` function.

6. Now press F5 to start the application. You should be able to drag a checker to any red square.

Providing Visual Feedback

When dragging an element, it's a good idea to provide some visual feedback indicating the object that was selected. By setting the `dropEffect` property in the `dragover` event handler, the cursor indicates if a drop is allowed or not. However, you should do more than that. Both the source and target elements should stand out visually so the user can easily see that if they release the mouse button, the piece will be moved from here to there.

To do this, you'll dynamically add a class attribute to the source and target elements. Then you can style them with normal CSS style rules. For the source element you'll use the dragstart and dragend events to add and then remove the class attribute. Likewise for target element, you'll use the dragenter and dragleave events.

EXERCISE 14-4. ADDING VISUAL FEEDBACK

1. You already have a dragstart event handler; add the following code in bold to the dragStart() function. This will add the selected class to the element.

```
function dragStart(e) {
    e.dataTransfer.effectAllowed = "all";
    e.dataTransfer.setData("text/plain", e.target.id);

    e.target.classList.add("selected");
}
```

2. Add the dragEnd() function using the following code that will simply remove the selected class when the drag operation has completed.

```
function dragEnd(e) {
    e.target.classList.remove("selected");
}
```

3. Add the dragEnter() and dragLeave() functions using the following code. This adds the drop class to the element and then removes it.

```
function dragEnter(e) {
    e.target.classList.add('drop');
}

function dragLeave(e) {
    e.target.classList.remove("drop");
}
```

4. Since you've added three new event handlers, you'll need to add code to add the event listeners. Add the code shown in bold to the existing script element.

```
var squares = document.querySelectorAll('.bblack');
var i = 0;
while (i < squares.length){
    var s = squares[i++];
    // Add the event listeners
    s.addEventListener('dragover', dragOver, false);
    s.addEventListener('drop', drop, false);
    s.addEventListener('dragenter', dragEnter, false);
    s.addEventListener('dragleave', dragLeave, false);
}
```

```
        i = 0;
        var pieces = document.querySelectorAll('img');
        while (i < pieces.length){
            var p = pieces[i++];
            p.addEventListener('dragstart', dragStart, false);
            p.addEventListener('dragend', dragEnd, false);
        }
```

5. Now you'll need to make a couple of changes to the drop event handler. You added the drop class to the target element in the dragenter event and then removed it in the dragleave event. However, if they drop the image, the dragleave event is not raised. You'll also need to remove the drop class in the drop event as well. Also, when creating a new img element, you'll need to wire up the dragend event handler.

6. Add the code shown in bold.

```
    // Create a new img on the target location
    var newPiece = document.createElement("img");
    newPiece.src = droppedPiece.src;
    newPiece.id = droppedPiece.id.substr(0, 1) + e.target.id;
    newPiece.draggable = true;
    newPiece.classList.add("piece");
    newPiece.addEventListener("dragstart", dragStart, false);
    newPiece.addEventListener("dragend", dragEnd, false);
    e.target.appendChild(newPiece);

    // Remove the previous image
    droppedPiece.parentNode.removeChild(droppedPiece);

    // Remove the drop effect from the target element
    e.target.classList.remove('drop');
```

7. Finally, you'll need to define the CSS rules for the drop and selected values. I've chosen to set the opacity attribute, but you could just as easily add a border, change the background color, or implement any number of effects to achieve the desired purpose.

8. Add the following rules to the existing style element:

```
.bblack.drop
{
    opacity: 0.5;
}
.piece.selected
{
    opacity: 0.5;
}
```

9. Press F5 to start the application. Try dragging an image to a red square, and you should see the expected visual feedback, as shown in Figure 14-4.

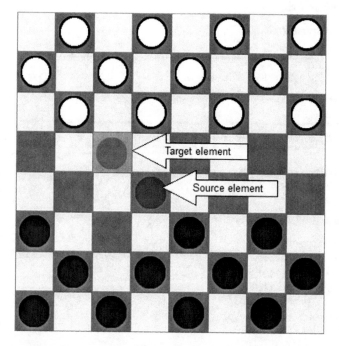

Figure 14-4. *Displaying the drag-and-drop visual feedback*

Enforcing the Game Rules

You've probably noticed that you can move a piece to any red square. The current implementation doesn't enforce any rules to ensure a legal move is being made. You'll now add that logic. This will be needed by the following events:

- dragover: To set the dropEffect to none for illegal moves
- dragenter: To change the style only for valid drop locations
- drop: To perform the move only if it's a legal move

You'll implement an isValidMove() function that will evaluate the attempted move and return false if this is an illegal move. Then you'll call this function in each of the three events listed earlier.

Verifying a Move

Fortunately, the rules in checkers are fairly simple. Because the dragover event handler is not added to the white squares, dropping a piece there is already disabled, which further simplifies the work needed. The following are the rules that you'll enforce:

- You cannot move to a square already occupied.
- Pieces can move only forward.

- Pieces can move only one space diagonally or two spaces (diagonally) if jumping an occupied square.

- You can jump only a piece of a different color.

- A jumped piece must be removed from the board.

■ **Note** You'll later add logic to handle promoting a piece to a king.

EXERCISE 14-5. ENFORCING THE RULES

1. Implement the isValidMove() function by adding the code shown in Listing 14-6 to the existing script element.

Listing 14-6. Implementing the isValidMove() Function

```
function isValidMove(source, target, drop) {
    // Get the piece prefix and location
    var startPos = source.id.substr(1, 2);
    var prefix = source.id.substr(0, 1);

    // Get the drop location, strip off the prefix, if any
    var endPos = target.id;
    if (endPos.length > 2) {
        endPos = endPos.substr(1, 2);
    }

    // You can't drop on the existing location
    if (startPos === endPos) {
        return false;
    }

    // You can't drop on occupied square
    if (target.childElementCount != 0) {
        return false;
    }

    // Compute the x and y coordinates
    var xStart = parseInt(startPos.substr(0, 1));
    var yStart = parseInt(startPos.substr(1, 1));
    var xEnd = parseInt(endPos.substr(0, 1));
    var yEnd = parseInt(endPos.substr(1, 1));

    switch (prefix) {
        // For white pieces...
        case "w":
            if (yEnd <= yStart)
                return false; // Can't move backwards
            break;
```

```
        // For black pieces...
        case "b":
            if (yEnd >= yStart)
                return false; // Can't move backwards
            break;
    }

    // These rule apply to all pieces
    if (yStart === yEnd || xStart === xEnd)
        return false; // Move must be diagonal

    if (Math.abs(yEnd - yStart) > 2 || Math.abs(xEnd - xStart) > 2)
        return false; // Can't move more than two spaces

    // If moving two spaces, find the square that is jumped
    if (Math.abs(xEnd - xStart) === 2) {
        var pos = ((xStart + xEnd) / 2).toString() +
                    ((yStart + yEnd) / 2).toString();
        var div = document.getElementById(pos);
        if (div.childElementCount === 0)
            return false;  // Can't jump an empty square
        var img = div.children[0];
        if (img.id.substr(0, 1).toLowerCase() === prefix.toLowerCase())
            return false; // Can't jump a piece of the same color

        // If this function is called from the drop event
        // Remove the jumped piece
        if (drop) {
            div.removeChild(img);
        }
    }

    return true;
}
```

2. The parameters to the isValidMove() function include the source and target elements. Remember, the source is an img element, and its id attribute is a combination of the color (w or b) and the x and y coordinates. The target is a div element, and its id attribute is just the x and y coordinates. I've added lots of comments to this code, so it should be fairly self-explanatory, but I will point out a couple of the more interesting points.

   - To determine whether a square is occupied, you can simply check the childElementCount property. This will be 0 for empty squares.

   - For white pieces, moving forward means the y coordinate is increasing, but for black pieces the opposite is true. To handle this, the function uses a switch statement to apply a different rule for each.

   - If the piece is moving two spaces, then the function needs to check the square that is being jumped. Its location is determined by averaging the starting and ending positions.

- If the square is occupied, then the code checks to see whether the piece is the same color. The code first gets the child element, which will be the img on that square. The color is determined by the prefix of the id attribute. The code converts the prefix to lowercase before comparing. I'll explain that later.

- If a piece of a different color is being jumped, then you'll remove it since the code already has the img element. However, you want to do this only if this method is called from the drop event, which is specified by the third parameter to this function. The other two events (dragOver and dragEnter) use this method to validate the move but don't actually make the move, and they will pass false for the third parameter.

3. Now you'll need to change dragover event to validate the move before setting the dropEffect. Replace the existing implementation of the dragOver() function with the code shown in Listing 14-7. The new code gets the id of the img that is being dragged from the dataTransfer object and then uses the id to get the element. This is passed in to the isValidMove() function along with the target element, which is obtained from the event object (e.target). The dropEffect is set to move only if this is a valid move.

Listing 14-7. The Revised dragOver Event Handler

```
function dragOver(e) {
    if (e.preventDefault) {
        e.preventDefault();
    }

    // Get the img element that is being dragged
    var dragID = e.dataTransfer.getData("text");
    var dragPiece = document.getElementById(dragID);

    // Work around - if we can't get the dataTransfer, don't
    // disable the move yet, the drop event will catch this
    if (dragPiece) {
        if (e.target.tagName === "DIV" &&
            isValidMove(dragPiece, e.target, false)) {
            e.dataTransfer.dropEffect = "move";
        }
        else {
            e.dataTransfer.dropEffect = "none";
        }
    }
}
```

■ **Caution**   As of this writing, Chrome, IE, and Opera won't allow you to access the dataTransfer object in the dragEnter and dragOver events. This does work, however, in the drop event. The work around in the dragOver event is to allow the move if the source object is not available. The game will still work because the drop event will ignore any invalid moves, but the user experience is not ideal. The dragEnter event is used to apply the drop class for styling purposes, and this will not work as well. For the rest of this chapter, I will be using Firefox to test the application.

---

4. Replace the implementation of the dragEnter() function with the following code. This code is essentially the same as the dragOver() function, except it adds the drop class to the element instead of setting the dropEffect.

```
function dragEnter(e) {
    // Get the img element that is being dragged
    var dragID = e.dataTransfer.getData("text");
    var dragPiece = document.getElementById(dragID);

    if (dragPiece &&
        e.target.tagName === "DIV" &&
        isValidMove(dragPiece, e.target, false)) {
        e.target.classList.add('drop');
    }
}
```

5. For the drop() function, wrap the code that performs the drop inside an if statement that validates the move by adding the code shown in bold. This time, the code is passing true for the third parameter to the isValidMove() function.

```
if (droppedPiece &&
    e.target.tagName === "DIV" &&
    isValidMove(droppedPiece, e.target, true)) {

    // Create a new img on the target location
    var newPiece = document.createElement("img");
    newPiece.src = droppedPiece.src;
    newPiece.id = droppedPiece.id.substr(0, 1) + e.target.id;
    newPiece.draggable = true;
    newPiece.classList.add("piece");
    newPiece.addEventListener("dragstart", dragStart, false);
    newPiece.addEventListener("dragend", dragEnd, false);
    e.target.appendChild(newPiece);

    // Remove the previous image
    droppedPiece.parentNode.removeChild(droppedPiece);

    // Remove the drop effect from the target element
    e.target.classList.remove('drop');
}
```

6. With these changes now in place, try running the application. You should be allowed to make only legal moves. If you jump a checker, it should be removed from the board.

Promoting to King

In checkers, when a piece moves all the way to the last row, it is promoted to a king. A king works just like a regular piece except that it can move backward. You'll now add code to check whether a piece needs to be promoted. To promote a piece, you'll change the image that is displayed to indicate it is a king. You'll also change the prefix, making it a capital *B* or *W*. Then you can allow different rules for kings.

You'll put all this logic in a single function called kingMe(), and you'll call this every time a drop occurs. If the piece is already a king or if it's not on the last row, the function just returns. Otherwise, it performs the promotion.

EXERCISE 14-6. ADDING PROMOTION

1. Add the kingMe() function shown in Listing 14-8 to the existing script element.

   Listing 14-8. Implementing the kingMe() Function

   ```
   function kingMe(piece) {

       // If we're already a king, just return
       if (piece.id.substr(0, 1) === "W" || piece.id.substr(0, 1) === "B")
           return;

       var newPiece;

       // If this is a white piece on the 7th row
       if (piece.id.substr(0, 1) === "w" && piece.id.substr(2, 1) === "7") {
           newPiece = document.createElement("img");
           newPiece.src = "../images/WhiteKing.png";
           newPiece.id = "W" + piece.id.substr(1, 2);
       }

       // If this is a black piece on the 0th row
       if (piece.id.substr(0, 1) === "b" && piece.id.substr(2, 1) === "0") {
           var newPiece = document.createElement("img");
           newPiece.src = "../images/BlackKing.png";
           newPiece.id = "B" + piece.id.substr(1, 2);
       }

       // If a new piece was created, set its properties and events
       if (newPiece) {
           newPiece.draggable = true;
           newPiece.classList.add("piece");

           newPiece.addEventListener('dragstart', dragStart, false);
           newPiece.addEventListener('dragend', dragEnd, false);

           var parent = piece.parentNode;
           parent.removeChild(piece);
           parent.appendChild(newPiece);
       }
   }
   ```

2. The kingMe() function simply returns if the id prefix is either *B* or *W*, which indicates this is already a king. It then checks to see whether this is a white piece on row 7 or a black piece on row 0. If so, a new img element is created with the appropriate src and id properties. If a new img was created, the function then sets all of the properties and events, removes the existing img element from the div element, and adds the new one.

3. Modify the `drop()` function to call the `kingMe()` function after a drop has been performed by adding the line shown in bold.

```
// Remove the previous image
droppedPiece.parentNode.removeChild(droppedPiece);

// Remove the drop effect from the target element
e.target.classList.remove('drop');

// See if the piece needs to be promoted
kingMe(newPiece);
```

■ **Tip**   When you implemented the `isValidMove()` function, the rule that prevents the piece from moving backwards applies only to b and w prefixes. Since a king has a capital B or W, this rule doesn't apply so the king can move backward. Also, when jumping a piece, the comparison was done after first converting to lowercase. This will allow a white piece to jump either a black piece or a black king.

---

4. Try moving the pieces around until you move one to the last row. You should see the image change to indicate this is now a king, as shown in Figure 14-5.

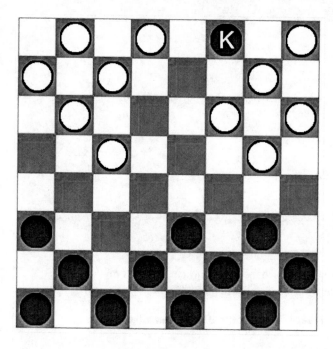

Figure 14-5. *The check board with a king*

5. Once you have a king, try moving it backward and also try jumping pieces with it.

Moving in Turn

You've probably noticed that the application does not enforce each player alternating turns. You'll implement this logic now. After each move is made (drop event processed), you'll set the draggable attribute to false for all the pieces of the color that just moved. That will keep you from moving a piece of the same color. However, there is one exception to this rule that will require a little extra work. If you jump a piece, then that same piece can make another move as long as it is another jump.

You'll start by implementing the general rule first. This will be performed by creating a new function called enableNextPlayer(). This function will use the querySelectorAll() function to get all of the img elements. The draggable attribute will be set to either true or false depending on the id prefix. Then you'll later add special logic that will handle the jump condition.

EXERCISE 14-7. TAKING TURNS

1. Add the enableNextPlayer() function to the existing script element using the code shown in Listing 14-9.

   Listing 14-9. Implementing the enableNextPlayer() Function

   ```
   function enableNextPlayer(piece) {

       // Get all of the pieces
       var pieces = document.querySelectorAll('img');

       i = 0;
       while (i < pieces.length) {
           var p = pieces[i++];

           // If this is the same color that just moved, disable dragging
           if (p.id.substr(0, 1).toUpperCase() ===
               piece.id.substr(0, 1).toUpperCase()) {
               p.draggable = false;
           }
           // Otherwise, enable dragging
           else {
               p.draggable = true;
           }
       }
   }
   ```

2. At the end of the isValidMove() function, add the code shown in bold. This will call the enableNextPlay() function when a drop is being performed.

   ```
   // Set the draggable attribute so the next player can take a turn
   if (drop) {
       enableNextPlayer(source);
   }

   return true;
   }
   ```

Note Normally it might make more sense to put this call in the drop() function. However, only the isValidMove() function knows that a jump occurred, and you'll need to add the override logic here. This needs to be after the general rule has been applied.

3. The drop() function creates a new img element and currently sets the draggable attribute to true. Now you'll need to make this conditional based on the draggable attribute of the existing piece. Add the following code shown in bold to the drop() function:

```
// Create a new img on the target location
var newPiece = document.createElement("img");
newPiece.src = droppedPiece.src;
newPiece.id = droppedPiece.id.substr(0, 1) + e.target.id;

newPiece.draggable = droppedPiece.draggable;

newPiece.classList.add("piece");
newPiece.addEventListener("dragstart", dragStart, false);
newPiece.addEventListener("dragend", dragEnd, false);
e.target.appendChild(newPiece);
```

4. Now you'll need change the dragStart event handler to ignore this event if the element is not draggable. Add the following code shown in bold to the dragStart() function:

```
function dragStart(e) {
    if (e.target.draggable) {
        e.dataTransfer.effectAllowed = "move";
        e.dataTransfer.setData("text/plain", e.target.id);

        e.target.classList.add("selected");
    }
}
```

5. Now you'll implement the special jump logic. If the piece just made a jump, you'll set the draggable attribute back to true so it will be allowed to make another move. However, you'll also add the jumpOnly class to the classList so you can enforce that the only move that it is allowed to make is another jump.

6. Add the code shown in bold to the isValidMove() function. This will look for jumpOnly in the classList and set the jumpOnly flag accordingly.

```
var jumpOnly = false;
if (source.classList.contains("jumpOnly")) {
    jumpOnly = true;
}

// Compute the x and y coordinates
var xStart = parseInt(startPos.substr(0, 1));
var yStart = parseInt(startPos.substr(1, 1));
```

7. Now add the code shown in bold to the isValidMove() function. The first part adds the rule to make sure a jump is being made if jumpOnly is true. The second part sets the jumped flag to indicate that this move is making a jump.

```
// These rule apply to all pieces
if (yStart === yEnd || xStart === xEnd)
    return false; // Move must be diagonal

if (Math.abs(yEnd - yStart) > 2 || Math.abs(xEnd - xStart) > 2)
    return false; // Can't move more than two spaces
if (Math.abs(xEnd - xStart) === 1 && jumpOnly)
    return false; // Only jumps are allowed

var jumped = false;

// If moving two spaces, find the square that is jumped
if (Math.abs(xEnd - xStart) === 2) {
    var pos = ((xStart + xEnd) / 2).toString() +
                ((yStart + yEnd) / 2).toString();
    var div = document.getElementById(pos);
    if (div.childElementCount === 0)
        return false;  // Can't jump an empty square
    var img = div.children[0];
    if (img.id.substr(0, 1).toLowerCase() === prefix.toLowerCase())
        return false; // Can't jump a piece of the same color

    // If this function is called from the drop event
    // Remove the jumped piece
    if (drop) {
        div.removeChild(img);
        jumped = true;
    }
}
```

8. At the end of the isValidMove() function, add the code shown in bold. This will override the draggable attribute if a jump was made and add jumpOnly to the classList.

```
if (drop) {
    enableNextPlayer(source);

    // If we jumped a piece, we're allowed to go again
    if (jumped) {
        source.draggable = true;
        source.classList.add("jumpOnly"); // But only for another jump
    }
}
```

■ **Note** The enableNextPlayer() function disabled all of the current player's pieces and enabled the other player's. Then this code enabled the piece that just jumped. So, both are enabled; this piece could jump again or the next player could make a move. Both are valid, so we need to allow them both.

9. Modify the drop() function to also add jumpOnly to the classList when creating the new img element by adding the code shown in bold.

```
// Create a new img on the target location
var newPiece = document.createElement("img");
newPiece.src = droppedPiece.src;
newPiece.id = droppedPiece.id.substr(0, 1) + e.target.id;

newPiece.draggable = droppedPiece.draggable;

if (droppedPiece.draggable){
    newPiece.classList.add("jumpOnly");
}

newPiece.classList.add("piece");
```

10. Now you'll need to clear jumpOnly from the classList when the next move is completed. You'll do that in the enableNextPlayer() function by adding the code shown in bold.

```
function enableNextPlayer(piece) {

    // Get all of the pieces
    var pieces = document.querySelectorAll('img');

    i = 0;
    while (i < pieces.length) {
        var p = pieces[i++];

        // If this is the same color that just moved, disable dragging
        if (p.id.substr(0, 1).toUpperCase() ===
            piece.id.substr(0, 1).toUpperCase()) {
            p.draggable = false;
        }
        // Otherwise, enable dragging
        else {
            p.draggable = true;
        }

        p.classList.remove("jumpOnly");
    }
}
```

11. Now test the application and make sure that each player must alternate turns. Also, verify that you can make successive jumps.

■ **Note** The `draggable` attribute is set to `true`, initially, for both the white and black pieces so either color can make the first move. If you wanted to specify which color went first, you would change the Razor syntax that creates the initial `img` elements to set the `draggable` attribute to `false` for one color. I did some research to see what color was supposed to go first but found mixed results. Some places indicated black goes first and others said that the white goes first. Some, however, said it's just a game, what difference does it make? I decided to implement this logic, so either can go first.

Using Advanced Features

Before I finish this chapter, there are a couple of things I will discuss briefly. First, I'll show you how to use a custom drag image. Then, I'll demonstrate dragging elements across browser windows.

Changing the Drag Image

When you drag an element, a copy of the element follows the cursor as you move it around the page. This is referred to as the *drag image*. However, you can specify a different image to be used. This is done with the `setDragImage()` function of the `dataTransfer` object.

There is a smiley face image in the `wwwroot\images` folder. Add the code shown in bold to the `dragStart()` function to use this as the drag image.

```
function dragStart(e) {
    if (e.target.draggable) {
        e.dataTransfer.effectAllowed = "move";
        e.dataTransfer.setData("text", e.target.id);

        e.target.classList.add("selected");

        var dragIcon = document.createElement("img");
        dragIcon.src = "../images/smiley.jpg";
        e.dataTransfer.setDragImage(dragIcon, 0, 0);
    }
}
```

Try the application, and as you move pieces, you should see the smiley face shown in Figure 14-6.

Figure 14-6. *Changing the drag image*

Dragging Between Windows

As I mentioned at the beginning of the chapter, there are separate events raised on the source element and on the target element. It is possible that these elements can be in different browser windows or even different applications. The process, however, works the same way.

To demonstrate this, open a second instance of the Firefox browser and navigate to the checkers application. You should see two browser windows each showing the checker board. Select a checker on one window and drag it to a square in the second window. You'll notice that you can drop it only on squares relative to its original location in the first window. When you drop it, the piece is moved to the drop location but is removed from the second window, not the image you initially selected.

The key to cross-window dragging is the dataTransfer object. This is provided in the dragenter, dragover, and dragleave events on the target object. It doesn't really matter where the drag initiated; this information is placed in the dataTransfer object and provided to any window that supports these events. When the drop event received this information, it removed the img element at the location specified in the dataTransfer object. Because the drop event was processed on the second window, the img element was removed from the second window.

The drag and dragend events are raised on the source element. Whatever logic was written on these event handlers is executed in the first window. Notice that the selected img element was muted during the drag but went back to normal when the drop was executed. This is because the dragend event fired on the source element clears the selected attribute.

When you control both sides of the operation as you do here, you can decide what data needs to be transferred and implement both sets of event handlers. In many cases, you can control only one side of the process. For example, a user could drag a file from Windows Explorer onto your web page. The dragstart, drag, and dragend events (or their equivalents) are raised in the Windows Explorer application, which you can't control. However, the dragenter, dragover, dragleave, and drop events are all fired on your web page. You can decide whether you will accept the drop based on the element it is being dropped on and the contents of the dataTransfer object. You also control the process that occurs when the drop is completed.

Summary

In this chapter, I explained all of the events that are raised as part of the DnD API and which elements they are raised on. The source element receives the following events:

- dragstart: When the element is selected and the mouse is moved

- drag: Called continuously while the mouse is moved

- dragend: When the mouse button is released

The following events are raised on the target element:

- dragenter: When the mouse first enters the target's space

- dragover: Continuously while the mouse is moved and over the target

- dragleave: When the mouse leaves the target's space

- drop: When the mouse button is released

The dataTransfer object is used to pass information about the source element. This is provided in all of the event handlers. It is used especially by the drop event handler to perform the necessary processing. This also enables dragging across applications.

The dragover event handler sets the dropEffect, which controls the cursor that is used. Setting this to None will cause the "not allowed" cursor to be used, signaling that the source cannot be dropped there.

To provide some visual feedback, the dragstart and dragend event handlers should modify the source element to indicate that it is selected and being dragged. Likewise, the dragenter and dragleave event handers should highlight the target element. This will provide an easy way for the user to see where the selected element will be dropped.

The sample application that you created implemented some complex rules for determining which elements could be dragged and where they could be dropped.

PART V

Appendixes

APPENDIX A

■ ■ ■

Sample Content for Chapter 4

Listing A-1 specifies the initial HTML content used for the exercises in Chapter 4. This is available from the downloaded source in the Default_content.cshtml file. I'm including it here in case you want to see it without downloading the code.

Listing A-1. Chapter 4 Sample Content

```html
<!DOCTYPE html>

<html lang="en">
    <head>
        <meta charset="utf-8" />
        <title>Chapter 4 - CSS Demo</title>
    </head>
    <body>
        <header class="intro">
            <h1>CSS Demo</h1>
            <h2>Introducing the new HTML5 features</h2>
            <h3>
                Use the new CSS3 features to build some of the most visually
                appealing web sites.
            </h3>
        </header>

        <nav>
            <ul>
                <li><a href="#feature">Feature</a></li>
                <li><a href="#other">Article</a></li>
                <li><a href="#another">Archives</a></li>
                <li><a href="http://www.apress.com" target="_blank">Apress</a></li>
            </ul>
        </nav>

        <div id="contentArea">

            <div id="mainContent">
                <section class="rounded">
                    <header>
                        <h2>Main content area</h2>
```

```
            </header>
            <p>
                Lorem ipsum dolor sit amet, consectetur adipisicing elit,
                sed do eiusmod tempor incididunt ut labore et dolore magna
                aliqua. Ut enim ad minim veniam, quis nostrud exercitation
                ullamco laboris nisi ut.
            </p>
        </section>

        <section>
            <article class="featuredContent">
                <a id="feature"></a>
                <header>
                    <h3>Featured Article</h3>
                </header>

                <div class="rotateContainer">
                    <p>This is really cool...</p>
                    <img class="rotate" id="phone"
                        src="images/phonebooth.jpg"
                        alt="phonebooth"
                        onclick="toggleAnimation()"/>
                    <br />
                    <p>
                        Lorem ipsum dolor sit amet, consectetur adipisicing
                        elit, sed do eiusmod tempor incididunt ut labore et
                        dolore magna aliqua. Ut enim ad minim veniam, quis
                        nostrud exercitation ullamco laboris nisi ut.
                    </p>
                    <p>
                        Lorem ipsum dolor sit amet, consectetur adipisicing
                        elit, sed do eiusmod tempor incididunt ut labore et
                        dolore magna aliqua. Ut enim ad minim veniam, quis
                        nostrud exercitation ullamco laboris nisi ut.
                    </p>
                    <p>
                        Lorem ipsum dolor sit amet, consectetur adipisicing
                        elit, sed do eiusmod tempor incididunt ut labore et
                        dolore magna aliqua. Ut enim ad minim veniam, quis
                        nostrud exercitation ullamco laboris nisi ut.
                    </p>
                </div>
            </article>

            <article class="otherContent">
                <a id="other"></a>
                <header>
                    <h3>Rounded Borders</h3>
                </header>
```

```
<div>
    <p>Details about rounded corners</p>
    <p>
        One of the most common features that you'll hear
        about is the use of rounded corners and we'll cover
        that here. Also, by configuring the div size and
        radius properly you can also make circular divs
    </p>
    <p>
        Lorem ipsum dolor sit amet, consectetur adipisicing
        elit, sed do eiusmod tempor incididunt ut labore et
        dolore magna aliqua. Ut enim ad minim veniam, quis
        nostrud exercitation ullamco laboris nisi ut.
    </p>
</div>
</article>

<article class="otherContent">
    <a id="another"></a>
    <header>
        <h3>Another Interesting Article</h3>
    </header>

    <div>
        <p>More things to say...</p>
        <p>
            Lorem ipsum dolor sit amet, consectetur adipiscing
            elit. Proin luctus tincidunt justo nec tempor.
            Aliquam erat volutpat. Fusce facilisis ullamcorper
            consequat. Vestibulum non sapien lectus. Nam mi
            augue, posuere at tempus vel, dignissim vitae nulla.
            Nullam at quam eu sapien mattis ultrices. Quisque
            quis leo mi, at lobortis dolor. Nullam scelerisque
            facilisis placerat. Fusce a augue erat, malesuada
            euismod dui. Duis iaculis risus id felis volutpat
            elementum. Fusce blandit iaculis quam a cursus.
            Cras varius tincidunt cursus. Morbi justo eros,
            adipiscing ac placerat sed, posuere et mi.
            Suspendisse vulputate viverra aliquet. Duis non
            enim a nibh consequat mollis ac tempor lorem.
            Phasellus elit leo, semper eu luctus et, suscipit
            at lacus. In hac habitasse platea dictumst. Duis
            dignissim justo sit amet nulla pulvinar sodales.
        </p>
    </div>
</article>
</section>
</div>
```

```
<aside id="sidebar">
    <h3>Other Titles</h3>
    <div id="moon"></div>
    <p>
        Check out some of the other titles available from Apress.
    </p>
    <section id="titles">
        <article class="book">
            <header>
                <a href="http://www.apress.com/9781430240747"
                    target="_blank">
                  <img src="images\office365.png"
                        alt="Pro Office 365"/>
                </a>
            </header>
            <p>
                Pro Office 365 Development is a practical, hands-on
                guide to building cloud-based solutions using the
                Office 365 platform.
            </p>
        </article>

        <article class="book">
            <header>
                <a href="http://www.apress.com/9781430235781"
                    target="_blank">
                  <img src="images\access2010.png"
                        alt="Pro Access 2010"/>
                </a>
            </header>
            <p>
                Pro Access 2010 Development is a fundamental resource
                for developing business applications that take
                advantage of the features of Access 2010. You'll learn
                how to build database applications, create Web-based
                databases, develop macros and VBA tools for Access
                applications, integrate Access with SharePoint, and
                much more.
            </p>
        </article>

        <article class="book">
            <header>
                <a href="http://www.apress.com/9781430228295"
                    target="_blank">
                  <img src="images\sharepoint_pm.png"
                        alt="Pro Project Management w/SharePoint 2010"/>
                </a>
            </header>
```

```
    <p>
        The intention of this book is to provide a working
        case study that you can follow to create a complete
        PMIS (project management information system) with
        SharePoint Server's out-of-the-box functionality.
    </p>
</article>

<article class="book">
    <header>
        <a href="http://www.apress.com/9781430229049"
            target="_blank">
            <img src="images\office:workflow.png"
                alt="Office 2010 Workflow"/>
        </a>
    </header>
    <p>
        Workflow is the glue that binds information worker
        processes, users, and artifacts—without it,
        information workers are just islands of data and
        potential. Office 2010 Workflow walks you through
        implementing workflow solutions.
    </p>
</article>

<article class="book">
    <header>
        <a href="http://www.apress.com/9781430224853"
            target="_blank">
            <img src="images\beginning_wf.png"
                alt="Beginning WF"/>
        </a>
    </header>
    <p>
        Indexed by feature so you can find answers easily
        and written in an accessible style, Beginning WF
        shows how Microsoft's Workflow Foundation (WF)
        technology can be used in a wide variety of
        applications.
    </p>
</article>
    </section>
  </aside>
</div>
```

```
<footer>
    <p>
        Last updated <time datetime="2015-03-07T20:32:22+05:00">
            March 7th 2015</time>
        by <a href="http://www.thecreativepeople.com"
            target="_blank">Mark J. Collins</a>
    </p>
</footer>

</body>
</html>
```

■ ■ ■

Completed Style for Chapter 4

Listing B-1 shows the completed style element from the Chapter 4 project. I've explained this in pieces, but I'm including it here if you want to see it altogether.

Listing B-1. Chapter 4 Completed style Element

```
<style>
    /* Basic tag settings */
    body
    {
        margin: 0 auto;
        width: 940px;
        font: 13px/22px Helvetica, Arial, sans-serif;
        background: #f0f0f0;
    }

    h2
    {
        font-size: 18px;
        line-height: 5px;
        padding: 2px 0;
    }

    h3
    {
        font-size: 12px;
        line-height: 5px;
        padding: 2px 0;
    }

    h1, h2, h3
    {
        text-align: left;
    }

    p
    {
        padding-bottom: 2px;
    }
```

```
.book
{
    padding: 5px;
}

/* Content sections */
.featuredContent
{
    background-color: #ffffff;
    border: 2px solid #6699cc;
    padding: 15px 15px 15px 15px;
}

.otherContent
{
    background-color: #c0c0c0;
    border: 1px solid #999999;
    padding: 15px 15px 15px 15px;
}

aside
{
    background-color: #6699cc;
    padding: 5px 5px 5px 5px;
}

footer
{
    margin-top: 12px;
    text-align: center;
    background-color: #ddd;
}

footer p
{
    padding-top: 10px;
}

/* Navigation Section */
nav
{
    left: 0;
    background-color: #003366;
}

nav ul
{
    margin: 0;
    list-style: none;
}
```

```css
nav ul li
{
    float: left;
}

nav ul li a
{
    display: block;
    margin-right: 20px;
    width: 140px;
    font-size: 14px;
    line-height: 28px;
    text-align: center;
    padding-bottom: 2px;
    text-decoration: none;
    color: #cccccc;
}

nav ul li a:hover
{
    color: #fff;
}

/* Rounded borders */
.rounded
{
    border: 1px solid;
    border-color: #999999;
    border-radius: 25px;
    padding: 24px;
}

aside
{
    border: 1px solid #999999;
    border-radius: 12px;
}

/* Make the radius half of the height */
nav
{
    height: 30px;
    border-radius: 15px;
}

footer
{
    height: 50px;
    border-radius: 25px;
}
```

```css
/* Gradients */
.intro
{
    border: 1px solid #999999;
    text-align: left;
    padding-left: 15px;
    margin-top: 6px;
    border-radius: 25px;
    background-image: linear-gradient(45deg, #ffffff, #6699cc);
}

/* Setup a table for the content and sidebar */
#contentArea
{
    display: table;
}

#mainContent
{
    display: table-cell;
    padding-right: 2px;
}

aside
{
    display: table-cell;
    width: 280px;
}

/* Setup multiple columns for the articles */
.otherContent
{
    text-align: justify;
    padding: 6px;
    -webkit-column-count: 2;
    column-count: 2;
    -webkit-column-gap: 20px;
    column-gap: 20px;
}

/* Add the box shadow */
article img
{
    margin: 10px 0;
    box-shadow: 3px 3px 12px #222;
}

.book img
{
    margin: 10px 0;
    display: block;
```

```css
    box-shadow: 2px 2px 5px #444;
    margin-left: auto;
    margin-right: auto;
}

aside
{
    box-shadow: 3px 3px 3px #aaaaaa;
}

/* Stripe the title list */
#titles article:nth-child(2n+1)
{
    background: #c0c0c0;
    border: 1px solid #6699cc;
    border-radius: 10px;
}

#titles article:nth-child(2n+0)
{
    background: #6699cc;
    border: 1px solid #c0c0c0;
    border-radius: 10px;
}

/* Text decorations */
h2
{
    text-decoration: underline;
    -moz-text-decoration-line: underline;
    -moz-text-decoration-style: wavy;
    -moz-text-decoration-color: red;
    text-decoration-line: underline;
    text-decoration-style: wavy;
    text-decoration-color: red;
}

h3:first-letter
{
    text-shadow: 2px -5px 1px;
}

/* Transforms */
.rotateContainer
{
    -webkit-perspective: 360;
    perspective: 360px;
}

.rotate
{
```

```
        -webkit-transform-style: preserve-3d;
        transform-style: preserve-3d;
    }

    /* Animate the moon phases */
    @@-webkit-keyframes moonPhases
    {
        0%    { background-image: url("images/moon1.png"); }
        12%   { background-image: url("images/moon2.png"); }
        25%   { background-image: url("images/moon3.png"); }
        37%   { background-image: url("images/moon4.png"); }
        50%   { background-image: url("images/moon5.png"); }
        62%   { background-image: url("images/moon6.png"); }
        75%   { background-image: url("images/moon7.png"); }
        87%   { background-image: url("images/moon8.png"); }
        100%  { background-image: url("images/moon1.png"); }
    }

    @@keyframes moonPhases
    {
        0%    { background-image: url("images/moon1.png"); }
        12%   { background-image: url("images/moon2.png"); }
        25%   { background-image: url("images/moon3.png"); }
        37%   { background-image: url("images/moon4.png"); }
        50%   { background-image: url("images/moon5.png"); }
        62%   { background-image: url("images/moon6.png"); }
        75%   { background-image: url("images/moon7.png"); }
        87%   { background-image: url("images/moon8.png"); }
        100%  { background-image: url("images/moon1.png"); }
    }

    #moon
    {
        width: 115px;
        height: 115px;
        background-image: url("images/moon1.png");
        background-repeat: no-repeat;
        -webkit-animation-name: moonPhases;
        -webkit-animation-duration: 4s;
        -webkit-animation-delay: 3s;
        -webkit-animation-iteration-count: infinite;
        animation-name: moonPhases;
        animation-duration: 4s;
        animation-delay: 3s;
        animation-iteration-count: infinite;
    }
</style>
```

■ ■ ■

Final Code for Chapter 14

Listing C-1 specifies the final code for the project in Chapter 14. This is available from the downloaded source in the Checkers.cshtml file. I'm including it here in case you want to see it without downloading the code.

Listing C-1. Chapter 14 Final Code

```
<head>
    <style type="text/css" >
        .board
        {
            width: 400px;
            height: 400px;
            margin-top: 20px;
        }
        .bblack
        {
            background-color: #b93030;
            border-color: #b93030;
            border-width: 1px;
            border-style: solid;
            width: 48px;
            height: 48px;
            float: left;
            margin: 0px;
            padding: 0px;
        }
        .bwhite
        {
            background-color: #f7f7f7;
            border-color: #b93030;
            border-width: 1px;
            border-style: solid;
            width: 48px;
            height: 48px;
            float: left;
            margin: 0px;
            padding: 0px;
        }
```

```
        .piece
        {
            margin-left: 4px;
            margin-top: 4px;
        }
        .bblack.drop
        {
            opacity: 0.5;
        }
        .piece.selected
        {
            opacity: 0.5;
        }
    </style>
</head>
<body>
    <div class="board">
        @for (int y = 0; y < 8; y++)
        {
            for (int x = 0; x < 8; x++)
            {
                string id = x.ToString() + y.ToString();
                string css;
                if ((x + y) % 2 == 0)
                {
                    css = "bwhite";
                }
                else
                {
                    css = "bblack";
                }
                <text>
                <div id="@id" class="@css" draggable="false">
                    @if ((x + y) % 2 != 0 && y != 3 && y != 4)
                    {
                        string imgSrc;
                        string pid;
                        if (y < 3)
                        {
                            imgSrc = "../images/WhitePiece.png";
                            pid = "w" + id;
                        }
                        else
                        {
                            imgSrc = "../images/BlackPiece.png";
                            pid = "b" + id;
                        }
                        <text>
                        <img id="@pid" src="@imgSrc" draggable="true" class="piece">
                        </text>
                    }
```

```
                </div>
                </text>
            }
        }
    </div>
    <script type="text/javascript">
    // Get all the black squares
    var squares = document.querySelectorAll('.bblack');
    var i = 0;
    while (i < squares.length) {
        var s = squares[i++];
        // Add the event listeners
        s.addEventListener('dragover', dragOver, false);
        s.addEventListener('drop', drop, false);
        s.addEventListener('dragenter', dragEnter, false);
        s.addEventListener('dragleave', dragLeave, false);
    }
    i = 0;
    var pieces = document.querySelectorAll('img');
    while (i < pieces.length) {
        var p = pieces[i++];
        p.addEventListener('dragstart', dragStart, false);
        p.addEventListener('dragend', dragEnd, false);
    }

    // Handle the dragover event
    function dragOver(e) {
        if (e.preventDefault) {
            e.preventDefault();
        }

        // Get the img element that is being dragged
        var dragID = e.dataTransfer.getData("text");
        var dragPiece = document.getElementById(dragID);

        // Work around - if we can't get the dataTransfer, don't
        // disable the move yet, the drop event will catch this
        if (dragPiece) {
            if (e.target.tagName === "DIV" &&
                isValidMove(dragPiece, e.target, false)) {
                e.dataTransfer.dropEffect = "move";
            }
            else {
                e.dataTransfer.dropEffect = "none";
            }
        }
    }
```

411

```javascript
function dragStart(e) {
    if (e.target.draggable) {
        e.dataTransfer.effectAllowed = "move";
        e.dataTransfer.setData("text", e.target.id);
        e.target.classList.add("selected");

        var dragIcon = document.createElement("img");
        dragIcon.src = "../images/smiley.jpg";
        e.dataTransfer.setDragImage(dragIcon, 0, 0);
    }
}

function dragEnd(e) {
    e.target.classList.remove("selected");
}

function drop(e) {
    // Prevent the event from being raised on the parent element
    if (e.stopPropagation) {
        e.stopPropagation();
    }

    // Stop the browsers default action
    if (e.preventDefault) {
        e.preventDefault();
    }

    // Get the img element that is being dragged
    var droppedID = e.dataTransfer.getData("text");
    var droppedPiece = document.getElementById(droppedID);

    if (droppedPiece &&
        e.target.tagName === "DIV" &&
        isValidMove(droppedPiece, e.target, true)) {
        // Create a new img on the target location
        var newPiece = document.createElement("img");
        newPiece.src = droppedPiece.src;
        newPiece.id = droppedPiece.id.substr(0, 1) + e.target.id;

        newPiece.draggable = droppedPiece.draggable;

        if (droppedPiece.draggable) {
            newPiece.classList.add("jumpOnly");
        }

        newPiece.classList.add("piece");
        newPiece.addEventListener("dragstart", dragStart, false);
        newPiece.addEventListener("dragend", dragEnd, false);
        e.target.appendChild(newPiece);

        // Remove the previous image
        droppedPiece.parentNode.removeChild(droppedPiece);
```

```
            // Remove the drop effect from the target element
            e.target.classList.remove('drop');

            // See if the piece needs to be promoted
            kingMe(newPiece);
        }
    }
}

function dragEnter(e) {
    // Get the img element that is being dragged
    var dragID = e.dataTransfer.getData("text");
    var dragPiece = document.getElementById(dragID);

    if (dragPiece &&
        e.target.tagName === "DIV" &&
        isValidMove(dragPiece, e.target, false)) {
        e.target.classList.add('drop');
    }
}

function dragLeave(e) {
    e.target.classList.remove("drop");
}
function isValidMove(source, target, drop) {
    // Get the piece prefix and location
    var startPos = source.id.substr(1, 2);
    var prefix = source.id.substr(0, 1);

    // Get the drop location, strip off the prefix, if any
    var endPos = target.id;
    if (endPos.length > 2) {
        endPos = endPos.substr(1, 2);
    }

    // You can't drop on the existing location
    if (startPos === endPos) {
        return false;
    }

    // You can't drop on occupied square
    if (target.childElementCount != 0) {
        return false;
    }

    var jumpOnly = false;
    if (source.classList.contains("jumpOnly")) {
        jumpOnly = true;
    }
```

```javascript
// Compute the x and y coordinates
var xStart = parseInt(startPos.substr(0, 1));
var yStart = parseInt(startPos.substr(1, 1));
var xEnd = parseInt(endPos.substr(0, 1));
var yEnd = parseInt(endPos.substr(1, 1));

switch (prefix) {
    // For white pieces...
    case "w":
        if (yEnd <= yStart)
            return false; // Can't move backwards
        break;

    // For black pieces...
    case "b":
        if (yEnd >= yStart)
            return false; // Can't move backwards
        break;
}

// These rule apply to all pieces
if (yStart === yEnd || xStart === xEnd)
    return false; // Move must be diagonal

if (Math.abs(yEnd - yStart) > 2 || Math.abs(xEnd - xStart) > 2)
    return false; // Can't move more than two spaces

if (Math.abs(xEnd - xStart) === 1 && jumpOnly)
    return false; // Only jumps are allowed

var jumped = false;

// If moving two spaces, find the square that is jumped
if (Math.abs(xEnd - xStart) === 2) {
    var pos = ((xStart + xEnd) / 2).toString() +
              ((yStart + yEnd) / 2).toString();
    var div = document.getElementById(pos);
    if (div.childElementCount === 0)
        return false;  // Can't jump an empty square
    var img = div.children[0];
    if (img.id.substr(0, 1).toLowerCase() === prefix.toLowerCase())
        return false; // Can't jump a piece of the same color

    // If this function is called from the drop event
    // Remove the jumped piece
    if (drop) {
        div.removeChild(img);
        jumped = true;
    }
}
```

```
    // Set the draggable attribute so the next player can take a turn
    if (drop) {
        enableNextPlayer(source);

        // If we jumped a piece, we're allowed to go again
        if (jumped) {
            source.draggable = true;
            source.classList.add("jumpOnly"); // But only for another jump
        }
    }

    return true;
}

function kingMe(piece) {

    // If we're already a king, just return
    if (piece.id.substr(0, 1) === "W" || piece.id.substr(0, 1) === "B")
        return;

    var newPiece;

    // If this is a white piece on the 7th row
    if (piece.id.substr(0, 1) === "w" && piece.id.substr(2, 1) === "7") {
        newPiece = document.createElement("img");
        newPiece.src = "../images/WhiteKing.png";
        newPiece.id = "W" + piece.id.substr(1, 2);
    }

    // If this is a black piece on the 0th row
    if (piece.id.substr(0, 1) === "b" && piece.id.substr(2, 1) === "0") {
        var newPiece = document.createElement("img");
        newPiece.src = "../images/BlackKing.png";
        newPiece.id = "B" + piece.id.substr(1, 2);

    }

    // If a new piece was created, set its properties and events
    if (newPiece) {
        newPiece.draggable = true;
        newPiece.classList.add("piece");

        newPiece.addEventListener('dragstart', dragStart, false);
        newPiece.addEventListener('dragend', dragEnd, false);

        var parent = piece.parentNode;
        parent.removeChild(piece);
        parent.appendChild(newPiece);
    }
}
```

```
function enableNextPlayer(piece) {

    // Get all of the pieces
    var pieces = document.querySelectorAll('img');

    i = 0;
    while (i < pieces.length) {
        var p = pieces[i++];

        // If this is the same color that just moved, disable dragging
        if (p.id.substr(0, 1).toUpperCase() ===
            piece.id.substr(0, 1).toUpperCase()) {
            p.draggable = false;
        }
        // Otherwise, enable dragging
        else {
            p.draggable = true;
        }

        p.classList.remove("jumpOnly");
    }
}
</script>

</body>
```

Index

Get the eBook for only $5!

Why limit yourself?

Now you can take the weightless companion with you wherever you go and access your content on your PC, phone, tablet, or reader.

Since you've purchased this print book, we're happy to offer you the eBook in all 3 formats for just $5.

Convenient and fully searchable, the PDF version enables you to easily find and copy code—or perform examples by quickly toggling between instructions and applications. The MOBI format is ideal for your Kindle, while the ePUB can be utilized on a variety of mobile devices.

To learn more, go to www.apress.com/companion or contact support@apress.com.